INVENTING THE BOSTON GAME

A VOLUME IN THE SERIES
Public History in Historical Perspective

EDITED BY
Marla R. Miller

INVENTING THE BOSTON GAME

FOOTBALL, SOCCER, and the ORIGINS of a NATIONAL MYTH

KEVIN TALLEC MARSTON

and

MIKE CRONIN

University of Massachusetts Press
Amherst and Boston

Copyright © 2024 by University of Massachusetts Press
All rights reserved
Printed in the United States of America

ISBN 978-1-62534-842-5 (paper); 843-2 (hardcover)

Designed by Scribe Inc.
Set in Adobe Garamond
Printed and bound by Books International, Inc.

Cover design by adam b. bohannon
Cover photo by Lewis Wickes Hine, *Amateur Football on the Boston Common. Location: Boston, Massachusetts.* Boston Massachusetts United States, 1909. October. Courtesy, Library of Congress.

Library of Congress Cataloging-in-Publication Data
Names: Marston, Kevin Tallec, 1977– author. | Cronin, Mike author.
Title: Inventing the Boston game : football, soccer, and the origins of a national myth / Kevin Tallec Marston & Mike Cronin.
Other titles: Football, soccer, and the origins of a national myth
Description: Amherst : University of Massachusetts Press, [2024] | Series: Public history in historical perspective | Includes bibliographical references and index.
Identifiers: LCCN 2024033371 (print) | LCCN 2024033372 (ebook) | ISBN 9781625348425 (paperback) | ISBN 9781625348432 (hardcover) | ISBN 9781685751135 (ebook) | ISBN 9781685751142 (epub)
Subjects: LCSH: Oneida Football Club (Football team) | Football—Massachusetts—Boston—History. | Football—United States—History. | Oneida Football Monument (Boston, Mass.) | Boston (Mass.)—Social life and customs—19th century. | Boston (Mass.)—Social life and customs—20th century. | Collective memory—Massachusetts—Boston.
Classification: LCC GV959.53.B6 M37 2024 (print) | LCC GV959.53.B6 (ebook) | DDC 796.33—dc23/eng/20241025
LC record available at https://lccn.loc.gov/2024033371
LC ebook record available at https://lccn.loc.gov/2024033372

British Library Cataloguing-in-Publication Data
A catalog record for this book is available from the British Library.

To our two Young Boys

From two Old Boys

CONTENTS

Illustrations ix
Preface xi
Acknowledgments xiii
The Oneida Team Members xvii

Introduction: The 1927 Luncheon   1

PART I—THE ONEIDAS AND BOSTON

1   1863: The Match   9
2   School Years: A Classroom, a City, and a War   23
3   Games: Spaces, Clubs, and Organizing Play   39
4   The Crimson: Harvard and Football   55
5   Brahmin Networks: Families, Professions, and High Society   73

PART II—FROM MEMORY TO MONUMENT

6   Dinner Guests: Books, Memories, and the Origins of Sport   91
7   The Boy in Bronze: Schools, Anniversaries, and the Birth of a Myth   111

8 Monument Men: Deaths, Rivals, and Making a
   City Legend   133

PART III—THE STEAL AND THE HOAX

 9 The Soccer Grab: Surprise Legacies, Halls of Fame,
   and Refurbishing a Usable Past   157

10 Postmatch Analysis: Friendly Tactics, Mischief, and
   Gammon, or a Hoax?   179

11 Conclusion: Boys Will Be Boys   205

   Epilogue   215

   Notes   217
   Index   283

ILLUSTRATIONS

IMAGE 1. The Oneida Football Monument — x
IMAGE 2. The Oneida ball — 10
IMAGE 3. The donation of the ball by the Oneidas, November 15, 1922 — 112
IMAGE 4. Round Robin sent to Gerrit Smith Miller and signed November 7, 1923 — 128
IMAGE 5. First National Bank of Boston advertisement — 150
IMAGE 6. The Oneida ball and the United States Soccer Football Association — 162
IMAGE 7. National Soccer Hall of Fame brochure, ca. 1992 — 171
IMAGE 8. The Oneida monument and the seven surviving team members — 190
IMAGE 9. Six of the Oneidas at the monument unveiling — 191
IMAGE 10. The rear of the Oneida monument — 192
IMAGE 11. The Oneida ball and its lettering — 195
IMAGE 12. Lovett's poem, "Old Friends" — 211

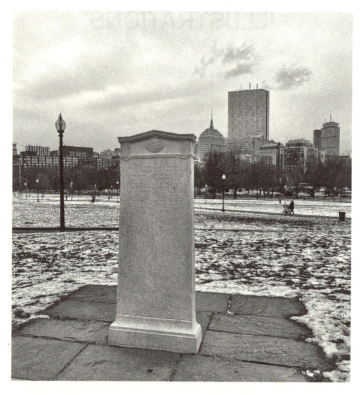

IMAGE 1. The Oneida Football Monument, Boston Common, Boston, Massachusetts, which was unveiled on November 21, 1925. Author photograph.

PREFACE

At the heart of this book is a football team that played its games on Boston Common in Boston, Massachusetts, in the 1860s. Part of the story is about the boys who took part and what kind of football this team played. The other part is about how and why, over decades, their nostalgia was preserved, self-memorialized, and finally transformed. It is not, however, a simple historical story. The origins of most modern sports are complex, a matter of evolution and development over time rather than a definitive moment of invention by a named individual. But humanity thirsts to know and understand how things began in sport, as in life. As such, sports and games have developed foundation myths so that their origins are known. In the game of rugby, it is William Webb Ellis who is said to have first picked up a ball and ran with it, thereby inventing the game, in 1823. Similarly, the foundation of baseball is accredited to Abner Doubleday, who played the first game in Elihu Phinney's cow pasture in Cooperstown in 1839. The foundation myths for both rugby and baseball are exactly that, myths, but both tales have proved enduring. This book deals with a similar origin story that relates to the American birth of two types of football—gridiron and soccer—and how in the early 1860s a group of Boston schoolboys began playing a modern form of sport.

On Boston Common there is a monument, one of many commemorating events and people from the city and wider American history, which specifically celebrates the first organized football team in the United States (see image 1). The Oneida Football Club is said, according to the monument, to have played its games between 1862 and 1865. It was made up of Boston schoolboys, who were mostly enrolled in fee-paying schools and preparing to take the Harvard entrance exam. They were boys who largely came from the elite families of Boston and in adulthood would go on to serve in public office, make fortunes in the worlds of banking and insurance, or else have leisurely lives, secure in the wealth of their family trust funds. This book explores how and why, in the 1920s, a small group of elderly men who had played football in the 1860s and were part of the Oneida Football Club chose to commemorate and memorialize a game of their childhood. It will establish that they did so by constructing a history for themselves and their play, allowing the narrative of their boyhood game to be linked to the contemporary pastime and national obsession that was 1920s American collegiate football. To construct this history, the men donated artifacts to museums, deposited self-penned histories into the leading Boston libraries and archives, and erected memorials to themselves.

The story of the Oneida Football Club and the ways in which its existence was documented and commemorated reveals much about the transformations taking place in Boston in the late nineteenth and early twentieth centuries. Running through this book are questions relating to history and memory and how the latter is a powerful tool in the creation of foundation myths, both local and national. Whether the boys playing their football on Boston Common was historically significant is almost irrelevant here. What is significant is how and why a group of elderly and well-connected men chose to create archival evidence, preserve artifacts, and erect bronze and stone memorials so that their boyhood game appeared as a seminal event in American and sporting history.

The book explores the Civil War context of the Oneida football games and compares what happened in Boston with the parallel development of ball sports in the United Kingdom. It also shows how the creation of a usable sporting past, particularly connected with the game of rugby, informed the actions of the former Oneida players in the 1920s. The story looks at the tight-knit elite social networks of late nineteenth- and early twentieth-century Boston and demonstrates how close friendships and associations developed through school and at Harvard University endured. Were these men just memorializing the importance of what they had done as teenagers as part of the historical preservation of the wider contributions of their tightly knit Boston Brahmin world? Or, helped by their social standing and their connections within the city of Boston, did they knowingly create a hoax, a deceptive history that gave birth to a questionable foundation myth that retrospectively positioned them as key to the development of gridiron football, America's biggest sport, and then soccer, the country's perpetual sport of the future?

ACKNOWLEDGMENTS

Some research journeys begin at a confluence of inspirations. In this case, a curiosity from Kevin's early doctoral days about a legendary club trickled years later into a postconference sidewalk conversation with Mike. This flowed further downstream into a call for papers for an edited collection on early soccer history in America. While Kevin might have been happy to leave the Oneida Club in the alluvion of drafts to that chapter, Mike buoyed him up, "Hey, there's a book in here!" Of course, Mike was quite right in retrospect. Well, at least this is how we remember it all. . . . But then again, as the Old Boston Boys remind us, memory has a funny way of becoming a self-fulfilling prophecy. So it is probably best to just stay the course and reiterate thanks to all those who participated in encouraging this pursuit or helping it float along.

The literary endeavor inevitably ends with a long list of debts, which follow here; we only pray they are not considered trespasses. For completing this book has required venturing into some fields whose boundaries were previously foreign to us and that remain better cultivated by other historians. This book was ever a balancing act between the broader context of, and beyond, Boston history (which at times threatened to aspirate the focus) and the narrow chronicle of a peculiar band of myth-making men (whose all-consuming biographies also at times endangered wider perspective). We hope that the forays here into nineteenth- and early twentieth-century New England (and specifically Brahmin) history as well as the history of memory, in particular, will be viewed by those more cultured in those fields as welcome divagations rather than vexing transgressions. Our underlying wish is that this history of curious commemoration will speak broadly to the universal elements of human experience.

This book has benefited from countless individuals. Beginning with those so dear to the historian's heart, librarians and archivists, we would like to express our thanks to the custodians at the many New England institutions that hold much of the material used in this book: Erin Hunt (Berkshire County Historical Society); Christian Guerra, Sarah Hutt, and Sarah Rodrigo (Boston Art Commission and Boston city hall); the reference staff at the Boston Athenaeum and Boston Public Library; the staff and archivists at Countway, Houghton, and Widener Libraries at Harvard University; Bob Malme (Hingham Historical Society); Shelley Cathcart, Nicole Chalfant, Donna Russo and Stephanie Herbert (Historic New England); Dan Hinchen (Massachusetts Historical Society); school archivist Heidi Charles (Noble and Greenough); Christian Dupont and the staff at the Burns Library, Boston College; Lori Fidler and Elizabeth Roscio (Revolutionary Spaces—formerly the Bostonian Society); and Christopher Fiorillo and Michael Frost (Yale University Library and the rich Walter Camp collection).

Closer to Oneida Gat Miller's hometown, we are grateful to the New York institutions that hold many essential collections and sources: the staff at Cornell University Library, Sydney Loftus and Barbara Schwartz (Madison County Historical Society), Taylor James Muench and Theresa Mannes (Syracuse Central Library), and the staff at Syracuse University's Special Collections Research Center. Further afield, our thanks go to Christopher Damiani and Lee Arnold (The Historical Society of Pennsylvania); Mayelin Perez (Van Pelt-Dietrich Library at University of Pennsylvania); the Library of Congress staff, and particularly genealogy librarian Sheree Budge and the now both retired sports and leisure librarians Dave Kelly and Darren Jones; the staff at the National Sporting Library and Museum in Middleburg, Virginia, for their help and in awarding Mike a fellowship in 2020; Lisa Greer-Douglass and Betty Reagan (National Collegiate Athletic Association Library and Archives); Sarah Cain and Matthew Short (Northern Illinois University) for answering a host of historical printing questions about the Beadle collections; Djorn Buchholz at the National Soccer Hall of Fame; as well as Greg Fike and Alidu Salifu from the United States Soccer Federation. Gratitude is owed internationally to Michael Schmalholz, Clément Le Minoux, Silvano Berti, and Dominik Petermann (FIFA Library and Archives); Jonathan Smith (Rugby School Archives); and Caroline Buit (La Chaux-de-Fonds Public Library) for setting up perhaps one of the last remaining microfiche readers near Neuchâtel.

Additional recognition must go to a number of individuals who provided unique access to materials and helped our research: Samuel Spirn, Joan and Alan Peterson, and Rachael Young. We are also grateful to Tom McGrath, as

Acknowledgments

devout a defender of the Oneida legacy as there is. A sincere thank-you, also, to those with whom many an email about nineteenth- and early twentieth-century football was exchanged: Adrian Harvey, Les Jones, Andrew Margolis, Stephen Siano, Robert Sproule, Nigel Trueman, and Earl Zukerman. Special thanks must go to Melvin Smith, perhaps the most passionate and dedicated researcher of them all, who shared mountains of material over much correspondence and for whose groundwork all historians of football must be indebted. Tatiana Wilde worked with us on the first complete draft of the book and proved an adept and insightful editor. She showed us how to keep the narrative at the heart of the book and gave us permission to let go of a mass of historiographical scaffolding.

We are particularly appreciative of the support during the writing and editing process to those who gallantly shared an expertise exceeding our own and thus enhanced this book significantly. Partially guilty for encouraging this book beyond the initial chapter for their collection, George Kioussis and Chris Bolsmann's knowledge and keen editorial eyes challenged and improved our writing (and both also generously shared material anytime they saw the word "Oneida," from archival collections including the Lovejoy Library of Southern Illinois University–Edwardsville). Tony Collins, Richard Holt, Chuck Korr, Pierre Lanfranchi, and Dil Porter provided invaluable feedback on the manuscript as well as debating ideas on podcasts and over coffee, a precious reminder of the intellectual camaraderie that has been the hallmark of De Montfort University's International Centre for Sport History and Culture for so long. This is also where Neil Carter, Robert Colls, Heather Dichter, James Panter, and Matt Taylor always provided support and encouragement. We are grateful to the anonymous University of Massachusetts Press reviewers whose pertinent stylistic, historiographical, and thematic suggestions we have done our best to incorporate. Working with the University of Massachusetts Press has been a delight, and they have guided this project from manuscript to finished book with a great eye for detail and a belief in the project's value. Thanks go to Matt Becker for all his work with us on the final stretch, to production and design editors Ben Kimball and Sally Nichols, and to Brianna Blackburn and the editorial team at Scribe.

Kevin is particularly grateful to his principal academic home for these last two decades, the International Centre for Sport Studies (CIES) in Neuchâtel, Switzerland. CIES has supported the research, conferences, and travel all essential to this project. Thanks to Roland Chavillon, Pierre Cornu, Anne-Catherine

Le-Mevel, Vincent Monnier, Denis Oswald, Vincent Schatzmann, and all CIES colleagues for the general support as well as to Jean-Louis Juvet and Sue Ingle, whose belief in Kevin is treasured still. Christophe Jaccoud and Thomas Bussett contributed particularly via innumerable discussions and genuine collegial interest, and it would be remiss not to thank CIES librarians Marie-Claude Borel and Maryline Burri, who obtained far more interlibrary loans than should be allowed. Special tribute must be reserved for the Society of American Soccer History (SASH) and several members who were instrumental along the way through supportive discussion, answering questions as well as flagging and sharing sources: Zach Bigalke, James Brown, Brian Bunk, Ed Farnsworth, David Kilpatrick, Gabe Logan, and Tom McCabe as well as founding stalwarts Roger Allaway, Jack Huckel, and Colin Jose. This would not be the same book without SASH. Kevin must thank his family for their unwavering support, particularly Teozen, with whom father-son writing outings have become an unexpected and joyful life revelation. The father awaits the son's first book with anticipation as the creative spirit pipes inspiration on through the generations. The thanks to his parents Philip and Gwenaëlle, sisters Miriam and Joëlle (with her and Nichlas's amazing family), and godmother Armelle are too great to be diminished by mere words. Merci à vous tous, je vous aime.

Mike's colleagues in Irish Studies at Boston College were always on hand to offer insights on the history of Boston and its geography. Thanks as always to David Quigley and John Burke for encouraging research endeavors such as this. In Ireland he is indebted to his colleagues Thea Gilien and Claire McGowan as well as to his friends and past collaborators Mark Duncan and Paul Rouse. Final thanks, as always, to his family, who lived with this project through the pandemic. While we all stayed at home during lockdown, they shared their space with the mass of papers that related to the lives of the fifty-two Oneida players as their complex stories were uncovered. For that reason, and for all the love, thanks to Moynagh, Ellen, and Samson.

If researching and writing are always toilsome to a degree, here we might quote Oneida Robert Means Lawrence about Jim Lovett's own labor in penning *Old Boston Boys*, "The work was doubtless congenial." Congenial indeed it was. In fact, we think we had as much fun in writing their history as the Oneidas did in making it.

THE ONEIDA TEAM MEMBERS

*Name appears on the Boston Common Monument.
+Organizer of the Commemoration of the Oneidas.

Full biographies are available online at UMass Digital Humanities Platform.

William Foster Apthorp, October 24, 1848–February 18, 1913.
Music critic and author.
Edward Lincoln Arnold, December 8, 1845–March 9, 1935.
Insurance agent.*+
James Arthur Beebe, August 12, 1846–November 27, 1914. Wool merchant and financier.
Joseph Smith Bigelow, October 28, 1848–December 24, 1930.
Bank president.
William Sturgis Bigelow, April 4, 1850–October 6, 1926. Medic and philanthropist.
Robert Apthorp Boit, April 29, 1846–March 6, 1919. Writer and insurance executive.*
Edward Bowditch, January 19, 1847–July 19, 1929. Domestic stove manufacturer.*+
John Henry Brooks, June 20, 1848–July 21, 1913. Railway investor.
Walter Denison Brooks, August 26, 1845–April 5, 1877. Book publisher.*
Joseph Taylor Brown, January 17, 1848–March 8, 1929.
Pharmacist and estate trustee.
Edward Burgess, June 30, 1848–July 12, 1891. Entomologist and yacht designer.

Walter Burgess, May 24, 1851–December 1, 1931. Real estate investor and yacht builder.
George Kuhn Davis, December 6, 1846–November 9, 1893. Clerk of the Oakes Ames estate.*
John Dixwell, March 21, 1848–April 19, 1931. Medical doctor.
John Robertson Duff, August 25, 1844–February 27, 1891. Wall Street trader.
James Dwight, July 14, 1852–July 13, 1917. Tennis player.
William Ellery Channing Eustis, November 24, 1849–October 29, 1932. Estate trustee and metallurgist.
James Malcolm Forbes, February 2, 1847–February 19, 1904. Estate trustee and horse breeder.*
Virgil Gilmore, October 21, 1845–June 9, 1918. Banker.
Russell Gray, June 17, 1850–June 7, 1929. Investor.
John Paouaa Hall, 1845–August 29, 1916. Stud farm manager.*
Arthur Sherburne Hardy, August 13, 1847–March 14, 1930. Mathematician, editor, and diplomat.
Francis Stanton Hubbard, December 21, 1847–April 3, 1925. Insurance underwriter.
Oscar Iasigi, October 18, 1846–January 18, 1884. Estate trustee.
Frank Jackson, February 2, 1850–June 3, 1921. Investor.
Robert Gould Jones, October 10, 1847–June 21, 1885. Wool broker.
Amory Appleton Lawrence, April 22, 1848–July 6, 1912. Investor and estate trustee.
Robert Means Lawrence, May 14, 1847–March 7, 1935. Medical doctor and writer.*+
William Lawrence, May 30, 1850–November 6, 1941. Cleric, writer, and investor.
Henry Cabot Lodge, May 12, 1850–November 9, 1924. Academic and politician.
James D'Wolf Lovett, May 31, 1844–September 29, 1935. Insurance underwriter.*+
John Wayland McBurney, August 22, 1848–January 4, 1885. Insurance broker and fruit farmer.
Charles Dudley Miller, July 3, 1847–October 6, 1894. Farmer and breeder.

The Oneida Team Members

Gerrit Smith Miller, January 30, 1845–March 11, 1937. Farmer and breeder.*+

Arthur Mills, November 17, 1850–January 1, 1907. Railroad freight investor.

George Richards Minot, March 3, 1849–January 24, 1894. Investor and estate trustee.

Henry Parkman, May 23, 1850–June 23, 1924. Lawyer and bank director.

Francis Greenwood Peabody, December 4, 1847–December 28, 1936. Academic.*+

Joseph Warren Revere, September 20, 1848–December 13, 1932. Mining engineer.

Henry Richards, July 17, 1848–January 26, 1949. Architect, paper manufacturer, and illustrator.

Arthur Rotch, May 13, 1850–August 15, 1894. Architect.

Winthrop Saltonstall Scudder, July 24, 1846–August 14, 1929. Publisher and author.*+

Frederick Cheever Shattuck, November 1, 1847–January 11, 1929. Medical doctor and academic.

William Eliot Sparks, October 23, 1847–September 5, 1886. Mechanical engineer.

Frederic Russell Sturgis, July 7, 1844–May 6, 1919. Medical doctor and academic.

Stephen Van Rensselaer Thayer, August 2, 1847–October 10, 1871. Explorer and banker.

Louis Thies, December 12, 1847–August 1870.*

Alanson Tucker, April 20, 1848–May 1, 1909. Dry goods businessman and estate trustee.*

Robert Clifford Watson, September 10, 1847–June 1, 1902. Fire insurance investor and rower.*

William Fisher Wharton, June 28, 1847–May 20, 1919. Lawyer, author, and politician.

Huntington Frothingham Wolcott, February 4, 1846–June 9, 1865. Soldier.*

Roger Wolcott, July 13, 1847–December 21, 1900. Lawyer, estate trustee, and politician.

Two codes diverged in a yellow wood . . .

INVENTING THE
BOSTON GAME

INTRODUCTION

The 1927 Luncheon

> Hoax, noun: a humorous or malicious deception.
>
> "The originator of the deception must, through either intentional or inadvertent action, create a message that transmits information about the world that is incorrect in some way."
>
> —from Peter Hancock, *Hoax Springs Eternal*[1]

On a mild spring Saturday in May 1927, six elderly men and lifelong friends gathered for a celebratory lunch.[2] In pictures taken around the time, they are aged but look healthy and well-groomed. The meal was eaten at the home of Mr. and Mrs. William de Yongh Field in Weston, on the western outskirts of Boston, Massachusetts. How many other people attended the lunch is unrecorded, but it is likely there were some from the couple's wider social network there. De Yongh Field was wealthy, had a farm, and lived on an extensive estate, so the food was no doubt plentiful.[3] The festive gathering was organized to acknowledge what the six men (plus one other not in attendance) had achieved in the previous few years. Reminiscing on a series of events orchestrated between 1922 and 1926, they could revel in having ensured their place in history: they were the seven living members of the Oneida Football Club of Boston, the first organized football team in the United States.

Most of the men were locals living in Boston—Edward "Ned" Lincoln Arnold, Robert "Bob" Means Lawrence, James "Jim" D'Wolf Lovett, Francis "Frank" Greenwood Peabody, and Winthrop "Win" Saltonstall Scudder—with two teammates living out of state in New York, Edward "Ned" Bowditch and Gerrit "Gat" Smith Miller.[4] Mostly retired, during their working lives they had been active in the fields of insurance, manufacturing, medicine, education, and publishing. Some of them were incredibly wealthy men, others quite comfortable—well connected and members of the myriad of clubs that made up Boston's elite social and cultural world. Just two—Arnold and Lovett—appear to have been living on more modest means.[5] Perhaps only Peabody, a leading scholar of social ethics at Harvard and a famed reformer of that university, would, without the success of their self-commemoration, have been considered famous or well known.[6] Steadfast in their childhood friendships as Boston transformed from the 1860s to the 1920s, together these men had worked cleverly to create a place in history for themselves and commemorate their club, which included at least fifty-two boys from the most prominent Boston Brahmin and old New England families.[7] Building more consciously each step of the way, the seven friends gifted artifacts to museums, deposited manuscripts in archives, and most audaciously, built a public monument to themselves. All these steps, taken over the course of four years, worked together to create proof that what they claimed—their history-making moment—was true, verifiable, documented, and memorialized. The Oneida commemoration was the perfect execution of what a contemporary writer, Van Wyck Brooks, coined in 1918: the creation of a usable past "placed at the service of the future."[8]

Because of the way that historical memory is constructed, the Oneida tale endures to this day. Each element of the story that they put in place in the 1920s reinforced the other. By the time of their own deaths, in the late 1920s and into the 1930s, just over half of the seven obituaries had begun to embrace the myth and position their supposed achievement as central to their lives and their legacy. As the seven passed away, it was recorded that, as teenagers, they had been members of the Oneidas (as they were collectively referred to): the first football club in the United States, unscored upon between 1862 and 1865. From them, the origins of the game of American football could be traced. By 1926, for example, the magazine *Boys' Life* was telling its hundreds of thousands of young scout readers that "the man who is said to have founded organized football in America is still living. . . . His name is Gerrit Smith Miller, known to his comrades as 'Gat Miller.' In 1862, while the Civil War was being fought, he organized and captained what is reputed to be the first football team formed in this country."[9]

Returning to the lunch in 1927, one of the men, James D'Wolf Lovett, had written a poem, *A Pilgrimage*, which he read to those gathered. The poem was later printed in book form, bound between a sky-blue cover, which featured the title, a crest, and the line "Read at a Meeting of the Oneidas: Saturday, May 28, 1927." It celebrated their club in an invented dialogue as Lovett spoke to their old round rubber football, the memory of which was honored on Boston Common:

> And *YOUR* monument will long
>   endure, singing its Football Song,
> When the remaining few of our dear
>   old Crew,
> Shall have silently passed along.

After the luncheon, another of the men, Winthrop Saltonstall Scudder, had deposited a bound copy of the booklet (perhaps the only one that was ever printed) in the library of his alma mater, Harvard University, where it remains to this day.[10] It was a droll poem that summed up an in-joke between friends and that to all of them, familiar as they were with each step of their self-memorialization, underlined what they had done and offered clues as to some of the claims they had made. In the decade after the 1927 lunch, the seven men all passed away, with the last of them—fittingly, their captain, Gerrit Smith Miller—dying in March 1937.

Nearly all the fifty-two boys in the club had grown up within walking distance of one another, attending the same set of schools and playing together on Boston Common. From school, the majority of the boys entered Harvard, where they appear to have dropped their football playing to concentrate on their adult lives instead in the midst of the Reconstruction era. And as these boys were part of the Gilded Age Bostonian elite, their passage through college and into a plethora of professions perpetuated the social networks and generational wealth that their forefathers had established. The boys remained tightly connected into adulthood. Most who stayed in Boston lived in the same parts of the city, particularly the exclusive Back Bay. They were members of the same clubs and involved themselves in philanthropic work that supported charities for the poor and sick and extended to the galleries, museums, and learned institutions of the city and abroad.

Decades following their deaths, the domino effect continued; the story had taken hold, such that a 1976 advertising campaign for Wrigley's Chewing Gum was able to state as a fun fact that "America's first football team was the Oneida Football Club, organized in 1862 by Gerrit Miller in Boston."[11] But however deliberately one places the dominoes, surprises can arise down the line. The same kids who chewed gum in bicentennial America were also playing soccer, that other football popularized in the United States by Pelé. In the subsequent years, the guardians of American soccer memory tackled the Oneida gridiron legacy and, by the 1990s, had claimed the club ancestry as their own. So the Oneidas' work, the founding myth that they memorialized, endured just as Lovett had so poetically promised, but perhaps not in the way he had imagined. The Oneida monument that was supposed to sing a football song had changed its tune to a less oval and rounder melody.

So how and why did a small group of elderly men put so much time and effort into carefully interweaving history and heritage? From 1904 to the mid-1920s, they produced a historical record that, because of who they were, was accepted into the archives, libraries, and museums of the city's leading institutions. No one questioned the veracity of their claims. They self-memorialized and produced a history, a collective memory, that they had done something exceptional and that modern intercollegiate gridiron, the sport that captured the imagination of millions of Americans filling university coliseums by the 1920s, stemmed from the game that they had played sixty years before. Their exceptional history was born in the midst of the construction of a wider "exceptionalist" narrative. With the Civil War relegated to the fringes of living memory and the Gilded Age just behind them, the aging Oneidas witnessed the era of progress as Europe dimmed and America rose in its twentieth-century self-consciousness. To draw on Sam Haynes's study of eighteenth- and nineteenth-century British sentiment of America, the Oneidas embodied the shift from their Revolutionary and early republic's forefathers' "deep-seated sense of cultural inferiority to a bold, if self-conscious declaration of their own exceptionalism" evident by the early twentieth century.[12] As their country roared into the 1920s, the Oneidas sought to remember the same rapidly receding past that was at the heart of the New England preservation movement vibrantly growing around them in the hope that it "would regenerate their heroic values."[13] Their monument was erected in the midst of what Erika Doss has called "statue mania" in response to "anxieties about national unity . . . unleashed by the rapid advance of modernism, immigration and mass culture."[14] The seven remaining Oneidas crafted their exceptional sporting story as Frederick Jackson Turner was articulating his Frontier Thesis and Werner Sombart was exploring reasons why the socialism of the Old World was missing in the New. Those two contemporary observations qualifying the American experience as unique were formulated in the midst of an emerging consciousness of the now pervasive term "American exceptionalism"—particularly in the case of Boston's understanding of its own history as the original "city upon a hill."[15] In this same time period, the aging Oneidas began to believe that they had done something different—something exceptional, in fact—and succeeded in attributing to themselves special national significance.

Yet the Oneida history did not end with their own efforts. After the men were long dead, their place in their self-created history assured, someone saw the monument that they had erected and chanced on an opportunity to rewrite the record. In the 1990s it was reclaimed and reinvented with a new meaning as a foundational story for American soccer. Later, even this was challenged by a defender of the long-dead Oneidas, who fought for them and their self-proclaimed history. The Oneida story explores the fertile verge between history and heritage, how they are open to manipulation, and how the meanings of a usable past can be continually twisted into the present.

This book is a history *of* the history of the origins of football and the problems that accompany foundation myths. It shows how monuments that commemorate a birthplace—in this case, that of football—possess interpretative power and how we must be alert to how memories are constructed or, in the words of historian Seth Bruggeman, "that the process by which memory is made at public monuments is always political . . . our task is to identify what is at stake and who is at play in the politics of remembering birth."[16] Furthermore, the Oneidas were also confronted with the risk that groups who attempt to rebuild "collective social memory"—to quote early sociologist Maurice Halbwachs, who wrote contemporaneously to their monument—"most often, at the same time as they reconstruct it . . . deform it."[17] Those who engage in memorialization are what Jay Winter called the "social agents of remembrance," and this book explores one such "fictive kinship group" personified by the Oneidas.[18] As such, this is also fundamentally a story of the complex nature of human intention. At the start of their memorializing endeavors, the Oneidas never intended to become mountebanks, but there is mystery surrounding their history, the one that was eventually celebrated in poetic knavery at the 1927 luncheon. Unveiling their evolving intent is a Sherlockian exercise in evaluating facts and changing circumstances, deciphering means, and uncovering motive. Yet at its heart, the Oneida story is one of old friends who created and memorialized a version of the past that gave them a self-appointed exceptional place in history. It remained ambiguous enough for surprises because these elderly men, of Boston's social elite, playfully constructed a fabled heritage that just may have hatched the greatest sporting hoax ever. They are the Oneidas, and this is their story.

PART I
THE ONEIDAS AND BOSTON

1
1863

The Match

In the off-site storage facility of Historic New England Library and Archives in Haverhill, Massachusetts, there are thousands of artifacts and documents that relate to the history of the region.[1] Tucked away on a shelf, in a climate-controlled storage room, and kept in a cardboard archive box is a black ball. It is a ball that was designed for some type of play, but quite unlike anything used in contemporary sport. It is not purely spherical, so it may not be a soccer ball, and neither does it resemble the oval shape of a rugby or American football (see image 2). It is squatter, a slightly rounded-off square shape, which is dented and collapsed in on itself in places as if the task of remaining inflated has proved too much. On touching the ball, it feels hard, and it emits a hollow sound when tapped. It appears to have been made of rubber, but over the years it has hardened and perished so it feels like thin wood. On one side of the ball, in white lettering, its purpose is suggested, declaring that it was won by someone (there is a crest, but no name) on November 7, 1863, from the High and Latin Schools. On the reverse are fifteen names (the players who played that day?) and, given the mid-nineteenth-century obsession with recording facts and statistics, the top of the ball spells out times—namely, the eighth, ninth, and tenth minutes, suggesting that something about these timings was significant.

But what is this ball, and what does it represent? It was clearly significant enough to have been kept, and subsequently someone saw fit to mark the ball with a date, a crest, the name of a defeated team, and a list of fifteen surnames. And given that the ball is preserved by Historic New England, it is clearly important to the history of Boston. The ball was once played with, was kept by the winning side in the manner of a trophy, and more than a century and a half later is still preserved by one of the region's leading archives

IMAGE 2. The Oneida football that the team won in 1863. The ball is made of rubber panels and marked with the date of the match and the names of the Oneida players who took part that day. It was gifted to the Society for the Preservation of New England Antiquities in 1922. Courtesy of Historic New England.

(it had also spent a score residing in the National Soccer Hall of Fame, but that is a story for later).

The ball was donated in 1922, fifty-nine years after it had been played with, to what was then the Society for the Preservation of New England Antiquities (the SPNEA, now Historic New England).[2] Visitors are told that it is the actual one that was played with in the match on November 7, 1863, and features the names of the boys who played for the Oneida Football Club (only identified on the ball by the team crest). The Oneida Football Club, whatever that term actually meant, had been formed by and involved a wider group of Boston boys who mostly attended Mr. Dixwell's School in the early 1860s. They played their game on Boston Common against boys from other city schools—namely, the Boston Public Latin School, the English High School, and Dorchester High School. According to later stories, the Oneidas were unbeatable and the club's name had been suggested by a teammate in reference to the lake near their captain's upstate New York hometown—though there may have been other closer rowing-related inspirations. It was decided in November of 1863 that they would play a select team—drawn from the finest players of the Boston Public Latin School and the English High School—to see which was the best side in the city.

Where did this all-important ball come from? It was clearly not a ball that the boys had made themselves but a manufactured ball, and one that would have been sold commercially, or at least made for them. And the manufacturing of sporting goods in the post–Civil War years was important in explaining "much of the popularity for athletic games and outdoor recreation [that] was due to standardized manufacturing."[3] But there is no evidence in the *Boston Directory* for 1861 or 1862 of a sporting goods shop existing in the city. There were a number of specialty shops, those selling billiard equipment or leather and rubber shops such as Alfred Hale and Co., which had all manner of goods for sale, and such shops no doubt found a profitable sideline in selling footballs to the boys and men of Boston.[4] By the time the boys were playing their games, there was also a transatlantic mail-order business that sold and shipped footballs and other equipment to the United States. In the same year that the boys took to Boston Common to play their game, over in London, the Lillywhites store opened for business, specifically selling sporting goods and making its entire stock available for shipment to the United States and elsewhere.

Given the dates of their play, 1862–65, it is likely that the Oneida boys played with an India rubber ball. Over the years in which they played, the Oneidas likely used a number of balls brought to the Common by different boys on match days. Some undoubtedly burst or were damaged, and they would have moved on to the next available ball. In this context it is likely that the boys used types of balls manufactured by a variety of companies. Put simply, they played with whatever they could source.

The Oneida ball held by Historic New England does not look like a makeshift, irregular pig-bladder ball but rather has the appearance of a mass-produced ball, and it is reputedly one that was manufactured by Charles Goodyear, a fact repeated on a myriad of soccer history websites.[5] He died in 1860, but it is claimed that a few years before his death, he made the first football in 1855. Awarded multiple patents between 1835 and 1852, he worked to improve the air pump, an essential instrument for his November 1847 deposition describing how to produce a hollow ball made from rubber panels that were stuck together with glue.[6] In 1853, Goodyear published *The Applications and Uses of Vulcanized Gum Elastic*, in which he set out the hundreds of potential uses for his rubber, covering everything from mechanical items to nautical wares, medical equipment, packing materials, and optical implements. In the section on sports and games, he states that footballs could be made with rubber "in the same way as hollow ware, or they may be made more substantially of gum elastic felt or vegetable leather. They are uniformly inflated with a tube as they are not otherwise made stiff enough to retain their shape without being too heavy."[7] If, as is often repeated, the Oneidas played with a Goodyear ball (the one now in Historic New England), it was manufactured between Goodyear designing his original football in 1847 and his death in 1860 (or else by another manufacturer who produced balls based on Goodyear's design at a later date).[8] The Oneidas did not begin playing until two years after Goodyear's death, so the ball's design was already a dozen years old by the time they used it on Boston Common. It was then stored between the 1863 game and the presentation of the ball, by Edward Arnold and the others, to the museum in 1922. For a ball that was said to be seventy years old at the time it was presented for safekeeping to the museum, it had survived remarkably well. A contemporary of the Oneidas, Clarence Deming, played his midcentury football elsewhere in New England but did recall later that the balls he used were "imported from the city, made of pure rubber, of vast diameter, blown up by brass pipe which turned a screw and, after vexing trials, locked the air in. This ball was, also, tender, flabby, addicted to leaks and a chronic habit of sudden collapse just as the game grew hot."[9] This description matches the preserved Oneida ball, but Deming's narrative does not make the balls sound reliable, and across their club's three-year lifetime, the Oneidas must have either constantly repaired or else replaced their ball.

The key point about India rubber balls is that they were more reliable and uniform than the pig-bladder balls that preceded them. This meant that the Oneidas, and other teams playing at the time, had a ball that could be reliably carried, thrown, *and* kicked until it lost its shape or burst. Indeed, this was true for the development of all the football codes to that date. In Britain it was rugby, with its central focus on the handling technique, that was the dominant game until the late 1860s. How much of that dominance was due to the unreliability of the balls that could be bought commercially and the fact that the pig-bladder balls of the period were better suited to being handled rather than kicked?[10] The Oneida boys played their game at precisely the moment mass-produced balls and a shift in technology allowed for a kicking game to be played more easily.

The match the Oneida boys played in the early 1860s was retrospectively deemed important. Although the supposed match ball would one day be presented to the SPNEA, in reality this was simply a game played between teams of boys doing what boys do: entertaining themselves through a form of play that embraced the idea of defined teams, a winner and loser, and some rough physicality that allowed them to expend an excess of testosterone-filled energy. That a group of boys was playing a form of football was nothing new or remarkable for Boston at this time. The importance of the Oneida boys was not that they were playing but *what* they were playing and the significance, although they would not have realized it at the time, of how their game would evolve and how powerful, as a maker and marker of memory and history, their later decision to memorialize their boyhood games would be.

Several city papers, including the *Boston Herald* and the *Boston Daily Advertiser*, reported that the title match in November 1863 was "an interesting game of football" involving the "well-known Oneida club" even though the coverage was dwarfed by the reports about the progress of the Union in the ongoing Civil War and the battle of the Rappahannock, which took place on the same day as the Oneida game.[11] In its few lines on the game, the *Boston Evening Transcript* referred to the combined forces of the Latin and English boys as "Rome" and noted that the Oneidas, victorious in three successive games, "now hold the championship of Boston."[12] The game was actually a series of games, but the meager press coverage hardly gives the reader any idea of the rough-and-tumble game the boys actually played. What was their football like? How was the field laid out, if at all, and did it have clearly marked lines or goals? Did they kick and dribble with their feet or handle and run with the ball? Was there an offside rule, and was tackling allowed?

Beyond the brief contemporary press reports, the only detailed description of the game was written by one of the players many years later. In 1906, the Oneida player James D'Wolf Lovett privately published a book about his childhood years and the various games and sports that filled the nonschool hours of his contemporaries. His *Old Boston Boys and the Games They Played* began, in print at least, the creation of a mythology.[13] The book includes a description of what happened on Boston Common in the famed match of 1863 and describes their football-playing days. As the book was written a full forty-plus years after the matches that the Oneidas had played, it is perhaps unsurprising that Lovett's description is lacking in clarity.

Lovett was deliberate, however, in making some clear distinctions between what was commonly known as the college, intercollegiate, or gridiron game, or just simply "football" (without the qualifiers "rugby" or "Association") in the American universities at the time, and the game that he and his adolescent friends played. There was little confusion in his mind about the obvious differences. Lovett explains that in the old days there were "no 'touchdowns' nor was the ground marked off by lines of any kind; in fact, there was no 'gridiron,' nothing but straight football," nor any mention of a fixed duration of play. When a goal was scored, the game was over. The boys played several games in an afternoon, since each time the ball crossed the boundary line that game was over, and a new one began. The mention of the "opponents' boundary line" is a vague one, however, since Lovett sketches an ambiguous picture of unmarked perimeter lines with Beacon Street Mall as one goal line, and the path between Flagstaff Hill and Charles Street as the other.

But how did they play? Lovett compared the college football of present-day 1906 (but before the 1905–1906 rule changes and introduction of the revolutionary forward pass) with his boyhood game, and he noted the "difference between guarding a line the entire width of the ground, and one a few feet long between the upright poles of today's game." So the Oneidas played without the defined goal lines (endzones) and goalposts so essential to the game in the American colleges. In 1906, eleven gridiron players had to defend a clearly marked goal line that stretched 160 feet wide and run up and down a field 330 feet long. In comparison, a rough measure of the space on Boston Common would be about 300–350 feet by 450–500 feet. The actual space used may have varied based on the number of players; accounts of Oneida and school games in the 1860s papers vary as to the number of players, sometimes ten, twelve, sixteen, or even seventeen per side.

Lovett never mentions the, even by 1906 standards, modern fixed "line of scrimmage" with players not in motion, but he does mention a "rush line" of five (his teammates, Cliff Watson, Frank Peabody, Walter Brooks, Frank Davis, and John Hall) who were "were tough propositions to run up against." Cliff Watson was also the strategist, able to "extricate the ball from more tight places than anyone else upon the team," while Gerrit Smith Miller was "our sheet anchor as 'tender out,' or 'full-back' as it is called to-day, and a tower of strength when the ball got past the rest of the team."[14] Was Watson then possibly filling the role of putative quarterback or rugby scrum half while Miller acted as some kind of early soccer libero?

The confusion from Lovett's 1906 account—an illustration of the problems of memory, given that he played in and watched these games in the 1860s—remained unclarified in later years. In 1926 surviving members of the Oneidas donated a file to the Massachusetts Historical Society.[15] In the file, the Oneida captain, Miller (or at least that's how the other members referred to him), attached a sketch of the team's sixteen-member tactical formation. The one-eight-four-two-one formation included "rushers," "infielders," "outfielders," and the "tender out or full-back"—a farrago of terms that hardly allows for a distinctive picture of their play. But perhaps this is the central point. In trying to remember retrospectively through any contemporary lens, comparisons will indubitably fail. And in making such leaps, to impose modern positions on the 1860s Oneidas, who were playing a game that was loosely defined and still evolving, are we seeking historical antecedents where none exist?

From Lovett's account of 1906, there was no time limit to the matches and only scoring ended the game. Both Lovett and the contemporary press presented the game as a series of best out of three, but this, like many other aspects of any agreed rules, was not set in stone. If the games were indeed settled by the first score, does then the marking on the ball from 1863 that states "Time. 1st 8 min. 2nd 9 min. 3rd 10." suggest that the Oneidas won that day three games to nil, and the minute times represent when they scored the winning goal in each of their three games? In the most detailed account of what appears to be a different game and not strictly an Oneida one, but still between the same Latin School and Dixwell's boys, the full series—that time a best of five—lasted two hours and forty-seven minutes, while the individual games went on for fifteen, twenty, forty, or even forty-five minutes until one side "gained the coveted goal." To achieve this score, which ended the game, a team had "to land the ball past their [opposing] goal."

From Lovett's descriptions, it appears that a score was achieved by kicking the ball toward a wide unmarked goal. An illustrative case in point was Lovett himself, who, as it was recalled by one teammate, had spent the afternoon loafing "around with his hands in his pockets, during the first four games [before he] woke up and finished the game, after forty-seven minutes, by kicking the winning goal."[16] The rare news coverage of Dixwell School games from the period underlines that kicking was the agreed scoring method, with William Newell credited with a "well directed kick" defeating the Latin boys in October of 1860.[17] Even in a subsequent 1924 retrospective account of the game, one Oneida's, Ned Arnold's, quick thinking stopped an opponent who was about to "kick the goal and win the game."[18]

It does appear that the Oneidas both kicked and handled the ball without the carrying counting for a score—a rule that became more important in the intercollegiate game only in the 1880s and '90s rule changes.[19] Lovett describes other teammates (Bowditch, Scudder, Means Lawrence, Wolcott, and Thies) who "played into each other's hands with skill and judgment," or Arthur Beebe, who patted the ball "with his hands, this way and that, steering it clear of the ravening wolves [opponents] who were pursuing and . . . deftly tossed the ball over the surrounding heads into the ready hand of an alert partner."[20] Equally, Lovett recalls Oneida Ned Arnold, rushing toward another player, both "intent only on kicking the ball"; Pat Jackson, who was adept at the free kick "with no one to interfere with him"; and Tom Nelson, who shook off his pursuers and "proceeded to kick the ball according to original intentions."

What defensive tactics were available to counter this kicking and carrying game? Perhaps unsurprising, rough-and-tumble tackling of opponents seems to have been part and parcel of these boyhood games. Sam Cabot was a "peace-loving boy" but also a "tough customer to run foul of, and whoever he tackled might as well give it up first as last." Lovett also refers to an episode when he saved the day by leaping and landing on another boy, who went sprawling and released the ball. Lurking, or the Oneida primeval version of offside, was, in Lovett's words, "an offense not to be countenanced for a moment, even if the boy guilty of it was on one's own side." The Oneidas seemed to have developed their own sense of boyhood justice and fair play. Lovett, in what might be his own rosy version of how they played fair back then and mindful of how college football had become renowned for its dangerous and ungentlemanly play by 1906, referred to lurking as a trick "very rarely resorted to in those days," wherein a boy would sneak around the side and kick the ball his way.[21]

Even if Lovett's account gives a glimpse of those boyhood football games, the purpose of his *Old Boston Boys* book was far more personal. It was never intended as a definitive rulebook or a guide to understanding the play of a bygone era. His was a private memoir written to honor old friends. It mixed testaments to youthful athletic prowess with the lifelong career achievements of a close-knit Boston elite. The tone is deliberately allegorical, with numerous references to the Civil War, which so marked that generation. The neighborhood boyish scrimmages were described as "football battles" and the players equated to torpedo boats, powerful battleships, or swift cruisers.

He even compared those who went in to kick the ball with the same "utter contempt for personal danger which Farragut so forcibly expressed" at the battle of Mobile Harbor, albeit without reference to the famous saying "Damn the torpedoes, full speed ahead!"[22]

Yet other than passing references to a handful of Old Boston Boys, casualties of the conflict, the "ever present Civil War" is more a backdrop than directly discussed.[23] In a rare personal moment, Lovett reveals that his brother enlisted twice. Indeed, having a relative fighting made the war a "much sterner reality than to those who had not" and a reminder that "times of peace can only be appreciated at their full value by those who know, by personal experience, what a long, heart-breaking war means."[24] Slavery, however, gets not one explicit reference, and only a couple passing words describe a few "negro boys" (one of whom was well known to Lovett).[25] In the end, the book was simply an ode to a childhood protected from the immediacy of war.

The omnipresence of war imagery and language in *Old Boston Boys* is telling, since the Oneidas had largely evaded the war's harsh battlefield realities, save one: Huntington Frothingham Wolcott, the only Oneida to serve and die as a result of the conflict. Speaking at the memorial service following the death of Wolcott's younger brother, Roger, in 1901, Henry Cabot Lodge, who had played with both boys on the Oneida team, said that "there is in memory no space between the elder brother at school and the next scene. In reality there was an interval of brave, active service, even while we boys at home played on as before. All this vanishes in recollection. He had gone to the front, he had come home wasted with fever, he was dead, that was all we knew."[26] So while the younger Oneidas remained home and played their games on Boston Common, Huntington Frothingham Wolcott fought for the Union and died.

The Oneida boys lived through a profound transitional era in the last decades of the nineteenth century: war, Reconstruction, immigration, westward expansion toward Frederick Jackson Turner's famous frontier, but also the diffusion and growth of modern football codes that have since achieved global cultural resonance. The changes to Boston football in the years after the Oneidas had ceased to play moved the sport away from their childhood games that had no written codified rules (that have survived) and made the game anew. Various authors have the Oneida game down as a forerunner of soccer in the United States or the direct founder of American football.[27] But with the diffusion of rules in the British Isles and beyond, diverging football games were sprouting across the Anglophone world and throughout the

British Empire.[28] Rugby rules were a source of inspiration in Melbourne for what was reshaped into autochthonous Australian rules. The Gaelic Athletic Association in Ireland went through similar phases of rule adaptation to create a truly Irish football code, part of a larger cultural revival movement to define and preserve language, literature, and culture.[29] The split between Rugby League and Rugby Union from 1895 caused further fragmentation and codification built on the foundations of an underlying class divide and differing views on what defined the amateur versus the professional.[30] The different kicking/dribbling football association organizations producing rules in Cambridge, Sheffield, London, and farther north in Scotland continued to evolve their rules until finally defining one transnational—and quintessentially British—body to standardize rules and facilitate competition, founded as the International Football Association Board in 1886.[31]

Closer to home, yet further evidence of the transnational concurrent development of football, the Canadians borrowed from rugby rules and the evolving collegiate game of their American neighbors in order to infuse their own solutions to similar problems encountered on the field.[32] The debates on rules and codification were felt in Boston too. A lengthy editorial in the 1872 Harvard *Advocate* student paper argued in favor of intercollegiate contests, and in order to do so, they said, "We should glance at the style of game played here and elsewhere. . . . The other colleges have adopted systems similar to each other, resembling very closely the English game," and "a change evidently must be made somewhere if we are to play with other clubs."[33] In a few short years, the American colleges had tweaked their rules and birthed a new code evolving in parallel to the many others.

The last thirty years of the nineteenth century saw individuals across the Anglophone world—such as Walter Camp in the United States, Michael Cusack in Ireland, Robert Tait McKenzie in Canada, and Tom Wills in Australia—contemporaneously tweak playing rules, borrowing and actively influencing football codes across oceans. This parallel evolution was based on a transnational exchange of people, products, and ideas, mixing commerce, printing, and sporting goods. The process moved play away from the uncodified games of innocent boys and toward the written, tested, and constantly revised diverging codes that forever modified the genus football into a family of footballs, often with their own national twists.

The radical changes in the world of the late nineteenth century, and in the games that people played, would have undoubtedly made it difficult for the Oneida boys to recognize what they considered their games later in life. They were, after all, at least several generations removed from the modern phenomenon and remained the few alive for whom football was still ultimately one game despite its locally, or even nationally, differing rules. As Tony Collins has argued, football in 1860s Britain (exactly when the Oneidas were playing) was still very much under the impression that there was only *one* football game and that efforts especially between 1867 and 1871 could still achieve "one universal code according to which all matches may be played," to quote the Football Association's call for more members.[34] The creation of the Rugby Football Union in 1871, of course, ended all hopes in the UK for a universal game, and from there branched off even more codified versions. Lovett's recollections in *Old Boston Boys* were penned in a period right before the implementation of the forward pass rule. But even before this fundamental transformation, Lovett noted in early 1906 that he was "sadly ignorant of the [merits of the] modern game of football . . . as compared with those of the old game, open, full of stirring episodes, and intelligible at any stage to every onlooker."[35] This initial experience with a common game, "foot ball," as it was often called well into the 1870s, had shaped the Oneidas' view of the game.

In reaction to the evolutions of the various football codes that were present by 1906, Lovett was diplomatic in admitting some difficulty in appreciating how American collegiate football had evolved. He expressed his preference for a different style of play, more open and less in need of a medical staff awaiting the next inescapable injury.

> I attended a Harvard-Yale game not so many years ago, and as I sat trying to study out what was being done in one corner of the gridiron, where both teams were apparently welded into one solid mass which every few seconds would sway and heave, perhaps a foot or two, in one direction, and then, as though having changed its mind, sway and heave back again. . . . And then the suits of armor, together with the presence of the ready surgeon and the waiting stretcher (and, for aught I know, the undertaker), made it all savor a little too strongly of the Roman amphitheater to be compatible with what football seems intended for, namely, a healthy and invigorating pastime.[36]

His and the Oneidas' pastime, recalled and so revered, was indeed past, but not before Lovett could preserve the memory of his old friends. Yet it was almost as if, in Lovett's words, he had hidden the spirit of the Old Boston Boys waiting to be awoken as the founders of modern sport: "Probably any boy of the present-day and generation, if told that fifty years ago there was neither baseball nor football (as we know them to-day); that tennis, polo, golf, lacrosse, and basket ball were unknown, besides many other athletic sports now so common, would at once ask, with surprise, not unmingled with pity, what the boys of that day did, anyway, for sport and recreation."[37]

In acknowledging that modern codified sports such as college football had taken hold of the contemporary public imagination, Lovett recognized in his 1906 book that something else—the game that he and his friends had played on Boston Common—had gone before. The boys, who were at the forefront of a sporting revolution (even though they would have never realized it at the time), were alert as they aged and progressed through their successful lives. Over time they began to believe that they had done something important. What and how significant it was remained a mystery—indeed, posterity had barely begun to play with the Oneida legacy—but Lovett, in remembering the championship match of 1863 and his Oneida Club, sowed the seeds for a future memorialization process.

Memory, however, pulls only against the tide of forgetting. The challenge arises when that memory, which has become legend, and that legend elevated to myth, is confronted by some forgotten truth or has its inconsistencies revealed. And yet, in order to record the past, preserving testimony and artifacts is essential, no matter the ambiguity they may conceal. Even history must be grateful for the fragments that remain. But history is more than just remembering, and the Oneidas are a case in point. The story of the Oneida boys, of their games in the years between 1862 and 1865, reveals just as much about the history and evolution of modern sport and the kinds of lives the Boston elite lived as about how malleable the past and associated acts of memorialization have been.

So who in sport history is the father of modern American football? Walter Camp of Yale fame, without a doubt.[38] More than any other, he was the man who changed and adapted the rules of a college game that was still a hybrid version of early rugby and soccer and made it into a specifically American version of football. He was remembered as such, and his heritage was ostentatiously memorialized at Yale, in Halls of Fame, and in the history books of American football. Historians have unanimously recognized his contribution to American football and culture. But who acted as the sporting midwife while Camp was running around his home in New Britain, Connecticut, as a toddler, unaware of football? The boys of the Oneida Football Club.

2
SCHOOL YEARS

A Classroom, a City, and a War

The story of the Oneidas begins in Boston when they were schoolboys. The Boston in which these boys grew up during the 1850s and 1860s was a city in transformation, expanding and being constructed anew through a massive land reclamation and building scheme. It was a city that had a fast-growing population as a result of waves of immigration. Other more bellicose tides splashed arguments for and against abolition across the city and then carried its young men south to fight in the Civil War. The Boston of the Oneida boys was significant in the history of the nation. It had had a central place in the Revolutionary War against Britain and was proud of its role in the foundation of the United States. Boston was established by the Puritans in 1630, and their aims for settlement were about more than simply surviving in a new land; they were lofty goals that came to define the city and its sense of itself. John Winthrop, one of the original settlers, who became Boston's first governor, summed up his dream by expressing his desire that the Puritans' new home should aspire to be, in biblical terms, "a city upon a hill"—although the phrase was more warning than aspiration, and the national narrative significance of the famous *Arbella* sermon was largely the creation of 1930s scholar Perry Miller.[1] Notwithstanding a posteriori reinterpretations, the city as a polity did embody a utopian vision, harboring what historian Mark Peterson calls "virtuous aspirations toward self-governing autonomy and an internal ethic of charity" before being consumed by the nineteenth-century nation-state's interests.[2] This was an ideal that not only shaped the future of Boston and the United States but also set the city apart.[3] The early settlers believed that they, and the place that they founded, had to respond to a higher calling. In pursuing those ideals, generations of Bostonians brought into being some of the key institutions and traditions of the city, a spirit that the Oneida boys would inherit and build on further.

A key philosophy in the Puritan mindset was the value of education. The creation of the Godly society, which they had traveled across the Atlantic to build, free from persecution, was underscored by their belief that educated citizens would be required for that task long into the future. The first manifestation of this philosophy was built in 1635, when the Boston Latin School opened its doors.[4] The aim of the school was to educate young men of all social classes, and its curriculum—based on learning classical or ancient philosophy, language, and history—was modeled on the traditions of the Boston Grammar School in England. The following year, and with a steady flow of Puritan immigrants continuing to arrive from England, the decision was made by the Boston authorities that a college for the training of clergymen, to minister to the growing population of the city, was required. Harvard College, as it was named in 1639, would take many of its students from Boston Latin, and like the school, it became a bastion of power and influence for the sons of the city's wealthy elite.[5] These educational institutions would be central in forming generations of young male Bostonians.

The boys of the Oneida Football Club mostly lived in the wealthier parts of Boston, many on Beacon Hill, while others resided in the country suburbs such as Brookline or Milton.[6] Around 90 percent of the Oneidas attended just one school. The Dixwell School was established by Epes Sargent Dixwell and opened its doors on September 29, 1851, nearly a decade before the Oneida boys would enter his classrooms.[7] His private school followed the approach of Boston Latin, where he had previously taught and been head, and attracted the sons of the elite who wanted the best possible preparation for their entrance examination to Harvard.[8] Including his time as headmaster of the Public Latin School and operating his own private school from 1851 to 1871, it is estimated that Dixwell successfully trained nearly 250 boys to pass into Harvard.[9] Dixwell mixed socially with many of the leading families in Boston and was particularly close to Cornelius Conway Felton, president of Harvard between 1860 and 1862, who had been Dixwell's roommate in college. Dixwell's links to the Oneida families began as early as 1836 with a marriage to Mary Ingersoll Bowditch, the aunt of future player Edward Bowditch. The family and financial ties surrounding the Oneida boys were such that Dixwell also invested all his capital at the time, estimated at five hundred dollars, in his wife's family investment firm, J. J. D. and J. I. Bowditch.[10]

The curriculum studied at Dixwell's followed closely the same classical course of education he had fine-tuned at the Public Latin School.[11] Classes were not structured by age but rather according to ability, and Dixwell followed a long Boston Latin tradition, of which he had been part as pupil, teacher, and head. Dixwell's approach was summed up as building on the seventeenth- and eighteenth-century educational philosophy of the Boston elite that "was thoroughly classical with a strong emphasis on moral learning."[12] During the nine to two o'clock school day (Saturdays until noon), as explained by Dixwell in an official notice sent to parents, the curriculum was a classical course of study that included the "Latin, Greek, French, and English languages; Arithmetic, Algebra, Geometry, Reading, Declamation, Composition, Drawing, Chirography."[13] Oneida member William Lawrence attended Dixwell's from 1863 alongside his brother, Amory, specifically because it "was the best fitting school for Harvard."[14] The biographer of Oneida member Henry Cabot Lodge noted how he had tackled the curriculum "satisfactorily but without distinction."[15] Lodge, in his own autobiography, acknowledged that Dixwell "exercised, I am sure, a good influence upon me, for he had no patience with slovenliness of mind; he also taught well, as I found when I reached the top of the school and came under him."[16]

The overriding aim of Dixwell's was to prepare boys for the Harvard entrance exam. It was a university that, although remaining small in the 1860s and 1870s, was desirable as a place in which to study, forge future professional and personal relationships, and be at the heart of Boston's social elite. This meant that there was an increasing competition for places. Dixwell was incredibly successful, claiming that he only had one student ever fail the exam—who was nevertheless admitted after a second attempt.[17] As admission to Harvard became more difficult and competitive through the mid-nineteenth century, so the average age of the Harvard student rose from when Dixwell himself had entered at age fifteen in the 1820s or Thomas Wentworth Higginson, a decade later, at a precocious thirteen.[18] By the time the Oneidas arrived at Dixwell's, this meant that boys were staying longer in school and transferring to college, not as early teenagers, but as young men. The extended years at school—the majority of the Oneida boys were between seventeen and nineteen when they entered Harvard—meant that the very nature of schooling changed. The aim, entrance to Harvard, was the same, but schools were teaching young men who were older, more responsible, and more worldly. It is hard to imagine those early teens who attended elite schools at the start of the nineteenth century, being given the freedom, or having the desire to organize an afternoon of sport for themselves. But by the time of the Oneidas, those schoolboys were young men who were capable, more trusted, and able to organize themselves in their extracurricular hours, whether it was for sport or singing clubs like the one Robert Apthorp Boit participated in while at Dixwell's.[19]

The drive to get into Harvard grew, and within a few years of the Oneida generation graduating, the college had become "by far the top choice of the Boston upper class" and remained so until well into the twentieth century.[20] An undergraduate of the mid-1830s observed that the stricter requirements already favored boys from "the Public Latin Schools of Boston and Salem, the academies of Exeter and Andover, and the famous Round-Hill School at Northampton."[21] Dixwell knew what he was doing. He was "a most accomplished man, an elegant scholar, a gentleman of the world." Not surprisingly, his institution quickly became "the best fitting-school for Harvard," the resort of boys from Brookline and other suburbs, as well as those from Beacon Hill.[22] Such was the success of Dixwell's, the percentage of private day schoolboys entering Harvard rose during the years the school was open (1851–72) and fell back as soon as Dixwell retired and the school closed.

Dixwell moved boys from his school and onto Harvard in big groups. And at Harvard, their education as well as their social networks were enlarged. When the Oneida player Amory Appleton Lawrence went to Harvard, his father deliberately sought lodgings for him in Gray's Hall so that Amory could fulfill "his desire to broaden his acquaintance and to know those who roomed in the college yard, as well as those who could afford the accommodations of private houses and club life."[23] After graduation from Harvard, Dixwell's former pupils went on to dominate civic, political, and economic life in the city and beyond. They were expected to succeed. Men like Dixwell trained them for the future so that when it came to their examinations for college entrance, the "boys from the Boston Latin, like those from Exeter and Dixwell's, seemed to touch the appreciation of the Harvard examining board a little more deftly than an applicant from any other place."[24]

The backdrop to the Oneida boys' years in school and at college was an era of profound change in their home city. While Boston had entered the 1800s as a prosperous city, it had by midcentury run out of space. As Oneida player William Lawrence noted of the early 1860s, "It seemed a long drive from the Common to our house in Longwood [just over three miles away], for just beyond Charles Street the blocks of houses stopped. The Public Garden was then a dirty waste, and at Arlington Street was the city dump, where ashes and other refuse was thrown by tip carts into the Back Bay."[25] It was a city where "the Back Bay was largely water, when no office buildings downtown were tall enough to require elevators."[26] Boston had been established as a port city and was built on an outcrop that was joined to the mainland by a thin slice of land to its south: the Boston Neck. This meant that, until the 1860s, the growing population of the city had to squeeze into the preexisting streets, as there was no easily accessible land onto which it could grow. This led to overcrowding, unsanitary conditions, and a host of social problems. The growth of the city was incredibly rapid. In 1800, Boston was home to 24,937 people (then barely a third of the size of New York and dwarfed by the million people who lived in London at the time), and in an age of industrialization and technological innovation (and the associated process of urbanization), it was a relatively compact and small-scale city that was not expanding at the rate of other metropolitan centers. Its relatively modest size was perhaps surprising given its position as one of the major transatlantic ports and as a gateway to the New World. By 1840 Boston's population had grown steadily to 93,383 with the city a key destination for those Europeans seeking a new life in the United States. A large proportion of the new arrivals in the period to 1840 were from Ireland, both Protestant and Catholic. Until that time, as the Catholics were in the minority, the Protestant newcomers—sitting closer to the established Boston communities in terms of religion, sensibility, and customs—formed the majority. Given this apparent homogeneity, the level of civic and press fears relating to immigration was, prior to the midcentury, relatively low (there were, however, notable sectarian riots and brawls, such as the Broad Street riot in 1837).

In 1845, the onset of famine in Ireland transformed the ethnic and religious makeup of Boston. By 1860, the city's population had nearly doubled in just two short decades. Despite this rapid growth, the demographer Frederick A. Bushee was still able to comment in 1899 that "Boston, on account of its early history or on account of certain traditions connected with it, is often thought to be a more purely American city than many others." A city that, he argued, was believed to "have preserved to a greater extent its old American character." Yet as Bushee demonstrated, by 1895, the 220,000 Irish-born formed just under half of the city's 487,000 residents and dwarfed the 80,000 classed as "Old Americans."[27] How was such change and growth in population from the midcentury managed so that the "old American character" of Boston was preserved?

In the half century from the onset of the Irish Famine to the close of the nineteenth century, Boston became an Irish city (in 2014, nearly 23 percent of Bostonians still classified themselves as Irish American, the highest figure of any city in the United States). The Irish who had fled the famine were initially met with distrust, opposition, and violence. The fear from the host population was based on the Catholicism of the new arrivals, concerns about diseases associated with the famine, and stereotypical images of the Irish as drunken, violent, and degenerate. In the post–Civil War era, the Irish entered the ranks of civic employees as police officers and firemen; they organized themselves within trade unions and as a political grouping and, by 1884, achieved the election of the first Irish-born city mayor, Hugh O'Brien. The rise of the Irish in the second half of the nineteenth century transformed Boston, and while they accessed political power at the local level, wealth and influence remained, for the time being, firmly with the Old Americans. It was in the years immediately before and then during the Civil War that Boston's elite reimagined their city, contributed once more to the redefinition of their nation, and managed the massive demographic and ethnic changes occurring.[28]

True, its population had grown exponentially in a short period of time and was accompanied by all kinds of social and economic issues. But in the years leading to the Civil War, Boston continued to transition from a maritime city, on which it had built its initial wealth, to an industrialized city that made those who controlled its banking houses and railway stocks—many of them the parents and grandparents of the Oneida boys—vast fortunes. Boston had always prided itself on being progressive and innovative and, no matter what was happening on the electoral scene, the wider city authorities, charities, philanthropists, planners, and thinkers all worked to try to create an ever-better city. It was a city of social liberalism and experimentation. A host of issues were supported in Boston such as temperance, prison reform, universal peace, women's rights, and the abolition of slavery. Most Southerners "viewed the notion that citizens should refrain from alcohol, coddle convicted prisoners, surrender their weapons, allow their wives out of the kitchen, and set Africans loose on the community as nothing less than a perversion of the entire natural order put forward by a pack of liberal radicals and professional do-gooders."[29] And despite such Southern dismissals and the challenges caused by massive immigration, Boston did offer a series of reforms and innovations in the decades leading to the Civil War.[30]

In 1852 the decision was made to fill in and reclaim what was known as the receiving basin, which lay to the west of Boston Common.[31] In his memoirs,

Oneida member James D'Wolf Lovett recalled that in 1859, he had been walking the junction of Beacon Street and Charles Street, where the land of central Boston ended and the water began. Observing the first trucks of landfill arriving to build the Back Bay, his father remarked in amazement at the scale of the project, "Maybe Jim, you will live to see this whole Back Bay covered with streets and houses, but it hardly seems possible."[32] Once filled, the area to be known as the Back Bay would become a new neighborhood.[33] The idea was to build a new suburb, close to the city, to house segments of the rapidly growing population. But this was not simply a housing project; it was also social engineering. It was a plan to ensure that the new immigrant populations were kept separate, as were the growing commercial and business premises of downtown, from Boston's professional and business classes. These people did not wish to become commuters; they wanted a wealthy, cultured enclave that would be home, separated from the poorer quarters, but still close enough to their downtown business interests. In 1856, Boston architect Arthur Gilman proposed that the Back Bay be based around broad, tree-lined avenues of fine houses so that the city would have something comparable to the wide streets of Haussmann's Paris or Hobrecht's Berlin.[34] The plan was warmly received and the commissioners set about bringing the Back Bay plan to life, an area of exquisite homes, public parks, churches, and cultural institutions where the best of people in Boston could live. Work started on filling the receiving basin and, as the land was filled, it was sold for development. What is remarkable, in hindsight, was not simply how visionary the project was, but that it actually made a profit for the city. Half of the money accrued was invested in an educational and cultural fund, which was spent on universities, schools, and museums. When the project was finished the city had made a profit of $3.5 million, and it was the Back Bay, as adults, where many of the Oneidas would move and make their homes.

The project was driven by the power of the steam shovel, railways that brought in landfill from the quarries of suburbs such as Needham and Dedham, and in human terms, the labor of thousands of Irish and other immigrant workers. It took until 1890 before the area as far back as Fenway was filled in, and until 1894 before the whole Back Bay project was complete. But as each street was built from the late 1850s through the Civil War and on to the end of the century, the social engineering and class elitism that lay at the heart of the project became a reality. Into the Back Bay area came the universities, the new Boston Public Library in Copley Square, churches, and cultural institutions such as the Museum of Natural History, many of which were funded and endowed by the families of the Oneida boys.[35] To take advantage of these institutions, the proximity of the Back Bay to the city center, and the tree-lined streets promising good health and tranquility, came the elites of Boston. Whereas Beacon Hill had been the home of the Brahmin elites in the first half of the nineteenth century, the Back Bay became the home of their descendants, their intermarrying offspring, and the newly wealthy.[36]

As successful as the reclamation of the Back Bay would eventually be, the beauty of its streets, and the value of the real estate, the actual starting point for the westward expansion of Boston was the Oneidas' playground: Boston Common.[37] The Common, as a spatial marker of a separation within the city, was part of the larger process in the nineteenth century that saw the cityscape sunder across class, race, ethnicity, and political belief. As Mark Peterson observes, "From the mid-1830s onward, from the time of the burning of the Ursuline convent, the mobbing of Garrison, and the Broad Street riots, the lines of fracture in Boston's social and political order—rich versus poor, black versus white, foreign versus native, Irish versus Yankee, male versus female, Cotton versus Conscience Whigs—generated an escalating sequence of violent incidents—violence that was increasingly linked to national affairs."[38] In more innocent terms, even Oneida Henry Cabot Lodge, writing about being a young boy in the late 1850s, noted how the Common featured as an interface between youthful inhabitants from different parts of the city: "[There] we also waged Homeric contests with snowballs against the boys from the South Cove and the North End, in which we made gallant fights, but were in the end, as a rule, outnumbered and driven back."[39] Despite such battles between boys for control of the Common, it was a space that, while public, was clearly identified with one tradition within the city: "Situated between two Protestant strongholds in the Back Bay and Beacon Hill, the Common embodied the city's Puritan Yankee past."[40] The Oneidas played their games on land that spoke to the traditions and values that they embodied. Boston was not simply a city being transformed by the building of new lands and suburbs, the events of citywide and national transport, or even the rapidly changing political climate that led to the Civil War; it was being changed by the rapid influx of people from within and beyond the United States. With the demographic growth of the city and all the pressures that came with it, places and spaces became marked. They were delineated, sometimes legally and others by expectation, in terms of who was included and given access, and who was excluded and forbidden. That such battles over identity and desirability (or undesirability) took place in such a small city space made the need to control access to certain parts of the city ever more important.

But against the backdrop of the Oneidas, and others, playing their football and developing their game on the Common, so began a far larger struggle that had erupted in American life. In 1861 the nation split apart over the issue of slavery and secession. Boston had a historic reputation for being independent and liberal-minded. And yet as the divisions that led to the Civil War loomed, the city contained competing factions and populations who did not all share a single vision for the future of the country nor how they should respond to the demands and actions of the Southern states.[41]

Of the main events that would bring about the conditions for war, it was perhaps John Brown's failed attempt to create a slave uprising, in October 1859, and his subsequent arrest and execution that brought matters to a head. On the day of Brown's execution, December 2, 1859, there was an outpouring of grief in Boston. Church bells rang across the city, gun salutes were fired, and thousands of citizens paused for a moment's silence. Prominent abolitionist groups, led by members of Boston's African American community, organized vigils in the city churches. Not everyone supported the marking of Brown's passing, with the antiabolitionist *Boston Post* remarking that it was impossible that day to get a haircut or have one's shoes polished.[42] Neither was the passing of Brown mourned by many within Boston's Irish community. While the issue of slavery and abolition may have been unfamiliar to many new arrivals, they reacted on the basis of their own economic opportunity and feared the freeing of enslaved people would lead to an economic downturn, increased competition for employment, and the potential loss of their jobs.

What was clear was that many in Boston's elite did believe in the cause of abolition, even funding Brown's attempts to instigate a slave rebellion. The founders of the Lowell textile mills, including Amos A. Lawrence (grandfather of Oneida boys Amory and William Lawrence), William Appleton, and Edward Atkinson, had sent Brown guns and money (even though their own advancement of king cotton and the wealth they had accrued was built on the backs of Southern enslaved people producing the raw material they required). Support extended further west to future Oneida captain Gerrit Smith Miller's home in Peterboro, where his grandfather regularly hosted Brown and plotted as part of the "Secret Six," which included other Oneida family relations: Thomas Wentworth Higginson and Samuel Gridley Howe.[43] The context marked Miller's youth, who remembered later in life the last time he "saw John Brown in the dining room" in April 1859.[44] Their activities demonstrated that Oneida families and many in Boston's social elite were forcefully abolitionist—like schoolmaster Dixwell, whose diary recorded his vote for Lincoln in November 1860. Any hope for postelection unity faded when South Carolina seceded from the Union on December 20, 1860, bringing civil war closer and causing Dixwell to lament, "O heavy year that has broken up my glorious country! God! direct us in the dark!"[45] There was further disorder on the streets and increasing instability in the Boston economy. Factories cut production, working hours were reduced and many businesses went bankrupt. The decision of South Carolina had spooked the wealthier classes of Boston, not knowing whether compromise would save the Union or if war was inevitable.

In April 1861, the Battle of Fort Sumter unleashed the Civil War. While a catastrophic outcome, it removed the uncertainty, a sense of waiting, from Bostonian life. The inhabitants—including the Irish who chose patriotism over economic self-interest—its politicians and business leaders, gathered behind the Union cause and the local economy benefited from a transformation to supplying the needs of the war.[46] Railroad and steamship companies made their stock available to transport troops, the local banks made $3.5 million available to the state to support mobilization, and leading businessmen financed the Massachusetts Soldiers Fund to assist those families whose men had gone off to fight.

Shortly after Sumter's shelling, Lincoln called for the creation of the Union Army and asked for seventy-five thousand troops to fight the Confederacy. Amid what Dixwell recorded as "great excitement," Massachusetts's Governor Andrew was quick to respond, sending fifteen hundred soldiers to Washington to secure the nation's capital from being overrun by Confederate forces.[47] Thousands of Bostonians from all social classes, including the older brothers and other male relatives of a number of the Oneida boys, signed up to fight, and the first volunteers were organized under the flag of the Massachusetts Eighth and Sixth Regiments.

In gathering support for the Union cause and in raising an army, Governor Andrew knew that he had to bring on board the social elites of Boston. If this group could lead the fight and send its own sons to war, it would be perhaps easier to bring the diverse social, economic, and ethnic groups of the city together against the Confederacy. Governor Andrew "knew that, above all, he needed the backing of Boston's commercial and social elite, the so-called

Brahmin caste."[48] The Brahmin class, including the families of many of the Oneida boys, were critical to the war effort, not simply for their control of wealth, industry, medicine, and education within the city and the state, but also for the symbolism of that group of powerful families throwing their weight, and the bodies of the sons, behind the Union cause. And it was not simply a question of gaining Brahmin support; it would also be, within the army, an issue of how that group offered leadership and a sense of honor. Put simply, weren't these well-bred young men—connected as they were to wealth and power, educated at the best city schools and in all likelihood at Harvard—the leaders that the Union needed? In short, the Brahmin class may well have been predisposed by its peer code, education, and shared social values to a military ethic (expressed as "Death before Dishonor") and would be needed to lead a Union victory.[49]

While in absolute deaths the total number of volunteers and draftees from Boston's lower social classes far outstripped the number of Brahmin dead, the killing of the latter was proportionally significant and was seen as a necessary part of the public sacrifice involved in war.[50] For those opposing the draft, there was the widespread practice of the wealthy putting forward a substitute to take their place in the army or else paying a commutation fee. To complement the picture, however, the constant press coverage in Boston of the death and wounding of the sons of the leading families spun a narrative that all families of the city, no matter whether rich or poor, were suffering and grieving equally. Military history writer Richard Miller underscores how the newspapers, many of which were owned by Brahmin elites, "tirelessly trumpeted the services . . . especially Harvardians; the sons of prominent families, their comings and goings and, especially, their deaths in battle and the details of their funerals were almost always conspicuously profiled."[51]

This seismic struggle that dominated American life was the backdrop of the entire lifetime of the Oneida Football Club (1862–85). It was a constant in their lives, and "at school the progress of the war was freely discussed and before Lee's surrender the young boys were being given military drill."[52] The boys undoubtedly had opinions on that struggle, and one of their number would eventually take up arms joining a number of their brothers, including Nathaniel Bowditch, brother of Edward, who died at Kelly's Ford on March 18, 1863, and Charles Lovett who enlisted twice.[53] But while the world around them dealt with death, upheaval, shortages, and uncertainty, the boys came together to play. They lost themselves in the joy of running, kicking, and throwing, fully embracing the battle for the ball and a goal. And perhaps they were grateful, as youngsters, that this sporting contest was their only battle on that day and not the actual fighting that dominated American life. Their play offered a respite from the news of war that swirled around Boston.

It had begun innocently, almost festively, for the boys, and Oneida William Lawrence remembered how "we children stood on the bank of the Worcester, now the Albany, Railroad, just behind our grove, and cheered the Sixth, as they went on their journey through Baltimore to spill their blood on Lexington Day, the 19th of April [1861]."[54] But soon he recalled how in 1862, when "the drum beat in the streets warned the boys that war was in the air . . . Dixwell's School, like many others, was formed into a military company."[55] In October that year, the headmaster's own diary was curt: "arranged to have boys drilled."[56] Clubmate Henry Cabot Lodge wrote in his biography that "while the Civil War was raging it was certain that no one forgot it and that its shadow hung dark over the land . . . in the history of that great period of conflict, it has seemed to me that the impressions of a boy, living safe-sheltered in a city and a State where no enemy ever set his foot, are not without importance."[57]

The answer to the continued need for battling bodies was a compulsory draft of men of fighting age into the Union army, something the South had already imposed. Passed as law in March 1863, the Union draft process accelerated after the battle of Gettysburg, and its rules demonstrated that this was a war of the rich to be fought by the poor. For a three-hundred-dollar substitution fee, the families of those with financial means could keep their sons out of the war. For the poor, this was not an option, and waiting for a visit from the dreaded draft man was an inevitability. The controversial nature of the draft and its focus on the working classes led to a riot, on July 14, 1863, in Boston's North End, a district inhabited mainly by Irish immigrants. Boston mayor Frederick Walker Lincoln took no chances and requested that Governor Andrew send the state militia to put down the rioters in the North End. News of similar events the prior day to the south had made their way to Boston. Dixwell recorded in his diary that a "terrible mob in New York resisting the draft" and that the rioters continued to "have it all their way" though he made no mention of the Boston riot.[58]

The officer in charge of the army was Major Stephen Cabot of the First Battalion Massachusetts Heavy Artillery (an uncle of Samuel and Arthur Cabot; the former played with the Old Boys, and Arthur competed later in the seminal Harvard-McGill games of 1874). Fearing for the lives of his men, who came under attack when they entered the North End, Major Cabot ordered them to fire a cannon loaded with canisters through the doors of the Cooper Street armory, where they had taken refuge.[59] Once the cannon fire had shattered the doors, Cabot's men began firing their weapons through the gaping entrance of the armory and into the crowd outside in an attempt to disperse them. In a few short minutes, the shots thudded into the crowd gathered outside. The fusillade of the crowd left as many as twenty lying dead or dying on the stones of Cooper Street. The brutality of the army response did put an end to the riot, and an uneasy peace, punctuated by occasional violence, ensued in the North End for the remainder of the evening.

Four months after the bloodletting of early midsummer, Cabot's two nephews and their friends continued the playful havoc of autumn games on Boston Common. While the Oneidas played and sweated to score their goals, other young men farther south scrambled and fought to stay alive. On the same Saturday, November 7, 1863, that the Oneida Football Club crossed its opponents' Boston Common goal line three victorious times, Union forces led by Major General George G. Meade attacked an altogether different sort of boundary—the Rappahannock River crossing held by Robert E. Lee. The Confederate general had withdrawn his troops to the south of the river in the wake of his defeat at Gettysburg. He hoped that they could winter there and that the river represented a line that he could hold over the cold months until renewing his campaign in the spring. In the ensuing battle, a Union victory and a farther retreat to the south by Confederate forces, Lee's forces were caught by surprise and quickly overrun. The fighting took place at close quarters in pontoons, rifle pits, and forts that had been built by the Confederates to defend the river. H. H. Lloyd in his account of the fighting wrote, "Discharging but a single volley, the assailants closed with their antagonists, actually grasping the bayonets pointed at their breasts. As friend and foe were mingled promiscuously, the batteries on both sides ceased, and ringing cheers and shouts and death-groans rose above the sound of musketry. Men grappled one another in their death-struggles, some fighting with clubbed muskets, others with their fists."[60] In total, over two thousand men were killed, wounded, or captured, with losses suffered by the Confederates four times greater than their opponents' and representing three-quarters of their forces. The defeat at the Second Battle of Rappahannock Station was described by the Confederate Colonel Walter Taylor as "the saddest chapter in the history of the army."

Two days later and perhaps oblivious to the chatter around them of that Union victory, the Oneida boys wandered home after a day of reading Sophocles and Virgil in the original Greek and Latin under the watchful eye of Headmaster Dixwell. The news from Rappahannock appeared front and center on the Monday edition of the *Boston Daily Advertiser* and was undoubtedly the talk of that evening's dinner, although the Oneidas were possibly more interested in showing off the "local matters" column to the right, where their match had been recounted briefly on the front page.[61] Perhaps the boys reflected on the distant fighting. Or perhaps they preferred to ignore the serious dinner conversation of the adults and instead saw the table settings as their pitch, reliving their own sporting battle in their heads, plotting imaginary running and passing lanes between glasses and cutlery. However rough-and-tumble their football actually was, their battleground was a public play space shared with other Boston children. The reality of the Common contrasted with that of many other young men sent south, where the future of the United States hung in the balance.

The eerie experience of war manifested itself soon enough. Just a month after the Oneida championship match of 1863, Dixwell added another former Dixwell boy as a casualty of the war in his diary. Oneida Edward "Ned" Bowditch's older cousin Henry Pickering Bowditch was shot in December and honorably discharged; but within three months he had voluntarily returned to the front with the Fifth Massachusetts colored cavalry regiment.[62] Even as the pull of war continued to draw young men to enlist, theoretically boys were protected by the age limit of the draft. But the line between warrior and boy was a thin one, and this war was waged by thousands of underage soldiers.[63] After watching from the sidelines throughout 1864, Oneida Club captain Huntington Wolcott was one of the young volunteers who traded games for guns because he "could no longer be restrained" despite being well under the conscription minimum of twenty years old.[64] Headmaster Dixwell revealed no emotion in his diary, only writing that his boys gave Hunty Wolcott a "sabre, belt and pack" as the boy departed a man for war in early February 1865.[65]

The war was effectively over within a fortnight when Charleston, the Confederacy's last stronghold, fell. When the African American Fifty-Fifth Massachusetts Regiment marched into Charleston, they brought the narrative of the war full circle and, as they passed into the city, they loudly sang "John Brown's Body." The war was nearly over, and once more Boston rejoiced, with a further mix of civic and private celebrations. The festivities turned to grief on

April 15 when news arrived that Abraham Lincoln had been assassinated. On the day of Lincoln's funeral, April 19, Boston was a city in mourning, with all businesses closed, transport suspended, and a saddened silence hanging in the air. Henry Cabot Lodge recalled, "The horror, the dazed surprise, the shock of the announcement, I shall never forget. During the four years just passed Lincoln had become heroic to my young imagination, looming up as a dim and distant figure which seemed to me to personify the country. The crime which ended his life raised him in my eyes to the proportions of a demigod."[66] Yet the event that may have left the greatest impression on Lodge's Oneida clubmates was the death of one of their own. In the words of William Lawrence, Hunty Wolcott "left his desk for the War, with a sword, and within a few weeks we gathered at his bier."[67] Lodge, who had even sat diagonally behind Wolcott in the schoolroom, recalled, "[The whole Dixwell School] went to the funeral and I saw him in his coffin, worn, haggard, aged, and yet still a boy, dressed in the uniform of the United States. This brought the war home to me as never before."[68]

In the immediate aftermath of the war and the process of planning the Reconstruction of the South, so life in Boston began to return to its prewar calm. Work on the Back Bay continued, the city's expansion headed ever farther west, and the slow process of ethnic and racial integration, which had been accelerated by the wartime experience, continued to change the urban landscape. In the long term, the industrial base of the United States shifted farther south and concentrated on New York. Boston—in particular, its social elite—cemented its wealth and status through the power of capital and investment. In the second half of the 1860s, the Boston business community would have considered that they had had a good war: "The war brought immediate prosperity, new solidarity for the republican party, and renewed patriotic pride among city leaders whose ancestors had fought at Concord, Lexington, and Bunker Hill."[69]

What was apparent from the ranks of grieving families and the war dead, whose names would adorn Harvard's Memorial Hall (but only the 136 Union dead; the sixty-four Confederate dead were not included), was that Boston's social elite, the types of families from which the Oneidas were drawn, had played a full role in the Civil War, with many paying the ultimate price.[70] It wasn't simply a question of sacrifice but also the way in which the young men of the Brahmin class had approached the war. They had embodied the supposedly best, and most honorable, qualities of the elite: "The gallant response by young

Brahmins and Harvard graduates, and as officers in the proud Massachusetts regiments, was satisfying proof that the old Boston values were still alive."[71]

The Oneida boys had played their football against the backdrop of the Civil War. More broadly, they played while further transformations were made to their city with respect to its ethnic makeup and in terms of the creation of the Back Bay. They attended school and played, fully aware of the national struggle that was being fought to the south. They watched troops move through Boston, and at the most personal level, some lost brothers to the war and even one of their friends and leaders, Huntington Frothingham Wolcott. The context and the ways that city and nation convulsed with change during the years in which the boys went to school and played their football in the Oneida Football Club (1862–65) are critical for understanding how and why the game that they played became so important to them in later life. The Oneida boys, with the exception of Hunty Wolcott, did not see active participation in a war that refashioned so much of the world around them. Where the boys did participate vigorously was in the games of Boston Common during an era in which the culture of play was also transformed.

3
GAMES

Spaces, Clubs, and Organizing Play

The football at the center of the Oneida story was a part of a particular leisure and boyhood culture—spanning the Atlantic across the Anglophone world. Their game was also anchored in one place: Boston Common. Where, how, and in what context the Oneidas played are as important to understanding the significance of their self-memorialization as to knowing what their game actually was. When the Oneida boys were playing their games on the Common, it marked the far western edge of the city; next to it was the Public Garden, and beyond that was the shallow receiving basin of the Charles River. But by the 1920s, when the Oneidas built their memorial, the Common had become the downtown heart of a much larger city. Boston Common had been a work in progress since the seventeenth century. This outdoor space would have a sporting legacy and an impact on contemporary America in ways that the Puritan settlers could not have imagined and would have no doubt been seen with a mow.

Originally purchased by the city in 1634, the Common was a fifty-acre area of open ground, secured for the use of Boston's residents. In the early decades of its existence, the area of commonage was used to graze cows and other animals—a vital provision in a growing settlement that was still reliant on self-sufficient agriculture. By 1830 the cows would be gone and grazing banned as the Common (always retaining its name) became a shared park for Bostonians in which to enjoy the outdoors, to sit, walk, and play. As with all public spaces, the use of and access to the Common was a mediation between different class groups as to who could use it, at what times, and for what purposes. It was the residents of Beacon Hill, the northern slope, who saw the Common as their personal garden. The creation of brick footpaths around and through the land in the early nineteenth century made it a fashionable place to walk and to be seen strolling. It became part and parcel of the daily life of the Boston elite; as Mona Domosh has commented, the "noble place of the Common was a direct reflection of Boston's aristocracy," where city elite saw themselves cultured, free from work, and natural.[1] The development of the Back Bay, as a suburb for the expanding Boston professional classes, formed a nabe of social influence with the Common at its heart. As Mark Rawson has explained, the Common and Public Garden "served as extensions of each other and informed the subsequent development of the neighboring Back Bay as an elite enclave. Together, the Back Bay, Public Garden, Boston Common, and Beacon Hill formed an unbroken chain of refined spaces."[2] Also, as a space that was protected by city laws, it stood as a permanent barrier against any encroachment of the undesirable version of the city into the Beacon Hill and Back Bay neighborhoods.[3]

In terms of order and control, the issue of games was adjudicated on early. The Common was decreed by city authorities as a place where games could be played, but the adjacent Public Gardens, a more ornate and intensely planted space, was reserved for walking, and all games—namely, "football or other athletic sports" were banned without the consent of the mayor or the Board of Aldermen.[4] Excavations of the Common in the 1990s show how the nineteenth century ushered in an age of playful childhood, evidenced by the discovery "of toys such as jacks, marbles, and dominoes. . . . By the time of the Civil War, Frog Pond had become a sea where aspiring young sea captains sailed their boats, and abandoned British trenches were garrisoned by young soldiers."[5] This was not formalized, and neither were spaces in the park explicitly marked out as being for child-centered play. As the Common became ever more demarcated, children's play was focused on playgrounds, and for the youths and men who would play sport, there were marked-out ball fields. Despite the prohibiting of rowdy ball games in the Public Garden, there was no objection made to the sons of the elite monopolizing space on Boston Common, provided they had the city's permission. One such permit from 1866 granted Lovett's baseball club three afternoons' use of the "ground on which they usually play . . . to the exclusion of others."[6]

In the first decades of the nineteenth century, baseball was becoming ever more popular, hastened in 1834 with the publication of Robert Carver's *Book of Sports*, which is often noted as producing the first printed rules for baseball, or what he refers to as "base or goal ball."[7] Carver's book, which included a woodcut of a game being played by boys on Boston Common, contains the rules for a range of children's games. While capturing youthful play, Carver's printing of a central spine of common rules is important as it demonstrates, even at the level of a game to be played by boys, that basic rules had become commonly understood. By 1845 the game had been organized and codified by the Knickerbocker Base Ball Club of New York and developed rapidly in the city and its hinterlands. In Massachusetts there was a different variant of the game, regularly played in the form of challenge matches on the Common during the summer, and in 1858 ten of the clubs involved formed the Massachusetts Association of Baseball Players. In the years leading up to the Civil War and after it, the New York rules, as opposed to the Massachusetts rules, became ever more popular and formed the basis for defining the modern game. In Boston specifically, no matter the number of clubs and the debates over the different rules, it was on the Common that the game was frequently played. It was, in effect, the city's most important open sporting space.[8]

A key figure in the evolution of baseball in Boston was John A. Lowell, who founded the Bowdoin Square Club in 1858. In 1861, he established a team made up of boys who attended the local schools.[9] This school club would later merge with the Bowdoin Square Club and be known, in honor of the founder, as "The Lowells." Central to the Lowell team were Oneida players James D'Wolf Lovett and Gerrit Smith Miller. Additionally, Oneida members also played for the Tri-Mountain team (Edward Arnold) and Harvard (Francis Peabody, Edward Bowditch, and Gerrit Smith Miller).[10] James D'Wolf Lovett was such a central figure in Boston's baseball landscape that he was selected to pitch for the Picked Nine that played against the professional Boston Red Stockings for their inaugural game on April 6, 1871; even his 1874 wedding announcement was flush with baseball imagery.[11]

As with the various forms of baseball that had been played on the Common from the 1830s, so football, especially played by schoolboys, became a regular sight in the winter months. One of the most complete records of football-style games has been Melvin I. Smith's *Evolvements of Early American Foot Ball*.[12] In over six hundred pages, Smith records football games in three evolving types beginning in the United States from the 1600s, with the presence of football at Harvard in 1741 and the playing of football on the street in front of the Roxbury Latin School in Massachusetts as early as 1768. More recently, historian Brian Bunk has contextualized the widespread practice of mid-nineteenth-century schoolboys as part of what he calls the "manly games of celebration and escape" most often experienced in nostalgic, holiday, military, or club settings.[13] This early record of football in both the college and school setting demonstrates how central kicking and throwing a ball, in the name of play, was to young men.

Colleges and schools would play a key role in the development of the game in the United States, and in Boston, boys and the Common were at the center. Smith points to an 1804 *Boston Repertory* article that "complained of boys playing football on the streets of Boston. They should be playing on the Boston Common."[14] In 1821 there he recorded both football and cricket being played on Boston Common, with reference to Robert C. Winthrop, a student at the Boston Public Latin School.[15] Other sources also describe this early football. Born in 1827, invited orator and future Bostonian Society president Curtis Guild recounted antebellum memories at the 1885 annual meeting of the city's Old Schoolboys Association (for public schoolboys). Guild described how the Common was "the playground of the Boston school boys" and a place where being from "a stuck-up private school" did not stop him then from mixing and playing football even if they "kicked it instead of running with it in our hands."[16]

By the 1850s, high school games became a feature of Boston life and there was enough recorded football activity that Smith found evidence for multiple games each year. In 1858–59 Smith detected a change in the style of game—namely, a move toward a more handling or carrying game. He also noted that the Boston schoolboys habitually attended Harvard's games and that "the chances were great that they also would play a carrying game this year as well."[17] Occasionally the games of this era also saw college students mix with high school teams who were "assisted by several lads (our magnificent Seniors actually!)" as revealed in the *Harvard Magazine*.[18] Football was not a uniform activity and a recreational version existed alongside the more violent hazing activity known as Bloody Monday that was finally banned by Harvard's faculty in 1860—in four academic years the class of 1860 had played eighteen matches, winning fourteen.[19] As a result, city football from 1860 was confined to schoolboys. But they could not play just anywhere. City ordinances banned football in the Public Garden, and so Boston Common became *the* place for football in the city.[20] It was there that the school game could thrive, where Dixwell boys challenged other schools benefiting from a vacuum left by collegiate prohibition. Shortly following the ban, a Dixwell-Latin match was "witnessed by a large crowd" come to watch what the papers called "a fine game for schoolboys when they play it in a proper manner."[21] If the city play at first seemed to be casual pickup, by midcentury most games were clearly based around schools' challenge matches on Boston Common.

Historians of American football agree, in a shared narrative, that the sport was born of a series of compromises and rule tweaks, made by the undergraduates of the elite colleges in the northeastern United States from the turn of the 1870s. This development of the game, particularly under the guidance of Walter Camp, meant that the United States did not take directly to the kicking code of soccer or the handling code of rugby but rather refined the rules to create a separate version of a handling game. However, the unanswered historical question remains as to what happened before that "big bang moment" or, in footballing terms, what happened before campuses became alive to the possibility of football in the 1870s?[22]

The standard telling of this part of the story, of what went before the rebirth of campus football in 1869, is often told this way: "the sport may have its earliest origins among high schoolboys in the 1860s. A number of leading football luminaries would accept the Oneida Football Club of Boston, composed of boys from several area high schools, as the first organized football club."[23] If any further details are added, beyond these basic facts (which echo the details of the memorial on Boston Common), they will usually include the date of the game, November 7, 1863, and the venue on Boston Common. In essence, historians view the matches in a similar way to the contemporary newspapers that recounted the event as an "interesting game of football." What few historians bother to ask, as they rush rapidly to the established collegiate origins of American football, is who the Oneida boys were, what they were doing, and why it was important. After all, the Civil War caused a rupture in the development of sport as stability, the space to play, was eroded. As Robert Pruter noted, "Just as schoolboy sports were about to take off, however, the Civil War erupted, deferring growth to the latter part of the 1880s."[24] But clearly, Boston schoolboys were playing football of some kind during the war years. What game were these boys playing in the years following the banning of football on college campuses in the 1860s? What did it mean that they were playing their games when the Civil War was in full flow? And how, if at all, does the reemergence of some form of football on college campuses from 1869 relate to the Oneida game?

To understand what the boys were doing, it is necessary to ask a number of questions in relation to their leisure time. How much free time did the boys actually have? After the hours at school, was there time for them to pursue games and hobbies? Were they present within the daily life of the family home? What is significant is that the Boston boys, the sons of the city's social elite, were exactly that: boys who lived at home with their families in Boston, who went to school every day, and then returned home. This was radically different to the situation in the elite British public (fee-paying) schools, where games such as rugby and soccer were first played and the modern, codified sporting revolution began. Across the Atlantic, British boys lived in the schools as boarders.[25] And there is also the question of scale. In 1861, Boston Latin had an enrollment of 262 boys, and the number at Dixwell was fifty-three. In Boston, the boys from Dixwell's formed the Oneida Club with a handful of boys from other schools. At the same time in England, Rugby School had an enrollment of 360 boys, while Harrow and Eton each had over 450. Not only were the English boys resident on school grounds as boarders, living, learning, and playing together; they also had large enough numbers of senior boys to create multiple teams. In the isolation of their own school, they could develop their particular forms of sport, be it the game that would become rugby, the Eton "wall game," or any other local forms. British public schools were rich and well endowed; their architecture spoke to power and learning and all of them, cloistered away as they were in mostly provincial towns, had private playing fields for their sole use. In Boston there would be no such decades-long development and refinement, within a boarding school setting, of a single school games tradition (as with rugby at Rugby School). Instead, the much smaller number of Boston boys had to come together from a range of schools, on common ground, to play their games in the full glare of the public eye before returning home for dinner. In this context, the Oneida Club only lasted for several years without a fixed, isolated setting and private fields on which to play and with a steady number of new boys inheriting and building on school sporting tradition. The Oneida Club—especially in the context of a civil war—faded away as quickly as it had seemingly emerged.

In a British context, the Victorians worried about the morality, or rather the potential immorality, of boys and young men. Schools like Rugby instigated a strict regime of discipline (usually enforced by the older boys), a full diet of classical learning, and daily Anglican worship to fill the days.[26] But the boarders were also given free time in which they could exercise and play, and it was in this space that a games ethic, ideologically branded as Muscular Christianity, emerged. Critically, students' free time was also a period of release from the control of the schoolmasters (just as boarding placed them beyond the reach of parental control). In a Victorian society that was becoming ever more rule-bound, stricter on the expectations of moral behavior, and increasingly controlling of the body and its physicality, games gave the boys an important outlet that they managed for themselves. It was from within this space, the time to play, that challenge matches between different houses within the school were organized. It was from these house challenge matches that the games of rugby and soccer, the handling and kicking codes, would emerge in the nineteenth century. The advantage the British public school setting had for the emergence of sport was structure. Games and challenge matches gave the boys the chance to measure the skill, strength, and abilities of one house above another. Essentially, as with modern sport, the boys were fighting over local bragging rights.

As an exported ethos, historian Clifford Putney observed that Muscular Christianity was "received with enthusiasm" by one Bostonian related to the Oneida circles: Thomas Wentworth Higginson.[27] But it was different in America because the United States did not have a centuries-old boarding school tradition in which the young men of the Boston elite left home for months at a time to pursue their education.[28] An upstate New York boy, Oneida captain Miller was an exception to the rule; the Dixwell School register lists exclusively boys residing in the Boston area.[29] The boys simply left their homes each morning and walked across the city to attend one of the schools, such as Dixwell's or Boston Latin, in preparation for entry into Harvard. The absence of a boarding house system, of structured leisure time within the school context, and the lack of interhouse rivalry meant that the game of football developed differently in the United States.[30] Moreover, the disruption caused by the Civil War meant that the progress of football codes in the United States was fractured.[31] Whereas Britain had boarding schools, political stability, and no domestic warfare, the United States suffered the rupture and dislocation of the Civil War.

This did not mean that the boys were bereft of any culture of voluntary association. Given the social networks of the Boston boys and the limited geographical scope of the city that they lived in, they were familiar with all kinds of social, leisure, and political life across the city.[32] Whether it was an awareness of the clubs that their parents belonged to, the myriad of political and abolitionist groups meeting across the city, or even their own experience of school-based drama, debating, or literary meetings, the boys fully understood associational culture. And even in sport, and the possibilities and ways in which clubs might function, especially in baseball—or else in winter activities such as coasting on sleds, ice hockey, or skating—the notion of a club would have been familiar. The boys may not have understood what modern, codified sport might look like, but they understood the pleasure of physical exertion, bodily movement, and, in the way of boys, the need to be the fastest, strongest, or highest scoring. This gave such activity an associational culture in the context of forming the Oneida Club and in making challenges with other schools.

They had also grown up in a world full of sports-related publications and would have been familiar with books about sport as well as coverage of major events in the newspapers and a range of specialist magazines that covered sporting interests. Also, the boys were growing up in a country where certain sports such as baseball, cricket, and rowing had become ever more popular and organized. From the sports they had experienced or were aware of, they would have been conversant with the need for rules, the sporting ways of conduct, and the need to organize competition in such a way that there was a clear outcome: a winner and a loser.

In that context, Oneida football does not appear out of nowhere. In 1848, Samuel Williams's *The Boy's Treasury of Sports, Pastimes and Recreations* was published. In one page the book offered an outline of the game of football, "a match made between two parties about equal in strength, two goals or boundaries should be marked out, a hundred yards asunder. The game consists in one party striving to kick the ball beyond the goal of their opponents, who at the same time [try] to drive the ball beyond the bound of their adversaries. . . . The party over whose goal the bladder is first kicked, loses."[33] In 1855, J. G. Woods's *Every Boy's Book: A Complete Encyclopedia of Sports and Amusements* outlined the game in the same way as Williams had done but added, in line with advancing the technology, that the ball was to be made of India rubber rather than the old-style inflated bladder.[34] Woods also stated that "the worst part of this sport is the tendency which the players have to kick each other's shins." Such books were popular in the 1850s and sold under many different titles; they spoke to the expectation that boys of a certain class would have access to, and indeed needed, pastimes. The football that is referenced in them sounds very much like the game the Oneidas played on the Common in the early 1860s, as later described in *Old Boston Boys*: a two-sided game where a win resulted from getting the ball across the goal boundary line of the other team. These games are not described in a way where the rules are strictly laid out, as was common by that time in descriptions of cricket or baseball. They were ball games, a type of football that was loose, about the battle for territory and the final hoped-for destination of the ball that signaled victory. Ultimately, this ambiguity in rules left a great deal of room for innovation and local specificities.

The boys would also have known what football might potentially entail from what they read in books or what they had seen at Harvard. But the Oneida game was not mirroring Harvard's tempestuous and pugilistic Bloody Monday.[35] The Dixwell-Latin match just weeks after the 1860 college ban was described in the press as having been played with "a good deal of skill and agility on both sides."[36] The Oneida boys were aware of a different way of playing, or a different meaning behind playing football, and one that was not necessarily the violent hazing form at Harvard. As John Krout wrote in 1929, "While Harvard and Yale students were bringing football into disrepute in college circles, New England boys had introduced a measure of skill into certain features of the sport."[37]

By 1864, at the very time the Oneidas were playing their games, things shifted in boys' books on sport. Where there had been the shortest of descriptions of football in previous books, White, Herrick, Wier, and Harvey's *The American Boy's Book of Sports and Games* offered an explanation of the terms and objectives of the game, but also critically reprinted the thirty-three rules of "The Laws of foot-ball, as played at Rugby."[38] Four years later the updated American edition of *Every Boy's Book* captures the ongoing division of football into distinct kicking and handling codes and remarks that "it would seem a pity at first sight that there is no authority like that of the Marylebone Cricket Club to revise the laws of foot-ball and insist upon their being observed in all places where the game is played. . . . To touch the balls with the hands is in some eyes a heresy, and in others an uncommon virtue." In concluding that "in the game of football the fewer the rules, and the simpler those rules are, the better," Woods offered a ten-point version of the Rugby School rules.[39]

What is apparent is that until those books were published from 1864 onward, which specifically promote the rugby rules, the game of football as outlined and advocated for as an amusement for boys is a fairly basic affair: two teams trying to get a ball over the opposing team's boundary, with the first team to do so winning. Within that basic description is the game of football that was played by the Oneidas, and by other schoolboys in Boston and elsewhere in the United States during the 1860s. The Oneidas do not appear to have invented a football code or a specific way of playing but built on an existing and traditional understanding of what constituted ball games among schoolboys at the time.

While such books are useful for tracking the evolution of football, its dissemination, and the eventual split, in a non-American context at least, between handling (rugby) and kicking (soccer), we cannot know if the Oneida boys read such tomes. Fiction was far more influential in disseminating ideas about football traditions than dry bullet points. Indeed, *Tom Brown's Schooldays* has been credited as one of the most influential books of the nineteenth century with over 225,000 copies in its first American edition printed by Boston's Ticknor and Fields.[40] An immediate success, the American version, *Schooldays at Rugby*, was a book familiar to the Oneidas.[41] Henry Cabot Lodge recalled that the book "was the favorite with all boys of my time. . . . No better book describing boys was ever written."[42] The book received a lengthy and raving review in the Harvard student paper, and continued references to Tom Brown underline how widely it was read, to say nothing of other periodicals that were available in Boston like J. D. Cartwright's description of football at Rugby School in the *London Society Magazine*.[43]

But the football of Rugby School was not only an imagined experience, and the Oneida boys also had direct links with the British institution. Henry Richards had two older brothers—George Henry and John Tudor—who attended Rugby School in the mid-to-late 1850s and undoubtedly would have experienced the traditions of school football on Old Bigside.[44] Another American boy—albeit not an Oneida—did recount his experience at Rugby in the early 1860s to his father back home in western Massachusetts. In several manuscript letters, William Barlow Morewood wrote home mentioning the seasonal organization of sport and how they had "almost got through playing foot-ball" by late October.[45] Thus, literary and personal testimony combined to bring the experience of Rugby and its football to old Massachusetts.

The Oneida boys then must have had some familiarity with the various ways the game could be played. By the turn of the 1860s and their later teenage years, they had already experienced kicking, handling, and chasing a ball. The Oneidas who strode out onto the Common between 1862 and 1865 weren't landing on the moon, a potentially inhospitable environment about which they knew little. They were walking onto Boston Common and its tradition of games and sports, which they were entirely familiar with. Who knows what manner of games and activities they had witnessed being played there? As Stephen Hardy noted, "Even before the Civil War, schoolboys had competed against each other on their acknowledged playground, the Common."[46] The game that the boys played may have been a rougher and more boisterous activity than was expected on the Common, but for them, the open park was the perfect place to play. Once there, the boys knew that they had gathered to play sport: challenges had been issued and times set. They were prepared. This activity had not emerged spontaneously. They had brought red bandanas to wear to distinguish the Oneidas from the other team and a ball to play with; they had agreed the limits of their playing area and those parts of the Common that would form their goal lines and how many boys would play on each team. The rules were clear, and transgressions like the "considerable lurking by Frank Peabody" in one 1862 match recorded by an onlooking classmate were understood to be frowned upon.[47]

The Oneidas played a game that was shaped by the contemporary world in which they lived. They were using what public space was available to them; they were building on their knowledge and experience of clubs and associational culture. Relying on what they had previously seen, experienced, or read, the boys put into practice what they knew about playing football. It was also a product of practicality: how much time they had, how many players, and what they could most usefully do, in terms of fun and competition, with the precious ball that they had secured for play. But what the Oneidas were doing was playing an early version of football that was common to many schoolboys and young men in the mid-nineteenth century in the towns and cities of the Northeast and mid-Atlantic.

The Oneidas had a shared identity as boys who attended, almost exclusively, Dixwell's school, and it was around this that the club, perhaps a representative interschool side, was built. Although not centrally part of his educational curriculum within school, did Dixwell encourage the football team organized by his charges, in the manner of the British reforming headmasters, as a way of instilling discipline? Dixwell did not mention sport once, in any form, in his autobiographical notes or his diary. Even if the headmaster stressed he "had little confidence in the benefit of corporal punishment," Dixwell was, however, adamant about his "determination to preserve the moral atmosphere pure and to train them to conscientious adherence to duty. . . . I believed that an undisciplined school like an undisciplined army was a disorganized mob."[48] In this sense, it is unclear how his presence, or indeed absence, from his school might have affected the arrangement of football games on the Common.

When Dixwell opened his school in 1851, thirty boys enrolled as the initial intake. Organizing football does not appear to have been an immediate priority. Smith recorded the new school's first football game only in the fall of 1855 with games in each subsequent year (the first score reported was a loss to Boston Public Latin School in 1857, with the first Dixwell victory in 1859).[49] In 1862, the press reported that the Common was again the venue for "a football match between seventeen boys of the Public Latin School and the same number from Dixwell's School, which resulted in the Latin School boys winning three games in five. . . . The playing was some of the best seen in Boston for some time."[50] Dixwell student Francis Lincoln recorded this game in his diary—going as far as keeping the cutouts in his journal and underling some "foul play on the side of Latin"—and also noted unnewsworthy interclass football like the second class challenging the first for a match in October 1862.[51] The way the games were recounted suggests that the sight of interscholastic matches on the Common was not unusual and comparisons could be made.

In 1863, something shifted in the way the newspapers recorded the team names. November that year marked the first reference to a "well-known Oneida Club," which played three games and won them all without giving up a game (goal) against the combined Boston Public Latin / Boston English High School team, the match commemorated on the ball that found its way to a museum decades later.[52] According to Smith, the following season Huntington Frothingham Wolcott was made captain after two leaders graduated from Dixwell's, and he led the 1864 team in victory over the English High School as well as a combined Roxbury Latin School and Dorchester High School team.[53] For the 1865 season, referred to on the Boston Common monument as the Oneida's final one, the newspapers instead refer to Dixwell defeating Boston Public Latin. Smith suggests that the period marked the school's last football game at a time when "the club had lost its name, and the team was again called the Dixwell Latin School" and the institution was deprived of its headmaster, Epes Sargent Dixwell, who "became ill and went to Europe for recovery . . . and was gone for the better part of the year."[54]

So in the years leading up to Dixwell's illness in early 1867—which, as his diary records, kept him at home for weeks at a time—and his subsequent European journey, the headmaster was present for the period of growth of schoolboy football on Boston Common. In describing the development of football, Robert Pruter has noted the significance of Boston schools, particularly how "interscholastic football arose first in the Boston public and private schools during the late 1850s, namely, Boston English, Boston Latin, and Dixwell Latin. Another public school joined the competition in 1863, suburban Dorchester High."[55] But 1865 appears to be the apex of the city scholastic game, since Smith records progressively fewer games between this group of schools. Overall, the Oneidas played at least ten games during the club's life-span, even if Smith notes some may have been rather labeled as Dixwell.[56] This may explain why the newspaper record is sparse regarding the Oneidas. While the Oneidas appear in 1863, the club name is gone from the newspaper record by November 1864, and the team was once more known simply as Dixwell's.

If the contemporary focus on school teams versus the Oneidas reinforces Bunk's observation that games involving formal clubs "were not widely played in the United States before 1863," the paucity of news is only a reflection of what was press worthy and is not in itself proof of their absence.[57] After all, the club was referred to during this period as "the well-known Oneidas." To quote David Kilpatrick in reference to another early club in New York, a lack of press coverage in this era also underscores how easily club football "seemed to have been forgotten" by the papers. Ed Farnsworth underscores how ubiquitous football was in this period, but it did not occupy the mind, "much less the effort of recording play."[58] In fact, the Oneida Club appears to be mentioned in the contemporary papers on only two occasions: the November 1863 title match and one game a year later in which the "2[n]d twelve of the Oneida Football Club" defeated Latin again in three successive games.[59]

Most importantly, Smith's research reveals a gap in reported Boston school football beyond 1866–67 after which "no more interscholastic games had been found until the 1872/73 season."[60] This begs the question of why Boston Common football, so popular in the 1850s and '60s, was all of a sudden abandoned. Something clearly happened in the years after 1865 to cause the effective ending of interschool football matches in Boston—a break that continued until the early 1870s when, in tandem with the college variety, games restarted. Undoubtedly, there is no singular reason for the vacuum. Broadly speaking, there was a convergence of various circumstances that all may have contributed in complementary ways. Firstly, the context of the Civil War changed with a focus on beginning national Reconstruction after 1865. Other leisure activities began anew. Lovett's scrapbooks record a great deal of baseball activity beginning from a handful of games in 1864 to a plethora of matches reported in the press between 1865 and 1868, precisely during the period when schoolboy football suddenly stops. When Harvard revived football from 1871, the games generated crowds and interest in a period of relative peace, becoming newsworthy. Are then the brief reports of schoolboy games on Boston Common in the first half of the 1860s also newsworthy, not because they are generating crowds, but because they offer light relief in the context of a civil war that affected the population such that Dixwell's diary summarized 1862 as "a sad year"?[61] Moreover, the reports of games also feature some of the "best" young men still in the city and not away at war. Perhaps also the question of climate may be relevant. The postwar boom of baseball reported between 1865 and 1868 was played between May and September, when the weather was more favorable to outdoor games. Incidentally, the autumn seasons between 1865 and 1869 saw a higher level of precipitation and colder temperatures than the decade between 1855 and 1865.[62]

The newspapers suggest that the game's retreat was not simply an issue for Dixwell's. With the reporting of games diminishing after 1865 for other city schools, perhaps this also reveals a change of habit, in moving from official interscholastic games to less organized pickup activity. In *The H Book of Harvard Athletics*, Morton Henry Prince (class of '75) recalled the late 1860s' "Boston Game" culture of regular play both on the Common and nearby: "we boys of the upper classes of Boston Latin School used to play football every day in the season during recess on Boston Common. In the afternoon the boys of all the preparatory schools who lived on Beacon Hill and the Back Bay would meet for a game on one of the vacant lots west of Berkeley Street, preferably the one adjoining Boylston Street, between Berkeley and Clarendon Streets, on the southerly side."[63] In this sense, it is important to recall that this was the messy period that saw the beginnings of codification moving away from what Tony Collins has called football's "primordial soup" of the 1850s and 1860s.[64] Boston boys were playing without any structure to adhere to, any universal set of rules, and without the boarding school or "Old Boy" apparatus that, although fragile as it was in the mid-to-late 1860s, aided the English Football Association (FA) to codify their rules, provoking the subsequent formation of the Rugby Football Union. The Oneidas also played before the FA rules were ever printed in New York by Beadle's in 1866 or even communicated in Gotham's press.[65] In this era, local custom dictated the laws of the game. The Oneidas appear as an organizational parenthesis in the Boston scene before a shift to impromptu play after 1865. In an institutionally bereft context, any leisure activity is a function of voluntary action, schoolboys or otherwise. So who could be responsible for the end of the Oneidas in 1865 and the gap in organized football until the early 1870s?

Even if there is no explicit trace of his involvement, was the role of Headmaster Dixwell somehow critical in supporting the playing of football? His presence coincides with the period in which the interschool games phenomenon began until its decline after 1866–67 (Dixwell until at least 1865). When reported on in the decade prior to 1866, it was as interscholastic challenges with the school name being used in press reports, suggesting some tacit approval from the headmaster of his charges representing the school in matches against other institutions of equal social standing. The lack of coverage after 1866–67 reinforces the suggestion of such a link or formal engagement between the school, the headmaster, and the boys who were playing—a connection that may have been affected by Dixwell's absence. As recorded in his journal, he "caught cold" at church in February of 1867 and had to spend significant time at home over the next few weeks.[66] In the summer, the headmaster went abroad on a several-month long tour until November that year. Thus, between the autumn of 1866 and the headmaster's return in late 1867 no Dixwell interschool football was reported for the first time in Boston for a decade. Does this suggest that the headmaster played some role, if not in the organization of the games, then in giving the match or games some official imprint that allowed them to take place and be reported on as interscholastic challenges? Despite Dixwell's return and renewed presence after 1868 until his retirement in 1872, school related football did not reappear as a regular phenomenon on Boston Common. This suggests that the headmaster was not the principal facilitator of football. What about his students, those who were commemorated as the members of the Oneida Club and the organizers of Boston football?

Dixwell's school remained stable in terms of student numbers until 1868 when enrollment began to drop. However, a number of club members were still on Dixwell's tuition books until the end of the 1867–68 school year.[67] Their disinterest in continuing football seems strange, since the boys organized their own pickup games regularly after 1865, as described by Prince above. But Oneida football was linked to specific schoolboys. Given that the club and school team ceased to exist at a specific point, the years 1865–66 were a key juncture. Was it because a specific core of Oneida players had left the school? Of the sixteen boys later listed on the monument, in fact only four were still at Dixwell's in 1864–65: Miller, Means Lawrence, Scudder, and Tucker. The first two then entered Harvard—Scudder and Tucker's next steps remain unknown until they respectively entered the college in 1867 and 1868—uniting with old Dixwell classmates and Oneida teammates.[68] By the autumn of 1865, all the older boys were gone, and Miller soon suffered a fall—mentioned by Dixwell in his diary that "[doctor] Wyman suspects epilepsy"—which caused his withdrawal from Harvard and may have been an impetus for him to stop contact sport.[69] Perhaps the interest in organizing a team, pursuing a tradition of a club with boys from different schools, simply faded. People and their interests do matter.

Whatever the complexities of the game that the boys played, and no matter how far they built on a preexisting sporting culture, they were not playing a codified game governed by printed rules and overseen by an established governing body. They were playing their own games for their own entertainment and unaware, at the time, of their pioneering role in the development of the game of football. The Oneidas were playing on the Common and defining their own basic rules, developing their own "Boston Game" tradition, organizing themselves, and making challenges. And they were not alone—they played against single schools who, although perhaps not as skillful as the undefeated Oneidas, were organized enough to put a team onto the field of play. These teams were not entering into a ready-made and well-defined sporting environment where public leisure provision was the norm. It wasn't until the late 1880s and into the 1890s that the city of Boston started considering sporting and leisure provision as part of its brief. But the Oneida Club's contemporary contribution as an early interschool organized club ended in 1865, playing no active role in the city's sporting future. There is no doubt a plethora of reasons why the Oneida Club disappeared in 1865, but one key issue was the progression of the bulk of the boys, a close-knit group of neighborhood friends, from school to college. By the mid-1860s, coinciding with the end of the Civil War and the start of Reconstruction, it was time for the boys to begin their adult lives perfecting their education as Harvard men.

4
THE CRIMSON

Harvard and Football

The Oneidas, as their own records stated, had a playing roster of at least fifty-two boys. In his short historical sketch about the club, Winthrop Saltonstall Scudder compiled a list—featuring many recognizable Boston Brahmin names—which was deposited in the Massachusetts Historical Society on October 18, 1926, by Oneida Robert Means Lawrence, also a member of the society.[1] Of these fifty-two, at least thirty-seven successfully entered Harvard, arriving mostly between 1864 and 1870. They were not entering the large, internationally minded institution that Harvard is today; they were joining a university that was small and also tightly concentrated around the male social elite of the city who made up the undergraduate body. These were the sons of both old Boston families as well as a new group of business and professional families who would do much to endow the college and through their philanthropy make their mark as people of substance. To cite Ronald Story, "The Harvard experience became an important part of the process of elite social, economic, and cultural consolidation in these years, and contributed to the cohesiveness, cultivation, and hauteur of the distinctive Brahmin upper class that was to flourish after the Civil War."[2] Such was the elitism, insularity and self-assuredness of the Harvard classes of the post–Civil War era through to the early twentieth century, that those who graduated were critiqued for developing a "Harvard indifference." In 1907 alum Theodore Roosevelt was able, in an address to the Harvard Union, to classify Harvard men as "too lazy, too selfish, too short-sighted, or too timid."[3] The Harvard that the Oneidas entered has been described as "the institutional extension of the aristocratic family, and to allow oneself to be nurtured indefinitely by their alma mater was the equivalent of refusing to leave the family nest, and it produced similar neurotic symptoms."[4] Henry Cabot Lodge's biographer noted of his time at Harvard, "In a more democratic institution he would have been considered a dude and a snob. In Harvard he was just another rich young man from Boston with no aim in life beyond receiving a gentleman's C and having a good time."[5]

Even in the mid-1860s attending Harvard was not cheap, costing around $400 a year in fees. In addition, there were the general costs for accommodation and other necessities of $700, which meant that a student needed access to annual funds of at least $1,100 (a Massachusetts school principal was, for context, earning approximately $2,000 per year at this time). The sons of the elites entered Harvard in such numbers that they dominated the year groups in the mid-nineteenth century. While there were as many as forty-four scholarships for between $100 and $300 per year available in 1866—covering at most 11 percent of the 419 students enrolled—Ronald Story has argued that pecuniary support diminished significantly, resulting in an "increasing monopolization of the college by the Boston elite."[6] From Harvard, these young men would enter the professions and the businesses of their families: by the 1870s, Harvard graduates comprised two-fifths of the chief officers of the large New England textile firms and half the directors of the leading Boston banks and insurance companies. Prominence in law, medicine, politics, and scholarship was at least equally great. And while Harvard catered to the sons of its own graduates and to a tightly interrelated elite social group, other universities opened in Boston to cater to the middle classes of the suburbs, such as Boston University (1839), Tufts (1852), the Massachusetts Institute of Technology (1861), and Boston College (1863). While the proliferation of universities and colleges in and surrounding the city would lay the foundations for Boston becoming a world leader in education, the availability of other universities for the middle classes to attend meant that Harvard could continue, well into the twentieth century, largely providing an education and program of social networking for a narrow, city-based elite. While about twenty Oneidas had graduated from Harvard before Charles Eliot was appointed in 1869, the remainder were attending the college as the new president began a series of reforms that transformed the institution over the next quarter of a century. With the hindsight of forty years, Lodge recalled he entered a college with "a narrow classical curriculum of its English exemplars, and I came out a graduate of the modern university."[7] The Harvard in which Lodge and most of his clubmates studied was an institution on the cusp of educational evolution in these post–Civil War years. So where was football and sport in the university of the Reconstruction era?

Harvard had been founded in 1636, and as the United States grew in geographic and population terms, so the idea of colleges as centers of adult learning and professional training spread. What would later be qualified as the Ivy League was a group of colleges that had all been established, with the exception of Cornell, before the time of the American Revolution. They were elite institutions concentrated in the Northeast of the country underpinned by high academic standards and a strong religious character. What was not part of the formal life of the colleges until into the nineteenth century was sport. Indeed, most forms of games or exercise, and certainly anything that could become rowdy or unseemly, were regularly banned by college authorities. What first emerged as something that was recognizably sport within the college experience, in a formal and codified fashion, was rowing, a sport with a hidden trove of later influences on football development and the Oneida Club. Far more informally was an early form of football.

The emergence of some form of football was common to most of the colleges. The game was recorded from the 1820s at Princeton and Dartmouth, Columbia from 1824, and Harvard's Bloody Monday from 1827, with Penn students playing games against local high schools from the 1840s, and Yale began its freshmen versus sophomores challenges in the same decade. These games were, apart from an agreed time and date for the match, barely organized, with few rules. They seem to have emerged as a beginning of term ritual in which the freshmen could be bloodied rather than being a form of sport that might have developed and moved toward some form of codification. What is clear from the college experience of these annual fall challenge matches (an excuse to rush at freshmen and cause bodily damage), was that they did not, unlike the parallel history of sport in the English public schools, seem to be showing any signs of development.[8] The events that were banned by the college authorities in 1860 were effectively the same violent rushes that had emerged in the 1820s.[9] Only the most basic rules dictating the number of players, the size of the pitch, or a point scoring system seem to have developed over four decades: for example, the list of eight points from neighboring Connecticut's Trinity College.[10]

One aspect of Harvard life that was absent during the Civil War years was the annual football game that had traditionally taken place at the start of the academic year. The game between two Harvard classes was, prior to 1860, a feature of college life, but football had always been frowned upon by the college authorities. Playing football on the grounds within Harvard itself was explicitly banned, with the College's Orders and Regulations of 1852 stating that within the college yard there was to be no "snowballing or kicking football in the yard, lying on the ground, smoking in the streets of Cambridge or in the College yard."[11] After much debate—even among the student body—the game was banned outright by the college authorities, no matter where it was staged, on July 2, 1860, thereby prohibiting the annual match between sophomores and freshmen—soliciting a joyous reaction from some in the class of 1863.[12] The game that was banned was violent and criticized for being little more than an unfair fight between well-organized sophomores who had planned for the contest and freshmen who did not know each other and had been on campus for only three days. With the game played on the campus Delta and not the Common, the students' behavior was there for the entire university to see. There was also the issue of how the students conducted themselves as they gathered for the match. Within the student body called out voices of temperance and shame.[13] In the June 1858 *Harvard Magazine* students decried,

> Those who stand as opponents on the Delta, on the night of the Football Game, go there excited and maddened by the intoxicating cup,—drunk! Students of Harvard! does not the mention, even, of your disgraceful condition cause the blood to glow and tingle in your veins with shame? Have you so little self-respect, that you can dare to appear before many witnesses, perhaps not drunk yourselves, but at least banded together with those who are?—so little regard for that institution whose foster-children you are, that you thus wantonly expose her to obloquy and contempt?[14]

The following September match was covered in a full *New York Post* column—reprinted in the *Boston Daily Advertiser*—admitting that "there is too much fighting."[15] Within two years the Harvard faculty had seen enough of a game too violent and disruptive. The students had no choice but to accept the ban and even marked the ending of their annual football contest by staging a mock funeral in which the class of '63 buried a ball and a headstone erected over the grave.

The last game played at Harvard before the ban on football featured Henry Ropes, class of '62. That game has always been situated, in football history, as the final match before the authorities acted on their abhorrence toward the violence of the game. It then followed that there was a decade-long hiatus, whereupon the game was finally revived and transformed by a new generation of college men. This overly simplistic trajectory has been summed up by Steven Apostolov, who wrote that the traditional Boston Game was doomed because "of its pre-modern character.... Had students decided to modernize the Harvard game and introduce more rules, certainly it would have taken a lot of time and practice to do so.... The primary preoccupation of Harvard University students was their studies, not the modernization or codification of pre-modern sport."[16] The significance of Henry Ropes underscores how solely sport-focused historians of football have been. Men like Ropes, who may well have worked to modernize the Harvard or Boston Game, to see how it could be played in the context of the advancing codes of rugby and soccer, were not preoccupied with their studies in the missing decade of football: they were engaged in a fight for the future of their nation.

Henry Ropes was dead within three years of the last pre-ban Harvard football game and within a year of his graduation. Having volunteered to fight and joined the Twentieth Massachusetts Volunteer Infantry, on July 3, 1863, he was reading a Charles Dickens novel near Cemetery Ridge, Gettysburg, when nearby a defective shell was fired by his own side. The shrapnel from the exploding shell killed Ropes, who died where he fell.[17] He was twenty-four. Of the 1,622 Harvard men who fought on both sides in the Civil War, Ropes was one of 246 who died, to say nothing of the injured. Whereas British men had domestic peace and stability in which they could think about sport, their American counterparts, Harvardians like Ropes, were fighting to stay alive. Precisely during the years when handling, hacking, and violence were debated and then regulated in England between London, Sheffield, and beyond, a different North-South debate was had across the Atlantic. Without regular football there was no opportunity for the ongoing and incremental development, codification, and association of the game that took place in Britain during a battle that sundered kicking and handling codes. As such, Harvard students and graduates could not heed the call that the "game can be reformed without being abandoned" as urged in that lengthy 1858 match report, the second to last to be played.[18] They did not, nor could they have, simply because they were engaged in a bellicosity of the most mortal kind. A focus on grave matters—war and its aftermath—meant that Harvard football would not be revived until late 1871. In this sense, the world of Robert Apthorp Boit and his Oneida clubmates differed greatly from that of his Boston-born but London-based cousin Julian Sturgis, who benefited from the continuity of peace to play football at Eton and Oxford throughout the 1860s and then win the 1873 FA Cup, the first American to do so.

During the initial Reconstruction years, football was not played at Harvard in line with the decade-long ban. The *Harvard Advocate* reported matches at Columbia, Cornell, and Dartmouth and some in the Crimson student body "could not help wishing for something of the kind here," asking, "Why do we not play foot-ball? It is a more dashing, spirited and manly game than base-ball . . . and if well played as in England, it has science and skill enough to satisfy the most devoted and fastidious connoisseur of base-ball."[19] At the turn of the 1870s, the game began to reemerge, but the new football was more complex than what had gone before and was undoubtedly informed by the emergence of the rules of rugby and soccer across the Atlantic. As such, the Harvard men who took to the football field in the 1870s had to decide what game they would be playing. How and why someone was declared the winner was not simply a matter of being first as in rowing but relied on a series of rules that dictated fine details such as what constituted the goal and how points were scored. A view of what university football looked like in the years immediately after the Civil War can be found in the recollections of Morton Henry Prince, the first secretary of the Harvard Football Club. Known as a sickly child at school, Prince's entry in the *American National Biography* recounts that at college "he transcended his sickly childhood by cultivating the strenuous life of a football player and club athlete."[20] Prince recalled that the college game, through to the 1870s, was the one that had been played in the elite schools of Boston and that these formed the first rules for the game as adopted by the Harvard University Football Club in 1873:

> The rules were simple and through tradition were well established. Theoretically, any number could play on a side, but practically only ten or fifteen played because not more than 20 or 30 turned out each afternoon for a game. Instead of goal posts, the goal, over which the football had to be kicked on the fly, was only an imaginary line across the whole width of the field at each end. . . . The ball was round and made of a non-elastic

rubber fabric material similar to that of which rubber boots are made. The rubber only made it airtight.... Kicking was the predominant feature of the game, but under a certain condition a player was allowed to run with the ball, "baby" (i.e., dribble) it, or throw it or pass it to an another, and these tactics were liberally used. A player holding or running with the ball could be tackled.... On the other hand, striking, hacking, tripping and other rough play was forbidden.... The style of play as developed under these rules and by tradition was thoroughly open, and remarkably individual, leaving nearly everything to the initiative, skill, and agility of each player.[21]

Involved in the revival of football at Harvard in the years following its ban and after the Civil War, Prince was familiar with the Boston Game that had been played on the Common by the Oneidas and other schoolboy teams. He wrote of his own undergraduate days, "When winter came the success of the three seasons—two autumns and one spring in 1871 and 1872—of sport had been so exhilarating that the football enthusiasts felt that the game ought to have a wider support and all the students be invited and encouraged to join and learn to play."[22] The fact that Prince was part of what he called "three seasons of football" but wished the game had a wider support suggests that the revival was initially based around a small group of young men who were familiar with the Boston Game as it had been played through to 1865. The Oneida matches are recorded as having finished in 1865, and Prince was playing the Harvard revival matches on the Common by 1871. As Prince suggests, the game as played by the Oneidas must have continued in some unorganized and unreported pickup form, in the six years to 1871. Were Prince and his fellow students of the early 1870s, the ones who revived football in a college setting, the missing link between the Oneidas and the Harvard game, boys who likely played an ongoing form of the game on Boston Common but did not identify it specifically with the Oneida Football Club?

Prince's recollections of the game did suggest a continuity of games from Boston Common to Cambridge. He wrote, "There were at this time, 1871, at college, in the several classes a group of Boston 'men' who for years had played football in the Boston schools and were enthusiasts of the game."[23] Significantly, Prince's group of Boston men involved in the revival of football at Harvard included George Wigglesworth (class of 1874), Arthur Cabot (class of 1872), and Robert Grant (class of 1873). These three are a significant link between the Oneidas and football at Harvard. Wigglesworth attended Dixwell's School in the last two years before it closed (and would marry another daughter of his headmaster, Epes Sargent Dixwell, which meant that he became brother-in-law to Gerrit Smith Miller) and was a classmate of the Oneida player George Minot.[24] Arthur Cabot's older brother was Samuel, a good friend of Jim Lovett. Both Cabots and Robert Grant entered Boston Latin (1860, 1862, and 1863 respectively) and were close friends with Oneida player Frederick Cheever Shattuck. The enthusiasm for football that these men shared with Prince and their active participation in pickup games lay the foundations for the game being formalized at Harvard.

At the end of the 1872 fall season and barely a month after the Great Boston Fire's decimation of the city east of the Common, a meeting was held on December 3 in Holden Chapel, and the Harvard University Football Club was formed. With several Oneidas still on campus as the university renewed with the game, was that tradition of Boston football the same one that the Oneidas had been part of?[25] None of the officers of the new club were directly Oneidas, although Augustus Hemenway, who had attended Dixwell's in the same class as three Oneidas, was the first treasurer of the Harvard University Football Club (and in the way of Oneida networks would marry William Lawrence's sister).

The emergence of football in the 1870s was not restricted to Harvard but happened across the elite universities. Beyond the student body's interest, also important in supporting the idea of football was the continued success of *Tom Brown's Schooldays* in the United States—evidenced by the raving reviews of the "excellent and ennobling" book and its availability in college libraries like Yale's.[26] The popularity of the book—well known to the Oneidas and extolled in the antebellum *Harvard Magazine*—and the culture at Rugby School, including the game, were heightened by a tour of the United States by the book's author, Thomas Hughes. During his multi-city and university visit in the autumn of 1870, he even "indulged in foot ball" with Cornell professor and university vice president William C. Russel, news that was reported with interest in the *Harvard Advocate*.[27] References to Tom Brown can be found regularly in the college newspapers of this era, underlining Hughes's reach in American culture with a generation having grown up with the book. American college faculty found a didactic tool in the football and character of Tom Brown, the legitimacy of which was embossed by the visit of the respected social reformer and marked a key shift from the prior decade. After his Cornell visit, the upstate university paper noted how Hughes observed "the awkward way in which foot-ball was played" on campus, prompting the *Era* writer to agree, "We do not pay the attention to physical culture that high mental cultivation itself demands."[28] Hughes's own recollections—printed in Boston and also in London—did not conceal criticism of Harvard's lack of physical culture. He wrote that, aside from rowing, "nothing else is stirring"; cricket was "too tedious, and is not, I believe, played at all. The same may be said of football, for . . . Bloody Monday has brought out an ordinance against the game."[29] Hughes's visit could not have been more serendipitous.

At this point the various colleges, especially those concentrated in the Northeast, returned to forms of football. More widely, after the end of the Civil War, the idea of play and leisure once again began to take hold of the imagination on campus. Mark Bernstein adds a further ingredient when he argues that during Reconstruction, "college campuses swelled with the returning veterans, many of whom brought with them a love of vigorous games and impatience with college prohibitions against them."[30] The thirst of college students for renewed football was undoubtedly quenched by Hughes's words of approbation at faculty dinners and by example even playing the game. Cornell reported the creation of a football association just weeks after Hughes's visit based on "an arrangement of stringent rules for the scientific playing of the old game," and Harvard's magazine reported that Dartmouth students agreed to oversight on regulations in exchange that the "Faculty now furnish the balls." While there is no direct evidence that Hughes urged faculty to revoke their bans, his speeches extolled the benefits of sport for the American college man—even sending a silver cup to Cornell's boat club—and Columbia, Dartmouth, Harvard, and Yale acquiesced to football directly following the Englishman's 1870 tour.[31] In Hughes's wake rose a tide of campus football.

A pair of other schools was ahead, however, in pushing for more football. In the fall of 1869, a group of students from Rutgers were challenged by those from Princeton to a series of three football games. In correspondence between the two, the rules for the challenge matches were agreed. The field was to be 360 feet long and 225 feet wide with a goal eight paces wide. Princeton alum Henry Van Dyke recalled the series years later: "Twenty men a side: round rubber ball: no carrying allowed: only kicking, dribbling, and batting with the hand."[32] The game would be played until one team had scored six goals. The first game was played on November 6, 1869, and took over three hours to complete, with Rutgers the winners by six goals to four. The second game was won by Princeton by eight goals to nil. The third game was never played on the orders of the college administrators, who felt that the sport was too distracting and gaining too much attention among the undergraduates.[33] After these first games, intercollegiate challenges came thick and fast. In 1870, Princeton played Rutgers again, and a new challenge was made between Rutgers and Columbia.

The appetite for intercollegiate football grew steadily. After initial interclass matches in November 1870, Yale students quickly formed an association and within two years organized a match with Columbia featuring the first college admission charge for spectators at twenty-five cents per person.[34] Yale favored a purely kicking version of the game. In 1873, Yale played Princeton, but that game ended after thirty minutes when the ball burst and was delayed until a new one had been bought—a lesson learned quickly, as future games were not planned without several balls on hand. Yale and Princeton would not play each other again until 1876, as they could not agree on common rules, evidencing the initial difficulty between various colleges in achieving regulatory accord.[35]

Rules were a big deal, since they were the only way to bridge local playing traditions; yet pitting institutional egos against each other was not simple. In 1871, Princeton had set up a football committee to try to establish rules, and such committees followed at other colleges. As had been the case with the English public schools, each college developed its own rules. Harvard built its rules around the traditions of the Boston Game and the rules of rugby. Yale and Princeton took to soccer, or predominantly the kicking form of the game. When playing intra- or interclass matches on their own campuses, under their own local traditions, negotiating such differences in the rules was not a concern. But trying to agree common rules between colleges for challenge matches led to regular disputes and disagreements about exactly what form of the game should be played. Whether they were trying to uphold their own campus traditions and versions of football or they felt playing "their" game would give them a competitive advantage, each college was fierce in insisting that their rules were the best. Some at Harvard did observe how the other colleges had "adopted systems similar to each other, resembling very closely the English game, in which most every thing is done with the feet" and even called to imitate them or "at least give the other game a trial" in order to play intercollegiate matches.[36] In October 1873, Princeton called a meeting in New York of the colleges in an attempt to define common rules, but only themselves, Rutgers, and Yale were in attendance.[37] While there was a debate at Harvard between trying new rules versus preserving sporting traditions—something that comes out clearly in the school's newspapers—the end result was that Harvard stood its ground. Writing in 1922, Prince recalled an essential problem,

> One fundamental principle of our game, determining the whole character of the play, was, I may repeat, that a player was permitted to pick up the ball, run with it, throw it, or pass it. He could also seize and hold an adversary to prevent his getting the ball. Quite contrary to this were the Yale rules, which were essentially the same as those of Princeton, Columbia, and Rutgers: no picking up, carrying or throwing the ball was allowed, nor was holding or pushing with the hands. The game was all footwork. . . . Regretfully, therefore, Captain Grant was instructed to decline Yale's invitation. . . . "We must either sacrifice entirely the principle of our game and learn a new one or abandon all thought of intercollegiate matches. We have chosen the latter alternative." And with this, the incident was closed.[38]

The letter sent from Harvard to Yale—reprinted in the latter's newspaper—explaining why they could not attend the meeting in New York further said, "I assure you that we consider the game here to admit of much more science, according to our rules. We cannot but recognize in your game much brute force, weight and especially 'shin' element. Our game depends upon running, dodging and position playing. . . . We even went so far as to practice and try the Yale game. We gave it up at once as hopeless. . . . I would send you a copy of our rules but we do not have a spare copy."[39] This seems rather disingenuous, however, especially given that the rules had been printed several times that year in the *Advocate*—including two weeks later alongside the code agreed in New York—and also reprinted in other college papers.[40]

Perhaps the disinterest in dialogue stemmed rather from the growing rivalry, stakes, and bitterness inevitable in intercollegiate competition. After all, the invitation to the October 1873 rules meeting arrived just a few months after the summer's college regatta, which had been steeped in controversy. The race was initially given to Harvard but afterward was awarded to Yale. There was some rowing-football crossover in both crews. Rowing for Harvard in the summer were members of the university's football club, including founding committee member Henry L. Morse.[41] The tension between mostly similar rowing teams continued the following year with Yale accused of fouling Harvard, resulting in "an outbreak of hostilities in the town." It was not until the 1875 regatta that the rules were amended with a total absence of fouls. It is not hard to imagine the bitterness from the July 1873 rowing race lingering into October when Morse and his fellow football committee considered an invitation to a football rules meeting that might include the same Yale oarsmen.[42] But Harvard's absence from the New York conference left them on the sidelines. The newly agreed rules banned the throwing or carrying of the ball, solidifying a kicking style exhibited to perfection by the Old Etonians who left Yale so impressed when visiting a few weeks later.[43]

With the other colleges having chosen the kicking code, Harvard began to look for new challenges. In May 1874, they played two games against McGill University of Montreal. The first match was played under Harvard rules and the second under the Canadian rugby rules. The key outcome of the game was not victory for Harvard but rather their embrace of the new game from Canada—and the cultural rapprochement between the elitist Harvard Brahmin and their well-accoutred McGill compatriots. In fact, the Harvard *Magenta* reported more about socializing and fox-hunting than the rugby played and underlined the contrast between the Canadians' "English foot-ball suit" and the "shabby-looking" and "dilapidated" Harvard men.[44] Initially designated as the umpire on the Crimson side, Oneida Oscar Iasigi's younger brother Augustus D. Iasigi ended up playing for Harvard.[45] The next big challenge for Harvard was arranging a match in 1875 against their rivals, Yale: rules were agreed, and the game played along the lines of those that the Bostonians had learned from the Canadians—essentially a handling game similar to rugby.[46] The Harvard and Yale match attracted two thousand paying spectators, which meant that Harvard's expenses for traveling south were covered. Harvard won the game four goals to nil, and it does seem as though it was some form of handling game that was played on the day, and Yale, like Harvard when they had met the Canadians, were impressed by this variant.[47]

The steady development of the game and the experiments with different forms led to a second meeting of the colleges—Harvard, Yale, Princeton, and Columbia—this time in Springfield, Massachusetts, in 1876, to agree on a common code.[48] The agreed-on sixty-one rules defined tackling, kicking, catching, the size of the field, the time of the match (two forty-minute halves), the size of the teams (fifteen players each), and the points-scoring system.[49] Yale withdrew immediately from the second Intercollegiate Football Association, having failed to get the team size set at eleven men each among other issues they disagreed with. Despite having left the association, Yale agreed to continue to play games against the other three colleges that season under the new rules and won each, thereby effectively claiming the first national championship. The fragility of these early intercollegiate associations—and mixing personal and institutional egos—was evident also in Yale and Harvard's withdrawal from the rowing association causing it to fold after the 1875 regatta.[50]

The next great leap in the development of football was the arrival, into the administration of the game, of Yale's Walter Camp. He had played for Yale and joined the Intercollegiate Football Association's rules committee in 1878, where he would remain a member until his death in 1925. There is no doubt that it was Camp's many rule changes that would redefine the game as played in the United States, break it from rugby, and produce the distinctive form of American football. Camp is hard-wired to the historical narrative, referred to as the father of American football as if he invented everything about the game. Yet Camp refined a game that had been agreed to, with a basic rule book that allowed games to be played and enjoyed, in Springfield in 1876. Those rules were being formulated in the year the freshman Walter was arriving on campus. It would be two more years before he joined the committee where he could influence the future direction of the game. Without diminishing Camp's contribution, perhaps history ought to think of him rather as a very good godfather, who takes the young child under his wing after the true parent has passed on.

So what type of game had been agreed to in 1876? Since the first intercollegiate challenge match of 1869, a number of colleges had been meeting and experimenting with the various forms and codes for football. In essence, the battle was in part a continuation of one that had taken place in Britain. The men of the American colleges were at one level deciding whether they should play a kicking code, soccer, or a handling code, rugby. But again, there are important differences between the British situation and that in the United States. The American colleges, in terms of student numbers, were much smaller than their British counterparts. American colleges did not recruit from a wide geographical spread, which was the norm in Britain, and as such, freshmen arrived from the local area or region and a small network of schools. They were familiar with one another and knew the local sporting variant. There was no mixing of codes within individual colleges and therefore no compromise or evolution of an agreed code, as there was no dissension about what the agreed local code was. There was not a large network of elite colleges in the United States with a high concentration of boys from multiple schools who brought with them a variety of footballing traditions. Distance, despite the advent and spread of the railroad system in the United States, was still an issue. Not only did college authorities frown on the idea of long-distance travel by undergraduates in pursuit of sporting fixtures, but the actual distances between the US colleges, while not insurmountable, were an issue in arranging challenges.

In the development of the competing British codes there was an ongoing, almost organic process as boys and young men passed through their schooling, to college, and into professions based in large urban centers. British boys and men did not suffer a critical four-year hiatus in the development of their football codes while a civil war was fought, and neither did they have to concern themselves with the physical and economic rebuilding of their nation. What American college boys and young men found when they sought to reinvigorate and possibly reinvent the game on campus at the turn of the 1870s was a clear choice: either soccer as formulated under the rules of the Football Association, founded in October 1863, or rugby as played under the Rugby School rules of 1845 and developed by the Rugby Football Union after 1871. There was also a third localized way: ignore the imports and continue with the traditions of the game that was played in their city or region and adapt them as necessary or when confronted by the need for compromise with other schools. In Britain there was an intense period of game development, attempted compromise, and eventual split between the two football codes. Precisely as the US colleges began to play again, the two games (or at least the two principles of kicking or handling) were already well formed. What is seen in the years from 1869 to 1876 is a relatively small number of games being played between a tiny number of colleges as they tried to figure out which version of the game they preferred. If there had been a larger number of colleges involved in the evolutionary debate surrounding football in America, then perhaps there would have been the type of split and a simple binary choice that took place in Britain—essentially, choose rugby or soccer. But in the United States, the number of colleges involved in this process of evolution was effectively less than six. If they could not collectively find an agreement as to what they could play together, then they would simply have no one else to play against. And this is perhaps where the power of Harvard, as a historic and socially influential establishment with its local ties to the Boston Game, is so important.

In 1873, the colleges had come together to try to establish common rules for the American collegiate game. They decided on the kicking code of soccer, but it was a choice that was soon to be proved as untenable. Why? Simply because, in 1873, Harvard had refused to attend the meeting and chose instead to dismiss the preferred kicking code under discussion. In this refusal to attend, Harvard was in a minority. So why did their nonattendance have such an impact? Why did their desire to hang on to the traditions of the Boston Game, a handling code, carry so much weight when everybody else wanted to kick? Harvard was respected among the other colleges at one level because it was simply the oldest with the deepest traditions, the home of the nation's established and most influential elite. In the development of sport, as had already been seen in the intercollegiate contests in rowing and baseball, playing Harvard was a key pull for spectators and a definite measure of status. In that context there is almost a business reason for wanting Harvard to be involved in whatever consensus was found for the new commonly agreed form of football, as evidenced later by the large paying crowd that attended the inaugural Harvard versus Yale football match in November 1875. Harvard was well connected politically, its alumni were some of the most successful businessmen of the era, and its traditions of philanthropy and school spirit were deeper than anyone else's. Harvard's presence, or absence, was a key deciding factor in the future viability of any version of a football code. The 1873 conference and the choice of a kicking code did not even last a year precisely because of Harvard's refusal to join.

Harvard was set, in 1873, on defending the traditions of their Boston Game. It was prepared to meet sporting modernity, in the form of McGill's rugby code in 1874, and would be won over by the appeal of that codified form. But that was still a handling code that maintained the base elements of Boston tradition. The Harvard game was not of itself a codified football game (until its 1872 rules), but the McGill rugby code was the nearest contemporary variant of a codified version of the Harvard game: a handling game, that also allowed kicking. What was agreed to in 1876, which would later be transformed by Camp into American football, was a handling game whose DNA can be traced back, both in its form of play and in the ways it flexed its cultural and institutional muscle and box office appeal, to Harvard and the Boston Game.

Writing years later, and by that time fully aware of the direction of the American football code, Prince recalled how Harvard was surprised and pleased to receive a proposal from McGill University in Montreal for a series of matches but underlined that

> As McGill played under the Rugby rules (slightly modified) it was proposed, in order to overcome the difficulty, that two matches be played, one under the Rugby rules and one under the Harvard rules. Of course, we eagerly fell in with the idea of the two matches. . . . We at once set to work studying the principles of the Rugby game, practising plays, and working out what could be done under the rules and particularly what tactics under the Harvard rules could be adapted. . . . The second match on the next day was a different affair [from the first game under Harvard rules]. We now had to meet our opponents at their own game. . . . Instead of the round "rubber" fabric ball used in the Harvard game, the ball was the English oval, leather-covered ball, substantially the same as that used today in the present American game. . . . The match was hard fought and evenly contested for it turned out to be a drawn battle, neither side scoring a goal or a touchdown in the three half-hours. . . . The fact that we held the McGill team to a draw at their own game speaks well for the skill and general excellence of our men at football, considering that they had only a few weeks in which to study and practice the game.[51]

While the evolution of the specific game of American football was a result of compromises and the eventual work of Walter Camp to create the basis of the distinctive game that we now know, it has very specific roots. The game of football as had existed on American campuses prior to the bans of 1860 could have potentially developed any number of ways. What was called to a halt in 1860 was a violent game of charges and skirmishes. During the years of the Civil War, football was absent at the collegiate level, first because the game had been banned and second as college undergraduates or alumni were focused on the business of war. What did exist were the Oneidas and other local school teams, although they were playing a game that appeared more sophisticated than Harvard's Bloody Monday game. How much they may have been influenced by Tom Brown and tales of games on the Close at Rugby School to develop their own Boston Game is impossible to ascertain. But one thing does seem certain: the young Oneidas were not gathering on Boston Common to charge, to fight, and to skirmish but to play, to score, and to win the game.

The football that emerged on campuses in the 1870s at some levels tried to pick up where it left off, but the old violent game was an anachronism, out of step with the force of modernity in life and in sport, and outmoded after the brutality of the Civil War. Available to the undergraduate classes of the 1870s was either rugby or soccer, in their putative forms, or else the continuation of some form of local tradition or code, and through to 1876 the colleges involved did try to work through these options before seeking compromise. Yet in their moment of grappling with sporting modernity and the options open to them in the form of soccer and rugby, the colleges were to a large degree dependent on the engagement of Harvard with any potential viable compromise as to what form football would take. Even the *Yale Record* admitted an excess of politeness and criticized its delegates who, through "short-sightedness and lack of diplomacy," agreed to the "Concessionary rules" for the 1875 game versus Harvard when "back-bone and discriminating stubbornness should [have taken] the precedence."[52] What Harvard held out for was a form of a handling game, which they had experienced in its rugby form in their engagement with McGill and that spoke back to the Boston Game and the Oneidas. Those Harvard men who revived and developed football at college in the 1870s had never experienced the old Bloody Monday game, but those men had been boys in the 1860s when the schoolboy form of football, engaged in by the Oneidas and others, was played on the Common.

One could argue what Walter Camp finessed and produced was a specific American football code based on Boston traditions, which was neither rugby nor soccer. This game of Camp's remained violent and physical and had to be radically reformed in the early twentieth century and refined again to prevent injury and death. Camp, then, was not the father of the twentieth-century American football game but rather a young man of the nineteenth century who grew up closer to the spirit, violence, and rushing of football as it had been played in the 1850s and 1860s. Camp reformed and remodeled the code as agreed in 1876 from his place in Yale. But he was not rethinking and refining a Yale or New Haven tradition; he was building on an intercollegiate acceptance of the cultural power of Harvard and the fact that the boys who had once played on Boston Common, and their network of successors, would not let the spirit of their game disappear. In the early evolution of American football up to 1876, handling won out over kicking, and Harvard won over Yale.

5
BRAHMIN NETWORKS

Families, Professions, and High Society

During the battle of words between a mother and her curly-haired son on whether he could join the Union Army and fight in the Civil War, Huntington Wolcott's mother offered sage advice. She argued that while fighting had to be done, there was a higher calling: "After the war is over, we shall need wise men, pure patriots in the councils of the country and high-minded statesmen."[1] Wolcott ignored his mother's plea, and with the support of his father plus a commission from Governor Andrew, he enlisted. He survived the fighting but soon after succumbed to typhoid and was dead at the tender age of nineteen. Fellow Oneida William Lawrence recalled Huntington's death in a tribute forty years later to the younger brother, Roger, the recently deceased Massachusetts governor: "On 9 June 1865, another Wolcott, patriot and soldier, a chivalrous boy, passed on. Again, the schoolboys met, and in his home in Boston, gathered round the bier of Huntington, their friend and leader."[2] As they stood over the body of their boyhood friend, the spirit of Wolcott's mother's advice must have been obvious to all the young men. Their lives could be cut short, the nation was divided, and for all their privilege, they had to contemplate how they would, as adults, serve one another, their community, and their nation. The Oneida boys were a tight-knit group. Their closeness was not only a product of sharing their school days and a sporting passion but also because they came from a wider, interconnected network of families that shared business and philanthropic interests and formed Boston's social elite. As they grew into adulthood, the Oneida network strengthened as many belonged to Boston's elite social clubs, worked in similar business and financial spheres, lived in the same socially exclusive neighborhoods, and sat on a myriad of boards that oversaw the city's educational, cultural, and charitable institutions. This powerful network served them well years later when commemorating their sporting youth.

There are many questions that can be asked of the Oneida boys as they journeyed from an antebellum childhood to a Gilded Age adulthood. Mostly, they were the children of a wealthy elite and living in one of the finest contemporary cities in the United States. Many of their families—with links to the textile manufacturing, trading, or banking worlds—had made significant fortunes in the decades leading to the Civil War. Many of the Oneida boys would enter their adulthood cushioned from the financial realities of the world by a healthy trust fund. The vast majority would journey across Boston to Cambridge on leaving school and enter Harvard. After college many of them would work for family interests, until they forged their own path through life. But what would these boys do with their privileged access to social networks and power? Would they be self-indulgent pleasure-seekers, narcissistically enjoying the benefits of wealth, or would they, as Wolcott's mother had asked, become wise men and high-minded statesmen?

The Oneida boys who attended Harvard were spread across several classes—especially 1869, 1870, and 1871—and many of them recalled later how they would recognize the faces of former schoolmates on campus. Harvard was a small place, and after 1850 more than 80 percent of its students came from Boston-based schools, with the private school contingent (including Dixwell) the second largest group on campus after those from Boston Latin.[3] Harvard was a university that had been funded by many of the boys' parents. A few boys would have entered campus buildings named after their forefathers; other boys had fathers and other male relatives on the faculty, within the administration of the university, on the managing Harvard Corporation, or else on the Board of Overseers. Many of the boys extended their time at Harvard and pursued postgraduate work, from Lodge taking a PhD in history in 1876 to others who studied at the medical school, such as Robert Means Lawrence and Frederick Cheever Shattuck, or the law school, as with William Fisher Wharton. While at Harvard the boys mixed still further, cementing their own social networks and extending them to include others they did not know from Dixwell's School or through their ball games on Boston Common. The various Harvard clubs and societies, such as the Hasty Pudding Club, were full of former Oneida boys. They also took part in sporting activities. A number of the boys were actively involved in the Harvard rowing crew: the ideal sport for a modern, upstanding, and strong young man. Others played baseball within the college, also representing Harvard at varsity level. While football did not see its formal resurgence until most of the boys had left campus, they were likely to have occasionally pulled on their boots again and taken to the familiar surroundings of Boston Common to take part in pickup games.

Many of the boys traveled across the River Charles to Harvard from their homes in Beacon Hill, while others journeyed from the affluent suburbs of Brookline or Milton. It was not however simply a case of a geographical closeness that tied the boys together or their shared school and sporting experiences. The boys were part of a kinship system, a social network; they were connected through the genealogical histories of their families and through intermarriage. Many of their families were associated not solely through shared DNA but also through extensive, intertwined, and mutually supportive business endeavors. They also had a multitude of common interests that brought them together: they had the same overriding political views (Republican), the same religious beliefs (many Unitarians followed by Congregationalists and Episcopalians), and an awareness of their collective role in the settlement and history of Boston and Massachusetts. Their shared worldview extended to similar philanthropic interests—namely, the support of educational institutions like Harvard, medical institutions such as the Massachusetts General Hospital, and cultural organizations ranging from the Athenaeum to the Academy of Arts and Sciences. The Mount Auburn Cemetery, where the majority would eventually be buried, was important to the Oneidas and their families. Founded by the grandfather of Oneida player William Sturgis Bigelow, the cemetery holds the final resting place of twenty-five Oneida players. While some of the boys, the wealthiest and best connected, existed at the very heart of this elite social network, all of them orbited around it with its range of business interests, kinship ties, private members' clubs, cultural institutions, and last resting place.[4] Even for those boys whose adult lives would follow very specific paths, sometimes taking them away from Boston, they would always return there and embrace the social network in which they grew up.

The key to understanding this tight-knit network is to acknowledge a pattern established by their fathers and grandfathers. This social elite strove to form and create long-term stability for themselves. In practice this meant, in business, that the traditional Boston families of wealth recovered from the cotton industry's post–Civil War collapse, in which they had made their fortunes, and invested profitably in the railroads and industry of a United States expanding westward.[5] The Oneida boys would follow these patterns of behavior, the management of their social networks, retention of their wealth, and the cultivation of a worldview that were all well established. The challenge for the Oneida boys was that their world was remarkably different to that of their parents. The United States had to rebuild after the years of the Civil War; the methods of industrial production and the financial infrastructures that had made their families rich would be transformed in the late nineteenth century, and the financial focus of the banking and business worlds would shift away from Boston and toward New York. The Oneidas' lifetime coincided with a transformation in Boston's fortunes: whereas the city had ended the nineteenth century as the second busiest American seaport, by 1920 it had fallen to sixth. Many of the city's main industries stalled, and in particular employment in iron manufacture, shoes, and textiles dwindled in the face of stiff competition from other cities and abroad. Boston did remain a significant banking and finance center as a result of the wealth and capital that had been built up in the nineteenth century, but "with no underlying economic base, Boston began a long decline."[6]

In Boston, political or civic power was also transitioning away from the old families of the city into the hands of the more numerous democratic Irish. With the loss of civic power, the Oneida generation would turn their attention to founding or supporting, in the last three decades of the nineteenth century, the maze of Boston clubs, charities, and cultural institutions.[7] Modernization—whether in terms of travel, communication, or technology—would have a transformative effect on their lives and the traditional certainties about their place in the world. The question for the boys, as they ended their years of play on Boston Common and entered Harvard, was how they would face the challenges ahead of them. Building on the Boston of their parents, how would they weave their own social and professional networks into a new generation of close-knit ties? And how, in the midst of societal change and transformation, would their networks be leveraged to make a schoolboy game of football a powerful statement of their position in Boston society, their place in history, and a recognition of the ties that bound them together?

The list of surnames of the Oneida Club members, according to Robert Holmes writing in the *Boston Globe* in 2012, "was as much a Massachusetts history lesson as it was a group of young men beating each other up on Boston Common."[8] The names are from some of the most famous families of Boston commerce and philanthropy and include a good number from Brahmin families. The boys were not simply playing with their social equals but alongside a network of siblings, cousins, and relatives. The team roster included five sets of brothers: Walter and John Brooks, Edward and Walter Burgess, Amory and William Lawrence, Charles and Gerrit Miller, and Huntington and Roger Wolcott.

The teammates' families also intermarried. Frank Davis's sister, Anna Cabot Mills Davis, married Henry Cabot Lodge. Gerrit Miller married the sister of teammate John Dixwell, the daughter of his old headmaster Epes Sargent Dixwell. John Dixwell's other sister married Oliver Wendell Holmes Jr., also a former pupil of Epes Sargent Dixwell, thereby tying together through family relationships the worlds of the Boston Brahmin, Washington politics, the legal profession, and the boys who once played football. Such ties were also evident in linkages with Harvard: Francis Peabody's father, Ephraim Peabody, was the brother-in-law of Harvard president Charles Eliot. One of Oscar Iasigi's sisters, Octavie, married William Apthorp, while another, Elizabeth, married James Dwight. Little did the boys know that one day they would be related through the ties of marriage as fathers, brothers-in-law, and sons-in-law. Such intermarriages continued into the next generation with the union of Frederick Shattuck's daughter to the son of Joseph Bigelow. More widely the teammates were interrelated through a network of genealogical relationships, with a third of the Oneidas having family trees that overlapped within two generations. William Bigelow and Frederick Sturgis, for example, were both great-grandsons of Thomas Sturgis, while Robert Clifford Watson's mother, Mary Taber Hathaway, was the sister of Sarah Swain Hathaway, mother of John Forbes, thereby making the two cousins.

In business and occupational terms, many of the Oneida team members were able to enter the worlds of law and finance, which were often tied to family interests that had been made highly profitable by their fathers and grandfathers and associated wealth (and its preservation) with a sense of civic duty.[9] Many of the Oneidas were born into affluence, and it was something that they strove, through investments and connections, to maintain and grow. As has been noted of this generation, "To be born into a wealthy family was a great advantage; it markedly increased one's chances both of becoming wealthy and of entering a highly desirable occupation."[10] That the Oneidas came from flush families was evident when Amory Appleton Lawrence began at Harvard. Rather than living on a budget, Lawrence had access to an account with Messrs. Lawrence and Co. from which he could withdraw money "as he pleased."[11] In the decades after the Oneidas left Harvard and began their adult lives, the United States created huge wealth. Millionaires in the United States boomed from just 100 in the 1870s to 4,047 nationally as reported by the *New York Tribune* in 1892.[12] What was $1 million in the 1890s would amount to approximately $29 million in today's world. What is noticeable in this *New York Tribune* listing is how dominant were the cities of Boston and New York. Within Boston approximately 34 percent of millionaires had Harvard degrees. In the 1892 list, when the Oneidas were in their midforties, seven of the former teammates featured. These were James Beebe, William Eustis, John Forbes, Amory Appleton Lawrence, George Minot, Stephen Thayer, and Roger Wolcott. When the *New York Tribune* compiled its list again in 1902, a further three Oneidas had become millionaires: Joseph Bigelow, William Lawrence, and Henry Cabot Lodge.

By the time that the boys had entered their fifties, one-fifth of the Oneidas were millionaires. Underneath these were the remainder of the Oneidas who had not reached the headline wealth of millionaire status but most of whom were, by the standards of the day, incredibly rich. The evidence of the extensive business networks acquired by the Oneidas is clear from the range and number of directorships that they secured. By the turn of the century, sixteen of their number were already dead, but those who lived to middle age were at the heart of business in Boston.

The directorships and trustees that the group had accumulated included those who listed a single connection, such as Winthrop Scudder's place on the board of the Liberty Shipbuilding Company. Others held multiple directorships, such as Amory Appleton Lawrence, which covered industrial concerns from the Ipswich Mills, through insurance in the form of the Massachusetts Hospital Life Insurance Company, and in banking the National Union Bank Everett Mills.

Many of these were family businesses, but others were financial institutions that lay at the heart of Boston's wealth as a mercantile center, most notably the Provident Institution for Savings and the Suffolk Savings Bank. That these banks had a number of Oneida members on their boards speaks volumes about the significance of this network of schoolboy friends who, as adults, lay at the very heart of Boston finance and banking. Beyond these named directorships were extensive individual and family holdings in the key railway companies of the area that linked Boston north to Canada, south to New York, and west to the Great Lakes. Others were charged with the management of family trusts or else lived off the proceeds. As is noted of the social strata from which the Oneidas were drawn, "There was a whole class of people who didn't have to work."[13]

Yet many of the Oneidas did work. While some managed their inheritances, others entered professions or else followed their passions and made them their life's work. Of the Oneidas, over half inherited considerable wealth, managed and lived off the family trust, or else worked in the family business. In trade, for example, James Beebe, although having considerable family wealth by virtue of his wife's inheritance, worked as a wool merchant. Joseph Bigelow managed the family mining and banking interests, while Robert Boit worked in the family textile business before it failed following the 1873 depression when they switched to banking. Other Oneidas did not directly enter the businesses of their families but pursued other interests, secure in the knowledge that their living standards would be underpinned by family wealth. William Apthorp trained as a musician and became the leading music critic in the Northeast; while receiving income from his family's real estate business, William Bigelow earned his medical degree from Harvard and qualified as a physician; and Edward Burgess qualified as an entomologist but would find fame as a yacht designer, with one of his yachts winning the inaugural America's Cup.

There were also those Oneidas who either chose not to work in ways directly related to their family wealth or else did not come from a family that had amassed a fortune. These men pursued careers after leaving school and college. John Dixwell and Robert Means Lawrence both qualified from Harvard Medical School and worked as physicians, while Frederick Sturgis qualified as a physician at Harvard and then moved to New York, where he worked as an academic and surgeon with an expertise in the study of venereal disease. Robert Clifford Watson worked in the insurance business and devoted much of his spare time to coaching the Harvard rowing crews.

The acquisition of wealth by the elite of Boston was a process carried out from the mid-eighteenth century and hastened by investments in the industrial and transport revolutions of the Northeast in the first half of the nineteenth.[14] One byproduct of this long period of wealth creation was the engagement of the city's elite, including many of the Oneidas, in a range of philanthropic activities, particularly in the areas of medicine, education, and welfare. As Olivier Zunz noted, "In the span of two generations of the Civil War, an unprecedented number of Americans became [so] rich and powerful . . . that these men . . . opted to give much of their newly acquired money away. . . . The new rich felt free to both envision and fashion the common good."[15] Much of the philanthropic activity undertaken by the various Oneidas related to their position in Boston society and their chosen career path. Roger Wolcott, who was a leading state politician, involved himself in high profile medical causes (the Perkins Institution and Massachusetts Home for the Blind) or else those which spoke to the military history of the United States (the Society for Colonial Wars and the Old South Association). Men of substantial means such as Amory Appleton Lawrence involved themselves in charities that cared for the less well off in Boston society, and he served on the same boards as Wolcott. Henry Cabot Lodge's philanthropic interests saw him take a place on the boards of the George Washington Memorial Association, the Bunker Hill Monument Association, the Massachusetts Historical Society, the Old South Association, and the Soldiers' Home in Boston. William Bigelow followed in the footsteps of his father as a great supporter of the arts, serving on the boards of the Museum of Fine Arts, the New Boston Music Hall, the New England Conservatory, and the Society of Arts and Crafts. Perhaps the most impressive list of engagement with charitable concerns belonged to Bishop William Lawrence, whose board memberships and trusteeships, befitting the city's leading churchman, included a score of charitable institutions. The Oneidas were men who understood, through their social contacts and their philanthropic and cultural work, how things got done in the city of Boston. When a small group of surviving Oneidas would begin work on memorializing their sporting pastime in the 1920s, they had a lifetime of connections across the city, with social standing and cultural capital to match.

Alongside business and charitable positions, the men of Boston's late nineteenth century social elite also joined a plethora of private and elite centered clubs that afforded a steady diet of social interaction and networking, and allowed the Oneidas to frequently meet, discuss the matters of the day and call to mind their shared childhoods. As the *Harvard Crimson* noted in 2000, "Years ago, a young Bostonian's quest for status began the moment he enrolled at Harvard. He needed to enter the right final club, the right country club, the right Boston club, the boards of the right charities and finally, if he reached the ziggurat of Boston society, Harvard's almighty Board of Overseers."[16] Above all the memberships of the private and highly influential clubs or positions on boards of banks and businesses was a place on the prestigious body that administered and managed the college. William Sturgis Bigelow, Amory Appleton Lawrence, Henry Cabot Lodge, Frederick

Cheever Shattuck and Roger Wolcott all held positions there in the first two decades of the twentieth century, while William Lawrence, originally elected as an Overseer, would hold the position of Fellow on the Harvard Corporation. These Oneidas were not only all Harvard graduates but men who had achieved high public office (Lodge and Wolcott), leading business figures (Amory Appleton Lawrence), members of the Harvard Faculty (Shattuck), major cultural philanthropists (Bigelow), or else civic and religious leaders of the city (William Lawrence). All of them were close to Charles William Eliot, the Harvard president until 1909 (who would address the unveiling of the first Oneida commemorative exercise), and would have been entirely familiar with his successor, Abbot Lawrence Lowell.[17] Lowell was Harvard president from 1909 to 1933, the period when all the Oneidas were on the Board of Overseers, and although a younger man who had attended Noble and Greenough School rather than Dixwell's, he would have been familiar to all of them through family (he was related to both Amory and William Lawrence and also to William Bigelow) and through the multifaceted business and trustee links of the Boston Associates from which many were descended.

The elite of Gilded Age Boston, of whom the Oneidas were very much part, became important cultural advocates from the 1880s. As the city was reimagined with the building of the Back Bay, new cultural institutions were built. Alongside the promotion of these new endeavors, the Oneidas, as befitted their status and connections, were members and officials in many of the leading clubs in the city. The Bostonians of the period had "almost an obsession for things snobbish. They were concerned with whether or not their children went to the right schools and to the right parties, with whether or not they joined the right clubs, and with whether or not they served the right wines at the right time."[18] This was the Oneidas' social world. And the social network, the clubs they joined, the committees they sat on, and the cultural institutions that they endowed were little changed from the time of their fathers. Of those who ran Boston's cultural institutions, their pedigree was clear and they were, as historian Neil Harris noted for the Museum of Fine Arts, "a carefully selected group of men."[19] The composition of such boards and the networks that tied such men together were true for the Oneida generation across the city's institutions.

One of the great Boston, if not national, institutions was the Athenaeum. It was founded in 1807 by the Anthology Club of Massachusetts. In essence a private library, the Athenaeum grew to house a vast collection of art and natural history and even had its own laboratory for the scientifically inquisitive. The Athenaeum's exhibitions of art would lead its members to be a driving force behind the establishment of Boston's Museum of Fine Arts. The Athenaeum, although a library, was in fact one of Boston's most exclusive private clubs. Its membership was made up of the wealthiest and oldest families within the city, and its founding members classed as proprietors. Proprietorships survived the death of a member and were passed down through the generations. To inherit the status of proprietor marked an individual as a person of considerable standing within society. Of the Oneida boys, three would serve the Athenaeum as officers in the position of trustees—namely, Henry Cabot Lodge (from 1879), Russell Gray (from 1882), and Roger Wolcott (from 1882). A further nineteen of the boys would inherit a proprietorship, with Alanson Tucker being the first in 1870 and continuing across four decades until 1903 when both Russell Gray and Francis Cheever Shattuck joined the ranks. Illustrating the tightness of their social world but also the elite nature of their schooling was one man's proprietorship that predated those of all the boys. Their headmaster from school, Epes Sargent Dixwell, had inherited his proprietorship in 1864, while the boys were still kicking their ball around Boston Common.

Less austere than the Athenaeum, and certainly less learned, was the Tavern Club. Founded in 1884, it was a dining and drinking club, whose membership was strictly by invitation and limited at any time to 125. The Tavern Club was used by its members for dining with guests and also featured a program of lectures and performances. Dinners in honor of notable guests prior to World War One included those held for Rudyard Kipling, Oliver Wendell Holmes, Booker T. Washington, and Winston Churchill. The 1893 list of members included Oneidas William Apthorp, William Bigelow, Henry Cabot Lodge, Arthur Rotch, and Frederick Shattuck.[20]

More upmarket than the Tavern Club, and with a much deeper history, were two intertwined clubs. The Somerset Club, originally the Beacon Club, functioned alongside the Union Club as one of the most elite, discrete, and private clubs in Boston. At least thirteen of the Oneidas were members.[21] Founded in 1863 as a result of divisions within the Somerset Club was the Union Club of Boston, one of America's oldest gentlemen's clubs. The breakaway, during the Civil War, established the new club in support of the abolitionist cause. Eighteen Oneida players were Union Club members.[22]

The St. Botolph Club was founded in the Back Bay on January 19, 1880. It followed a circulation asking for expressions of interest in a club that would contain an art gallery and stage monthly exhibitions. Its rules outlined the organizational focus on "the promotion of social intercourse among authors, artists and other gentlemen connected with or interested in literature and art." It was, like most of the clubs of the time, a men-only affair, and on opening, it had attracted 262 of the city's leading individuals as charter members. One of the prime movers in establishing the St. Botolph Club was Henry Cabot Lodge; eleven other Oneidas were members.[23] The club was forward-thinking in what it exhibited, and in its early years, "the club's gallery showed some of the most advanced art available in the United States and therefore played a significant role in the development of American art."[24]

The embrace of art through the St. Botolph Club mirrored the establishment, a few years earlier, of the great cultural institutions of Boston, including the Museum of Fine Arts (1876), the Public Library (1848), and the Boston Symphony (1881). In her study of twentieth-century American elites and the arts, Jennifer Lena argues that this cultural space is "the invention of a group of influential, rich Bostonians, called the Brahmins . . . between 1850 and 1900, bourgeois urban elites who built organizations that could define, isolate and sacralize."[25] The Oneida generation of wealthy Bostonians, the post–Civil War elite, held political power in the city until the 1880s when the occupationally organized Irish took control of city hall. The social elite, although still organized politically in the form of the Republican Party (Lodge, Parkman, and Wharton were highly influential locally and nationally), turned their attention instead to the control of culture and philanthropy. If the elite could no longer control politics at 45 School Street, then they would create and manage the city's social institutions.[26]

The Museum of Fine Arts was founded by the membership of the Athenaeum. Regarding the first board of trustees in 1876, Neil Harris observed that "at first glance it might have seemed merely a collection of wealthy Brahmins: Eliots, Perkinses and Bigelows took their places; almost all of the twenty-three elected trustees were descended from old Yankee families and were men of wealth. All but one were Proprietors of the Athenaeum, eleven were members of the Saturday Club, five served (or would serve) on the Harvard Board of Overseers, half were members of the Somerset or St. Botolph clubs and quite a number were blood relations. They had, for the most part, grown, studied and worked together."[27] Over the years the board, committee members, and donors included Oneidas such as William Lawrence, Arthur Rotch, and Roger Wolcott as well as a number of their wives who served on its various art committees. Another Oneida, William Bigelow, whose father had been one of the founders, was the leading western collector of Japanese art of the period and by the 1890s had amassed a collection of forty thousand pieces, which he donated to the museum.[28]

The various organizing and governing committees of the cultural bodies that many of the Oneidas sat on were "non-profit corporations, governed by a self-perpetuating board of trustees."[29] The model of the corporation as an organizing tool was one that had served elite Bostonian society well: they had used corporations to raise capital for the investments that had made them wealthy and in governing those charitable institutions that they supported philanthropically. These clubs and institutions were also those most focused on social networking: private spaces where men of power, wealth, and influence would meet. Generally, the membership of the Athenaeum, Union and Somerset Clubs included the political power brokers (both local and national) as well as those from the business world. Undoubtedly the issues of the day were addressed in such august surroundings, and problems that could be solved through a discreet conversation with someone in politics, an allied business, or the broader family network were worked through over an evening in the club. In addition to the broadly business-centered nature and social networks that existed in their leading clubs, Boston and the wider Massachusetts area were full of a larger network of special interest clubs.

Many of the former Oneidas continued their boyhood interest in sport and belonged to sporting clubs in later life. Important in Boston, from the point of view of social exclusivity, was a network of sport clubs based around single sports but that also offered a season of socializing and networking among people and families from similar backgrounds. These included private sporting clubs such as the Longwood Cricket Club—famous for its tennis courts and being where James D'Wolf Lovett was given honorary status in 1896 for his "long membership and also [his] great interest in cricket and sports"—and one of Boston's oldest yacht clubs, the Beverly, founded in the home of the Oneidas Edward and Walter Burgess in 1872.[30]

Baseball, certainly while they were still young enough to play during the years of college and immediately afterward, filled the leisure hours of many of the Oneidas. Gerrit Smith Miller and his brother were active in clubs around the Peterboro area where they lived and had been involved in the Lowell Club before they left Boston (winning the New England championships in 1864). The Lowell Club was one of the key early organizations for the game in Boston, captained in its early seasons by James D'Wolf Lovett. Miller, Robert Clifford Watson, and Edward Arnold were also regular Lowell players, and the latter served as vice president and was renowned in the city as an aggressive pitcher.[31] Beyond the club scene was the fledgling Harvard baseball club, where Oneidas Edward Bowditch, William Eustis, Francis Peabody, and Robert Watson all played. A triumvirate of teams—Lowell, Harvard, and the Tri-Mountain team—competed annually under the auspices of the New England Baseball Association for a silver ball, gifted by John A. Lowell, as a trophy.[32] The eventual memorialization around the Oneida Club would be carried out by seven men—namely, Arnold, Bowditch, Means Lawrence, Lovett, Miller, Peabody, and Scudder, all of whom (with the exception of Means Lawrence and Scudder) were closely tied up with mid-1860s baseball in Boston. The baseball bonds remained strong, as later correspondence reveals, with Lovett and Miller regularly addressing each other into the 1930s by the salutation "Dearest old teammate."[33]

The Oneidas were not only friends but also neighbors living in a part of Boston that had been designed to include many of the institutions and clubs to which they belonged. The Oneida network was one that was tightly knit and socially significant as well as being largely centered on a relatively small network of streets. It is striking how most Oneidas largely chose, and were able to afford, to live in two specific settings. By the time the Oneidas were married and beginning to start families, many of them chose to purchase plots or houses in the newly regenerated Back Bay. The density of Oneidas in a few streets speaks volumes about their shared position in the city's hierarchy of social class and their ability to purchase the city's new prime real estate. Of the nineteen Oneidas who settled in the Back Bay, on Commonwealth Avenue there was Beebe, Amory Appleton Lawrence, William Lawrence, Lodge, Minot, Parkman, Rotch, Tucker, Wharton, and Wolcott. Nearby on Marlborough Street were the houses of Brown, Gray, Iasigi, Jackson, and Shattuck. On Dartmouth Street could be found the houses of Means Lawrence and Thayer, while Dwight lived on Beacon Street. Across the River Charles in Cambridge resided Jones, who lived with his parents until his early death; Lovett, whose daughter also lived for a time with him; Peabody, who was on the Harvard faculty; and Scudder.

An important part of elite living in Boston into the early decades of the twentieth century was the possession of a country address.[34] Milton was particularly desirable.[35] The Brooks brothers both had property there, connected to the family's Wayside farm. Eustis built an impressive estate in 1878 on land that was gifted to him and his wife by both their families. Forbes built his own Forbes Farm nearby, and Wolcott inherited his family's Blue

Hill estate. Another signifier of social standing was a summer home, which offered an important retreat from the stuffiness of the city and access to more informal, outdoor living and busy weeks of summer entertaining. J. Bigelow and Brooks, for example, both owned summer houses in Cohasset to the south of Boston, with Dwight in Mattapoisett, Eustis on Cape Cod, Beebe in Falmouth, Thayer at Newport (Rhode Island), and Wolcott at West Chop on Cape Cod.

Existing as they did in this tightly knit social, political, and cultural world marked the Oneida group out as significant members of Boston's social elite. It was a world in which most of them were entirely comfortable and content to live. They understood networking and how to use and preserve power. What did mark the Oneidas out as different from the wider elite was that their small cohort had all belonged to a boyhood club and played football together on Boston Common. The networks that the Oneidas were part of, as they became elderly men, and their sense of their place within the city and how to exist at the heart of the cultural and historic fabric of Boston would be mobilized and leveraged as they later molded their boyhood pleasure into monumental form.

But in order to build a monument, one needs a purpose and a story to tell. As dusk settled on Gilded Age Boston, the Oneidas grayed. Many an Old Boston Boy passed away, and there was an inescapable scent of nostalgia in the air. What could be more natural than to look back fondly on one's own past and remember the good times and forget the bad? Fortunately for the Oneidas, they had one member who enjoyed writing. In the dark winter of 1904, James D'Wolf Lovett penned a few anecdotes about coasting down the snowy slopes of Boston Common in the 1850s. At least one of his friends, Samuel Cabot, thoroughly enjoyed the reminiscences and asked for more. So from the northeast corner of Boston Common, where the city had only recently erected the monument to Robert Gould Shaw and his Fifty-Fourth Regiment, Lovett had awoken the memory of Old Boston Boys. In the shadow of the Granary Burying Ground, the Beacon Hill Monument, and the Old South Meeting House began a slow and steady process of commemoration which snowballed from remembering a playful past into fabricating a usable one, ultimately placing the Oneidas at a moment of genesis in the nation's sporting history.

Prior to exploring the story of the memorialization of the Oneidas, it is worth assessing, in the context of social networks, who these particular men were who would craft the history of the team and make claims for its significance. The key Old Boys in remembering the Oneida Club were "Ned" Arnold, "Ned" Bowditch, "Bob" Means Lawrence, "Jim" Lovett, "Gat" Miller, "Frank" Peabody and "Win" Scudder. It was these seven Oneidas who would oversee the creation of the club memory and they who would present the list of who had been a club member. While all these men were well connected, they would not all be considered as part of the upper social strata of Boston society. Miller and Bowditch, although successful in their respective fields, lived away from Boston, out of state, and were not part of the city's mix of gentlemen's clubs and philanthropic endeavors. Robert Means Lawrence was a successful physician, resided in the Back Bay, and was a member of the Somerset, Union, and Longwood Clubs. Peabody was a theologian at Harvard, lived in Cambridge, and was a member of the Union Club. Art editor Scudder sat as a director on company boards, had a successful career in publishing, was a member of the Union Club, and lived in Brookline and later Cambridge. In contrast to their teammates, neither Arnold nor Lovett created substantial income during their working lives, both working in insurance brokerage and boarding or renting their lodgings. If not all the men who would commemorate the Oneida story held the same wealth, capital, and social status as their fellow club members, these seven were nevertheless linked through a childhood bond.

That special club connection kept them close, whether for shared business interests (Bowditch sending Miller his proxies), homely comfort (Bowditch arranging for Miller to order a stove at his company's wholesale rates or Miller sending Lovett "a splendid present of preserves" from his farm), or just friendly fishing expeditions (Lovett recalling Miller "whoofing up the stream" as they caught trout together).[36] The mundanity of enduring friendly and professional relations aside, the club roster also just happened to be a storied list of the richest and most powerful men in Gilded Age Boston. And these same names were essential to the city's sporting history—a history whose fading memory was only preserved in shared souvenirs like Lovett's July 1896 letter to Miller recalling "our [Lowell baseball] debut at Medford." By the turn of the century, funeral invitations were more frequent, such as the 1899 gathering for old headmaster Dixwell, serving as regular reminders of the reach of the Oneida network.[37] With one-third of the fifty-two Oneidas having followed their old headmaster across life's goal line by February 1904, advancing age was as good a time as any to wax nostalgic and awaken "Old Boston Boy" memory—the key to how and why the Oneidas came to be commemorated.

PART II
FROM MEMORY TO MONUMENT

6

DINNER GUESTS

Books, Memories, and the Origins of Sport

A few days after Thanksgiving 1904, seventeen men convened at 109 Commonwealth Avenue on a bitterly cold and wet Tuesday evening, a moment that marked the beginnings of the Oneidas' commemorative claims. Samuel Cabot, the well-known chemist, had opened his house in the Back Bay for a jovial gathering of old friends and contemporaries who had been prominent Boston oarsmen, cricketers, and baseball and football players as well as gymnasts and boxers.[1] Most guests were from Boston, either within the Back Bay or nearby Beacon Hill, but at least one, Gerrit Smith Miller, had traveled three hundred miles from his upstate New York home. The illustrious company included five Oneidas—Miller, Boit, Hall, Means Lawrence, and Lovett—and several other friends whose sporting commemorations would be recorded by pen but never immortalized in stone. Two notable Oneidas were absent: Win Scudder and Frank Peabody (though his brother Robert did attend). While the old acquaintances undoubtedly discussed current events and the day's newspaper headlines—the ongoing mysterious Bingham murder investigation, Secretary William Taft's visit to Panama to plan the future canal, or the factory worker strike in Fall River—they had gathered for a specific purpose. After reading Lovett's newspaper sketches reminiscing about the traditions and "lost arts" of childhood winter coasting published earlier that year, Cabot had suggested that Lovett write a broader collection of boyhood memories.[2] It was to this end that Cabot offered to host the dinner. The discussion ebbed and flowed from memories to anecdotes and was undoubtedly colored by the kind of hyperbole only permitted between friends. The "delightful dinner" was a success, and thanks to the "exuberant flow of reminiscent conversation," Lovett was gifted with mountains of material.[3]

Within a year and a half, Lovett had penned the two-hundred-plus-page book entitled *Old Boston Boys and the Games They Played*. The book begins with memories of school life across the city's public and private schools and goes on to span a variety of sports and leisure activities that the well-to-do Boston boys were involved in during the mid-nineteenth century. The first pages recount childhood games, hockey, coasting, skating, and swimming, among others. Then it covers rowing (also at Harvard), fire engines and cricket, football, gymnastics, and boxing. But the core of the book chronicles baseball, Lovett's true sporting love. Football only takes up nineteen pages of the entire book, of which only five actually describe the Oneida Football Club.[4] The Oneidas, then, are not foregrounded as having been significant in Boston's sporting history but are instead squeezed in between accounts of snowball fights, marbles, and jumping contests. Even the photo print of the famous ball won from the Latin and English School boys in November 1863 is just one image among thirty-two other sketches, photographs, and portraits of which none relate to football.

It would be foolish to interpret the book as a memoir solely to the football club and miss the wider context of sport and leisure that was a common thread of this account of innocence and youth. The monograph had a clearly stated purpose, and that was to recount boyhood memories and provide enjoyable reading that "may interest the old-timers" who were none other than a large circle of childhood companions. The tone of the book is that of personal memoirs, the kind that are shared with friends, relatives, and most likely grandchildren, the latter of which Lovett himself does not seem to have had.

As essentially an intimate yet collective memoir, the book was not initially written for the wider public. Lovett's nephew, illustrator Dana Gibson of "Gibson girl" fame and from whom Lovett had requested help with the visuals, wrote several times to his uncle while he worked on the manuscript in 1905 and 1906. Gibson and dinner host Cabot were "most enthusiastic" about the project and suggested a special edition at a good price that "would be subscribed to by the boys (now men) of those times."[5] Lovett, who worked as an insurance agent for the John Hancock Life Insurance company, liked to write and sporadically contributed to the *Evening Transcript*. He may have worked on the book in episodes in the vein of other serialized sports histories possibly attributed to him.[6]

By the spring of 1906, Lovett had written over two hundred pages and collected dozens of photographs, sketches, and portraits lent to him by the friends at the dinner or mentioned throughout the many stories. The most important image, from the perspective of the Oneidas, was the picture of the famous ball from the 1863 championship match. Obtaining a picture of the ball was difficult, however, since there was no photographer in Peterboro, New York, where the artifact rested in Gat Miller's possession. So Miller informed Cabot that he would have the ball sent to him in Boston so that he "could have just the kind of photograph [he desired]."[7] Though the intricate club crest and white gold lettering inscribed on the ball shone brightly for the impressed reader, the names of the championship team were not visible and only included in a caption.[8]

With the material in hand, Lovett did not have to look far for a publisher, since his monograph was printed by the Riverside Press in Cambridge, where incidentally another Oneida worked as art editor: Win Scudder, who also wrote an endorsement to promote the 1906 edition.[9] It seems that Scudder had a hand in the printing. When he informed Lovett of the delivery of his personal copy in early June and sent him the copyright receipts, his correspondence with the author was on headed paper from the press.[10] Cabot organized a first run of 250 books—the full subscription list is preserved in the Massachusetts Historical Society. At four dollars per volume—approximately 125 present-day dollars—the book may have been a "good price" for the Brahmin wallet, but it was certainly *not* cheap, nor was it for general sale to the public. So unsurprisingly, the private printing subscription booklet reads like a Who's Who of a well-off but waning Gilded Age Boston. Among the approximately two hundred names—some ordered multiple copies—are seventeen of the fifty-two Oneidas.[11] If copies were reserved for two of the elite schools—Groton and St. Mark's—other public institutions like the Boston Public Library, Brookline Public Library, and the YMCA also ordered one book each, making at least a handful of copies available beyond the immediate confines of the Brahmin world. Finally, two additional copies were sent swiftly to the Library of Congress, received and stamped even before Gat Miller received the first of his five copies numbered 3, 4, 5, 6, and 7 in early June.[12]

Lovett was evidently pleased with his work but also surprised at the positive reception from known, but nonetheless illustrious, company. Congratulatory and thank-you letters poured in from friends and Old Boys across New England; down to New York, Philadelphia, Washington, DC; and as far as Ohio and Michigan, including none other than President Theodore Roosevelt—albeit via his secretary—whose copy numbered 249 had been the second to last book listed among the subscription orders.[13] Even if the book was entitled *Old Boston Boys*, it appears that a number of *girls*, both young and old, liked it just as much. Lovett's niece and sister "thoroughly enjoyed" the book, and Sue Miller, Gat's wife, praised it as "beautifully written and smiles and tears chase each other through the pages as one reads."[14] Beyond the most intimate circle, Mary Clark Eliot—a daughter of the American Revolution and wife of Harvard president Eliot's nephew and attorney, Amory Eliot—found the book "all charming" and commended Lovett, "If a woman who never plays a game and doesn't care for sports finds your book absorbing, what must men with those tastes think of it?"[15] Replying a few days later, Lovett expressed his gratitude: "I received your kind words of praise for my book with profound surprise and pleasure. I had hoped that it might please some of the old boys by recalling to their minds some bygone scenes but I never dreamed that it would elicit from any of my 'girl' friends any sign of interest."[16]

Beyond friends and family, how was the book received? Because *Old Boston Boys* was a private affair directed at a small readership, it is unsurprising that the book was ignored by the wider press in 1906, save for a handful of local clippings preserved in Lovett's scrapbook and his papers. Reviewed at the end of June 1906, the book received regal treatment in the *Boston Sunday Herald*, which reserved a full two-page spread reprinting a number of images and portraits.[17] Four days later the *Evening Transcript*, which referred to Lovett's original piece on coasting and the subsequent 1904 dinner as the inspiration, recounted the hockey, snowball fights, and boating, with excerpts from the book.[18] The final piece of local press—no copy was kept by Lovett—came in the form of a short book review in the *Boston Daily Globe* toward the end of summer 1906.[19]

Albeit glowing, the sparse press coverage was local and not commercially focused—not listing a sale price, and only two of the articles actually gave the printer's name. Yet the most striking thing is conspicuous by its absence: any mention of the Oneidas. While football does get a brief mention in the newspaper reviews, the club is not presented as the first-ever club nor even highlighted by name. It is the schools that are the focus, and football is just one leisure pursuit among many. This is not altogether surprising, since the book recounted a plethora of sports and games and was never designed as a history of the Oneida Football Club. In fact, there was simply no reason, in the newspaper coverage in 1906, to place the Oneidas front and center. Yet rereading this in the light of later commemoration, the fact that the club, and its part in the origins of football, is entirely absent from the press is telling. The visibility of the Oneidas was limited to Boston high society and those who actually read *Old Boston Boys*, which was precisely the point, since the book's initial intent was to serve as a collective memoir for friends.

In writing such a book Lovett was in the perfect position to pen an ode to his own glory. However, a close reading hardly leaves the reader with the impression of a self-authored hagiography. To wit, his own friends actually accused him of excessive modesty in the "Four Words from His Contemporaries" printed at the back of the book. Miller wrote that "the charm of Jim's unselfish, modest nature pervades it from beginning to end," and the late Samuel Cabot noted that "because a long disuse [of the first person singular pronoun 'I'] had probably rendered him [Lovett] incapable of rightly spelling that important personal pronoun in all its cases and forms . . . in spite of his vehement opposition, that if there was not enough 'ego' in the narrative, we, his less important contemporaries, should exercise the reciprocal privilege of giving our recollections of him."[20] Even the secret garden of personal diaries revealed the true admiration others had for Lovett. Championship team member Robert Apthorp Boit dedicated well over a page of his diary to reflect on the book, of which he had ordered three copies. After a litany of "the best runner, the best jumper, the best foot ball player, the best baseball player," Boit journaled that Lovett was the "most kind hearted, gentle, modest of boys."[21]

Notwithstanding praise from his friends, Lovett only occasionally wrote himself into the story simply as one of a band of brothers, never elevating his own achievements. It is only when reading others that one begins to appreciate the sporting prowess behind the pen, or at least that which garnered the admiration of his friends and respect from his contemporaries so evident in the letters he received following the book's printing. From renowned painters like Edwin Howland Blashfield—who admitted that Lovett had been a boyhood hero for him, on par with Union generals Grant and Sherman—to senators like Henry Cabot Lodge, who wrote to dinner organizer Sam Cabot and described Lovett's skill, strength, and grace; the archive speaks the words of those who saw him play in the 1860s calling him the "ideal of an athlete . . . among all his contemporaries, amateur or professional. The grace and ease of his skill in all games was remarkable."[22]

Admiration from artists and politicians was undoubtedly pleasant but paled in comparison to the praise from one's direct, in this case sporting, peers. The great baseball player Henry Chadwick called him "an esteemed ball player" in his congratulatory note on receiving a copy.[23] A. G. Spalding later intimated to Lovett that he had "heard so much about your prowess at that time that I could not quite understand why the new Boston Club [the relocated Red Stockings] should want us western farmers to man its team."[24] Indeed, Spalding and the famous Wright brothers, Harry and George, pioneer professionals, had seen Lovett firsthand when they played against him in that inaugural game in 1871—Wright's new Boston Red Stockings club versus Lovett and a select Boston nine.[25] It was reported in the press, albeit many years after the fact, that the team's manager Harry Wright had actually offered Lovett $1,200 to pitch for the team in the early professional days of the 1870s.[26]

While Lovett had been a good athlete, he was more the consummate amateur than professional. In response to yet another congratulatory letter lauding the sporting "demigod," Lovett explained that he had been urged to join the newly founded Boston Red Stockings but "as a profession the game had no charm for me."[27] He left a lasting impression. Years later, in the months following Lovett's death, the still-living George Wright remembered him as "one of our grandest athletes, a gentleman, as well as a true sportsman."[28] Perhaps it was best put by Edmund Sears, a younger contemporary of Lovett, in a printed tribute on the occasion of his funeral, where he wrote that there was "no widely known and oft quoted figure in the baseball world [who] could be quite as appealing as was that masterful player and stainless gentleman, James D'Wolf Lovett."[29]

So there was no authorial aggrandizing in *Old Boston Boys*. At this point in 1906 the only moral risk was whether Lovett (and friends) were exhibiting an excess of collective hubris. At worst, Lovett might hazard a loving reprimand from close friends for letting the successfully paginated glory go his head. When some, like Sam Cabot, held Lovett up with such high esteem as a "true sport, as well as a true man," it certainly would not have been a surprise had he developed an overly inflated sense of importance. In reality, Lovett seemed too self-aware. In replying to Mary Eliot that summer acknowledging the temptation, he wrote, "that my own hat might bear a little stretching if I received many such kind notes as yours."[30] Given the largely local and friendly focus of the memoirs, one can hardly point fingers to judge Lovett and his friends for the nostalgic reveling of old age. For as they recorded their own boyhood recollections in book form, they did so primarily for themselves and as true gentlemen amateurs.

Yet as this band of sixty-year-olds aged and paused to remember their boyhood play, they were also witnessing a new millennium dawn on Boston, seeing New England—and their country—change before them. The Gilded Age that the Brahmin had built and lived through was coming to an end, and the landscape of the Hub, as once called by Oliver Wendell Holmes, was shifting. Beantown, as Boston is locally referred to, was being surpassed in population and financial and cultural importance with the rise of other cities like New York, Philadelphia, and Chicago, led by a generation of industrial nouveaux riches. Even among the social and business elite in Massachusetts, the range had widened such that the Oneidas were conspicuous in their— and their direct descendants'—absence in the 1908 edition of *Who's Who along the North Shore of Massachusetts Bay* and the *Men of Boston and New England* published in 1913.[31] This shift was coupled with the enormous demographic flood of immigrants to Ellis Island beginning in the 1880s, which spurred reactions of all kinds. Indeed, on the same day in June 1906 that the *Boston Evening Transcript* reviewed *Old Boston Boys*, news appeared about the passage of the Naturalization Act, beginning a series of reforms and restrictions on immigration.[32] The old Massachusetts families were not immune to the great wake of alien arrivals, described rather polemically by Henry James in his *The American Scene*, written during his travels through Boston and other American cities in 1904–1905. The Boston Brahmin followed James's gaze and saw that there was "no escape from the ubiquitous alien into the future, or even into the present; there was an escape but into the past."[33]

It was, as explained by James Lindgren, those same "unsettling changes in population, economy, and society [that] defined the era's cultural politics and set the context" for the 1905 campaign to preserve Paul Revere's home in the transformed and now fully Italianized North End.[34] That project set the framework for the creation of New England's foremost historic preservation agency, Boston's Society for the Preservation of New England Antiquities (SPNEA), just four years after the publication of Lovett's memoir. While feeling the forces change around them, these families were still powerful, controlling most spheres of influence in Boston life. In some sense, the origins of Massachusetts were still alive in these old families, which continued their legacies into the twentieth century. They were, after all, the inheritors of the tight-knit elite of eighteenth- and nineteenth-century Boston, who had led the revolt against the British, abolished slavery, and saved the Union but who now saw their place being rapidly transformed. Thus, the desire among Boston's elite to preserve and memorialize *their* heritage was strong. Buttressed by the production of enormous industrial and financial wealth, the Brahmin could leverage history and heritage to proclaim the significance of their part in creating modern Boston. However, the burden of urgency to protect Massachusetts's pioneering role in society had not yet included sport, whose national history had not yet been written.

Old Boston Boys was but an innocent and self-directed volume. Indeed, as Lovett penned the naive memoirs of a playful Boston Brahmin childhood, the search for sporting origins was still at its geniture. The Anglo-American generation that had grown up on both sides of the Atlantic through the industrialization and urbanization of the second half of the Victorian century was only just waking to the idea of the relevance of origin stories for their leisure activities. Only as these ball games morphed into city and national spectacles followed by large crowds across the Anglophone world did the debate on "firsts" and ownership truly begin. The quest for the genesis moment of a football—all codes, that is—and baseball was a commonly shared conundrum for the true amateurs of turn-of-the-century Anglobalized sport.

The discovery, reconstruction, and affirmation of origin stories for football and baseball followed different paths. If the result was a legendary innovator for rugby football and native inventor for baseball, the association game was given a less romantic but democratic story of institutional standardization and compromise, while American gridiron football was a scientific evolutionary tale of English ancestry. But in each case, the apostles of turn-of-the-century sport debated, researched, and in some cases ultimately fudged their sporting creationist myths in the same twenty-two-year period between 1885 and 1907. Most significantly for the Oneidas, as these origin stories were crafted, Boston's place was marginal at best. This was the bas-relief to Lovett's *Old Boston Boys*.

For football, the impetus for an origins debate came from a book by Montague Shearman and James Vincent published in 1885, the year that the association game in England accepted professionalism while rugby continued to faithfully abide by the doctrine of amateurism. *Foot-Ball—Its History for Five Centuries* outlined the most detailed history of the game to date, more extensive than several previous accounts. The lead author was a public school boy himself, not from Rugby but from one of the London institutions, Old Merchant Taylors. Shearman set out to recount the "ancient and honorable history" of football leading up to the two dominant codes in 1885.[35] The authors passed from ancient games to Puritan England mob village football before offering a detailed account of the principal school games. Even if the book highlighted Rugby School's rules first before discussing Winchester, Eton, Harrow, and Charterhouse, there was no romance for Rugby as modern football's inspirational birthland. In lieu of any meritorious historical agency, the authors' view was rather pragmatic, environmental, and bluntly spatial, as they simply argued that "the size of the Close at Rugby rendered it possible for the boys to play the original game without fear of being hurled when collared against stone walls, or iron railings, or upon surfaces of gravel."[36] The text was actually rather critical of the game of rugby for its roughness in collaring (tackling), hacking, and tripping, even linking it to the banned form of mob football of the sixteenth century, and even dared note that other schools allowed running with the ball.[37] So if Shearman and Vincent had the merit of setting apart the game of rugby from other schools, they did not do so on the account of a legendary boy named Webb Ellis who, by some deliberate act, altered the rules in an ingenious manner. Little did the authors know, but they were about to test Newton's third law as they set in motion a football origins debate in which the inertia of Rugby's school pride was not to be underestimated.

It took nearly a dozen years, but Shearman and Vincent's account awoke the spirit of Old Rugbeians, who took it upon themselves to address the "misleading, if not altogether erroneous," statements about their beloved school game that the two authors had brazenly qualified as "primitive."[38] A committee of Old Rugbeians was duly composed to conduct their own inquiry. Despite any conclusive evidence to corroborate the testimony of an old schoolboy, Matthew Bloxam, from the late 1870s (based on nothing more than unconfirmed hearsay), the committee proclaimed that "at some date between 1820 and 1830 the innovation was introduced of running with the ball" and "that this was in all probability done in the latter half of 1823 by Mr. W. Webb Ellis."[39]

If we accept that Webb Ellis did something aberrant to transform the nature of the game, the full effect of those changes was not codified for a further two decades. However, despite the committee's nuanced conclusions, the Old Rugbeian Society decided to put his actions of 1823 back at the center of the story and commemorate Webb Ellis's transformative role. Thus, in 1897, rugby football had a founder and a creation story.[40] But the Old Rugbeians were not satisfied until three years later, when they placed a commemorative plaque at Rugby School in January 1900, duly engraving Ellis into sporting history.[41] The plaque had been commissioned by the society for eighteen pounds and finally erected—at no cost—on the close, where the events of 1823 supposedly took place.[42] The plaque reads, "This stone commemorates the exploit of William Webb Ellis who with a fine disregard for the rules of football as played in his time first took the ball in his arms and ran with it thus originating the distinctive feature of the rugby game AD 1823." Committee investigations and reports cannot be reproduced on a memorial plaque and certainly should not stand in the way of a good story. As noted by rugby historian Jenifer Macrory, the plaque's wording was a mistake clouding the "careful and unsensational" conclusions of the committee; the result was that the school set out to "celebrate the game, but instead created a myth" of an antihero and "rebel in a good cause."[43]

Much like the motivation of Lovett in writing his book, the Rugby plaque seems to have been a rather private affair with no intent to seek public recognition. Neither does it appear to have been reported widely. Even Rugby School's newspaper, the *Meteor*, only included an announcement toward the end of the year.[44] Only then, nearly a year after the tablet's unveiling was the news reported, picked up in Manchester before making its way internationally.[45] By Christmas 1900 and into early January 1901, the news had reached across the American continent; it appeared in Kansas City, Chicago, New York, Fort Worth, Los Angeles, and as far as Hawaii. Strangely, it seems the news went unreported in Boston despite making the papers in the western part of Massachusetts.[46]

By the time the Oneidas gathered for dinner in 1904, the origins of the carrying half of football in the British Isles had been questioned, researched, and proved to be held in the history of Rugby School, even if the resonance of this story had yet to be more than a passing paragraph in the newspapers' miscellaneous columns. On US shores the sporting historiography up to 1904 had not been silent over this period, but football's history from an American perspective was simpler, easier to trace, and had no need for a boyish sporting genitor.

For one, the omnipresent American collegiate game was acknowledged as a direct offshoot from rugby, a fact so well known that it needed no further investigation. Moreover, the adapted Rugby School rules used by Harvard and McGill in 1874 and adopted by the colleges in 1876 were only a starting point. Since both the American universities and the English Rugby Football Union continued to significantly alter the rules after the mid-1870s, the question of who founded the game of rugby was inconsequential in the US. Secondly, there was only one football code that commanded the attention of the masses during the autumn, with baseball commanding the spring and summer.

Over the last quarter of the nineteenth century, association football had been essentially absent from the sprouting university athletic stadia. While present in the recreational activities of immigrant and industrial communities, as well as the military, the round game was not worthy of the official histories of the Ivy League–educated social elite.[47] Finally, and unsurprisingly, as this period was before the "discovery" of Webb Ellis, his character is absent from the American historiographic record up to 1900.

In effect, when Lovett sat down to write in 1904–5, there was never any doubt that the collegiate game so popular by then was a direct descendant of rugby even if Webb Ellis had not yet appeared in any of the US-printed texts. The American view was simply that the Ivy League, and subsequently the American universities at large, had perfected the game, giving them the self-satisfaction of their own superior scientific ingenuity. Following the Civil War appeared several general books promoting sports and their rules, although the first books that discussed football and its history—at least in some detail—did not appear in American print until the 1890s, nearly a decade after their British counterparts.[48]

Books took two forms in the postwar years: university records of the memories, statistics, and past glories of athletic competition or practical treatises on how to play the game. Building on the early Beadle rule books published in the 1860s, the sporting goods company Peck and Snyder solicited Charles W. Alcock of the FA in London to edit the first detailed description (published in 1871) of the different football games targeting an American audience but without any substantial historical background.[49] In 1875 Harvard produced a two-volume one-thousand-page school history, which was the first time a US university included athletics in such a book. While boating and baseball filled more than seventy pages each, football was only mentioned in one paragraph by Thomas Wentworth Higginson, the same man who had Oneida links going back to his abolitionist days.[50] Class of 1841, Higginson described football a generation removed from the Oneidas as "a much simpler game, as we played it, than that described in 'School Days at Rugby,' and much simpler than now played as the 'Harvard Game.'"[51] Princeton followed four years later with a short account of football contained in a series of sketches on the history of the school. The description traced an old form of the game back to a first club in 1857—though football did not become a staple of the collegiate experience until 1869. Witnessing a clear transition during his recently completed eight years on campus (1869–77), Henry Van Dyke regretted how rugby "has begun to usurp the place of our time-honored, old-fashioned football."[52] The publication of the Princeton book coincided with the ten-year anniversary of its initial intercollegiate match, which had included Van Dyke. That *nothing* was made of this important *first* illustrates how little commemoration was important in this early period.

In 1884, baseball man Henry Chadwick produced a lengthy book of pastimes for boys that gave an overview of the three known variants—English rugby, English association, and the American collegiate game (a modification of the first). He noted how the idea of the American college version was "to eliminate from the game some of the objectionable features of the Rugby rules" and that the official regulations were available from a certain Walter Camp at Yale University.[53] The New Haven, Connecticut, school soon had a 160-page volume written by alumnus Richard Hurd in which he proudly proclaimed the college's status as the first to have a rowing club and the first to have a published sporting history. Noting a long football tradition until the dark ages of 1858–70 when the game was banned across universities, Hurd credited the revival and subsequent shift to Rugby's rules to one student, David Schaff (class of 1873), conveniently omitting any mention of Harvard and Boston.[54]

Schaff, whose story evolved erroneously, was one of Yale's early revivers but soon faded in importance.[55] Instead, that rules man from New Haven was fast becoming a reference for all things football. Walter Camp had penned a few articles about the game in various periodicals and produced the official rule book for the Intercollegiate Football Association from 1882. But his contribution to the development of college football was such that, as Roger Tamte has argued, history mixes "his life story into the game's story so deeply that neither can be told apart from the other."[56] It was thanks to his extensive writing career that Michael Oriard qualifies Camp as having "done the most" to shape the sport and create his later reputation as the father of football.[57] Moreover, Camp's prolific writing influenced the historical narrative. Camp's 1889 book on university sports—reprinted twice in the next four years—left no doubt as to the origins of the collegiate game. He carefully credited Harvard for introducing rules that were "an outgrowth or development of the English Rugby game" to American schools.[58] In 1891 appeared an extensive book in which he claimed the first American game under Rugby rules was the 1876 clash and granted equal space to Princeton, Yale, and Harvard. The text was one of the rare US-printed histories in this period to actually mention the association kicking game on American shores.[59]

The year 1893 was prolific for more university-driven histories and promotional books.[60] They were either silent on football history or continued to anchor the college game in its English rugby roots from the origin points of the 1869 Rutgers-Princeton and 1876 Yale-Harvard games, omitting any connection to a kicking game other than as old, abandoned traditions. Some like Chadwick were quite critical of the college sporting phenomenon. In part, this was in reaction to the ongoing debate about gridiron violence, peaking again that autumn. In the wake of the 1893 football violence scandal, Camp published an impressive statistical apology to American college football and again affirmed the rugby link dating from 1876.[61] Camp continued two years later, with Deland, and for the first time included an extended history section. Rugby was given the prominent origin position in contrast to the unnamed dribbling game, though Camp claims that "neither was free from objectionable features."[62] In describing early football in the US, Camp spoke only of local traditional Thanksgiving kickabouts (including in New England), Yale's early football from 1840, and the 1870 revival thanks to David Schaff, said to be "formerly of Rugby."[63] Significantly, the new history went as far as *removing* any mention of the primacy of Harvard, which until then had been part of his foundational narrative. Camp's beloved Yale could thus lay claim to the first introduction of rugby rules in America, predating the Harvard-McGill games. It is worth noting that, similar to Princeton's 1879 athletic history, Camp's book was also published in Boston—and by Scudder's Cambridge-based Riverside Press no less.

In the years around the turn of the century, three new university athletic histories appeared.[64] Some advanced an earlier unrecorded tradition of football closer to the association game until the all-important introduction of rugby in 1876 or conveniently traced the start back to their university's "first" match, 1872 for Yale or 1869 for Princeton. With each passing year and new book, the early American sporting historical record became clearer and more extensive. Harvard, which had been the first institution to publish its athletic legacy, had not yet issued an updated version covering the incredible developments to intercollegiate sport between 1875 and the turn of the century. This left the school in the peculiar position of having been the first to write about itself but before football had truly taken off. Some, like the prolific Camp, praised Harvard for bringing rugby rules to the colleges, though he did not fail to mention that "Yale adopted them and they then became common to all the American colleges."[65]

Thus, by the time of the Old Boston Boys' 1904 dinner, the American historiography had established three key points. First, until its disappearance in the 1860s early football at the universities was more of the kicking style. Second, English rugby was the undisputed source for the American colleges, which adapted and perfected it (in their view) from the 1870s onward. Finally, Boston's place was as a marginal intermediary at best, with Yale and Princeton actively claiming their place in the list of firsts. Neither does Boston football emerge as truly important in Lovett's book. Rather, it was just another game that captivated the Old Boys' memories. Given the number of pages that Lovett wrote about the national pastime, baseball must have occupied at least a significant part of the dinner discussion as the boys recalled these games and possibly their origin. If the contours of the origins of football both in the UK and in America had been well defined by 1904, there was, however, a *live* and ongoing debate on baseball's origins. The other half of the sporting origins background so essential to understanding Lovett's book in its contemporary context is baseball's identity crisis. Similar to the rugby-Webb Ellis investigation, the baseball origins debate illustrates how central the question of pride was.

Around the same time that rugby entered its soul-searching phase, baseball's A. G. Spalding had led an ambitious international tour to promote baseball and American values in 1888–89.[66] At the close of the tour's celebratory dinner at the premier Delmonico's restaurant in Manhattan, National League Commissioner A. G. Mills had launched into a speech about the "strictly American origins" of baseball that had been determined through "patriotism and research."[67] This augmented an ongoing debate among enthusiasts about whether baseball was indeed a national creation or had evolved from the old British import of rounders. The debate climaxed precisely in the two years around the Old Boston Boys' dinner (between 1903 and 1905) and was argued in a series of articles written on both sides.[68] Spalding defended the nationalist claim and Chadwick that of an evolutionary link to a prior English game. The debate was so much in the public consciousness that Lovett explicitly referred to it in *Old Boston Boys*, although he did not express an opinion one way or the other. Rather than enter into the debate—maybe because he had liked cricket so much that an English origin would not have bothered him—Lovett focused on baseball's beneficial qualities: "Whatever the origin of our National game may have been, it is to-day a good, healthy recreation, calling for recruits who must be sound mentally and physically, and therefore a game making for the good of our young men."[69]

But the issue was a burning one. Even the newspaper review of *Old Boston Boys* in the summer of 1906 also made direct reference to it.[70] There was a need to clarify things once and for all. So both sides to the argument agreed to the formation of a national commission to determine the facts and arbitrate the matter. Finally published at the end of 1907, the Mills Commission report came to a similar conclusion to that of rugby, ignoring evidence, crafting their story to enshrine one character, Abner Doubleday, as the founding father of the national American game.[71] Interestingly, a story of English origins for football had posed no problem to the northeastern colleges between the 1870s and '90s. Perhaps the residual tendency of those American high-brows whose exercise of what historian Sam Haynes called a filiopietism "characteristic of the conflicted loyalties of many well-to-do New Englanders" until the middle of the nineteenth century was finally balanced by growing pride in autochthonous tradition.[72] Whatever the explanation, in contrast to British rugby's myth-making and baseball's nationalist struggle, football in 1904 America had not yet faced its Webb Ellis or Delmonico moment. Instead it was facing serious challenges to its legitimacy as a suitable sport for young American gentlemen.

For more than twenty years the collegiate game had been under fire for being too violent and dangerous. Despite universities routinely banning the sport and withdrawing from intercollegiate competition due to injuries and even deaths, support for the game was broad among students and alumni whose interest fueled a revenue-generating spectacle. Hoping to assuage the fears of school administrators, the sport's regulatory committee, under the guidance of Walter Camp, progressively tweaked the rules to remove certain kinds of blocking, tackling, and mass momentum plays like the "flying wedge." If the problem of violence was not enough, the debate of the evils of professionalism had grown from the early 1890s. The situation climaxed in 1905 with no less than President Theodore Roosevelt getting involved to reform the sport.[73] In his diary, one Oneida who had just attended the 1905 Harvard-Yale contest reflected on the "great row breaking out about the game." Robert Apthorp Boit's view was reflective of many of his generation for whom the solution was to "discard all this professionalism, allow no trainer, allow no coach who is not a bona fide undergraduate. . . . This would do away with most of the existing evils."[74] Football, in the words of Brian Ingrassia, had become a "commercial activity that could corrupt universities while destroying young men's bodies, minds and morals," and the game was only beginning its Progressive Era reforms.[75] But with collegiate football in the midst of a national crisis of public opinion, it was hardly the best time to go about boasting to be its founder.

So when Boit and his friends met for that 1904 dinner, they inhabited an awkward place in the sporting timeline, and unsurprisingly, they showed no consciousness of it. While they may have discussed Harvard alum Hollowell's long list of proposed reforms for football printed in that evening's *Transcript*, the old friends did not convene to claim ownership of the modern game or that it was somehow their collective progeny.[76] Indeed, establishing official origin narratives for football and baseball was hardly the object of *Old Boston Boys*, a book designed to be a private memoir of a forgotten youth.

That said, after the 1906 printing, the book did not remain only on a handful of Back Bay Brahmin bookshelves. Lovett had received early advice from Cabot and his nephew Dana Gibson when they had opted for the initial subscription model that could "ensure a financial success, then a popular edition could be printed."[77] As the monograph was indeed a success, it was reprinted twice in two years; once in 1907 with the same Riverside Press and then a third time in 1908 by a new publisher, Little, Brown and Co., which featured in the *New York Times* book reviews no less.[78] In contrast to the two first printings, this new popular edition was widely promoted and received significant press coverage across New England, from New York to California and through the Midwest, the clippings kept preciously by Lovett in his scrapbook. With a more affordable $1.50 price tag, the 1908 edition was now available to a wider readership and no longer just reserved for intimate Boston high society, such that A. G. Spalding underlined how Lovett "gave the country such an excellent contribution in [his] 'Old Boston Boys'" and earned him the right to review Spalding's own baseball history book in 1911.[79] This inserted Lovett's book into the sporting canon—the one that recently affirmed baseball's nativist origins—at a time when football was still being rescued from the clutches of its 1905 crisis.

With the book's third edition, Lovett had his moment of fame, all while the sun began to set on his old teammates. While his memoir began to spread knowledge of the Oneidas in the subsequent fifteen years, twelve more clubmates passed away—in addition to dear friend and dinner instigator Cabot, who died of pneumonia only a few months after the book was initially released in 1906.[80] As their memory slowly disappeared into the penumbra of early football's past, Lovett's book and Miller's old Oneida ball gathered dust as artifacts of old Brahmin memory. The book was slowly supplanted by a growing football historiography and the ball disappeared from view, kept safely by Captain Gat in upstate New York. Indeed, a continuous supply of football books flooded the bookshops both in the US and abroad. With them came the first shaping of the American football origin stories for the pre-1870s college era, which would omit the Old Boston Boys in favor of an English boy from Rugby School.

If the football histories printed up to the 1904 dinner had affirmed a standard narrative of evolution from the English rugby rules, in the subsequent fifteen years, the newly minted Ellis myth finally traversed the Atlantic and began to appear in the American sporting historiography. It appears that Walter Camp, in his 1910 book, is the first to have made the link between football in America and Rugby's rebel, Webb Ellis. Camp included a photo of the plaque on the Rugby campus but also described earlier forms of football from classical Greece to imperial Rome before tracing the game through Edwardian and Elizabethan England up to the founding of British public schools.[81] He then continued with his standard narrative from his 1890s books which ignored any schoolboy or organized football in America before the 1870s, save for the old Yale tradition of games on the College Green going back to the late 1850s.[82]

However preponderant Camp's voice had become by this time, it was not the only one. Within less than a year, Princeton veteran Parke H. Davis published his five-hundred-page football history. He went even further than Camp, adding an origins link, albeit by allusion, to the prophet Isaiah of "some form of a game" in biblical times, before weaving his way through the now standard story of Athens, Rome, and England.[83] In a change from Camp, however, Davis chose to begin the American timeline of football earlier than any prior account, going back to 1609 colonial Virginia. His account also offered a new synthesis of the history of the game in America and an ode to the central role played by Tom Brown in *Schooldays at Rugby* and the Webb Ellis story. Davis ingeniously traced New Jersey football back to before the American Revolution—that sacred date of national beginnings. He recounted in detail the first intercollegiate game of football from 1869 which generated a "pleasant aftermath" and underlined the spherical ball used in the 1874 Harvard-McGill game, thereby delegitimizing the singularity of that later event.[84]

As a result, Davis's account—like Camp's, silent on Boston schoolboy football—was the first to reach beyond Cambridge and New Haven as the hallowed birthplaces of football in America. Davis proffered a localized American school-rules background before the 1876 adoption of the Webb Ellis–inspired Rugby School rules. Importantly, the reader is left with a strong impression of continuity before 1876 and that the origin point is more complex than Camp and Deland's Harvard-Yale foci, written lest we forget by a Yale player, coach, and rules administrator (Camp) and Harvard's one-time coach (Deland).[85] Perhaps unable to help himself, Davis placed at his alma mater a tradition of "a definitely organized game of football twenty-five years in advance of any other college." Overall, for Princeton alum Davis, American football's history belonged not to Boston or New Haven but to all of the colleges who birthed the modern game in 1876. That year, as Davis reminded his readership, was "memorable as the centennial of American independence, [and] also marks for the collegian the formal establishment of the present game of intercollegiate football."[86] An American game on the centenary of independence? It was almost predestined and surprising that not more writers seemed to seize such beautiful symbolism.

In the years just prior to the outbreak of World War I, a cornucopia of books appeared—including another two by Camp—in multiple languages as the football phenomenon spread across Europe and the printing center in the United States seemed to shift from Boston to New York.[87] Even non-English books recycled the same rudimentary story of Thanksgiving day games, savage mob football with the round black rubber ball eventually banned by the universities, and finally the saving grace of Harvard and Yale, which civilized the sport in the early to mid-1870s.[88] Camp and Davis had published hundreds of pages of history between them, so what more was there to add to the duo? For one, if the university story had been told, what of football in the high schools? After all, it was widely recognized that all forms of modern football grew with English public school boys before they became university men. Was there no place for American high schools in the history of the American game?

High schools were barely even an afterthought. Even the rare mentions suggest that schoolboy play was a development contemporary to the college phenomenon of the 1870s.[89] But what of Boston's apparently vibrant 1860s school football scene, if we are to believe Lovett and his friends? The Latin School, where several Oneidas were educated, including Lovett and Means Lawrence, had published a massive history and register of all former students in 1886. Football and baseball were mentioned, but only in one footnote about the 1810s referring to a "large space which we boys made use of for foot ball and base ball"—not Boston Common, which was still a cattle grazing area and not yet the manicured city park of the 1860s.[90] Another antebellum school, the South Boston Hawes School, had published an early memoir to the school in which Horace Smith recalled the "kicks and bruises that we received in the strife to get the ball at home," again without mention of the Common.[91] A rare mention of schoolboy football on Boston Common was recorded by Curtis Guild, who recalled many games there in the late 1830s and 1840s.[92]

Yet none of these testimonies resonated beyond their local setting, and as such, it is unsurprising that schoolboy games did not feature in the university-driven historiography. Even the wide promotion of the 1908 edition of *Old Boston Boys* only mentioned the Oneidas by name once in the dozens of book reviews; they preferred to focus on baseball, coasting, rowing, and the many other sports described.[93] Thus, by the end of the 1910s, the Oneida matches on Boston Common and schoolboy games virtually anywhere else were essentially forgotten. So in the years following the publication of *Old Boston Boys*, twilight stretched the boys' fading shadow. Only Lovett's book and the ball kept by Miller remained as discrete witnesses of this Oneida first football nation. Lovett and his fellow Oneidas did not realize it at their dinner in 1904, but all this background—the creation of football and baseball origin myths, a developing historiography, and their book and ball artifacts—was part of a nascent historical problem. With the book printed in 1906, Lovett and his friends simply reveled in their boyhood memories. Commemoration in *Old Boston Boys* was not, a la Webb Ellis, about honoring some creationist myth of American football originating in Boston.

These Old Boys had gathered in 1904 only to remember and, most importantly, not to forget. At that moment, the wistful echo of the coasting and ball-playing Oneidas was still audible as the old men wandered down the Back Bay, through the streets of Beacon Hill, and across Boston Common. Lovett had already hinted at this in his original newspaper article which had spawned the book's commemorative impetus. Having lived through the Civil War, the tidal waves of industrialization, urbanization and immigration during the second half of the nineteenth century, those still living were the only ones alive to remember. In his original article from February 1904, Lovett had nostalgically described the gathering of buoyant Beacon Hill boys coasting until eleven o'clock in the evening. The reader could sense Lovett's melancholy, as their innocence was swept away with the onset of the Civil War: "Most of the laughing, careless crowd enlisted at the first note of the country's call and their boyhood came to a sudden end as the drum and fife stirred all hearts to sterner things. Some came back, but many, alas, stayed behind with the great silent army, and it is for us who are left to keep their memories green until we, too, are enlisted in the same ranks."[94]

So we ought to respectfully leave the Old Boston Boys in their nostalgic, youthful innocence. In the dusk of old Boston play, it took a rising tide of anniversaries and historical preservation to wake the Oneidas for one final game. Indeed, had it not been for a series of important commemorative events at the turn of the 1920s, the club may have faded entirely from the football story. Their memory might have been constrained to the occasional readers of Lovett's book who perused the few pages dedicated to football or only shared privately in correspondence between old friends as Lovett's papers bear witness to.[95] And those Old Boston Boys would never have been remembered and granted the legendary status of a Webb Ellis or Doubleday. But there were yet a few brave Oneidas who rose to stake their claim, almost a dying one, in a stirring series of acts of historical self-remembrance of the paternity of football in America. Their goal line still uncrossed, they set out to score once more.

7

THE BOY IN BRONZE

Schools, Anniversaries, and the Birth of a Myth

This is a very welcome gift and a great help to our small collection representing early athletics.

—William Sumner Appleton Jr., 1922

In November 1922, William Sumner Appleton Jr. was quite pleased with a rather unique gift to Boston's Society for the Preservation of New England Antiquities (SPNEA). Among the nearly thirteen thousand items donated to the growing collection in the twelve months between March 1922 and March 1923 was a "fine old rubber foot ball of the Oneida Foot Ball Club of Boston" for which the secretary of the SPNEA thanked the donors in writing.[1] In a solemn pose for posterity, six of the remaining Oneidas—Lovett, Bowditch, Scudder, Means Lawrence, Peabody, and Arnold—were photographed as they deposited their old ball at the SPNEA's premises at Otis House on November 15, 1922 (see image 3).[2] To their missing captain and owner of that ball, Gat Miller, the six teammates wrote that they met together "for the purpose of choosing a suitable place in which this ball may have a permanent home in its old age."[3]

The Oneidas had heeded Appleton's broad call to preserve New England's historic past by conserving "smaller antiquities in a museum, sectional and national in character."[4] In its first few years, the Society's drive for such a collection was "slow but steady, and in general the objects [had] not been of startling interest or value."[5] However, over time, gifts began to pour in, and with a growing collection that "would fill our present quarters several times over," the SPNEA acquired Harrison Otis Gray House in 1916, where Appleton

IMAGE 3. On November 15, 1922, six of the seven surviving Oneida players gathered to present the Oneida football to the Society for the Preservation of New England Antiquities. Courtesy of Historic New England.

arranged for a modest museum, still in use today by the society's successor Historic New England.[6] A number of Old Boys and Oneidas had supported the growth of the SPNEA, several holding life memberships, others with yearly subscriptions or making donations.[7] When the six Oneidas bequeathed their football in 1922, they were following a well-established practice that had seen teammate Stephen Van Rensselar Thayer's wife donate traditional wallpaper and Russell Gray gift two books.[8]

The donations list is full of often what appear to be mundane artifacts, but this was nothing other than the manifestation of the SPNEA's clearly stated purpose of "preserving for future generations the rapidly disappearing architectural monuments of New England and the antiquities connected with its people."[9] Indeed, when announcing a new collection of photographs and images, Appleton was clear: "Gifts are earnestly solicited. Do not discard those you think uninteresting, but send all you have to spare and let our librarian do his own discarding."[10] In a way, the rapidly disappearing artifacts were a proxy for the people who had owned them and a culture that was fading. As James Lindgren has explained, the SPNEA was an outgrowth of the nineteenth-century historical and antiquarian preservation movements. At its heart was a complicated question: "Whose culture would prevail as the nation went through the throes of immigration, industrialization, and modernization?"[11] At this point there were competing ideas about how to understand traditional Puritan New England and the place in history of these same old Massachusetts families so dedicated to the preservation of the past. Abram Van Engen has argued that the first of those visions was the grand idea that American liberty could be traced back to the Pilgrim landing at Plymouth Rock.[12] Central to this, and to understanding the significance of the Oneidas' commemorative actions, was an important anniversary. This anniversary became a focal point in consolidating a myth of origins so important to the American historical narrative.

A significant birthday does not come around often, and such tributes offer the possibility to reinvent oneself or give new meaning to old events. At the turn of the 1920s, the Boston papers were awash with news of grand celebratory plans to fete the tercentenary of the Mayflower landing in 1620. The planning in Boston had begun years before and was largely led by local artist Walter Gilman Page and regularly reported in the SPNEA *Bulletin*. The events were an enormous celebration of American history and, of course, Massachusetts's central place in the national story, with a colossal budget of nearly two million dollars.[13] Page, who had been a founding member of the board of trustees of the SPNEA and worked closely with Sumner Appleton Jr., led the planning commission, which decided for obvious reasons to host the outdoor festivities at another time than the historic December landing date. An enormous pageant was scripted and prepared for the summer of 1921, including over a thousand residents and children. In addition to the spectacle, special issue postal stamps and minted coins, significant landscaping, and monument-building endeavors were undertaken at Plymouth, and they even included events in Holland and Plymouth, England, hosted by the newly elected first woman member of Parliament, American-born Lady Nancy Astor, well known to the Oneidas and all Boston socialites.[14]

The event placed old Massachusetts at the center of national attention and elevated the Pilgrims' status as an origin point for America. The pageant drew tens of thousands over the two weeks in the summer of 1921 and was capped by a grand oration from Oneida member Henry Cabot Lodge, ending with a stunt that wooed the unknowing audience. In order to reinforce the prophetic power of the Puritan spirit that would be transmitted down to millions of sons of the Pilgrims all the way to the Pacific seas—as famously proclaimed by Daniel Webster at the 1820 Plymouth bicentenary event—the senator's speech was interrupted by a seemingly spontaneous telephone call from the governor of California.[15] Engaging in a spectacle that reinforced a myth of national origins, even if it was staged, was not beyond even the great statesman, for it was an Anglo-Saxon storytelling pursuit celebrating the republic's origins in the Old Bay State. The power of a vision—that old stock was the wellspring of the foundation of American ideals—was something so essential that it was well worth playful poetic license and built on two centuries of New Englanders retaining "the folkways of its Puritan descendants" more than any other region.[16] In the promotion of the Pilgrim story in the decades following mass immigration, it was no less the founding of a nation's spirit and its meaning that was at stake. Lodge's own views illustrated how Gordian the knot tying together identity and immigration was. A staunch advocate for certain types of limitations and a supporter of the Immigration Restriction League, Lodge also believed optimistically in "the spirit of progress" as essential to the American Republic, insisting on character above all and praising the contribution of assimilated newcomers. Through the pageant, the growing national myth around Plymouth as an important "foundational moment" was stressed by orators like Lodge who hailed the Pilgrim colony as a cornerstone "of the foundations upon which the great fabric of the United States has been built up."[17]

Origins and their meaning have great sway over a society, since they shape common belief and direction. The temptation to mold such original meanings is hardly limited to a nation's ideals or a people's identity. Indeed, many spheres of culture can be subject to such interest. While anniversaries sprout all the time, specific foundational dates—like the Plymouth celebrations—are rare and therefore all the more important to seize before they pass into the morass of mundane memory. By the time the Oneidas donated their old football, a significant sporting anniversary in 1919 had just passed uncelebrated, leaving the past still virgin territory for those who might wish to stake a claim. As the Western world emerged from the Great War, Princeton had apparently sent an invitation to Harvard's Athletic Committee to join in a "Football Pageant" around the fiftieth anniversary of the 1869 Rutgers-Princeton first intercollegiate game, yet no such event ever took place.[18] Only remembered

The Boy in Bronze

in passing comments in Harvard's *Crimson* and Princeton's *Nassau Literary Magazine*, the memory is nonetheless perpetuated in the still ongoing fight over the Revolutionary War cannons.[19] That same year, baseball also missed the opportunity to celebrate the eightieth anniversary of Doubleday's invention of the national pastime, which was not picked up again in earnest until its centenary in 1939.[20]

Circumstances alone do not produce memorialization, and just because there is an anniversary to celebrate does not mean that someone will celebrate it. Consequential commemoration is the fruit of conscious initiative, which requires intent and organization. To wit, the history of the Harvard-Yale rowing rivalry was actually celebrated on the occasion of its sixtieth anniversary in 1912 with a book printed by Harper and Brothers.[21] In the case of the Oneidas, the year 1923 offered them a similar opportunity, and unlike Princeton, Rutgers, or baseball, they seized the moment. This was different from Lovett's *Old Boston Boys*, which had not commemorated a specific event or organization. It had been essentially an effort to record the collective memory of an undefined group of Old Boys, which according to all logic ought to have stayed on a dusty bookshelf once its moment passed. Indeed, if the Oneidas were just boys who played football on Boston Common, a game that seemed at the time to have few standout qualities or any historically significant value, what could be more ordinary than young boys playing their games and the wider world forgetting them years later?

On the one hand, the early 1920s were a cocktail of Prohibition, jazz, and national soul-searching, and the aging Oneida generation was largely removed from this roaring scene. But on the other hand, the antiquarian movement around the SPNEA appealed to the Boston Brahmin to remember, preserve, and commemorate their own history. This is why the Oneidas donated their football in 1922, a quaint relic from another Boston, another America, the old stock. In a city that was awakening to its many "firsts"—the kind of awareness of origins that inspired the massive 1920 Pilgrim Tercentenary celebrations—the ground was fertile for planting seeds of commemoration of all sorts, including sports.

While the history of football by the early 1920s was now well established through the writing of Walter Camp, Parke H. Davis, and the many college-specific publications, one key story was missing among the Ivy League greats: Harvard's. Much of the newest literature focused on the technical aspects of the game, and in terms of additional foundation stories, the books offered a modicum of new history.[22] Little, that is, until a few weeks after Christmas

1922, when Harvard announced the imminent publication of its complete athletic history.[23] Released in February 1923—forty-eight years after its first school history, which had included some sport but no real record of football—the book was massive. Yet it was a handful of mentions that made all the difference to the old Boston schoolboys in terms of their historical significance.

For the first time in American collegiate football historiography, explicit and extensive recognition was given to the "well-established game which had been played for many years in the preparatory schools of Massachusetts, particularly in those of Boston."[24] The account in the Harvard book was written by Morton Henry Prince, a Boston physician and Harvard alum who also happened, unsurprisingly, to be a Latin School graduate himself—though he was younger and entered the Latin School in 1865 just when the Oneida Club ceased playing. Prince sketched an important genealogy of Boston football back to the well-established game on the Common played regularly by the "boys of the upper classes of the Boston Latin School, and Dixwell's," the tradition being a "school of football from which every year a number graduated to enter Harvard."[25] His account never cited Lovett's *Old Boston Boys* directly nor named the Oneida Club, but the descriptions of the game seem inspired by reading his fellow Latin schoolboy and one-time next-door neighbor's book.[26]

Prince also referenced one novel source that was, until then, internal to the Harvard community. Printed in the December 1915 edition of the Harvard alumni magazine and unreproduced elsewhere, it seems, a unique article by Parke H. Davis had expanded significantly on the pre-1870s period. Like Prince, Davis had not gone as far as quoting Lovett's *Old Boston Boys* but also must have read it. In a 1915 source directed at a singularly Bostonian-Harvardian audience, Davis had made the first reference to "the exploits of a famous club of that period, known and still well remembered as the 'Oneidas'" and omitted any mention of the classic Webb Ellis tale.[27] Prince's new encyclopedic account built on Davis's and outlined a direct lineage to the boys who had "introduced 'Boston' football [and] were trained in the Boston Latin, Dixwell, and other preparatory schools" and, in so doing, also disappeared any reference to Webb Ellis.[28] While bereft of any specific names to honor, Prince's February 1923 account formed a canvas on which it would not be difficult to paint the portrait of some key figures. When combined with several concurrent events, this new story of a "Boston Game" instigated a sort of new sporting archaeology around the origins of American collegiate football.

Shortly after the release of the *H Book of Harvard Athletics* occurred an exchange between two men—Arthur L. K. Volkmann and Winthrop Scudder—that kindled a commemorative spark. The erstwhile Boston schoolmaster drew Scudder's attention to a rather festive event being planned as reported in the *Boston Evening Transcript*.[29] Across the Atlantic, London-based *Westminster Gazette* editor G. F. Philip Bussy and *Transcript* correspondent J. P. Collins explained that Rugby School was preparing to celebrate the 1923 centenary of Rugby rules instigator William Webb Ellis. On March 3, 1923, the front page of the *Boston Evening Transcript* featured a photo of the Webb Ellis plaque, and the authors lauded Rugby School, its history, and its headmasters, making it a "character-factory, in all that the great English public schools claim to be."[30] The second page, a full sheet headlined "The Father of All Football," included another lengthy piece just by Bussy, which covered the sport of rugby. He explained the game's history, the story of the schoolboy Ellis, the Old Rugbeian Committee's investigation, and the asseveration that "this young rebel against the conventions of his day was the father of all football in which the ball is carried rather than kicked—of the American game as well as of that of Rugby Union."[31] Bussy praised British schools for the early development of football and credited the modern game to "their 'old boys' who have gone on playing," working to regulate and control the sport, specifically in fighting professionalism. He finished his five-column article with a mention of a suggested centenary match in honor of Ellis, at the school made famous by Tom Brown, between the finest players from England and Scotland as well as a joint Welsh-Irish side.

The "suggested" centenary match was actually farther ahead in its planning than Bussy had let on, the plans appearing to go back to at least early 1922.[32] Interestingly, the discussion was hardly restricted to British rugby circles, and the well-informed French quickly encouraged the celebrations—hoping for an invitation—with their leading sport newspaper, *L'Auto-Vélo*, reporting on some official plans even before the hometown Rugby papers got the news.[33] Word of the centenary had also reached Massachusetts well before Volkmann flagged it to Scudder, with the *Boston Herald* first reporting in September 1922 on "talk in England of celebrating the coming centenary," though the story was telegraphic, without mention of the special match but with a reprint of the text of the Webb Ellis tablet.[34]

As we know, the person of Webb Ellis and his "fine disregard for the rules" was certainly not lost on the 1922–23 Boston reader. In the preceding decade, the Ellis story had finally traversed the Atlantic and been transcribed—not as a legend but as a truth—into American sporting historiography, thanks to Camp and Davis. Davis had gone even further to affirm without question the conclusions of the Old Rugbeian Society that "fairly proved that this tradition is founded upon actual fact."[35] This simplistic view of an origin story had not been challenged in American writing since the publication of those two authoritative sources—that is until January of 1923. Three months after having first reported on the coming centenary, the *Boston Herald* ran a longer piece announcing the celebratory match that would feature the best amateur players from England, Scotland, Wales, and Ireland. Not insignificantly, the article recalled the Ellis plaque at Rugby, though with a different tone: "It may be that the tale is merely tradition and that Ellis had nothing to do with the innovation now ascribed to him." As if sowing the seeds of doubt to a sporting creation story was not enough, the article finished with a curiously inviting statement about placing tablets at American colosseums: "If the average American stadium puts tablets on its walls for the honor of players who therein displayed their prowess, what a Valhalla it would become."[36]

This January *Herald* article outlined a particularly American perspective, which is intriguing when considering how Scudder and Volkmann discussed Bussy's subsequent extensive praise of Rugby School and its sporting traditions. The London correspondent's five-column *Transcript* piece just a few weeks later referred to the tablet and described Ellis as "never likely to be forgotten. . . . The matches between Oxford and Cambridge and perhaps even those between Harvard and Yale are constant tributes to the revolutionary spirit of the small Rugby boy."[37] Those were powerful words to print in a city so rich in American history, particularly around independence and the foundation of the country. For, if the "revolutionary spirit" had a symbolic home in the eyes of New Englanders, it was most certainly Boston, not Rugby. In the absence of any journal or correspondence from Scudder, we cannot know how he reacted to Bussy's article. Similarly, we have no specific record that Scudder actually read the newly released Harvard athletic history. Nevertheless, even if he was not listed among the hundreds of alumni having earned the coveted Harvard "H" for athletics, at least seven Oneidas and another ten who appeared in Lovett's *Old Boston Boys* were.[38] As such, the book undoubtedly circulated in the Brahmin community throughout 1923, and it is highly unlikely that Scudder remained ignorant of Prince's new genealogy of Boston football.

The final piece of the puzzle was education, both a precious Puritan ideal on American shores and the celebrated linchpin of the British Empire.

Inseparable from Bussy's description of the 1923 centenary of the sport of rugby was the school itself, where the historical tablet had been placed twenty-three years earlier. It was there that the centenary match would be played. The school was central to the celebrations—celebrations that occurred in the midst of a wider "rush to rugby" across Britain, which underscored the perceived intrinsic link between the sport and the school.[39] A former schoolmaster, Volkmann could not have been insensitive to the role of the educational institution. The German-born educator was about ten years younger than Scudder and the Oneidas and was a graduate of Cornell rather than Harvard. But he became a pillar of the Brahmin world, teaching at Hopkinson's—the successor school to Dixwell's—until 1895 and then running his own school until 1917–18. After the US entered the First World War, Volkmann's German origins made him a source of suspicion and he was forced to close his school and merge with another private institution, Noble and Greenough.[40] The combined school purchased the enormous former Nickerson estate and moved to Dedham, Massachusetts in 1922. After an initial athletic grounds project in 1913–14, which saw the development of nearly five acres of sports fields in Brookline, the move to new hundred-acre grounds positioned the institution much closer to the long-admired British public school model.[41]

This was the context in which the Rugby centenary news made its way to Boston and from Volkmann into fellow Union Club member Scudder's hands when reading the *Evening Transcript*. From all this, it is clear that Scudder possessed a useful template from which he could orchestrate a memorialization of his own in Boston. Anniversaries and origin stories were in the air: the Rugby centenary plans, the missed opportunity to celebrate the sixtieth anniversary of Rutgers versus Princeton in New Jersey, and all the prior origin debates around baseball a decade earlier that stressed the importance of national roots. Given New England and Boston's obsession with important American firsts, it was only natural for Scudder to read Bussy's piece and begin to engineer a commemoration of the Oneidas. Indeed, just as New England had created a usable past in 1920 to celebrate its Pilgrim heritage as a starting point for the story of a new country, Morton Prince had gifted the Oneidas an origin point from which to weave some Old Boston Boys into the historical tapestry of Harvard and intercollegiate football. Until then, the foundation story of football had been intimately connected to Rugby School. However, in the new *H Book*, Prince made no mention of the Webb Ellis origins of rugby and instead introduced the pioneering native Boston schoolboys. With this dual omission and first mention (since Lovett's book), Prince contributed the essential cornerstone to an origin story still alive in its construction. When Volkmann shared the Rugby centenary news, the plans across the Atlantic resonated with Scudder. He drew the natural scientific parallel—the Darwinian evolution of his old Boston schoolboy football into the intercollegiate game described by Prince—and saw the potential to celebrate the American educational and sporting tradition on the new campus of Dixwell's descendant, Noble and Greenough.

After all, they did know that they had played old football games on the Common well before the universities transformed it into the 1920s gridiron beast it had become. The seven surviving Oneidas had the ball to prove it, the one just gifted to the SPNEA a few months prior. The notion that they must have been at the origin of this phenomenon was only logical, for the history of the country was in their blood. With lineage back to the Puritans, ancestors having fought the British at Bunker Hill, grandfathers standing for abolition, and brothers bleeding for the Union, these old friends were among the oldest living descendants of true national pedigree. They came from the old stock, so of course they were first, they *must* have been first. America was born out of *their* Puritan and Pilgrim ancestors' ideas, *their* patriot spirit. It was *their* families' blood that had been spilled in building and preserving their country, so how could they have been anything other than first in sport? Their manifest belief in the destiny that their sporting achievements should be trumpeted in the historical narrative was only natural, almost inevitable, just as these families had recorded for many other (and far more important) political, economic, and social spheres of influence. So after Volkmann shared Rugby's celebratory plans, Scudder began working and thinking about an Oneida commemoration.

In history and in acts of commemoration, it is not simply "what" is important but also "who," "where," and "how." The inspiration for the stone tablet at Rugby provided the template, but what would they commemorate? How should the facts be presented, who ought to be recognized, and where? They could hardly claim to be the founders of intercollegiate football in the United States given that there was little doubt that the university game had evolved after 1876 from the already defined rugby rules under the guidance of the omnipresent Walter Camp. So another angle must be found. While Lovett's *Old Boston Boys* book had never asserted that the Oneidas were the first football club in America, it did lay claim to them founding a club.

The Boy in Bronze

But was it the first club? No other record of a club existed in the American football historiography at that point, so perhaps. Next, Scudder needed a place to commemorate the club. However, Dixwell's—the school the majority of the Oneidas attended—no longer existed. The only school that still operated under the same name in the 1920s was Boston Public Latin. But of the seven ball donors, only Lovett had spent all his schooling there. This was problematic if they wished to place a plaque at a school, like the one at Rugby. It could not be at Boston Public Latin.

So between the spring of 1923 and the colorful New England fall, a compromise had to be found. The Oneidas needed to define the story and identify a location that would fit with the characters it featured. Honoring the club as a group was a good way to remember old friends as they had just done in donating the ball; the names of the players were already on the ball, after all. One name, however, had been singled out. It was not Lovett, despite him being hailed as such a grand sportsman in the wake of publishing his book—he was, after all, a baseball man at heart and a Latin boy. No, if one person must be singled out, it had to be a Dixwell boy. Indeed, in identifying who should be honored, who best but the captain and most senior member aside from Lovett, Gerrit Smith Miller? In recounting the origins of the club in *Old Boston Boys*, Lovett had not actually revealed who founded the club. But Lovett had clearly highlighted his old friend's role as a "most valuable addition" who immediately took "a prominent place" in school football at that time as the first captain of the Oneidas.[42] Miller, then, was an excellent choice. He represented the notion of a successful man with all the ideals worthy of praise. In choosing to tip their hat to their captain in upstate New York, the surviving Oneidas chose not only a solid sportsman and admired friend but also someone who existed outside the usually tight confines of day-to-day Boston high society.

In an America about to pass the Reed-Johnson Immigration Act of 1924, which would dramatically restrict the arrival of new huddled masses, "Gat" Miller came from old stock; his first paternal ancestor, John Miller, immigrated in 1649 from Scotland, and Gat's great-grandfather had founded the town of Peterboro, New York.[43] Having a famous abolitionist grandfather (Gerrit Smith) who ran several times for the US presidency, Miller made his name revolutionizing dairy farming with his work in importing and breeding Holstein cattle.[44] After having married his old headmaster Epes Sargent Dixwell's daughter, Susan Hunt, and moved back to the family farm, Miller also served in the New York State legislature and supported various philanthropic causes.[45] Miller was the natural choice.

But the Oneidas still had to resolve the problem of location. Through Volkmann, whose private school had recently merged with another old day school founded by G. F. Noble in the 1860s, there was direct ancestry through headmasters back to Epes Sargent Dixwell, under whose tutelage nearly all the Oneidas had studied. And the consolidated Noble and Greenough School (Nobles) had incidentally just moved outside of downtown Boston to open a new campus a year earlier. With the inauguration in 1922, the school was following the turn of the twentieth-century trend of building boarding schools in rural New England, some with stone Edwardian architecture, and campuses largely on the British public school model.[46] Scudder only needed to discuss the idea of a memorial plaque with the school's leadership. If facilitated by Volkmann himself, it would have been one of his last acts before his death in August 1923.[47] But it would not have been difficult for Scudder to arrange himself. His son Theodore had been a Nobles student in the early 1900s, and with nearly half of the board of trustees of Nobles being active Union Club members as late as 1921, Scudder would not have been a stranger to the school's leadership.[48]

With the pieces coming together, Scudder and his crew of Means Lawrence, Lovett, and Miller advanced plans for a tablet to be engraved and a ceremony for November 7, 1923, at Noble and Greenough School. At the start of the fall, Scudder did seek to verify some important facts about the Oneida Club. He wrote two letters to the authorities of the modern game—Walter Camp and Parke H. Davis. Both replied to Scudder affirming the Oneida claim to primacy as an organized club.[49] Camp's reply is particularly amusing, since he directed Scudder back to Lovett's *Old Boston Boys* for further reference, revealing how that book was taking on importance as a historical source even if it amounted to little more than circular reasoning. Though we do not know exactly when between the spring and fall of 1923 the tablet was commissioned, it is striking how quickly the whole project came together. At the least, this demonstrates that the Oneida claim elicited no questioning or doubts in the minds of any and all involved. Yes, Scudder had written to authorities Camp and Davis, but it was almost as if it were a late afterthought. Given Lovett's book, the donated ball, the literature, and the recent Harvard *H Book* that affirmed the historicity of Boston schoolboy football, along with the wider context of Boston and New England "firsts," it is easy to see how natural their claim would have seemed to them at the time.

What is odd, however, was the timing. The year 1923 was perfect for a sixtieth anniversary celebration of the club's founding, since according to Lovett's initial account in *Old Boston Boys*, he noted the date to be in 1863.[50] While the contemporary press reported games between schools the prior year—also recorded without the club's name by fellow student Francis Lincoln in his diary—there is no mention of the Oneidas before the fall of 1863.[51] For some reason, however, the plaque was prepared with 1862 as the chosen date. In reconstructing their past, Scudder and his friends must have come across some evidence that they had in fact started the club in 1862.[52] As for the actual memorial event, the famous match on November 7, 1863, against the Boston English High and the Public Latin Schools provided a sixtieth anniversary date. The date was set, then, and a modest event planned.

Incidentally, it was to be less than a week after the celebratory event and international match for the centenary of Webb Ellis's moment of glory at Rugby School on November 1.[53] The Rugby centenary plans had progressed in parallel. The British press had continued to recycle the Ellis tale, often reproducing an image of the plaque, quoting from it, and affirming its status as the origin story for the handling codes of football.[54] The event took place with a significant crowd of Old Rugbeians in attendance, as the *Rugby Advertiser* photos can attest.[55] While not invited on the pitch, in the end the French were represented by one touch judge, Paris-based Scot and longtime secretary of the French Rugby Federation, C. F. Rutherford.[56] At least a small delegation of the French Rugby Federation was present, as the president was invited to give a toast—the only non-British orator—at the banquet held in London for which the menu also fully honored *la langue de Molière*.[57]

Back in Boston it appears that the Miller tablet unveiling was principally planned as a local event for the Nobles School and its students. However, it became news for the *Boston Globe*—which even published the train times from Boston South Station to Dedham, Massachusetts, for members of the public interested in attending—and covered the day after by the *New York Times*.[58] The organizing group of Scudder, Means Lawrence, and Lovett cannot be accused of misleading those in attendance, as the speakers spoke more of the importance of character than sport history, citing the example of Miller and the other Oneida boys. The bronze plaque—modeled on the stone one from Rugby—stated only that Miller was the founder and captain of the "first organized football club" in the country.[59] The school archives contain a memorandum about the event on official Nobles-headed paper, which recounts "Scudder's untiring efforts thus to honor his old friend" and explains how the event was directed principally at the school community.[60] Medals were minted as a gift to the school to annually honor the best students in several fields (still awarded at the time of writing). Three were named after individual Oneidas, while the other two bore the names of old headmasters: athletics (the Miller medal), baseball (Lovett), rowing (Watson), Latin (Dixwell), and modern languages (Volkmann). These were accompanied by a hundred-dollar fund ($1,500 today) for each medal to cover future production costs and future interest to provide a scholarship—the Gerrit Smith Miller scholarship—for a boy from New York State to attend the school. Miller donated the sum to cover the three athletic medals, Dixwell descendant George Wigglesworth for the founding headmaster award, and Volkmann's wife for the final one. As for the tablet, it is unclear. The newspapers are somewhat contradictory as to whether Miller had paid for it or Scudder solicited eighteen friends.[61]

It may be naive, however, to think that such an event could be contained to a local gathering honoring the memory of old friends and edifying character examples for schoolboys to follow. The headlines in the press took the inevitable shortcut. The *New York Times* read, "Tablet Honors Football Founder" and included the statement "the reputed founder of organized football in America."[62] On the day of the event the *Boston Globe* headlined, "To honor the founder of organized football," and the article reported that both Camp and Davis acknowledged the Oneidas as "the first to organize football."[63] The *Boston Herald* article, with its "Miller, Football's Founder" headline, went even further to claim that the Oneida Club was the "first football club in the world."[64] Also reporting on the event the following day, the *Boston Globe* printed another headline, "Unveil tablet in honor of founder of football in the United States," and recounted the ceremony highlights.[65] Only the *Boston Transcript* abstained from overt hyperbole, stating that the tablet was to honor the founder of the Oneida Club, "which was the first of its kind," although the paper did make a direct link claiming that the game "once played so simply . . . by the Oneidas has now grown into an industry."[66] A few weeks later, a paper near Peterboro trumpeted its local hero as the "Founder of Football" but strangely stated the date of the club's first game as November 1863.[67] These stories were relayed, and the news reached from Maine to Washington, DC, to Nebraska, all with the similar abridged foundational version.[68] Thus, the only truth a reader nationally would retain was that Miller was the *founder* of the club that *founded* football and not that the club "is believed to have been the first exponent of which there is any record of organized football in this country," as was buried toward the end of one article.[69]

But one should be wary of extrapolating too much from the press in discerning the Oneidas' true intentions. Their focus seemed to be commemorating one of their own, Miller, at what was the descendant link to his old school. This commemoration was recorded, edited, and printed by Scudder largely for personal preservation purposes. The booklet *An Appreciation*, produced during the winter of 1923–24, appeared as a nicely bound supplement to Noble and Greenough's school paper and was donated to the Bostonian Society in March of 1924.[70] At least one copy was given to the school itself and is still in the archives, while the Library of Congress also received a complimentary copy in the same month of March 1924.[71] The focus was local, on Boston institutions, and for preservation rather than deliberate self-promotion or news creation.

It is not because the newspapers stretched the facts that anyone should condemn the Oneidas for placing a tablet at their old school in 1923 in the name of personal glory-seeking. It was impossible for them to imagine what the game of intercollegiate football would become under the guise of the young and growing National Collegiate Athletic Association (NCAA) and the newly born National Football League (NFL) or the manner in which the game would come to dominate national traditions in the way that the College Bowls or Super Bowl Sunday have since. In the same way that the Old Rugbeians had no conception that their plaque would create a powerful origin myth that would lead the International Rugby Board to name the Rugby World Cup the Webb Ellis Trophy, neither did the Oneidas know that their legacy would inform the history of gridiron into the twenty-first century or that American soccer would later claim the boys for itself.

Furthermore, despite having been announced in the press, the man being honored by Noble and Greenough was not even in attendance on the day. Perhaps Miller's absence reveals his humility in not wanting to be the center of attention, especially when the focus in his mind was the group; one paper explicitly explained Miller "stayed away out of modesty."[72] With his personal correspondence leaving a gap between 1913 and 1927, we are left to wonder. The absent captain had sent a message to be read out to those in attendance: "Give my love to each one of the undefeated Oneida Football team, and tell them the Tablet is in honor of us all." Underlining that fair play so dear to the Anglo-American gentleman, his motto was proclaimed by the school trustees board president: "Defeat with honor is better than victory with dishonor." While not expressed with the same poetic eloquence gifted to Lovett, the words encapsulated the unquestionable archetypal belief of his generation so bathed in the Muscular Christian message of striving masculinity. In truth, the absence of a celebrated hero allows those gathered to laud his character and merits but not shower the man with excessive adulatory praise. A hero's presence paradoxically transforms a didactic moment into a self-congratulatory event of, albeit friendly, idolatry. And so, in Miller's absence, the event remained honorific and educational, focused on painting his emulous character as a role model for schoolboys.

From the record provided in Scudder's booklet, the tenor of this event was straightforward: honoring an old friend while inspiring a younger generation. While Scudder's edited *An Appreciation* tends toward hyperbole at times—comparing Miller to the Duke of Wellington and stating that he was "revered, honored and loved by every man, woman and child" in his hometown of Peterboro—there was truth to their praise of his loyalty.[73] Yet the unveiling was not only about "Gat" Miller. The notable Bishop William Lawrence—younger cousin of Robert Means Lawrence, who had organized the event with Scudder and Lovett—spoke of the other old Dixwell boys and how those "schoolboys grew to be eminent men."[74] The Boston papers also included excerpts of the speeches and listed former Old Boys and their achievements. And who was to argue, since among the *Old Boston Boys* were a state governor (Wolcott), a current senator (Lodge), a Harvard theology professor (Peabody), and many Boston businessmen, industrialists, and politicians.

The final speech of the day was reserved for the doyen of them all, former Harvard president Charles W. Eliot. His words focused again on character, a focus shared by Muscular Christians on either side of the Atlantic. The educator summarized the spirit of Harvard: "It is the spirit of service to one's fellow-beings, to one's city, one's state and one's Nation: it is the doing of good as best one can, with an unselfish spirit that does not think of personal advancement."[75] Speaking about the Oneidas, President Eliot placed the emphasis not on sport but on character. In fact, nothing recorded in the press, or by Scudder, had Eliot discuss football in any detail. Not recorded in the commemorative booklet but printed in the press, the longtime educator remarked, "I should think you would think this is a rather curious spectacle; I should think you might wonder what all these old gentlemen are doing here, magnifying, lauding putting up a tablet to an old comrade of theirs, a comrade chiefly of their athletic sports. But really, this is a striking instance of the influence of character in youth upon one's comrades, an instance of the strong impression it can make, as proved by the presence of these old gentlemen, all of them nearly 80."[76]

The celebrations ended with a fascinating juxtaposition. That Eliot should speak to the character and loyalty of "these old gentlemen" was in itself not surprising, although he would have only had the chance to know Scudder and Tucker as students for one year, since he became president in May 1869; all the other championship Oneidas graduated in 1868 or July 1869. Rather, the irony was that Eliot was probably the greatest adversary football ever faced. His often quoted tirade of 1905 recorded in the *School Journal* objected precisely to the game's "moral quality" (or lack thereof) and the "state of mutual distrust it arouses between two otherwise friendly colleagues."[77] Having just published his *Harvard Memories*—bereft of any mention of football—here was the staunch defender of a Harvard *without* football standing alongside its newly proclaimed "founders" in 1923.[78] Indeed, the irony continued precisely at the close of Eliot's speech, when rose Charles Wiggins, current Noble and Greenough headmaster, who read the cable received that day from W. W. Vaughan, headmaster of Rugby School: "Rugby School sends its congratulations and greetings." The link to sport was evident and despite Eliot's long battle against the game, the phenomenon had taken hold by 1923. By then Eliot had grown old; he retired in 1909 and died in 1926. Perhaps the sands of time between his crusade against turn-of-the-century football and the ceremony at Nobles eroded his unequivocal doubt in the sport's moral qualities so he could stand side by side with the Oneidas as long as football upheld character-building.

It was, in the words of the *Boston Globe*, an "unusual ceremony [and] they were unusual persons."[79] Reflecting on the 1923 Oneida commemoration reveals the limited scope of the event, even if Scudder, Lovett, Means Lawrence, and Miller had clearly made the connection with the international centenary match being played at Rugby School. According to the *Boston Globe*, attendance was limited to the Oneidas, various guests, and fifty-some students; *An Appreciation* notes seventy-five in total—a much smaller event than that at Rugby. Scudder's booklet, which was only printed in limited copies for distribution at the school and among friends, notes that before dispersing, around forty of those present signed a "Round Robin" to send to Miller as a souvenir, a copy of which has been preserved in Lovett's scrapbook. The text read "Football as an organized game is honored by having Gerrit Smith Miller as its Founder—1862" (see image 4).[80] This was a private memento for the absent Miller even if it followed the press shortcut that football had a founder and his name was Gerrit Smith Miller. However minor it may have

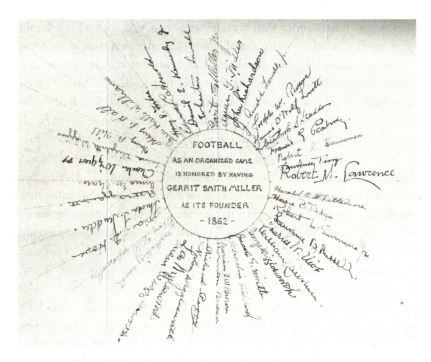

IMAGE 4. A Round Robin that was signed on November 7, 1923, and sent to Gerrit Smith Miller to honor him as the founder of the organized game of football in 1862. Courtesy of Revolutionary Spaces.

seemed, this was the first internal stretch in the fabric of the Oneida story, albeit one that was invisible beyond the confines of the school community and friends present.

Just as Rugby School had illustrated twenty-five years earlier, it was terribly difficult to reduce a complex story of rule changes, customs, and hearsay onto a short commemorative plaque. For granite tablets, bronze plaques, or the 1920s newspapers, it was far easier to have one character and tell an engaging yet simple story. So rather than face the challenge of defining the full story of the Oneidas or examine in depth where else beyond Boston early football may have been played, in the person of Miller, Noble and Greenough could extol the qualities of one man as an archetype. Had the event gone unreported and unembellished in the press, perhaps the focus would have remained a character exercise and the hyperbole limited to friendly admiration. But someone, presumably Scudder, who set up the event, had informed the papers. And they would not try to nuance how the Oneidas played an older more kicking-style game or that there had been a complex process within the universities to adopt Rugby rules and then modify them into some new sport. The press wanted a hero, and in Miller they had their headline.

The key point here is that while the media would seek (perhaps wrongly) to position the Oneida story as a point of origin for "foot ball" in the United States, the fact that the newspapers did so is consequential. In an age of mass media, the power of a newspaper's sporting headline was significant particularly in the construction of "football as narrative," as Michael Oriard has demonstrated.[81] That the newspapers disseminated an idea that could be recalled and recounted into the future was all that was necessary for collective memory to become myth and the tenuous hitched to hard fact. The story became a visible point of origin, now indisputably memorialized in tablet form.

What were the effects of this commemorative exercise? Firstly, in the following months, Miller filled in the one missing line on his curriculum vitae since 1869: the elusive Harvard degree. At commencement on June 19, 1924, Miller, along with thirteen other men, was awarded an honorary degree from the institution he had had to leave after just one year due to illness. No mention was made in the account of the ceremony of Miller's sporting achievements. Rather, he was recognized for his incredible contribution and work in dairy farming.[82] Nevertheless, it is not unreasonable to wonder how Miller's moment of football fame may have propelled his name onto suggested lists for honorary degrees between the November 1923 tablet and the July 1924 commencement ceremony. No similar recognition was reserved for Lovett or Arnold, both of whom were Oneidas but had never set foot as students on the famous Delta. Indeed, both had been slighted during the news coverage of the tablet unveiling, Jim Lovett once being referred to as "Bob" and poor old Ned Arnold often omitted entirely.[83] Fortunately, the Oneidas' own chronicler, Scudder, had included them properly in his official account of the tablet unveiling. The booklet was donated and reviewed by historical societies, and the contents were then condensed and reprinted in the bulletin of the SPNEA in July of 1924, including a photo of the plaque and the seven surviving members.[84]

The second consequence of the tablet commemoration—thanks to the role of the media—was the true birth of an origin story for the Oneidas. Until this point, their story was just a collection of memories from a dinner, in a book, and on a ball. From the tablet's unveiling, the new press and print literature sowed the seeds for the potential future recognition of Miller's team as a starting point for the history of football in America. In the midst of what historian Daniel Boorstin has coined the Graphic Revolution and specifically the transformative period of the 1910s and '20s, getting in the news was essential in order to obtain celebrity status, hitherto something to be absolutely avoided by anyone with a reputation.[85] With the press eager to fabricate fame through exaggerating stories or factual shortcuts, the natural process of attaining hero status was abridged. The Oneidas were on the cusp of this paradigm change. They were not a contemporary news story as were the many celebrities born in the 1920s newspapers. For the Oneidas had truth to their claim, and they were only trying to remember and honor one another, held up emulously for the next generation of Boston boys at Noble and Greenough. Yet not even they could foresee the power of print. To wit, an article in Lovett's own company paper announced with pride the school tablet's unveiling under the headline "Original Football Team" and boasted that one of the company's own was among the "fifteen youths who are the fathers of organized football."[86]

So by 1924, old friends had gathered to honor one of their own at a school born of the traditional Boston education from which they had benefited. Scudder and Lovett mailed copies of the booklet about Miller to friends and Old Boys, as testify the many thank-you letters they received.[87] Miller finally had his Harvard degree, and Scudder had deposited a memoir there for posterity. Lovett made another donation to the SPNEA of a picture of the famous Volant rowing crew from the 1860s and finally became a subscribing member of the society.[88] Perhaps now the "fathers of organized football" could rest? But if the Oneida saga teaches us anything about human nature, it is that we are a surprisingly entrepreneurial species.

One year after the unveiling, the *Literary Digest* printed a lengthy article entitled "Who Started All This Football, Anyway?"[89] Beginning from the plaque at Rugby and the Ellis story so firmly entrenched in the historiography on both sides of the Atlantic, the author recounted American football's kicking-to-rugby switch in the universities between 1869 and the all-important date of 1876, when the colleges finally agreed to a set of common rules. The article ignored Boston's schoolboy football games, with of course no reference to Miller's Oneidas. Walter Camp was credited with establishing the early supremacy of the game, and the article noted how the Yale man was "occasionally referred to as the father of modern football." But had not the Oneidas

The Boy in Bronze

just been proclaimed the "fathers of organized football"? It is unlikely that the article went unnoticed in Boston, especially in its call for a statue in the vein of Aristonico Caristo, the Athenian hero of early Greek football or *pheninda*: "In proof of this appears the figure of one Aristonico Caristo, to whom the Athenians raised a statue because of his eminence as a player of the football game known as *pheninda*. Enthusiasm! We bellow through megaphones, throw hats over cross-bars, and dance snake dances. The Athenians were a less frothily exuberant folk; they put their hero into imperishable marble. When will Boston raise a statue to a Mahan or a Casey; or New Haven one to a Coy or a Mallory? Echo answers—'When?'"[90]

Camp the father of football? A statue in New Haven? It was almost as if the *Literary Digest* was egging on Boston. Summoned for one final match, did the aging Oneidas have the resilience to respond, or would their goal line be crossed by some other upstart claiming paternity on the great game of football?

8
MONUMENT MEN

Deaths, Rivals, and Making a City Legend

> Then—"A Football Monument," I
> said, "has lately been erected
> To the old Oneida Team." At this
> he was visibly affected.
> Then I told of the graven Football
> and the phrase, as on a scroll,
> That no opponent, anywhere, "Had
> ever crossed our goal."
>
> —Lovett, *A Pilgrimage* (1927)

In the months following the tablet unveiling, the Oneidas must have been satisfied with the recognition granted to old Gat Miller. A dear friend had been honored, his memory (and vicariously theirs) perpetuated, and they had even been granted a few lines of newspaper glory. They had, after all, accomplished a great deal in historical preservation terms. The group had donated their old ball in late 1922 to the city's premier antiquarian society. In a printed booklet gifted to a handful of libraries and numerous institutions, Scudder had recorded Miller and the club's story, the one memorialized on a school plaque all in parallel to the Rugby centenary celebrations across the pond. In one sense, it was mission accomplished, and over the next eighteen months, while others around them passed away, the surviving Oneidas carried on as living monuments of the old life on Beacon Hill and in the Back Bay. Yet during this time when friends' obituaries and funeral invitations were frequent, Scudder and his band were inspired to steer a second commemoration project toward the heart of their city to mark a sporting *hors du commun* on

Boston Common. A small bronze tablet on the secluded campus of Noble and Greenough—however grand its stone castle walls were—was apparently not enough. Nor was it sufficient to donate medals and scholarships to motivate students, such a noble educational goal. While reported in the news, these were private affairs for a small community. Thus, the memorialization efforts continued to evolve and culminated in a public monument that was uniquely celebrated in private verse at a festive 1927 luncheon.[1] As Lovett's poetry reveals, if the nostalgic reflections of an undefeated youth are to be celebrated in life's autumn years, it should preferably be in frothy rhapsodic humor.

Jest is not enough, however, and bereft of a specific purpose or object to honor, monuments are never built. Whether for the living or the dead, engraving the image of someone or something in stone appears to be humanity's preferred method to ensure posterity. Sport is no less a human activity than any other, and the roots of its statuary go back to ancient Greece.[2] Hence the calls by the *New York Times* and the *Literary Digest* for a statue to a contemporary Boston or New Haven football star in the image of a Casey, Mahan, Coy, or Mallory. However impressive their careers were, erecting stone likenesses to those who are still young and even playing was admittedly awkward in 1924, or at any time.[3] The pull to honor and remember is nonetheless powerful and awaits the opportune time—often when, to cite historian Pierre Nora, the *milieux de mémoire* sit on the fringe of disappearance.[4] Indeed, it is the living who inhabit and guard these *milieux*, and when they pass, another thread of that collective memory unravels. For death and memorialization make good bedfellows.

Between the summer of 1924 and the spring of 1925, the city of Boston lost two eminent citizens while the American football world mourned two great advocates. At the intersection of these four lives lies a key to understanding what the Oneidas did after the school tablet commemoration. The first two, both Oneidas, were born within ten days (and a ten-minute walk) of each other in 1850 and were contemporaries of Scudder, Miller, and Lovett's gang. Henry Parkman, prominent lawyer, banker, Massachusetts state representative, and senator, passed in the summer, while the great statesman Henry Cabot Lodge, who left few ambivalent one way or the other, died in November. The other two, pillars of the footballing world, both collapsed suddenly within five months of each other. On October 27, while preparing for the Cornell matchup a few days away, recently arrived Columbia football coach and Crimson alum Percy D. Haughton fell ill in the middle of a team practice and died shortly after being rushed to the hospital. Stolen from football at age forty-eight, the Harvard man's death came as a shock to the game, and his funeral in Boston was well attended.[5] If Haughton's death had caught national attention—front-page news in the *New York Times* and the *Boston Globe*—and was widely recounted in the Harvard community, the coverage of Walter Camp's surprise passing echoed even further. The coverage of Camp's death was sweeping, and his papers at Yale include an entire folder of dozens of news clippings from across the country, almost always including the paternal title in the headline or text.[6] While front-page news from New York to Los Angeles through Chicago and many other cities, only the *Boston Globe* explicitly connected the two deaths.[7] In an exercise of Oneida amnesia, the Boston papers flashed headline after headline reminding its citizens who the true "father of football" was.[8]

Four men taken by death: two witnesses of old Boston Brahmin memory and a pair of giants from football history. Nearly all four funerals were linked through the celebrant; only Camp's service in New Haven was not presided over by the Oneida bishop William Lawrence.[9] The two Oneidas, Lodge and Parkman, were well into their seventies. Of the two football greats, Camp was sixty-five but still vibrantly participating in the intercollegiate rules committee. The first two were part of the passing of the Brahmin world, the last generation who knew both the Civil War and the Gilded Age. For the latter two, the media expressed a sense of injustice at losing Camp and Haughton too soon and calls to memorialize them came swiftly. The differences in how these four deaths were recorded, received and reacted to is telling. It is interesting that neither Parkman, called "one of Boston's best-known citizens," nor Lodge, whose death and funeral were widely reported in the press and in a fifteen-page homage by the Massachusetts Historical Society, were quickly linked to a grand commemorative impetus. The closest initiative was Lodge's name being attributed to a bird sanctuary near his home on Nahant, but there were no immediate plans for statues or monuments to either.[10] Within the Harvard community, the four were remembered differently in the university's alumni magazine—Haughton with two obituaries over fourteen pages accompanied by a full-page photograph, Lodge with a seventeen-page article without any image, Parkman by a one-line notice, and Yale alum Walter Camp not even mentioned in passing.[11]

In contrast to the minor musings of ornithic commemoration for Cabot Lodge, chirpy calls for football memorials came straightaway. A thousand letters were mailed by classmates and former Harvard students for a Haughton memorial in Boston.[12] This quickly paled in comparison to the national movement to commemorate the "Father of Football" from New Haven. The *New York Times* had barely reported Camp's death as, in the same breath, it announced that a memorial "will probably be erected."[13] Haughton was not forgotten in Boston or New York, and a similar committee at Columbia began raising funds for a new room named in their deceased coach's honor. Work on a Boston memorial began under the supervision of city architect Charles Howard Walker and within a few months involved renowned sculptor of the Lincoln statue in Washington, DC, Daniel Chester French, who expressed "how much pleasure it would give [him] to be associated."[14] But Boston continued to print even more news about the quickly advancing plans to honor Camp, which seemed to dwarf attention to the memorial efforts for Harvard alum and Columbia coach Haughton. His commemoration continued but now in the shadow of the Yale giant.

Thus, less than eighteen months after the Oneidas obtained initial recognition with a small plaque on the wall of a secluded Boston private school, one of the country's leading universities and Harvard's eternal rival began plans for a Camp memorial. It was to be as grand as the man they wished to honor, with Yale alumni quickly expressing a desire to recognize he who had become a collegiate football legend. Within a few weeks of Camp's death, Dr. Clarence Mendell, Yale's athletic association's president, wrote to the coach's widow that a joint university–athletic association committee would steer the financing and planning of the proposed Walter Camp Memorial.[15] Soon, the scope of the project went well beyond the confines of the Yale community. Action was spontaneous and came from all over. Walter Powell, who had worked under Camp's direction in the navy during World War I and was a close friend of E. K. Hall, wrote to Walter Camp Jr. exposing that he had already garnered much support from fifteen or twenty of the most prominent coaches in the country in support of a memorial project. Powell wrote again within a month to explain that the response "has been far beyond our expectations. . . . Many are willing to go to work immediately to help raise the necessary funds."[16] Suggestions over the spring and summer for the location and nature of the memorial ranged from New Haven to Washington, DC, naming the field or even a scholarship trust to be awarded. This undertaking was significant. By September 1925 the initial plans called for towers at the entrance of the cavernous seventy-thousand-seat Yale Bowl and were illustrated in a booklet produced by the joint Yale–National Collegiate Athletic Association committee to enlist pledges or contributions from universities, colleges, and schools.[17] The commemorative power of 1920s stadia, as Brian Ingrassia underlines, is just another example of how Progressive Era football had become an accepted "cultural ritual" across the full spectrum of American society even up to its Brahmin high-brow layer.[18]

Such a project undoubtedly made the small tablet on the wall of Noble and Greenough appear rather modest. In comparison with Yale's archives, the relative paucity of sources for the Oneida monument limits our full understanding of what inspired the Oneidas to initiate a second commemoration. While it is clear that the process was underway by the start of the autumn 1925, it is difficult to know exactly when the project was born. The oldest documents on record for the planning of the Oneida monument are two letters dated September 8, 1925, between the Oneidas and the Boston Art Commission and the architects and the City Park Commission. In the summer of 1926 Scudder had noted that their monument had been a two-year old project, which would date this back to somewhere mid or late 1924.[19] But no document about the planning of an Oneida monument has been uncovered that predates Camp's death, and nothing from the archive in 1924 ever speaks to a monument project. Even the lengthy article published in the July 1924 SPNEA *Bulletin* referred only to the Miller tablet for the Nobles School event and was entirely silent on any further plans.[20] Moreover, not a single piece of evidence from what remains of Lovett, Miller, and Scudder's correspondence scattered across multiple archives or Lovett's extensive scrapbook even mentions a monument before those letters in September 1925. As such, it is impossible to know for certain if the widely reported discussions held in the weeks and months following Camp's death about a Yale memorial were a motivating factor in the Oneida project. It is equally impossible to ignore the striking parallel with how the 1923 Rugby centenary was a direct inspiration for the Miller plaque at Noble and Greenough.

Nevertheless, the Oneidas had organized themselves by September 1925. Their committee was four men—Miller, Means Lawrence, Lovett, and Scudder—who submitted their request for a memorial tablet to "record the organization in 1862 of the Oneida Football Club of Boston, the first organized football club in the United States," to be placed on Boston Common "where their games were won."[21] The whole process appears to have moved quite quickly, as opposed to the Camp Memorial, which had become a national matter and was advancing only gradually.[22] By October 1925 then, the Oneidas had approval and could prepare a new commemorative event. Despite the plans being announced in the press, one week before the unveiling the Oneidas penned a lengthy complaint to the architects and openly threatened to withhold payment.[23] The point of contention lay in architect I. Howland Jones's plan to display a carved wreath on the top of the monument in the place of a football. The Oneidas insisted that a ball "of the appropriate proportions with the lacing showing" be used and considered abandoning the entire project: "The Committee feels so strongly about this change that it will not accept your design or the Monument until the football is substituted for the wreath. Indeed the Committee will abandon the erection of the Monument altogether rather than erect it with the wreath which you propose. They do not desire to crown themselves, or appear to do so."[24] It was the last piece of correspondence before the monument's unveiling. Notwithstanding the absence of images showing the full monument at the unveiling, given the subsequent events, it seems the wreath never appeared. But much to their dismay, there was no graven football.

Yet the event had been planned, and the *Boston Globe* had already announced the monument listing the sixteen club members' names, its designers, the city's approval, and its location to honor "the first organized football club in the United States."[25] A week after the letter of complaint, the ceremony went ahead on the Common in front of some one hundred individuals. The press confused which of the Oneidas were present, some omitting Arnold and Bowditch entirely. Speeches were given by several Oneidas, which highlighted the main characters of the club and its undefeated record but also the patriotic aspects of this story. Means Lawrence presented the club as "the first organization of its kind in this country, and dating from 1862."[26] Peabody stressed the enjoyment of a sport without its modern pressures and chose to honor the memory of Wolcott, the Oneida boy of seventeen who "died for his country to preserve the Union."[27] At the same time, the professor stressed perspective and encouraged those present not to overemphasize the moment, discussing how the Oneidas of 1862 had not the contemporary problems of the collegiate sport, since their "game was sheer boyish pleasure, and there were no spectators."[28]

The city, the Latin School, and Harvard were all represented jointly by one person. Despite the grandeur of tone as reported by the press, the event was not important enough for each institution to send an individual representative, so Capt. Edward F. O'Dowd received the monument on behalf of the city. The event did include at least one famous spectator in attendance. Erstwhile baseball star, George Wright, explained to the press that "Lovett was one of the greatest all-round athletes of his day."[29] After the presentation speech, the stone tablet was unveiled by Miller's granddaughter Dorothy and Lovett's daughter Alice. While the moment was nicely captured in a photograph printed in two Boston papers, only two mentioned that names were carved onto the stone; both, however, curiously stated that the reverse side listed only the seven survivors rather than all sixteen names listed in the articles.

The press shaped the meaning of the event by taking shortcuts in their headlines, referring to the "Monument to First Football Team Dedicated on Common" in the *Boston Herald* or the "Memorial to First Football Team in United States on Common" in the *Christian Science Monitor*.[30] Not satisfied with padding headlines with founding firsts, the newspapers competed in hyperbole. The media nonsense went as far as to juxtapose a crowd that gathered *later* that day and nearly *five miles away* at Harvard stadium with the small congregation of less than one hundred individuals on the Common that morning. The *Boston Traveler* headline read, "Unveiled as Crowd of 54,000 Flocks to Stadium" and the *Globe*'s report the following day claimed "Ceremony on Common While Thousands Were Pouring into Stadium—Oneidas Played the Game in 1862–65."[31] Admittedly, the Oneidas had been deliberate in their choice of the date for the unveiling: the same day as the Harvard-Yale football clash. But at best, the link between the two events was spurious, at worst anachronistic. Because the distance between Boston Common and Newspaper Row on Washington Street was a short walk, the reporters had been able to write and photograph the monument event that morning and still have the Oneida story printed in time to appear in the paper *before* the Harvard-Yale game kicked off in the afternoon. The fact that reporter Joe Toye of the *Traveler* bothered to report seeing a couple of Italian boys from the North End who "gazed respectively and quite interested in these old gentlemen" around the monument reveals the sparsity of the crowd.

The difference in reporting across the country is telling of the local newspapers' co-creation of the unveiling as a media event. Between Boston, New York, and Washington, DC, to name just three cities, the papers presented the story in vastly different ways. The news reached the Five Boroughs but was reported rather differently. Six pages into its nine-page sports section and squeezed between the box scores of Manhattan high school football games, the *New York Times* did grant the Oneidas a few lines, including correctly printing the seven surviving members' names. Yet the paper made no explicit link between the Boston Boys' historical first and its extensive coverage of the Crimson-Bulldog matchup. After five full pages reporting on the Harvard-Yale game and the many other collegiate contests, the paper simply noted that the Oneidas were the "first organization of its kind" and the "precursor of modern college football."[32] The *New York Sun* article gave a bit more detail, although published nearly a month later, and underscored "the scant notice" given to the ceremony attended by "a scant one hundred persons, many of them curious."[33] Further south in the capital, no news made it even in the following day's Sunday sports section. While the Harvard-Yale game was covered in detail, the only mention that weekend of football history was in the widely syndicated Uncle Ray's Corner in the *Washington Post*.[34] Indeed, ignorant of the monument unveiling in Boston, Ramon Coffman traced the origins of early "rush" games between freshmen and sophomores and the growth of the game from the 1869 intercollegiate Princeton-Rutgers contest and finished his Saturday column without any mention of the Oneidas.[35] It was his third piece on football history in less than one week, the second of which began by quoting in full the Webb Ellis plaque at Rugby.[36] Even the *Boston Herald* could headline the Oneidas as the "First Football Team" and still print a story in the same issue about the history of football entirely ignoring the local Oneidas.[37] The fact that the Boston Oneida story was essentially inconspicuous in New York while entirely obscured in Washington, DC, is telling. It illustrates not only how local the Oneida monument unveiling still was in its significance—despite making the national papers—but also that theirs was still a live, developing story yet to have moved from news to history.

Of course, the Oneidas cannot be held responsible for how a gullible and hungry press reported the story, since the media gave life to news in ways of their choosing. Whether headlines or which parts of a speech to recount, reporters and editors chose what was newsworthy and how stories ought to be shaped. Only Toye of the *Traveler* and the *Herald* included Peabody's remarks about not taking the monument or the unveiling too seriously. Others cropped that from his speech and focused on the easy hyperbole. Perhaps it was the surprising absence of the invisible bishop who had been responsible for the moral emphasis in 1923. This time he does not appear to have attended the event, an odd fact given his extensive support for the school tablet. Little in any of the reporting put the emphasis on character building with the Muscular Christian undertones so evident in Bishop Lawrence's speech just two years earlier. As a result, most of the coverage simply related the foundation story as the essential part.

In contrast to the speeches in 1923 at Noble and Greenough, the tone of the reporting for this more public event was decidedly less moralistic or educational. It is easy to understand why the press took the bait, since, as an event, the monument unveiling was perfectly staged. In his speech, Peabody affirmed two facts about the club: that they were never beaten and "that from this aboriginal game has sprung the amazing progeny of mighty contests which have almost supplanted baseball as our national game."[38] The *Boston Herald* had reported that Harvard's football tradition died out with the Civil War but that "the Oneida claim is that theirs was the first organized team in America. Their contention evidently has been accepted."[39] The date chosen by the Oneidas not only fell on the most important football game that year in Boston, against archrivals Yale, but it was also the fiftieth anniversary of that same Harvard-Yale rivalry. Unmentioned by the papers, was it a coincidence or just a providential nod from above? Indeed, even those things beyond their direct control genuflected to the Oneidas. With a wink to their destiny and as if to say the gods of football were still with them, on the day of their monument unveiling, Boston's goal line remained uncrossed with Harvard holding Yale scoreless.

Despite the unveiling and the successful construction of the narrative about the new "founders of organized football," the saga of the Oneida monument was far from finished—the stone tablet still lacked the graven image of a football. It seems that in the spring of 1926, the Oneidas revived their cause. The architect, Jones, wrote to Parker at the city's art commission in late May alerting him to the possibility that the Oneidas may again plead to have a large oval football carved. Jones seriously objected on the basis that "what they propose is entirely out of scale with the monument and is the wrong shape and completely changes its character."[40] The architect correctly foresaw the Oneidas' persistence, and one month later, the monument committee of four sent another letter to the Boston Art Commission asking to carve the oval football, the final missing element to "record the fact that organized football began on Boston Common." The letter, signed by all four, including Peterboro-based Miller, was firm. The Oneidas asserted their position and took aim directly at Jones before insisting on the completion: "We have asked the opinion of several eminent architects and of teachers of design. They with one voice approve of the football as the appropriate symbol on a football monument and heartily accepted by our committee but rejected by the junior member of the firm.... We respectfully ask your committee to give us an order to complete the monument.... A Football Monument without a pigskin, the acknowledged symbol of the game, is not to be considered."[41] After some name-dropping, stating that the monument inscription had been "improved and approved by Dr. Charles W. Eliot, Dr. Henry P. Walcott, and Bishop William Lawrence," the Oneidas complained that Jones had refused to carve the football unless enclosed in a circle and tried to force a "mortuary wreath" upon them, likening the architect's designs to a "masonic design, or a geometrical problem."

The wreath that was initially perceived as a crown had now become macabre, and the surviving Oneidas certainly did not want to be buried prematurely, at least not before writing their page of history. A series of exchanges by letter and in person ensued in July and August, with Parker informing the Oneidas that the city's art commission had voted on the measure. The city agreed that if a football were shown on the original approved plans, then it "should be completed in that detail."[42] Parker worked his magic, and despite Jones's insistence in supervising the football carving and opposition to the design submitted by the Oneidas, a solution was found to complete the monument while safeguarding the designer's rights not to see his work altered without his consent and approval.[43] Scudder had used a different tone in his personal communication with Parker, perhaps realizing that the Oneidas' letter in June went beyond the standards of Boston socialite decorum. He wrote to Parker expressing his appreciation for "attending to [his] ridiculously unimportant affair from the point of view of [Parker's] august Commission" and recognizing Parker's absolute authority "over all works of art belonging to the city."[44] Conscious of having plunged Parker into a "tempest in a teapot," Scudder agreed that Jones should prepare the carving design, giving the original designer the final say and the Oneidas their football carved by a young sculptor and Harvard alumnus, Joseph Coletti.[45]

But Scudder may also have been playing behind the scenes through his social connections in institutions like the Union Club, whose west facade faced his old playground of Boston Common.[46] Nonetheless, there appears to have been no love lost between Scudder and Jones, as evidenced by the latter's lassitude. In closing the saga, Jones's letter to Parker finalized the details, and the architect signed with irritation, "I sincerely hope that this will be the end of the whole dam [sic] thing"—a copy of which was sent to Scudder.[47] Indeed, it seems that the Oneidas' threat to hold off payment was in earnest and had been effective. Nearly a year after the unveiling, and incidentally on "Walter Camp Day," Lovett cut two checks now that the oval ball had finally been carved—one for Jones's firm for a hefty $1,742.16 and the other to Coletti for seventy-five dollars.[48] As Coletti finished the carving, Scudder wrote Parker saying that thanks to his "kind and vigorous intervention, the red-haired gentleman has succumbed at last and the football is engraved on the monument."[49] That same day, October 18, 1926, Means Lawrence deposited a document in the Massachusetts Historical Society, whose extended list of club members honored a total of fifty-two Oneidas. The typescript entitled *An Historical Sketch of the Oneida Football Club of Boston 1862–1865*, edited and written by Scudder, ended with a mention of the Camp colonnade project—the subscriptions still ongoing—and the possible commemoration of the 1869 Rutgers-Princeton match, before closing with a poem by Lovett. Scudder's conscious construction of a narrative that began with old Boston's first football team in the 1860s and concluded with the colleges through reference to Walter Camp and the first Rutgers-Princeton game placed the Oneidas as obvious genitors of the American collegiate game.[50] In their minds, the connections between the commemoration of the Oneida Club and those of Camp and Rutgers-Princeton illustrate how conscious they were about competing claims to footballing paternity.

At last, one would think the Oneidas could finally rest. They had their monument, had newspaper glory as the founding football team, and had managed to claim first place in the commemoration race, planting their flag in the ground on the most important public space in the city that birthed American liberty. And they did so before Yale's Camp colonnade and Harvard's Haughton memorial, neither completed until 1927.[51] Scudder, however, could not quite let go yet and wrote again to Parker a few months later, visibly consternated about the state of the ground around the monument, which "looks like an Irishman's back yard," and expressed, "We Oneidas would like to do something to overcome this."[52] In suggesting Coletti again for the work, Scudder could not help himself in adding his pleasure about learning that Jones was pleased with the end result. Scudder subsequently explained the source of the problem they wished to prevent: "small boys wiping their feet on the monument."[53] Parker appears to have acquiesced, and by Christmas Lovett wrote to Miller to say, "[The] outlook now seems good for a railing about the monument . . . and I shall be glad to see it, at last, <u>finished</u>."[54]

One can read the situation with irony bordering on the sardonic: *Old* Boston Boys complaining about *young* Boston boys wiping their feet on a monument erected to commemorate the *same* adventurous foolhardy boyishness on

Boston Common. The old Oneidas perhaps forgot that, before and after wiping their feet on the monument, the younger generation Scudder denounced was probably using the space on the Common to play. Indeed, Lovett had reminded his readers in *Old Boston Boys* that the Common was "the only playground in Boston to which we had access," a situation not dissimilar to the 1920s city-dwelling boys criticized by Scudder.[55] After all, the Oneidas had built a monument in a *public* park. One might argue that those young Boston boys were just following the example of the Old Boston Boys.

Indeed, why all the fuss? After all, it was just a granite tablet in a public park. Of course, it was specially carved with a ball and a few names mentioning boyhood games. But the monument was, of course, far more than that. The stone had meaning, at least for the Oneidas. Yes, Peabody had attempted to de-emphasize the monument's importance in his address at the unveiling in 1925, but his speech did not stop there. In fact, the theologian compared the Oneidas to the young rebels of the Revolution and concluded with a mention of the Civil War. Peabody also referred to the well-known Boston story of local schoolboys who, according to legend, had confronted British general Gage in 1775, whose reply was "It is impossible to beat the notion of liberty out of these people, for it is rooted in them from childhood."[56] Then Peabody concluded grandly,

> If we may associate small events with great ones, the schoolboys of 1862 playing their games, with the young rebels of 1775 defending their coasts, may we not hope that as future generations pass this modest stone, they may say: "It is impossible to beat the notion of honorable sportsmanship out of Boston boys, for it was rooted in them on this spot more than 60 years ago."? . . . Does the Statue of Liberty [referring to the Sailors and Soldiers monument to Boston's Civil War dead a stone's throw from the Oneida tablet] which crowns it persistently turn its back on this little stone which records no martial glory, or may we fancy that the stately figure inclines its head a little this morning and smiles with gentle approval as it sees at its feet this simple record of the friendly games so long and so lovingly remembered by some Boston boys?[57]

In Bussy's original article from 1923—the one that sparked the Oneidas' commemorative endeavors—had the editor not praised the "revolutionary spirit" of a small Rugby boy?[58] Whether or not Peabody had this in mind, his parallel with liberty—the quintessence of Boston independence, omnipresent in all the SPNEA preservation and Pilgrim tercentenary celebrations the prior years—closed the circle nicely.

As in 1923 with the school plaque, the Oneidas played down the unveiling to some extent and cannot be held responsible for the exaggerations of the press. However, commissioning a monument on the most prominent space in one of the country's oldest cities about a purportedly insignificant event and then insisting on its *un*importance in a series of *public* speeches syndicated nationally by newspapers might raise a few eyebrows. Clearly, the monument had a great deal of meaning for the surviving Oneidas, as testified by Scudder's letter to Lovett on the day the football was finally carved. Addressed to Jim and his only daughter Alice, who had been one of the two women to unveil the monument the year before, one can almost hear the emotion as Scudder completed his mission a year after the monument's unveiling: "Your humble servant has now entered the class of loafers and is taking the four o'clock train to join his long lost wife in New York at the Seville. . . . After three years of strenuous work, with my chief occupation in life gone, I feel like a lost soul."[59] Scudder had indeed been the principal laborer behind the scenes. He was largely responsible for taking the Oneidas beyond the intimate confines of just honoring friends to the public realm of commemoration for posterity. The four others had credited Scudder directly for the accomplishments in a letter of pure laud for their friend. Indeed, it was Win, after a "random remark concerning an old football," who was truly responsible for bringing the old ball down from Miller's home in Peterboro, New York, to the SPNEA in Boston in 1922.[60] According to the letter from Miller, Arnold, Lovett, and Means Lawrence, it was Scudder who was behind the tablet in 1923. It was he, editor by profession, who had prepared the subsequent tribute, *An Appreciation* of Miller in 1924, and even commissioned the bronze school medals to be produced in France for the occasion. In thanks, Miller, Arnold, Lovett, and Means Lawrence gifted Scudder a gold watch fob of a football and seal in Russian lapis lazuli.[61] The four friends expressed their admiration for Scudder's "astonishing 'touchdown,' the ambitious (not to say audacious) project to erect, on the 'Sacred Soil' of Boston Common, a monument whereby to inform the world where the first games of organized football in the United States were played."[62]

So in what was truly a monumental moment for them, the Oneidas had succeeded in recording their own historical significance as an ode to their friendship. Despite scoring their touchdown, the Oneida story did not immediately oust Camp as the legitimate father of football in the historical record. The books published following the monument unveiling revealed just how local the Oneida story was. If Alex Weyand's nearly five-hundred-page football history included a first-ever historiographical mention of Miller and Dixwell's, Harford Powel Jr.'s extensive tribute to the great Yale coach traced football history to its origins from Rugby School not to Boston but to Camp's alma mater, one of the oldest American schools still operating: Hopkins.[63] Indeed, Camp's memory was omnipresent, and the fall of 1926 the coach was honored nationally with "Walter Camp Day" celebrated by over two hundred universities at more than one hundred games around the country, showing the reach of the "Nestor of American Football" in the national sporting consciousness.[64] Such was Camp's dominance that a fortnight before Christmas 1926, the *New York Times* printed an article in its Sunday edition entitled "The Famous Oneidas" beginning with the question: "Outside of Boston how many know that Gerrit Smith Miller invented modern football?"[65]

The *New York Times* was right. Few outside of Boston knew. Immediately following the monument unveiling, the Oneida story was hardly ubiquitous and still remained mostly a Boston tale, only picked up occasionally—for example, by the University of Chicago's Amos Alonso Stagg in his 1927 *Touchdown* book but not in later publications like Herbert Manchester's impressive *Four Centuries of Sport in America* or John Da Grosa's fascinating genealogical tree of the origins of football.[66] The summer of 1927 saw the Camp Memorial construction begin, and Yale University announced in its official press release that the former coach was "known wherever the game is played as the 'Father of American Football.'"[67] So even if the Oneidas' story was gaining traction beyond their own circles through the occasional press mention and budding historiography, the narrative was often abridged and did not necessarily link to the grand list of Brahmin names carefully noted by Scudder in *An Historical Sketch*.[68]

As the remaining Oneidas passed away, they lingered in the shadow of Camp, whose paternity of football was unquestioned nationally. It was not helpful to the Oneidas' case that their story was rarely remembered at their deaths. Between 1929 and 1932 nine Oneidas from the extended list passed on. None had died since William Sturgis Bigelow in 1926, but those three years between the Great Crash and 1932 were brutal for the club. Yet of all the necrologies, the only ones to link to the Oneidas were for Scudder, the great orchestrator of their commemoration, with his multiple obituaries in Boston and New York recalling the art editor as a "football pioneer" and an "original member of America's first football club."[69] Strangely, not even the grand yachtsman Walter Burgess, whose obit included a lengthy three-column account of his sporting past, or William Channing Ellery Eustis—whose baseball background was highlighted—were ever presented by the press as members of the Oneida Club.[70]

In these years, the newspapers may have forgotten to name the club, but among themselves the fading Oneidas continued to remember. The remaining Oneidas who were the closest continued to see one another, and Lovett recounted his teatime visits to see Frank Peabody and Bob Means Lawrence, underscoring in November 1931 that "these meetings of the old boys cannot occur too often. The number of the Oneidas is narrowing down but, glory be, there are a few kicks yet left in the old toes of Billy, Bob, Gat, Jim and Ned and Frank."[71] Lovett opened his next letter to Miller a week later with the words "just six years yesterday the monument was unveiled on the Common."[72] Indeed, from 1932 to 1935 there was enough life left for them to enjoy the hospitality of friendly visits and even savoring an occasional lobster.[73] Over the period, Lovett and Miller spent weeks together in Peterboro at the Miller homestead. When Lovett was in Boston, the two regularly wrote to each other about listening to games on the radio, praising how "Harvard—Yale was a great one . . . Notre Dame—Army the most sensational!" and commenting that Babe Ruth's Depression pay decrease "should cut a little deeper."[74]

It was a time for final reminiscences. In his ninetieth year, Lovett wrote memoirs of his childhood days and family life at his old Beacon Hill home. He wrote them not for his own grandchildren—he had none—but for others in the family who "may like to read about the little boy who laughed and cried and played and went to school, so many years ago."[75] Oddly, in his forty-six-page family history, he never once mentioned the Oneidas nor his baseball prowess. Perhaps the story was sufficiently told, simply not that important anymore, or perhaps Lovett was staying true to his reputation of great humility. The press, however, was interested in stories like his. *Boston Evening Transcript* sportswriter George C. Carens penned a lengthy piece in his column "The Pulse," which appeared on Lovett's birthday, equating him to a combined Babe Ruth and Freddy Frankhouse and calling the nonagenarian the "link between prehistoric and modern days in Boston sports annals."[76] The article even included a photo of the famous Oneida ball, promoted the *Old Boston*

Boys book, named Lovett as a "pioneer in America's present national games," and erroneously gave him credit *primus inter pares* in the founding of the Oneida Club.[77]

The year 1935 was hard as Lovett noted that the "circle of old boys is growing smaller." In March he wrote to inform Miller, "Our good old friend, Bob [Means Lawrence], is <u>very</u> ill and not expected to live," and he called an equally ailing Edward Arnold to inform him as well.[78] It was to be Lovett's last call with old Ned, and within two days both Bob and Ned were gone. Lovett wrote again to Peterboro to encourage Gat "to stand closer than ever shoulder to shoulder and so close the gaps in our little circle made by the passing of our two loved old boys, Bob and Ned."[79] When the obituaries appeared for Means Lawrence, one of the two Boston papers highlighted the Oneida story, which was the first such mention—aside from Scudder—in the club's collective necrology.[80]

The summer of 1935 was Miller and Lovett's last meeting. Longing for the flavor of the Peterboro raspberries, Lovett sent a postcard featuring the Harvard football stadium, a retrospectively symbolic piece of final correspondence before his trip to upstate New York in mid-August.[81] After a several-week visit, the ninety-one-year-old Lovett returned home and passed on September 29. His last letter to Miller was equally emblematic, beginning with his customary "dear old teammate" salutation, and recounted the visit of Scudder's grandson, Teddy, with whom he "spoke enthusiastically of our wonderful 'come back' and of Win and the old Oneida team days."[82] Lovett did not live to see the opening of the Harvard football season or the 1935 World Series. In contrast to some of his more illustrious teammates, it is telling that his death was largely just local news. The media stressed his role in football—enshrined in a public monument—more than his baseball prowess and certainly more than any other life achievements.[83] Both Boston obituaries underlined the sporting pedigree for the "ruddy-faced supple old gentleman" with the *Boston Herald* headline mentioning that he "Was in [the] First Recorded Game in America."[84]

By the fall of 1936, only four Oneidas were still living, including the last two remaining monument men—Frank Peabody and Gat Miller. Lovett had regularly mentioned Peabody in his letters to Miller, but the scope of the Peabody-Miller friendship remains unknown, as there does not appear to be an archival record of correspondence between the two.[85] The Harvard professor was the first to die in December 1936, a few months before Miller. As widely recognized individuals, both their deaths were regional news, but the Oneida football link was tenuous at best. Peabody was remembered in the press for his leading role in intellectual life and for having transformed religious study and ethics at Harvard—and also credited for abolishing mandatory chapel attendance.[86] Boston did not remember him as a footballer. Similarly silent on any Oneida link, the *New York Times* did, however, highlight the emeritus professor's baseball pedigree as "the first man who ever went to bat against Yale."[87] Miller's death in 1937 also made national news and was picked up as far away as Chicago. Yet it was only in Boston where his obituary headline included the bold claim of his being the father of football in the US. Elsewhere the accent was placed on his cattle breeding and abolitionist family heritage. Even Miller's lengthy obituary in the New York Historical Association's *Review* was essentially uninterested in his football links.[88]

In the years surrounding the passing of the last Oneidas, the press chose to pick up (or not) the Boston story and its characters in different ways, most often illustrating the local flavor of yet another in the city's long list of firsts. But since the true national football story had been settled with Camp's demise and before the stone tablet on Boston Common could have much influence, most of the country's papers were uninterested in parochial obituaries discussing another Boston first. By the 1930s, a grand narrative had already emerged in the books and popular histories that credited the colleges with the game and honored Camp as the father of the sport. So even in their lifetimes, the Oneida "monument men" were never really recognized as such beyond the periphery of Boston or the rare, syndicated news story. At least at the city level, the story still carried weight.

Beantown's papers had reported extensively on the Oneida tablet and monument events of the mid-1920s, and when the opportune moment arrived, they recycled Boston's foundational story. Sometimes, these were prompted by personal contributions or reflections—as in the case of the focus of Lovett's ninetieth birthday—or a more corporate interest. To wit, in the weeks after Lovett's death in 1935, the city's First National Bank of Boston took out a half-page tribute featuring a yet-to-be-seen lithograph of the Oneidas playing on Boston Common and a photograph of Harvard stadium (see image 5). Honoring "America's first football team," the piece referred to the contemporary collegiate football phenomenon and told a brief story of the club—albeit without mentioning any individual names—thanks to which "Boston saw the beginning of it all!"[89]

IMAGE 5. A lithograph of the Oneidas playing on Boston Common that featured in a newspaper advertisement for the First National Bank of Boston and appeared in the *Boston Evening Transcript* and other local newspapers on November 21, 1935. Courtesy of Revolutionary Spaces.

But to influence the nationally established narrative, it would take more than just local newspaper advertisements, a city monument, and some printed memoirs. Entry into the historical canon is a laborious, organic, and desultory process, which generally occurs postmortem. In the case of the Oneidas, their story took on a life of its own after the monument men had passed on having left their mark not only in stone but also in ink—through Lovett's *Old Boston Boys* and Scudder's short publications on Miller in 1924 and the club in 1926, both deposited in historical societies, archives, and university libraries. Since the turn of the century, the narratives in earlier football books had either ignored the Oneidas entirely or quickly waved at them in their passing parade of factual but unimportant figures. It was not until Francis Peabody Magoun's 1938 attempt at a revised and definitive history that the Oneidas were finally given prominence and grafted onto the historical record.

While not as lengthy as previous publications, Magoun's *History of Football—from the Beginnings to 1871* was unquestionably the most scholarly to date and included footnotes to Scudder's *An Historical Sketch* and Lovett's *Old Boston Boys*.[90] Unsurprisingly, the philologist and literature professor—a Harvard man through and through and, most importantly, also a Nobles alum—highlighted the importance of the Dixwell boys and the contribution of the Oneidas.[91] Despite no apparent relation to his Oneida Peabody namesake, Magoun credited the Boston boys for some of the genesis of the modern football phenomenon.[92] Intriguingly, Magoun's book was written in English but released by a German publisher. As such, it is unclear how widely available this book was in Boston, New York, or even London.

For the Oneida story, the relevance of the archive was evident. The power of the press influences popular memory, but the archive does not speak at the same pace nor necessarily to the same audience. If the press had seized on the newsworthiness of the untimely death of Walter Camp, it was a nation of journalists and editors working with the power of syndication who were able to inform popular history around the "father of American football." Rankean historical empiricism, narrative, and the explosion of the preservationist movement—so evident in the Boston institutions where the Oneidas carefully deposited the record of their club—meant that the impact of Scudder and his teammates' act of preservation did not *become* history until the academy began to mine those preserved archives. When Rhea published his comprehensive history of sport and leisure in 1940 and referred to Scudder's typescript on the Oneidas from the Massachusetts Historical Society, he did so without any reference to Magoun's book.[93]

With the arrival of new scholarly work on the history of sport, the Oneida story was moving from the worlds of memory and news into the historical canon. After the 1920s, the monument on the Common became evidence of memory and fact corroborated in an archival document (Scudder's *An Historical Sketch*) and a published book (Lovett's *Old Boston Boys*) that could be now reconstructed as a historical account. The work by Magoun and Rhea, completed in a more academic setting, illustrates how the uncovered archive corroborated the printer's word and triangulated the mason's monument. But academic history did less to spread knowledge than its popular cousin, which was aimed at a broader readership. In the same year that Rhea's book was released, Dean Hill, the captain of the 1910 Georgia Tech team, published a wonderfully illustrated book on the history of football, which benefited from powerful endorsement and promotion.[94] Beginning with the tale of Webb Ellis, Hill anchored the American narrative in the 1869 Princeton-Rutgers "first" college football game before passing to the omnipresent role of the "father of football" personified in photos of the Walter Camp memorial colonnade at Yale.[95] Hill also made swift teleological work of the fact that the early games were a "running, kicking, continuous game with no holding of the ball, and played under mixed rules agreed upon just before the start of the game" and noting how the round rubber ball had yet to evolve into the modern pigskin.[96] The states outside the Northeast featured prominently in Hill's book, demonstrating how national the sport had become by then. Moreover, the author was anything but a Boston boy, having attended Phillips Exeter in New Hampshire, and then college in the Old South. Unsurprisingly then, the Boston Oneida story and monument were entirely absent from his book, which placed the emphasis on the sport as a national collegiate game, not an Ivy League one, and even less about Beantown.

While a successful city legend, it was almost as if the Oneida story could not break through its local perimeter and shine nationally beyond ephemeral moments of obituary fame. Seeing the Oneidas as an essential piece of the *national* sporting foundation story had not materialized. With two of the extended list of Oneidas still alive in 1940—Bishop Lawrence and Henry Richards—perhaps their story was just too incarnate. As evidenced by Camp, one must generally die to begin a new life in legend. On November 6,

1941, the eve of the seventy-eighth anniversary of that famous Oneida match inscribed on the ball, the bishop passed the celestial goal line at the age of ninety-one. The death of the Episcopal clergyman was front-page news in Boston, reported as far as Atlanta.[97] The "Banker Bishop's" two-column obituary in the *New York Times* dwarfed even that of infamous former impeached New York governor William Sulzer, which appeared in the next column.[98] Among the 1,500 gathered to pay their respects at his funeral were Massachusetts Governor Saltonstall and banker J. P. Morgan. But at his death, Lawrence's sporting pedigree went unremembered, its presumable insignificance drowned in a litany of more illustrious deeds, accolades, and memberships. Even the juxtaposition of the front-page funeral announcement under the headline "Harvard Upsets Army" had offered a perfect opportunity to link football to the bishop, but the Oneida Football Club featured nowhere.[99]

The last Oneida, Henry Richards, lived another eight years, and in club tradition, his death in Maine was news back in Boston and as far as New York. As the oldest living MIT graduate and second-oldest Harvard alum, the centenarian was newsworthy just on that alone. The obituaries recounted his Dixwell studies, various public offices, and professional accomplishments but once again were mute as to that youthful club on Boston Common.[100] With Richards's passing, all the Oneidas from Scudder's 1926 list were gone. Perhaps it was fitting that the last man standing was the one with the deepest direct connections to the football origins debate through his two brothers' time as students at Webb Ellis's illustrious school.[101]

With Lawrence and Richards's deaths, the last living link to the Oneidas was gone, along with a connection to the football of bygone days, both in Boston and all the way back to Rugby. Their passing left their story, their artifacts, and the developing narrative in the unpredictable hands of posterity. What might happen to their story? Their fame as inventors of football was short-lived and, until then, often only attributed to three or four of the already small band of monument men. Still, the Oneida gridiron team had taken the lead in the match for the history of football codes, gaining a place on the podium of origins as a city legend. The Oneidas had run their last play—a tactical memoir erected in stone—and now looking down from above they were surely convinced that the game was over. Indeed, few team sports have tamed time as much as American football. Already by the turn of the twentieth century, the obsession of a modern scientific approach had established total control over the now sixty-minute clock.[102] There was no mystery to the length of a game, and the final play was just that. Except that the other football, the round association one, had a quite different approach to time, handing the referee enormous discretionary power. In 1921, just before the Oneidas began their commemorative endeavors, the International Football Association Board (IFAB) had granted referees the ability to extend the game to account for lost time, an almost divine intangible supremacy on the life of a football match.[103] Amazing things can happen in added time, altering the history of football, even a final result so certain that it appears graven in stone.

PART III
THE STEAL AND THE HOAX

9

THE SOCCER GRAB

Surprise Legacies, Halls of Fame, and Refurbishing a Usable Past

> Somehow when that full story is told, the modest Oneida monument seems scarcely enough. There ought to be a big one over in the middle somewhere to "The Boys of Old Boston who Made This Their Playing Field And Who Here Set The Pattern Of American Manhood Through Individual Competition, Loyal Team Work, Mutual Respect And Fair Play."
>
> —*Boston Sunday Herald*, June 1948

> The First National Bank of Boston gave a boost to soccer with its promotional piece... It was in the form of a blotter which depicted a scene in color of the first soccer football team in the US which was organized in 1862 in the Bean City. It was known as the Oneida Football Club.... Following efforts from this corner, the bank officials agreed to permit soccer clubs to reproduce the drawing for other promotional pieces.
>
> —*Long Island Star Journal*, December 1948

Two quotes diverged at the printing press. In 1948, the words of two sportswriters revealed contrasting possibilities for the Oneida legacy. Well-known national sports journalist Bill Cunningham profiled the club in a lengthy front-page piece in the evening edition of the *Boston Sunday Herald*.[1] Cunningham gave significant credit to the deceased Lovett and his still-living daughter Alice, referring often to passages in *Old Boston Boys*, including an abridged list of names from Scudder's *An Historical Sketch*, before closing with an ambitious call for further recognition. But six months later and two hundred miles down the coast, national soccer expert Milt Miller introduced, either unwittingly or deliberately, an unexpected turn to the club's legacy. In his regular "Soccer Shots" column, Miller reacted to a new drawing of the Oneidas kicking a round ball and drew the natural conclusion that this was the origin of the association game in America and finally gave Boston its place in the timeline.[2] Where before only existed the calculated and playful quest to be remembered as the founders of American football, there now appeared a sudden vision of the Oneidas as initiators of the kicking game. Milt Miller's fleeting comment had sown a seed for a new Oneida history.

Becoming history is not a straightforward or predestined process and the path is fraught with missed opportunities and surprises. At this point, the Boston schoolboy story was not fully visible, ever taking umbrage of Camp's national shadow, and had yet to become the precollege historical reference par excellence. To wit, not even Morris Bealle's lengthy ode to Harvard football, which contributed significantly to the collegiate football historiography in 1948, included a mention of the Oneida boys as precursors of the great Crimson tradition.[3] If any book ought to have included the old Boston story, one would have expected the freshly published Harvard history to do so. Just as anniversaries had played an important role in stimulating the school tablet in 1923, new opportunities for recognition beckoned to the Oneidas.

Projecting their postmortem prominence onto the stage of national interest, in the persona of their captain Gerrit S. Miller, was the 1949 anniversary talk (around the 1869 Rutgers-Princeton match) regarding the creation of an American football hall of fame. Two cities were considered by the newly created National Football Shrine and Hall of Fame: New Brunswick, New Jersey, and Cazenovia, New York. The former was the home to Rutgers University; the latter was Miller's hometown and not far from Cooperstown, New York, which already hosted baseball's hall of fame (opened in 1939).[4] In the end, Cazenovia eventually lost to New Brunswick, even if the actual building project was postponed, and so New Brunswick won little else than housing some paperwork and archives. Perhaps the small upstate New York town was too provincial and far away from Harvard to benefit from powerful alumni support. Nevertheless, the fact that Miller and his club were front-page sporting news—syndicated by the Associated Press across the country—as a nominee for a national hall of fame actually illustrated how far their usable past had

The Soccer Grab

come as an essential foundation narrative.[5] Legendary and legitimate enough to vie to host the sport's hall of fame, the name of the Oneidas was finally whispered by the winds of history, and national fame beckoned at their doorstep.

Incidentally, in the months that followed the Oneidas' national spotlight moment, a series of ostensibly unrelated events occurred in Philadelphia, Boston, and as far away as Brazil, which cleared an unexpected path off the Oneida's self-constructed walk of fame. Indeed, halls of fame were fashionable, and in the Quaker capital, the still fresh Philadelphia Old Timers Association decided to create a shrine celebrating the city's football history.[6] But this was football of the association kind, not gridiron. Fifteen individuals were honored, and an extended twenty-nine were recognized on February 26, 1950, at the Lighthouse Club. No more national a memorializing process than the Oneida's initial efforts in the 1920s, the Philadelphia soccer endeavor was first and foremost a local one, not immediately endorsed by the national governing body, the United States Soccer Football Association (USSFA).[7] The federation, which had existed since 1913, was enthusiastically preparing for its first World Cup appearance since 1934. For the US team, the 1950 tournament in Brazil was a mitigated success. Finishing last of their group on goal difference, they did, however, manage to upset the historically great English. In federation's player selection committee chairman Fred Netto's words, "In defeating England, the kings of football, we accomplished an unbelievable victory."[8] This result became an essential reference point on the American soccer timeline for years to come. In an effort to preserve the moment, the round ball from the match was proudly displayed at the USSFA's offices on Fifth Avenue, New York City.[9] Balls are important artifacts; their shape is not an insignificant matter.

While the American soccer community continued to bask in the glory of the victory in Brazil, the Oneida legacy continued in Boston. In June of 1951, Noble and Greenough once again awarded their annual James D'Wolf Lovett Baseball and Gerrit Smith Miller Scholarship and Athletics medals. Their names were better preserved on the school medals and intramural clubs than they had been in stone, however.[10] A few weeks after the school ceremony, Arthur J. O'Keefe, the secretary of the city's Park Department, wrote to the Boston Art Commission informing them that the Oneida's stone monument needed repair. O'Keefe began by noting that the William Lloyd Garrison statue—erected in 1886—needed gold lettering and then called attention to the unreadable inscription on the monument to the "First

Football Team" underling that "Professor Peabody of Harvard was one member of that team."[11] The letter has a handwritten note dated two days later: "Have to do something about it." Indeed, it seems that name-dropping still worked, and within a few weeks a quote from John Evans and Co. was submitted and quickly approved.[12] The Oneidas were fortunate that erosion was their only enemy and that the Brahmin pen was mighty enough to preserve their stone.

On the eve of the annual Yale-Harvard game in November 1951, the Harvard spirit moved in mysterious ways, using Boston paint to taint Camp's colossal legacy. Some overzealous Harvard students smeared crimson paint in the shape of the letter H across the columns of the Walter Camp Memorial Gateway. The Yale athletics director shamed the individuals, pointing out that the colonnade in New Haven was "a national football memorial."[13] It was suggested that sandblasting might be necessary to remove the graffiti.[14] Back in Boston, the restoration of the Oneidas' memorial was simpler. Three days later, the stone had been recut and the inscription restored.[15]

As the Oneidas watched on from above, reassured that their monument would remind passersby of their gridiron legacy for years to come, the seed of Milt Miller's 1948 soccer claim found fertile enough ground for the story to sprout a narrative parallel to the American football one. Firstly, and not unlike the Boston story, another locally inspired movement to honor a sport's legacy was given national orientation, though this time it was for the round ball in that other parallel sporting universe. At their annual meeting in 1953—on their fortieth anniversary—the USSFA voted to endorse the hall of fame created in Philadelphia.[16] Like its gridiron cousin, the soccer hall of fame did not yet have a physical home, but the foundations were laid with a now national annual dinner and awards ceremony to celebrate the kicking game's history in America.

But just how old was that game, and when did its history begin on American shores? In its first hall of fame class of 1950, the Philadelphia Old Timers' association had inducted Dr. Gus Randolph Manning, US soccer's first president in 1913. Manning served the national federation until his death at age seventy-nine in 1953. Having been dubbed the "Father of Organized Soccer," history clearly began with him, at least in the eyes of the 1950s American soccer community.[17] However strong his aura was, ten years had passed when the USSFA approached its golden anniversary and some had begun to reflect beyond living memory. Sam Foulds, a US immigrant born in Canada of English parentage, had taken interest not only in playing, coaching and administrating the sport in Massachusetts but also in its history. He attended the fiftieth annual meeting of the USSFA in 1963 and spoke during the discussion about juniors and promotion of the game. He urged the national body that more needed to be done to promote the game to the average American who did not know that "we have had soccer in the United States since colonial times.... In Boston, in 1862 we had the first organized soccer team.... If you want to go to Otis Harrison Grey House, you can see the ball used, a circular ball made of rubber with a canvas cover.... We have roots in soccer before our so-called college football, before basketball, before hockey."[18]

Yet where had Foulds learned of this round ball? It is possible that he simply discovered the ball on a visit to Otis House. Foulds made no mention of the monument and its pigskin-shaped carved ball or Milt Miller's 1948 article but only of the Oneidas' round rubber artifact in the SPNEA. The monument was on the city list of monuments in 1961 but without any mention of the ball graven in stone.[19] Alternatively, he might have read about the Oneidas the year before in the 1962–63 USSFA annual citing the widely circulated US soccer periodical *Soccer News*. The annual reprinted the image used on the First National Bank of Boston ink blotter spotted by Milt Miller in 1948, which illustrated the Oneidas playing what appeared to be a kicking game (see image 6).[20] Aside from the one-off 1948 mention, the USSFA annual appears to be the earliest other written connection between soccer and the Oneidas. The federation's rulebook from 1960 had included an intriguing timeline with key soccer milestones going back to 1609 (the same reference to Henry Spellman's *Relation of Virginia* uncovered by Parke Davis in his 1911 football history), but nothing about the Oneidas or their founding date of 1862. Had the link been common knowledge in 1960, then presumably it ought to have appeared in the detailed list that included two other key entries for 1862—the banning of football at Harvard and Yale and the publishing of Thring's rules.[21] By the fiftieth anniversary of the national soccer federation, two of soccer's leading writers of the era, Miller and Bill Graham, had sufficiently relayed the usable Oneida story for individuals like Sam Foulds searching for the game's forgotten American ancestry.

The years from 1962 to 1963 appear as a turning point in the Oneida link to soccer. Not only were they cited officially in the USSFA institutional world but one of the first PhD dissertations was written entirely about American soccer. Defended by Robert Charles Baptista on the topic of intercollegiate soccer,

A CENTURY AGO — WHO NEEDS RULES?

Soccer News Picture
The first soccer team in the United States, according to a release from the First National Bank of Boston, Mass, was organized in Boston in 1862. Known as the Oneida Football Club and made up of boys who played informally in school it met all comers on its own field on Boston Common. For three years its goals line was never crossed. A red handkerchief sufficed for a uniform. Above is an artist's conception of the game as played in those days.

22

IMAGE 6. As soccer grew in popularity in the United States in the post–Second World War era, the national association sought to claim a long history for the game. The depiction of the Oneidas playing in the 1860s features the round ball and is explicitly claimed as being a game of soccer. Courtesy of the Society for American Soccer History.

the Wheaton College (Illinois) instructor and coach had made a number of research trips to the East Coast, though none to Boston. However, he still found and referenced Lovett's *Old Boston Boys* and Scudder's *An Historical Sketch*. Baptista described the Oneidas, whose "variation of football" mixed kicking and handling and "would profoundly influence the college game."[22] He walked a thin line of not explicitly labeling the Oneida game as soccer per se. His description of the Boston Game prefaced a longer treatment of early intercollegiate football, each match another step in codifying the rules, following more closely those of the English Football Association and only ending with the infamous Harvard-McGill matches of 1874. Yet he still named that period until the early college games of the 1870s "the eclipse of soccer."[23] Thus, for Baptista, the Oneidas were implicitly part of an earlier soccer-style tradition that died out in the universities after the early 1870s. Drawing such a link between the Oneidas and association football was a vastly different claim than the Oneidas' original one. It also reveals how the archive is an omphalos for the reconstruction of history. Had the Oneidas not written, preserved, and deposited records of themselves, later scholars like Baptista would never have been able to infer such a link.

Admittedly, the Oneidas served as a convenient placeholder between the early mob football on campuses banned by university faculties by the 1860s and the revival period with all its rule adjustments from 1869 to 1876. But only the Oneidas appeared in the official timeline during the intervening years with no other clubs or teams. So how should one interpret their brief parenthesis? On the one hand, bronze tablets, stone monuments, ceremonies, and select memoirs from the 1920s remembered them as an ostensive preface to the intercollegiate game—a foundational position for which Gat Miller's home of Cazenovia had almost managed to be crowned the hall of fame in 1949. On the other, Baptista seemed to suggest otherwise, altering, or at least questioning, the Oneidas' paternity. The soccer scholar's claim rested on one text published just a decade prior—becoming the standard football history book—and whose ambiguity toward the Oneidas would influence their legacy.

Allison Danzig's *The History of American Football: Its Great Teams, Players, and Coaches*, printed by educational publisher Prentice Hall, was released in 1956. The widely published sports journalist began his book not with football but with a contumelious critique of baseball, which had continued to believe in false origin myths. Bordered by a photo of Walter Camp with the caption "The Father of American Football," Danzig opened his account with the claim that football's history had never been concealed by a fake origin story a la Doubleday. He was unequivocal: "It is from soccer, or Association football, and Rugby that the American game of football evolved."[24] He then recounted a so-called formative period from 1609 to 1876 when the games mostly focused on kicking a ball rather than running with it. Danzig highlighted the Oneidas as the first "definite and formal football organization" in the country, quoting directly from the monument inscription. But in placing the Boston Game in this "formative period" before a stated "conversion to rugby," the Oneidas were stuck in a sort of sporting history no man's land, and Danzig was unclear on how to interpret them. He contrasted the Boston Game with the mob kicking version banned by universities at the start of the 1860s while also contrasting it to the later association style of Princeton and Rutgers. In the same breath Danzig wrote how Boston boys could run with the ball, he noted that compared to McGill's rugby rules, the Harvard game "was largely soccer." So when compared to mob football or the association game, the "Boston Game" was more rugby, but when compared to rugby, it was more soccer. For Danzig, the Boston Game was part of the pre-1876 intercollegiate era but unique enough to fall somewhere in between the soccer played in New Jersey / New York / New Haven and the rugby played in Canada. Yet Danzig's reader was still left with the impression that the Oneidas deserved credit for being sufficiently different to force the evolution toward American football and away from a kicking (soccer) game.

What mattered in Danzig's work was that it was an authoritative text (albeit not without errors), which opened a breach in the Oneida story. In their search for a national history of American soccer, Baptista and others in the 1960s saw the gap and began to ask questions and assert a new truth: that the Oneida story might reveal something behind the graven stone pigskin on the monument. If some in the American soccer community, like Foulds, had begun to affirm a long soccer history traced back to the round Oneida ball, it was far from common knowledge in 1960s soccer circles and even less known beyond this isolated sporting subculture. Throughout the Cold War and Civil Rights eras, soccer in America thrived but mostly on the margins of the cultural mainstream as the National Collegiate Athletic Association (NCAA) finally began a national university championship in 1959 and saw exceptional growth in the subsequent years.[25] While no extensive scholarly study of the history of soccer in the US had yet been written, the topic finally picked up in the academy.[26]

The Oneidas were now being identified as an origin point in the still nascent scholarly work on the kicking game. But much like the early appearance of the Oneidas in their American football timeline, it took time for the soccer story to catch on. Moreover, it had to contest with a monument to a manifest Oneida-claimed gridiron legacy. No such monument existed to help the Oneida soccer cause. This reveals the importance of the archive where Baptista had found the clubs' sources. Others like James Robinson,

The Soccer Grab

who wrote his doctoral dissertation in 1966 on his hometown city of St. Louis, mentioned the Boston boys, though without naming the Oneidas as such or citing Baptista; he discussed the traditional evolution story (classical antiquity to Webb Ellis) and a passing reference to soccer in New England.[27] Popular publications also ignored the Oneidas. John Allen's 1967 book *Soccer for Americans* and Julie Menendez and Matt Boxer's 1968 *Soccer* swept over the early history in one or two lines vaguely referring to soccer "first played in the U.S.A. as early as 1830" or "first introduced in the United States in the 1870s" but always bereft of any details.[28] This was, of course, because aside from the handful of academic studies largely unavailable to the public, the most usable history of soccer lay in living memory rather than the deliberately deposited yet discreet archive. Furthermore, in the 1960s popular imagination, soccer in America, in the words of immigrants Boxer and Menendez, was still "a foreign game to be played by foreigners."[29]

In establishing an Oneida link, soccer faced the same problem as the club's original quest to enter the gridiron historiography: theirs was first a local story largely beyond the reach of even the interested university researcher. The Oneidas had cunningly hidden the lede, obvious as it may seem in retrospect, on the stone tablet. Yet it required a detective's eye to triangulate the monument, the written archive, and the visual testimony of the ball. Indeed, even with Lovett's book and Scudder's typescript available in libraries across Boston and beyond, it took more than a passing comment at the 1963 USSFA general assembly for anyone to take notice that soccer might be traced back to Gat Miller and his companions on the Common. Even appearing in the timeline of the soccer federation's widely circulated rulebook was not enough, to say nothing of a handful of dissertation mentions that gathered more dust than public attention. To break through it would take something more, especially since soccer remained a minority in the hegemonic American sporting culture, in particular their popular histories. Moreover, the Oneida monument on Boston Common reminded passersby that theirs was an oval gridiron story, not a round soccer one, and continued to inform city journalists, like Tim Cohane and Francis Rosa of the *Boston Globe*, who recycled the old tale of the club founding American football particularly around anniversaries like the centenary of the first intercollegiate match in 1869 between Princeton and Rutgers.[30]

When soccer enthusiast Forrest Tyson completed his doctoral work a few years later, he lamented the lack of information both in popular and academic sources. While his 1976 dissertation cited Allen and Baptista several times—though without picking up the Oneidas—Tyson did include a mention of unnamed 1860s Boston schoolboys who "engaged in competitive play on the Boston Common Parade Ground."[31] Interestingly, this was not from any of the primary sources but from a locally produced and specifically targeted booklet printed by the newly founded Massachusetts Soccer Association's president, Alan Peterson. The British immigrant, an emblematic example of the parent-led youth soccer movement that was exploding in the 1970s, wrote a short booklet on the sport, including a history of the game, which clearly demonstrated he had consulted the standard histories of football.[32] Like Tyson and others, the Oneida name was not mentioned, but the Boston schoolboys are clearly one and the same. As with other references in the prior twenty years, the Oneidas and the Boston Game sit somewhat awkwardly pasted-in as the earliest appearance of soccer before the working-class British immigrants truly developed an association football culture from the 1880s onward—whose history has only recently been unearthed.[33] But yet again, there they were. In this way, the Oneida story was gradually being reshaped to serve as a new historical origin point in American soccer, and entirely unwittingly. What had changed? How was it that in the second half of the twentieth century and fifty years after their gridiron monument was erected, the memory of these Boston boys and their little round rubber ball was now being attributed to some other sport?

At the turn of the 1970s, a cultural change was afoot and about to walk unannounced over a well-manicured Oneida legacy. The period ushered in a new generation, and after years of the proverbial predictions of being the fastest growing sport since the 1910s, soccer finally began to reach across the full American cultural spectrum. For once, the prophetic calls of contemporary authors were actually right when they proclaimed "soccer will no longer be the immigrant sport" as "it is on the threshold of attaining in the United States the status and recognition it enjoys throughout the rest of the world."[34] After having ignored soccer entirely or associating it with Eastern and often Soviet Europe—"the game every Russian youngster plays"—the same *Boys' Life* magazine that extolled the emulous Miller and his club as the first football team in 1926 sensed a change and asked its scouting readership, "Can Soccer Score in America?"[35] But like an invisible tsunami, the demographic revolution birthed in the prior decade was racing toward the shore of the 1970s.

For the first time ever, so many children (girls included) were exposed to the sport in a national youth soccer boom that flooded parks and public

The Soccer Grab

fields, as a tidal wave of new organizations swept the US.[36] Amplified by the star power of Pelé's arrival in 1975 and the media attention around the New York Cosmos, soccer became legitimate mainstream news consumed by a new generation of post-Vietnam peace-loving young people. As the country celebrated its bicentennial, the ethnic moniker was finally being lifted off the sport.[37] Blinded by the glamour of the Cosmos and the omnipresent Saturday morning autumn family soccer outing, few at the time wondered whether anything had come before the grand North American Soccer League (NASL). Less important was some arcane past when the spotlight was on the big league of Pelé, Cruyff, and Beckenbauer. The NASL had finally taken soccer from its ubiquitous locally focused and grassroots ethnic sideshow to the main stage, front and center. For those who had been slaving away on the ethnic margins of American cultural relevance since the 1880s, this might have irked them. But undoubtedly many rejoiced in finally achieving some national recognition for their game. While initially only those closest to the Oneida story seemed to have heard their founding tale—especially those in Massachusetts and writing scholarly dissertations—the national spotlight and cultural paradigm shift fueled the need for historical legitimacy for a game with a supposedly rootless national past.

The whole time, the round Oneida ball had remained at Otis House, visible to any curious visitor or soccer aficionado. Sam Foulds's comment in 1963 about soccer's history going back to Boston schoolboys was not a flighty one made in passing. As one of the faithful disciples of the sport, he was intent on preserving the heritage of a game played consistently since the turn of the century in immigrant and working-class ethnic clubs and communities. Foulds set out to write a book with Paul Harris, a soccer writer and active referee with the rising American Youth Soccer Organization (AYSO) based in California. Their goal, an ambitious one, was "to settle, once and for all, the argument over America's soccer heritage."[38] Their book may also have been a response to Chuck Cascio's 1975 book *Soccer U.S.A.*, which repeatedly rehashed the game's un-Americanness, ignored the Oneidas and any early history, and mostly focused on the World Cups and the professional renaissance of 1968.[39]

When the two authors finally produced the first focused attempt at a history of soccer in America, printed in 1979, none of the Oneidas were alive to dispute how they or their game were portrayed. Foulds and Harris dedicated three pages to the Oneidas, introducing them with the following opening line: "The origin of soccer in its primitive phase is a matter of conjecture . . . [with] the answer wrapped up in the mythology of the past."[40] Though unreferenced, Foulds and Harris were faithful to the primary sources, having obviously consulted Lovett's and Scudder's accounts and the round ball visible at the museum. They recounted the Boston schoolboys' story, pulling from the original *Boston Advertiser* article in 1863, and discussed the donated ball as well as the tablet and monument. The book even has a photo of the monument, though intriguingly the authors chose the back side, where the perhaps inconvenient graven oblong ball was invisible. Admittedly, the authors did not obsess around the Oneidas as a foundational moment. But the book does position the club clearly in a soccer lineage different from the one the boys had claimed back in the 1920s.[41]

Foulds and Harris were not alone in trying to uncover American soccer's early history. Their book was part of a broader movement to preserve and uncover the game's hidden history and included the creation of a new hall of fame in upstate New York. About an hour and a half from Gerrit Smith Miller's hometown of Cazenovia lay a small town called Oneonta. The region had lost the American football hall of fame competition in 1949, but one of the local men's college soccer teams had recently won the 1977 NCAA Division I championship. This served as the impetus for a group of citizens, led by Albert Colone, the city's parks and recreation director, to build a National Soccer Hall of Fame (NSHOF) with a library and archive, gathering useful artifacts and memorabilia from all the older hall of famers inducted every year by the recently renamed USSF's continuation of the Philadelphia-driven Old Timers association.[42] Starting from an initial exhibition in 1979 at Hartwick College's Yager Museum, the NSHOF moved into the old Wilber mansion in 1981. While in a sleepy, remote town, Oneonta was only a thirty-minute drive from Cooperstown, where baseball's hall of fame drew hundreds of thousands of visitors annually, a key part of the soccer hall's initial business plan. Within two years, the project received the USSF's official blessing and a New York State educational charter.[43]

As interest in soccer history began to take off, the Oneidas were only a distant relative in the genealogy of the game. With late 1970s soccer booming under the lights of NASL primetime, journalist Zander Hollander released his extensive 1980 *American Encyclopedia of Soccer*. Notwithstanding an absence of specific references, it was the first compendium of its kind and included a germane entry for the Oneida cousins placing their game with its "features of soccer and rugby" in the historical evolution of American soccer.[44] Despite their inclusion in Hollander's *Encyclopedia*, there did not appear to be any doubt in Foulds's mind about who the "Grand Old Man of soccer" history was. In an editorial a few months after Hollander's book was released, Foulds proclaimed "Elder Statesman" Gus Manning—elected to its hall of fame in 1950—as the "true 'Founding Father'" of American soccer.[45] Because the kicking game already had a founding father with the initials G.M., this newly unearthed G.M. (Gerrit S. Miller) was nothing more than a prehistoric reference point in a new national origin story still live in its construction.

At the start of the 1980s, the NASL pro league was on its last legs, and it folded following its 1984 season. It became yet another entry under defunct American professional soccer leagues in the sport encyclopedias of which now soccer had its own.[46] Notwithstanding the growth both across the youth sector and through the fleeting professional NASL medium, soccer had not succeeded in completely shaking off its perception as a foreign sport. Mainstream journalism still quipped that the game was un-American—the most emphatic assertion was the out-of-context use of Senator Jack Kemp's comments in 1983 that soccer was a "European socialist" sport.[47] From a historical perspective, demonstrating soccer's link to endless waves of immigration was easy, but it would not solve the game's identity problem still evident in the cultural mainstream. Although some in the academy, like Daniel Ciccarelli, were continuing to study it, there was still little scholarly work on the issue in the 1980s and certainly nothing to mirror the way Harold Seymour's academic anthology had made serious baseball history accessible to all since the 1960s.[48] This is what prompted widely recognized coach and former US Olympic hopeful Len Oliver to note the lack of "rigorous, analytical studies of soccer in America" and summarize the state of research on soccer up to the mid-to-late 1980s: "So there is a history of soccer in America, one that is interconnected with the lives of working-class people, but it remains for the most part undocumented. With the new interest in social and working-class history, perhaps soccer's link with its ethnic roots will unfold."[49]

But it was not only uncovering soccer's ethnic roots that was of interest or at stake for the soccer history promoters behind the NSHOF in Oneonta or authors like Boxer, Foulds, and Hollander. It is telling that even Len Oliver—himself native-born of Scottish immigrants—had not referred back to the early Oneidas when writing precisely about the native history around soccer in America.[50] So despite several books and dissertations that mentioned the early Boston story and a growing hall of fame in New York State, still not everyone knew that the United States might have a soccer history that was not *only* immigrant, ethnic, foreign, or just begun with the Cosmos.

Essential to the often-heard claim that American soccer did not start with Pelé was the challenge to prove it with indisputable evidence. In a strange parallel to the baseball origins debate nearly a century earlier, there was an almost innate drive within American soccer circles to prove that the sport had old native roots. Much like the antiquarian movement of New England that sought to preserve and showcase the old-stock Americans, such a project required artifacts whose past meaning could be reshaped into a new narrative.[51] And there was one usable artifact that was on the Oneonta NSHOF's wish list: the old Oneida ball. In 1984, the budding NSHOF newsletter announced an exhibition called "Nineteenth Century Soccer in America." Gat Miller was at the center and "emphasis placed on his special relationship to soccer" alongside "the star of the show": the Oneida ball on loan from Boston's SPNEA.[52] With the arrival of the old rubber sphere to Oneonta, nicknamed the "City of the Hills," the home for soccer history now had a prize artifact and, with it, almost a natural claim to the Oneida legacy. After Foulds and many others who had labored tirelessly to preserve and unearth this "forgotten past," as historian Dave Wangerin later called it, the NSHOF finally had its Valley of the Kings moment.[53]

In 1989, with a US-hosted men's World Cup on the horizon after a failed bid for 1986, a new campus and soccer field project emerged to attract the millions of youth players' families from around the country to the NSHOF in Oneonta.[54] Hall development and planning director Will Lunn shared information with FIFA in Zurich, Switzerland, about the project plans for a museum in 1992 as well as brochures—featuring pictures of the Oneida ball and claims for the oldest soccer club but slightly incongruous dates, a point to return to later (see image 7).[55] Riding the wave of the US Women's World Cup victory in 1991—the world champions granting further claim to American soccer being a legitimate sport—the NSHOF organized a series of events around its Hall of Fame Week in the summer of 1992, including a soccer history symposium at which Foulds and others spoke. On the back of a successful event was the formation of the Society for American Soccer History (SASH), which published its first newsletter in the winter of 1993–94 with an editorial by Foulds summarizing the history of soccer back through the Boston "pick-up football games, which all had elements of soccer," played

Historic exhibits detail America's soccer heritage, including World Cup play.

Alfredda Iglehart, the first woman to be inducted into the NSHOF (1951), taught the fundamentals of soccer to over 1,200 boys during her 30 year career. Many of her students went on to become professionals and one of them, Millard Lang, is also a NSHOF inductee.

Oldest known soccer ball in America. The date, 1863, marks the first anniversary of the Oneidas, the first organized soccer club in America. International researchers believe the ball to be one of the oldest surviving in the world.

The U.S. team that startled the world by defeating England, 1-0, in the 1950 World Cup.

IMAGE 7. The National Soccer Hall of Fame opened in Oneonta, New York, and grew throughout the 1980s. Development brochures were produced that captured moments from soccer history and included the Oneida ball and a caption that claimed them as the first soccer team in the United States. Courtesy of the National Soccer Hall of Fame and with thanks to the USSF and the FIFA Museum.

by the Oneidas, the "first organized football (soccer) club in America."[56] This was a significant shift from his prior view about American soccer's founding. But history never stands still, and the American soccer community was consciously advancing its discovery and creation of a real national origin story with the Oneidas at the center.

Yet one problem remained. Any curious visitor was faced with a perplexing contradiction between the Oneonta display and the engraved pigskin on Boston Common. The famous Oneida ball at the NSHOF in upstate New York was *round*. Yet the club's stone monument planted on Boston Common showed an *oval* American football. During the decades from the 1960s to the 1990s in which soccer began to rediscover its past, the old Oneida monument had gradually eroded. By the time the 1994 World Cup was awarded to the United States, the stone tablet was listed among numerous city memorials needing restoration.[57] Sadly, Sam Foulds did not live to see the tournament, passing in January of 1994, but his historical work was used to underscore further legitimacy to the US soccer story. The competition's official newsletter proclaimed Boston had a soccer history since 1862 with the Oneidas paraded as the "first American soccer club." Travel magazines included advertisements urging tourists to visit the Oneonta NSHOF to learn about "the days of the Oneidas" alongside articles that claimed, "A year before [the English Football Association] . . . the Oneida Club of Boston had adopted the experimental rules of association football . . . and launched the game of soccer here."[58]

When the tournament ended, attention turned to its legacy, which included the foundation of a new professional league, Major League Soccer (MLS), set to start in 1996 with a team playing in greater Boston. In Foulds's stead, and aware of the state of the monument, NSHOF director Albert Colone wrote to Boston mayor Thomas Menino in March of 1995 explaining the history of the club, its round rubber ball on display at the NSHOF, and how "something was obviously lost in the interpretation and translation" between the games in the 1860s and the monument's rugby-shaped ball. Colone requested to "appropriately re-engrave the ball on the monument and to figuratively reclaim the sport's rightful spot in American history."[59] The city responded positively, happy that someone was taking the lead in restoring yet another worn public memorial. After some back and forth with city officials, Colone repeated that the NSHOF was committed to "the historical correction and refurbishment of the Oneida club monument" with plans for restoring the memorial, landscaping, and beautification.[60] He underlined that the reengraving would be news of significant interest and would "open many eyes across the country," to which the city art commission director, Mildred Farrell, replied that she "was pleased that [he had] decided to correct and completely restore" the monument.[61]

The work was finally completed in June 1996, and the monument was rededicated in mid-October. Ultimately a media nonevent, it garnered much less attention than the first unveiling in 1925 despite being again planned to coincide with a big football match: the first MLS championship match at Foxboro stadium. Well-known soccer reporter Frank Dell'Apa of the *Boston Globe* hardly gave it more than one line.[62] A more detailed article did appear later (possibly in *Soccer America*) citing the late Sam Foulds that "the Oneidas played a version of soccer," a view evident in his regular use of a stamp on correspondence reading "Soccer, America's Original Football, Founded 1862."[63] With a new tradition of American soccer history growing, the NSHOF hosted another symposium in June 1997, featuring a presentation on the Oneidas.[64] Within two years, the story reached new MLS commissioner Don Garber, who "visited the site [of the monument]" and now championed the Oneida Club as a national first.[65] And just like that, with a monument recarved to show a round modern soccer ball and a growing historical movement, the Oneidas were reappropriated as soccer scored a late extra-time equalizer to the club's long-standing gridiron legacy.

But with time still in the hands of the referee, there was no certainty that soccer's monumental late score would be enough. On his normal morning walk across Boston Common in the late 1990s, local resident Tom McGrath stood facing the inexplicable. As a teacher at nearby Wentworth Institute, he had given a struggling student an assignment to research an American football monument on Boston Common in hopes that the sporting topic would help motivate his pupil.[66] To his surprise, the student returned saying that there was no monument to gridiron in the park, only a soccer one. Confounded by why and how such a change had been made, McGrath embarked on a nearly two-decade journey of historical inquiry and heritage activism. He became so interested in the Oneidas that he began researching and writing a children's book about the club and its members' historical significance and even registered the name Oneida FC with the city so that it could not be usurped by a local rugby club.[67] His crusade to preserve the Oneida legacy is the last chapter of the Oneida story.

McGrath contacted the city mayor's office and art commission as well as the SPNEA with the results of his research. In July 2003, he wrote to Sarah Hutt of the Boston Public Art Commission claiming to have uncovered that the NSHOF had "put one over on the Boston Art Commission."[68] For McGrath, the NSHOF had the monument changed when they said it would only be cleaned and restored. He also contacted the SPNEA and according to an internal note, McGrath believed that the NSHOF "has the ball 'fraudulently'" and expressed that it should be held in a more appropriate museum like the New England Sports Museum.[69] In correspondence with the SPNEA's assistant registrar, Adrienne Sage, McGrath urged to clarify if the loan to the NSHOF was free or with a royalty fee. His view was that the ball "may be a football or a soccer ball" and suggested that any number of other interested organizations including the Professional Football Hall of Fame or even Harvard might "pony up some cash for SPNEA."[70] This appears to have been the stimulus for updating the NSHOF's loan agreement for the Oneida ball just a week after McGrath had raised the issue. With a new and lengthy appraisal by antique (and sport) specialist Robert J. Connelly—paid for by the NSHOF—the SPNEA now had a revised insurance estimate on the ball.[71] The SPNEA waited a few months but then followed McGrath's suggestion, recalling the ball in November 2004. While Sage underlined that the SPNEA was "pleased that the ball has been on public view at [the] institution . . . the loan was never intended to become long term," and she requested its return.[72]

However, for McGrath, the ball was only one-half of the story. As early as 2003, he had expressed thoughts about restoring the monument, a view that at least some in the city's Office of Cultural Affairs encouraged, even inviting him to present to the Boston Art Commission.[73] Despite McGrath's claim that the NSHOF duped the city of Boston, the archival record tells a more nuanced story. One area that was—and remains—unclear is how the 1996 monument restoration was paid for. McGrath appears to have been right that initial payment was messy. In the fall of 1997, Farrell had written to Colone rather upset that the local Boston society, the Friends of the Boston Public Garden and Common, had advanced the money to fund the restoration and had still yet to be reimbursed by the NSHOF over a year later.[74] Complicating the matter was that Colone was no longer with the NSHOF. An internal dispute at the hall of fame in Oneonta ended with Colone and the NSHOF's board of trustees parting ways in the winter of 1996–97.[75] If the Boston archives are silent as to any final resolution regarding the financing, they leave no doubt about the city's knowledge of Colone's aim for the restoration: the NSHOF was "committed to the historical correction." In several letters, the longtime director had underlined the NSHOF's intent to "correct the oversight of the monument's original erectors."[76] Colone's request had never concealed a covert soccer invasion of Boston Common, but his claiming "oversight" may, admittedly, have been one step too far.

McGrath was correct to assert that the original oblong football actually represented the Oneidas' true wishes. Indeed, while the Oneidas' ball was round, the monument men's "oversight" was, in fact, deliberate. As we know, Scudder and his friends had been adamant about an oval pigskin carving in 1925 regardless of the fact that it was obviously different from the historic round ball they had donated to Otis House three years earlier. The Oneidas had consciously sought to claim an oval legacy despite the ball's distant round parentage. It is in some sense ironic that seventy years later Colone would reclaim the Oneida flag for the association code, a round ball game desperate for a legitimate mainstream history alongside the traditional big-three American sports.

What is interesting for the Oneida story is how the Boston institutions shifted their view on the ball and club's historical legacy. If there did not seem to be any qualms inside the SPNEA about the NSHOF holding the ball into the late-1990s, once McGrath raised questions about the ball and monument, the tone changed inside Boston's cultural institutions. The SPNEA received several inquiries about the ball and regularly referred the requests without any issues to the NSHOF until the early 2000s, when the newly renamed institution's view expressed an internal shift that the "ball has been interpreted as a soccer ball, but it really is a football and we want to make sure it's described that way."[77] In its first newsletter as Historic New England, the curators explicitly linked the Oneidas' "Boston Game" as central in the evolution of American football and affirmed that "while this lumpy, deflated, round rubber ball in Historic New England's collection does not conjure up images of three-time World Champion New England Patriots, it is indeed a football."[78]

There were now two competing narratives for the history of the Oneidas, their monument and precious ball. Even with the ball back at its spiritual home in Otis House, the narrative around the ball and the club had changed. Having been on view at a *soccer* museum for twenty years (1984–2004) and with the refurbishment and correction of the monument on Boston Common in 1996, the Oneida story had become just as associated with soccer as American football history. Even the NCAA's extensively researched centennial publication—which does not appear to have used a photo of the Oneida ball as initially requested—labeled the Oneidas' game as "to have been more soccer than anything else."[79] With the NSHOF brochures continuing to promote a story of the "oldest ball" with exhibits about Gerrit Smith Miller, who founded "the first soccer club in the United States," history had somehow been altered.[80]

Such an appropriation perturbed McGrath who continued to orchestrate his own historical *re*-revisionism. What might be done? The ball was back in Otis House. But a soccer ball remained carved in stone on Boston Common and was clearly, in McGrath's view, a violation of the Oneidas' intent. His view was not to erase soccer, however, and he had argued that the Oneida game "evolved into Soccer and American Football," which was probably why he had suggested that "a baseball and bat and soccer ball are appropriate accoutrements placed near to the [Oneida] tablet."[81] McGrath was aware of the stakes and how culturally important soccer had become, admitting that he was "shooting [him]self in the foot by lobbying that the ball be replaced" and if he were only interested in selling children's books—to the "over 20 million boys and girls" who kicked soccer balls, as opposed to the far fewer who played American football—he would not insist.[82] But "misrepresentation of the soccer ball on the tablet" irked him, as evidenced by his substantial correspondence in the Boston Art Commission and Historic New England archives.[83] He did not mince his words—calling it vandalism several times—when writing to the mayor's office of arts and cultural affairs. McGrath argued that the 1996 soccer refurbishment was "an abridgement of history by the self-serving [NSHOF]." The local resident labeled the current state of the monument as oxymoronic and as historically impossible as a "'Boston Starbucks Coffee Party,' 'Boston Cream Twinkies,' 'Boston Baked Snow Peas' . . . [or renaming] the 'Boston Massacre' the 'Boston Slumber Party.'"[84]

With the zeal of a concerned citizen, the self-appointed guardian of Boston's heritage continued his Oneida quest, building alliances with the Harvard Varsity Club (for the ball) and the Friends of the Public Garden (for the monument), where he was a dues-paying member.[85] In 2007, McGrath had nearly completed his book and arranged a lunch with Henry Lee, the president of the Friends of the Public Garden. Lee informed Sarah Hutt at the city's

The Soccer Grab

art commission that "McGrath seems determined to preserve and correct the Oneida monument" but that he "will not hold [his] breath in anticipation.... I will let you know of any monetary windfalls."[86] The issue was the cost, and it appears that McGrath was unable to garner sufficient financial support, so the project was tabled.[87] Perhaps Lee was cautious because he had been president in 1996 of the same Friends of the Public Garden when it appears the society paid for the first monument refurbishment without clarity as to who bore ultimate financial responsibility.[88]

But McGrath was a man on a mission. Symbolically in 2012, on the eighty-seventh anniversary of the monument's unveiling, the *Boston Globe* ran a story on the Oneidas for which journalist Bob Holmes had interviewed McGrath and Hutt and thanked many of the city's historical institutions. Despite the archival evidence to the contrary, Holmes presented the 1996 restoration as soccer subterfuge and reassured readers that "efforts are underway to restore the soccer ball to a football."[89] Soon after, and in a strange twist of fate, the US Soccer Federation's 2013 centennial history book omitted the Oneidas in favor of a passing mention of 1860s colleges in its opening chapter.[90] The Oneidas were not forgotten by McGrath, and around Christmas that year, Sarah Hutt circulated the full application from the Friends of the Public Garden with the stated goal to "return [the] marble figure to original design intent depicting a American football."[91] The local society had chosen more diplomatic language than the *Globe* calling the 1996 soccer ball restoration a "miscommunication" in its correspondence with the city.[92] Finally presented to the Boston Art Commission on April 7, 2014, the monument *re*-refurbishment project received its full support.[93] Working behind the scenes, McGrath finally succeeded in having the monument changed back to an oval pigskin, with the work being completed in September.[94]

For seventy years the monument stood as a testament to the Oneidas' history as the founders of American football. Then flowing out of the soccer revolution both culturally and in the growth of its own historiography, the association game scored an added-time goal in 1996. American soccer claimed the Oneida ball as its own, recarving the Boston boys' role as its own originators. That soccer revisionist truth stood for twenty years of extra time until Tom McGrath launched a last gasp Hail Mary seeking to restore the Oneidas to their original gridiron glory—or, at least, intent. But those who build monuments have no control over the future, and the Oneida case illustrates the "tension around sport statue ownership" between those who commission such monuments and the surrounding contemporary culture.[95] For an Oneida goal line supposedly "never crossed," soccer carving a monumental extra-time goal in 1996 and Tom McGrath's 2014 American football bootleg remind us that sport is never without surprises until the final whistle. And with the World Cup returning to American shores in 2026, we are left to wonder if soccer might try again. . . .

10

POSTMATCH ANALYSIS

Friendly Tactics, Mischief, and Gammon, or a Hoax?

> Every game, in which a ball or any other form of missile has its place, defies the historian who tries to find its origin.
>
> —Scudder, 1924

> Having been proved that the Oneida Football Club was the first to be organized in the United States, it seemed eminently fitting to some of the old members of the Club, and a few of their friends, including families of Members of the Club no longer living, that a record of it should appear on Boston Common.
>
> —Scudder, 1926

Historian Marc Bloch once warned against the dangerous ambiguity of the idol of origins, which often "confuses ancestry for explanation."[1] In their commemorative enterprise, the Oneidas were aware of the obstacle to ascertain origins, at least before initiating their monument project. In his edited article for the 1924 SPNEA *Bulletin* recounting the Miller school tablet, Scudder's opening words reminded readers that the search for football's beginnings boldly brazens the historian.[2] And yet, less than two years following that didactic exercise for the boys of Noble and Greenough, Scudder drove a runaway train of self-commemoration and affirmed what was previously thought to be unknowable: the Oneidas were the originators of organized football.[3] In so doing, Scudder and friends had tripped on Bloch's line separating "ancestry and causality," passing off as history what was in fact heritage. As noted by Richard Holt, there is a difference between the two: "History is how we explain the past; heritage is how we preserve it."[4]

As the story goes, or at least as the Oneida monument on Boston Common declares, football in the United States was "invented" there: "On this field the Oneida Football Club of Boston, the first organized football club in the United States played against all comers from 1862 to 1865. The Oneida goal was never crossed. This monument is placed on Boston Common, November 1925, by the seven surviving members of the team." For all the millions of people who have walked past the monument since 1925, few have probably paid it much notice. For those who have stopped to look, it must appear a straightforward and quite simple commemoration to something clear cut. In essence the Oneidas were the first organized football club in the United States. They existed for three years, never gave up a goal, and seven men—the surviving teammates—arranged for a monument to be built. The Oneidas had gazed back at sporting ancestry and commemorated their shared past by honoring friends and games played in a Guttmannesque premodern sporting world. Just as their living Brahmin milieu was fading, the Oneidas enshrined their own memory on a monument on Boston Common, a poignant example of historian Pierre Nora's *lieux de mémoire*.[5] But the "foot ball" they played in the 1860s had evolved contemporaneously on both sides of the Atlantic (and beyond) away from their boyhood games into association football, rugby union and league, Gaelic football, and Australian rules football. Tony Collins explains how this happened through a transnational and concurrent process of diffusion and exchange across the nineteenth-century Anglophone world, one in which "myth-making and invented traditions were common."[6] Commemoration, however, runs against this chronological current and expresses our natural, if perhaps flawed, epistemological tendency to explain origins simply and backward—or, in Gavin Kitching's words, as "a time when something that now 'exists' did not 'exist.' Hence it must have been 'invented.'"[7] There lurks the idol of origins.

There is mystery in the Oneida origin story, an oblique shadow behind their monument, one that has stretched the length of the 160 years since their matches on Boston Common. Their acts of historical preservation left sufficient space for interpretation such that their story—as a sporting creation myth—took on a life of its own, developed and reappropriated as reimagined meanings popped out from the monument's shadow in the years after 1925. Thus, when looking at the entire history of the Oneida story from 1862 to

Tom McGrath's recent 2014 audible, is it sacrilegious to wonder about this door left so equivocally open to multiple retellings? Surely the Oneidas are not responsible for how their story was shaped by the contemporary media or continued to evolve long after they died. Or are they? Was their origin story real, or was it all a hoax, an embellished yarn spinning further and further beyond their control with each iteration—a dinner, a book, a ball, a tablet, a monument with multiple *Sketches*, *Appreciations*, and donations in between? In preserving their heritage, were the Oneidas out to gull history?

Sport has witnessed its share of hoaxes, and Boston is no exception. The Boston Athletic Association has seen more than one bilker at its marathon over the years, the most infamous being Rosie Ruiz in her record-breaking but fraudulent 1980 run.[8] Her ultimately unsuccessful case reveals that every hoax involves a process and intent. In his analysis of the motivations behind the successful delivery of hoaxes, psychologist Peter Hancock noted a number of necessary conditions.[9] He argues that there has to exist a constituency who are ready to be deceived and to whom an artifact, an item, or information can be presented to convincingly support a claim. Once the deceiver has decided on what evidence they will use for their hoax, they must manufacture a (generally accidental) discovery, which is then supported by a champion. But Hancock underlines that for a hoax to work, it "must not be too perfect" and possess characteristics that are open to interpretation. It is that imperfection that provides the crucial ambiguity to maintain the relevance of the story as the hoax persists over time. Before the Oneida story morphed into a book, museum donations, or commemorative plaques and stone monuments, it began not in an attempt to deceive or to claim first place. But from its start as friendly reminiscence, did the Oneidas' heritage project evolve into a ruse? If we take Hancock's argument as the playbook for a good hoax, then did the Oneidas' tactics follow it? In this postmatch analysis, we decrypt the Oneida mystery and unveil some surprises about pieces of their narrative.

Beginning with the necessary audience, there was unquestionably a Gilded Age Boston elite who feared that the identity of their city (and even their country) was floating away amid the flood of immigration. This was at the core of the institutionalized preservationist movement by private groups that, as Lindgren has argued, aimed to "ensure their own cultural primacy in New England's identity."[10] Believers in the historicity of the best of Boston having originated in old-stock Americans were aplenty in early twentieth-century Brahmin high society. Indeed, they had been commemorating their own for some time, with monuments sprouting all over the Common and across the city since the middle of the nineteenth century.[11] Part of the "statue mania" that Erika Doss explains "gripped nineteenth- and early twentieth-century Americans and Europeans alike," all of the Boston memorials were completed within a few years of the death of those honored. Memorials were always in the form of a statue or at least a plaque with the person's likeness—like that to former governor Roger Wolcott, one of the earlier Oneidas to die, unveiled in 1907 at the Massachusetts State House, overlooking the Common from atop Beacon Hill.[12] In this sense, the Oneidas were hardly original and just spoke to the same constituency already doing the same thing.

But it was not only Boston's Brahmin elite whom the city chose to remember during the Gilded Age, as public statuary in the city was a broad phenomenon.[13] Indeed, during an era of such massive immigration, honoring the memory of various constituencies who contributed to the American national narrative was both essential and contested. Over the prior decades, tensions with immigrant communities began to reveal a kind of American identity crisis as the new arrivals (mostly Southern and Eastern Europeans) faced a complex national dynamic of assimilation versus hyphenation. Only a year before the extensive celebrations in New York of the four hundredth anniversary of Columbus's arrival in the Americas, which included multiple monuments, New Orleans saw one of the largest mass lynchings in the country's history with eleven Italian Americans murdered by an angry mob.[14] It is impossible to separate the movement to build monuments to key figures or immigrant peoples from the wider socioeconomic context and demographic shifts of the era.

Returning to the Oneidas, building monuments in the heart of Boston was in vogue in 1925. In fact, their memorial was one of three unveiled on the Common that year in addition to two other tablets dedicated in the surrounding streets of old Boston.[15] In particular was an ethnic statue project for Tadeusz Kościuszko, the Polish hero of the Revolutionary War, who already had statues across the country, but not yet in the city that claimed a birthright to American independence.[16] Announced in celebration of the 150th anniversary of his arrival, the link to the American story was at the center. However, Kościuszko, whose statue was to be displayed in the Public Garden just opposite the Oneidas' old playing field, was anything but an old Boston Brahmin. Backed by the support of Mayor Curley and several prominent Bostonians, it was to honor the Polish people of New England.[17] When seen in context, the Oneida commemoration is hardly different from other initiatives during this time. Just another monument built for its believers.

Moving to Hancock's second element, the Oneidas produced multiple artifacts—objects, documents, and visuals—over several decades, which shaped their narrative. The first and main Oneida artifact is the old club ball. It first appears in the historical record when Lovett was preparing his book. Miller had the ball sent to Cabot in Boston to be photographed as it "will make a good subject for the book."[18] From the first image in the 1906 book to the ball's donation to the SPNEA in 1922, it is paraded as indisputable evidence of the historicity of the club's achievements from the 1860s. Second in importance to the ball is a red handkerchief also donated by the club to the SPNEA. The primitive uniform served to illustrate the team's early sense of organization. In addition to the physical objects, the club members produced written accounts. Beginning with Lovett's *Old Boston Boys* (1906), the Oneidas created and deposited their sketches honoring Gerrit Smith Miller (1924) and the entire club (1926) as well as a lengthy article in the SPNEA's bulletin (1924), all as testimonies to the history of the first organized football team in America. Alongside the printed word, the Oneida story also existed in visual accounts. Indeed, images from key moments (the 1922 ball donation) or the official commemorative photograph of the six Oneidas standing by the monument in Scudder's *An Historical Sketch* proffered verifiable evidence. These usable artifacts, documents, and images also shaped and reshaped the story.

These items were discovered and rediscovered in varying ways—some more manufactured than others—and supported by champions. After an initial remembering at the 1904 dinner, which spawned a book, we saw how the legacy of the Oneidas was "discovered" a first time with the ball donation in 1922 followed by the school plaque at Noble and Greenough alongside Rugby School rediscovering the Webb Ellis 100th anniversary. The Oneidas "rediscovered" their pioneering role again two years later as a response to Yale's massive commemoration of Walter Camp as the "Father of American football." Espial continued through the expanding historiography of American football adding the Oneidas in its timeline, which prefigured yet another discovery, this time by soccer unearthing its Oneida origins and the round ball that justified the culmination of a monument refurbishment in 1996. The Oneida story could not have developed unless championed by key figures. Whether it was for the school tablet where Charles W. Eliot and Bishop William Lawrence spoke at the dedication, for the monument on Boston Common—remember the name-dropping of physician Henry Pickering Walcott added to the president and bishop to get the oval ball carved in 1926—or the printed validation given by football authorities like Walter Camp and Parke H. Davis, the Oneidas had many champions.

But a credible constituency, artifacts and their championed discovery are just the basis for a hoax. As Hancock explains, an openness to interpretation and ambiguity are crucial for the story to have a life of its own. In the Oneida case, the artifacts and their discovery do reveal some problems, even if none of this surfaced to the public eye when they were presented. Let us begin with the ball, that truest of Oneida artifacts. The historian is confronted with several problems in terms of its authenticity as a truly historical object and in terms of what was painted on it. The ball was said to have been kept by Miller until it was taken out of storage and photographed for Lovett's 1906 book—the first visual evidence of the artifact. The only other image of the ball comes from when the Oneidas were photographed for its donation in 1922—the photo still in Historic New England's archive. No other visual evidence of the ball has been uncovered from before the book photograph or between 1906 and its donation. Of course, it had been presented publicly at the 1923 tablet unveiling and was on display at Otis House from the mid-1920s. So in theory, it was there for all to see—names and goal times—as indisputable evidence, but only after the Oneida story had been written.

It begs the question of if the ball and its painted record of the match are corroborating evidence or whether it was manufactured as part of the commemorative process while the book was being prepared. Was it perhaps a total fake, purchased sometime after the famous 1904 dinner in order to have a nice image for the book? Given the beating that these balls must have taken, is it truly absurd to question whether the ball was the same one used so many years prior? Lest we forget that in *Old Boston Boys* Lovett described how Ned Arnold and another boy kicked a ball simultaneously during one such game "with the result that it was ripped asunder like a paper bag."[19] Balls were precious commodities in those days, even if there was a store selling rubber "foot balls" on nearby School St. in 1862.[20] If we accept that the ball in the photo was an authentic one that had survived the rigorous 1860s match play by Arnold and his friends, did these schoolboys so intent on playing regular games on the Common really take a ball "won" during a game, albeit a memorable one, and immediately retire it for collection? It is hard to imagine them having an inexhaustible supply of balls such that they could take one, have

Postmatch Analysis

it painted for memorial purposes, and retire it for collection. Nevertheless, if the precious sphere had immediately been retired following the famous 1863 championship match—thus being authentic—was it just forgotten until the storytelling at the famous 1904 dinner prompting Miller to exclaim with delight to his friends that he still had it stored away somewhere in upstate New York? Authenticity would also mean that the old ball had endured the test of time after forty years of storage in Miller's farmhouse, through Peterboro's bitterly cold winters and hot humid summers. In the 1906 *Old Boston Boys* photograph, the Oneida ball looks remarkably well-preserved for a forty-year-old everyday plaything. At the least, the ball's survival from regular play and overall authenticity seems worthy of question.

If we set aside the doubt about its general historicity as the actual ball from the 1863 match, another aspect that raises serious authenticity questions is the lettering painted on the ball and when this was actually done. As we know, there are only two images of the ball from this period: one from 1906 and the other from 1922. The book's 1906 photo shows only two panels of the sphere with their painted lettering and a caption stating that there were fifteen names painted on it. The words read "Won by [crest image] Nov. 7th 1863. from High & Latin Schools." On the photo from the 1922 donation, the same panels are visible, but one can just barely discern the edge of the inscribed names on the ball resting in Lovett's hands. If we can assume that all the lettering was painted on the same occasion, the question remains whether it was done in 1863 or sometime later. Admittedly, there were places in Boston where one could get engravings and such painting done in the 1860s. And at least some of these Brahmin boys certainly had the means (or parents) to pay for a nice, embellished paint job. Such commemoration was common practice, evidenced by the collection of sixty-one painted Lowell Club baseballs—at least one listing Miller and Lovett's names—on display at the Boston Athletic Association circa 1910.[21] Nevertheless, the Oneida football's forty-year-old lettering is not beyond doubt given how pristine it looked for its first public appearance in 1906, so magically preserved after farmhouse storage absent modern archival climate preservation technology.

The ball and its painted inscription are exhibited as the evidence for the club's historicity. At first glance, this buttresses the club's argument, since Lovett's account of the championship match in *Old Boston Boys* is silent on the details. In fact, the goals and minutes never appear in the book. This is strange given the attention to detail Lovett gave to the rowing and baseball sections, which featured countless mentions of times and scores. It is possible that Lovett simply excluded the details as unnecessary because the ball already told the story in its old painted letters—despite being invisible in the book image and caption—but its absence in the prose does stand out. Nonetheless, the information on the ball is indeed the same as in the 1863 *Boston Evening Transcript* article—the only contemporary source that recorded the game length and scores. Neither the *Boston Herald* nor the *Boston Daily Advertiser*—both of which had reported the Oneida match—gave the score or times. Interestingly, there is no copy of any of the 1863 articles in any of Lovett's papers, his scrapbook, or even his richly annotated copy of *Old Boston Boys* that rests in the Massachusetts Historical Society augmented by countless newspaper clippings.[22]

In writing, Lovett relied on additional material shared by dinner attendees and other Old Boys. Some of the Miller and Lovett correspondence includes friends sharing fond memories or details clearly used in the final manuscript. However, the archive is silent about the specifics of the championship match, the ball, and the painting of letters. In 1905 Miller had only stated that he would send Cabot the Oneida ball because there was no photographer in Peterboro but made no mention of the painted lettering. Was it possible that sometime between the 1904 dinner and the 1906 book printing someone (maybe Cabot himself) may have found the *Boston Evening Transcript* article recounting the game and the three goals after the tenth, ninth, and eighth minute of each successive game? Then in arranging the photograph of the ball, the timings were carefully painted on the ball with the names of the team members in a deliberate a posteriori act to memorialize the event? In this sense, it is unclear how to interpret Miller's words on receiving his copies of the book. He wrote to Lovett saying that "Sam [Cabot] was very successful in reproducing the 'Oneida—High & Latin School' football! It would have warmed the cockles in dear old Cliff's heart if he could have seen it."[23] Perhaps Miller only meant that championship teammate Clifford Watson—who died in June of 1902—had passed away just too soon to see the image. Or maybe he was intimating that the ball had been doctored somehow and therefore Watson could never have seen it in its "reproduced" 1906 form.

As the lettering exists at present, something else stands out on the "reproduced" ball: only two names are accompanied by an initial. This is different from Lovett's full caption in 1906, which listed first initials with each last name. The first easily spotted, on its own line, is "Wolcott. H.," which was obviously an abbreviation for Huntington as opposed to Roger. The other is part of a sequence: "Davis. Brooks. W. Tucker." Following the Wolcott logic, the *W* should designate the first initial immediately preceding the last name. This would easily identify Walter Denison Brooks, whom Lovett mentioned as a member of the team.[24] This pleads in favor of the historicity of the letters actually dating from 1863, because Walter also had a younger brother, John Henry Brooks.[25] Distinguishing between brothers living in the 1860s would have made sense at the time. However, distinction may also have been needed, possibly more so, in 1906.

Notwithstanding Huntington (their club's heroic Civil War casualty) and Walter having passed away decades before writing, Lovett did not have any memory problems recalling them.[26] The Oneida chapter did refer to the two deceased players, but if Lovett also mentioned the other Wolcott, Roger, he only spoke of one Brooks: Walter.[27] At the time that Lovett's book was published, Roger Wolcott had just passed away (1901), while the younger John Henry Brooks was still living in Boston. Thus, in 1906 Brahmin society, the last name Wolcott would certainly have been more easily associated with the late Roger (whose statue at the Boston Statehouse was to be unveiled in December) rather than his long-dead brother, Huntington. Similarly, instead of mistaking the living John Henry for the dead Walter, it would make sense in 1906 to clarify the correct Brooks with an initial. As such, the two initials would undoubtedly help 1906 Brahmin readers remember the erstwhile deceased rather than confuse the names on the "reproduced" ball with the living (John Henry) or the freshly commemorated (Roger).

Aside from the lettering, also painted on the ball is the club emblem. It only appears on two objects: once on the ball and again, two decades later, on the privately printed *Pilgrimage* poem.[28] Admittedly, there are some rare examples of old fonts from the 1860s that do plead in favor of the Oneida crest's historicity. Baseball historian John Thorn explains how clubs painted balls as mementos and used intricate emblems, like the Harvard baseball club in the 1860s. The Baseball Hall of Fame holds two of Miller's other old balls from his old Cazenovia (New York) team. Apparently dated 1864, the ball's lettering style bears some resemblance to the Oneida emblem's "F" and "B" letters.[29] However, other later emblems such as the gentlemanly Corinthians logo—the English club that toured the US in 1906 after a canceled, but widely reported, initial attempt in 1905 that would have seen them play Harvard—or the original Real Madrid crest from 1902 recall the special lettering of the never-seen-before-1906 Oneida monogram.[30]

The other artifact presented as historical proof is the red silk handkerchief, which has never received the same attention as the ball. It has not recently been on display at Historic New England and is presumed lost. There are, once again, some unanswered questions. The first mention comes not in *Old Boston Boys*—entirely silent regarding the object—but around the November 1923 school tablet. Lovett's account of the Oneidas, and Boston football generally, is the oldest and most complete account that exists. If there is any source that might mention something, it ought to be Lovett's 1906 book. However, despite multiple mentions throughout *Old Boston Boys* of handkerchiefs for rowing and even a history of Harvard's baseball uniforms, Lovett *never* mentioned a handkerchief, a uniform, or any distinctive dress in regard to football or the Oneidas. Only later, at the 1923 school tablet unveiling, did Boston papers refer to a "red bandana" or "crimson handkerchief."[31] The artifact seems to have been absent from the 1922 donation; the SPNEA's newsletter only included the ball in the list of 1922 gifts.[32] Moreover, despite being in vogue particularly with footballers just weeks before it was said the Oneidas donated theirs, there is no sign of a handkerchief in the 1922 donation photo.[33] If the men had wished to memorialize the silk souvenir, then why was the object not front and center like the ball? But there is no record of the handkerchief in the bulletin, in correspondence, or anywhere in the donation file—nothing prior to November 1923. Instead, the artifact entered the commemorative record through the newspapers that reported how the men had brought it to the tablet unveiling at Nobles; from there it appeared in Scudder's official commemorative booklet.[34] Was the relic truly linked to the football club, or was it an a posteriori invention paraded for storytelling to the Nobles schoolboys?

The association of handkerchiefs to the Oneida name was not unique and revealed deeper links between rowing and the football club. In the 1850s the *Harvard Magazine* recounted the tradition of such handkerchiefs—initially a prize—and associated the crimson color with none other than the university's prize boat: the Oneida, sculled to victory in the inaugural 1852 race against Yale by at least one cousin related to the later football team.[35] By the time the regular regattas between Harvard and Yale began in 1859, the legendary Oneida boat that had "held undisputed supremacy" since the 1840s had been sold beyond the university, but a club bearing its name continued to exist through at least the class of 1861. That class had supplied two members to the crew that defeated Yale in the 1859 race. Proudly wearing his red handkerchief was Oneida footballer John Forbes's older brother, William Hathaway Forbes, perpetuating a distinctive headdress tradition that continued after the Civil War with several Oneidas also rowing for Harvard between 1866 and 1868.[36] Thus, in 1923, Blanchard's freshly published compendium of Harvard sport had revived Brahmin memory of the bond between handkerchiefs, the Oneida name, and their associated supremacy over Yale in an opening chapter on the history of the crimson color.[37] This was the context in which the Oneidas produced the hitherto unmentioned relic.

The ambiguity around the football handkerchief does raise questions as to whether the artifact was authentic to Oneida football or a reimagined legacy of Oneida rowing. Had the footballers imitated their Harvard rower cousins and brothers when playing in 1862? Or had a recently remembered rowing handkerchief actually been given to Scudder's crew in 1923 so they had another relic to display to the Nobles schoolboys?[38] The power of the artifact continued and appeared again twenty-some years later on the ink blotter produced by the First National Bank of Boston. That drawing of the Oneidas with silk bandanas was the one subsequently promoted by US soccer at the start of their Oneida discovery. Later, for the 1984 soccer exhibit, it was a *replica* that was on display and it is unclear when the actual artifact disappeared from view.[39]

As artifacts, the ball, its lettering, and the handkerchief are hardly unequivocal. Was the ball's intricate lettering corroborating evidence, or was it rather deliberately prepared for Lovett's book in a first discrete act of manufactured commemoration? With only partial photos and none prior to 1906, there is little evidence proving the ball's authenticity back to 1863. Rather than mark a decisive imprimatur on the Oneida story, the painted letters trace a shadow of doubt onto the ball's authenticity. Unmentioned before November 1923—and never listed among the SPNEA donations—the distinctive club handkerchief was only "discovered" and added to the historical record after Blanchard had published his mammoth Harvard athletic history in February and alongside the school tablet.[40] Indeed, the doubts surrounding these artifacts and that it is impossible to know for certain express precisely that ambiguity that Hancock describes as necessary for a hoax.

This obliquity is amplified by the difficulty in interpreting the various images preserved in Oneida documents. Photographs are an undervalued source of history despite the fact that visuals can be important in the "persistent reflection which forms the core of the process of historical truthfulness."[41] Nonetheless, photos are an equivocal source of truth, open to all kinds of manipulation, which can "contribute to the manufacture of meaning."[42] The Oneida images from 1926 are a case in point. Scudder's *An Historical Sketch of the Oneida Football Club of Boston 1862–1865* is *the* archival document most used to tell the club's story. It provides the definitive public written and visual testimony of the monument erected in 1925. The problem, however, is that the photographs are actually montages.

The first features the sunlit faces of the six survivors (and Bowditch inset) standing proudly around their monument (see image 8). This image is unique to *An Historical Sketch* and found nowhere else, not in the newspapers nor in any archive. While some newspapers featured an image of the monument

IMAGE 8. An image depicting six of the surviving members of the Oneida team at the monument unveiling in 1925 along with an inset photo of the seventh surviving member, which was produced for Scudder's *An Historical Sketch* in 1926 and donated to the Massachusetts Historical Society. The photograph did not appear in any of the Boston area newspapers of the time. Public domain.

Postmatch Analysis

unveiled by Alice Lovett and Miller's granddaughter, only two papers actually included a photo of the six men from the unveiling (see image 9). However, neither shows the six Oneidas standing by the monument like the image in *An Historical Sketch*; they are simply lined up in front of a row of houses that are without any doubt numbers 49, 50, and 51 Beacon Street (with Spruce Street running in between numbers 49 and 50).[43] The newspaper images are of mediocre quality, but the Lovett scrapbook contains a clear original photograph of that sunny monument morning.[44]

When examining those two images, the stances, facial expressions, and even shadows of the six Oneidas are identical. Notwithstanding the flat and grainy image in *An Historical Sketch*, it is the shadows that give the montage away. How could the six men have shadows on their faces, pants, canes, coats, and hats so clearly visible and yet the rest of the photo have such flat lighting? Unbelievably, there is no sign of a shadow around the monument. It is evident that someone cropped the original 1925 photo, separated the six

IMAGE 9. An original photograph that was taken of the six Oneidas who attended the unveiling of the monument on November 21, 1925, and included in James D'Wolf Lovett's sporting scrapbook. Courtesy of Revolutionary Spaces.

IMAGE 10. The majority of images of the Oneida monument on Boston Common show the front. Here the rear of the monument, with fifteen names of the Oneida team engraved, is shown. Public domain.

men and then created an entirely new image, inserting three on either side of the monument and finally drawing in Peabody's right arm, which is hidden by Miller in the original. Furthermore, the newspaper pictures of the six from 1925 were taken *a year before* the stone monument even featured the carved football—still the subject of contention between the architect and the Oneidas and not completed until twelve months later.

The second photo in *An Historical Sketch* portrays a similar montage issue (see image 10). Here, the monument runs at an impossibly contradictory angle in comparison with the first image of the six Oneidas standing on either side. The monument is not parallel with the angle of the paved walkway, as in the first image.

Indeed, when one looks closely at the two images in *An Historical Sketch*, the monument's angles are identical, and its edges appear suspiciously cut out from some other photo. One wonders if the two pictures used by Scudder were actual photos at all. Or perhaps they were the first plans submitted in

Postmatch Analysis

September 1925 or the second designs of the football carving, which were being discussed in the spring of 1926? To be sure, there is no clear answer to these questions, but one is justified in having monumental doubts.

As visual evidence then, the photos are not authentic, even if it should be said that the caption of the monument photo featuring the Oneidas included a caveat. The official commemorative photograph was described as "From a photograph November 21, 1925, on the Field where they played." It read "From a photograph." Not "A photograph" but *From* a photograph." Admittedly, the montage was not deliberately obscured and even asserted in the text by Scudder when he wrote that "Appended to this sketch is a reproduction of a photograph."[45] A "reproduction" may have been the exercise of artistic license, but it harkens back to Miller praising the "reproduced" ball in 1906. The consequence of the Oneidas' exercise in "reproduced" authentic heritage is a story riddled with ambiguity.

If the artifacts and the images are less than unequivocal, even more problematic to the Oneidas is the actual list of club members. In 1906, Lovett provided a first list of the 1863 championship team. When the ball, with its painted names and two initials, was gifted to the SPNEA in November of 1922, the donation was accompanied by a one-page typescript—more specific than the 1906 book's caption, which had only printed last names with first initials—printing the full names.[46] Four years later, the archive was supposed to have spoken the final truth with Scudder's full roster of fifty-two names in his 1926 *An Historical Sketch*; a list simply expanding on the original fifteen names. This list, however, became a wicked problem for the Boston club, and two changes occurred. Less than one year after the ball donation, not all the names cited were the same in the coverage of the Miller plaque unveiling at Noble and Greenough. In addition to a pair of late substitutions, one more Oneida player had sneaked onto the pitch. In the booklet and SPNEA article commemorating the 1923 event, there were now apparently *sixteen* members of the 1863 championship team. Avowed in the 1924 publications, the list was extended by Scudder in his 1926 *An Historical Sketch* after the monument unveiling with thirty-six more club members, including a few surprises. These discrete alterations to the club lineup made by Scudder between 1922 and 1926 further obscure the Oneidas' story.

In analyzing the substitutions first, Frank Davis and Lawrence Tucker were replaced by George Davis and Alanson Tucker. The former both appeared in the 1906 caption—and then with full names in the 1922 donation file—but disappeared when the Miller plaque was unveiled in 1923 at Noble and Greenough. The dual substitution is all the more curious given that Lovett had explicitly referred to both Frank Davis and Lawrence Tucker multiple times and never once mentioned a George Davis or an Alanson Tucker, who appear *nowhere* in *Old Boston Boys*.[47] While no existing document explains the change, the probable explanation is a younger brother switched for older brother.[48] From 1923 onward, all subsequent lists—including the extended one three years later—as well as all documents, correspondence in the Boston archives, and the newspapers refer to George Davis and Alanson Tucker. Frank and Lawrence had been erased from the club roster and also from a precious artifact.

If there are questions surrounding the initials on the ball for Wolcott and Brooks, the lettering is even more scabrous when considering how the Davis and Tucker brothers' substitution impacted the list of Oneidas. Beyond the fact that there were no initials distinguishing the Davis or Tucker brothers—something that makes even less sense when considering the choice to do so for the Wolcott and Brooks duos—the initial "W" reveals further artifact manipulation in doctoring the ball's lettering. The post-1922 Davis and Tucker substitution appears to explain why the painted "W" has a mysterious dash inside and appears just as much an "A" (see image 11). Even if it is impossible to affirm a mistake or a subsequent alteration, we know that Lawrence Tucker was a part of the championship team between 1906 and 1922 but then was erased from the record. An "A," however, would certainly correspond with his previously unmentioned brother Alanson. Both Tucker brothers were alive in 1906, but only Lawrence had ordered a copy of the book. It could explain the bizarre discrepancy between what was originally a "W" and then changed to an "A" after the 1923 substitution. It would also elucidate the bedimmed outer lines, more faded than the central "A" part, and the inconsistent placement of initials after "Wolcott. H." but before "A. Tucker." Perhaps Scudder's late lineup change needed to be reflected on the ball regardless of how messy it might look on the rubber panels. There are no clear answers and one can only wonder about the quirky lettering, the silent archive, and the fact that these 1923 substitutions were played on men long dead.

Less confounding, but still pertinent to the club roster, was how Scudder had added a sixteenth member to their illustrious championship team, one who had passed away in February 1904 just months before the important

IMAGE 11. The Oneida football featuring a panel with the names of four players. Author photograph.

dinner: John Malcolm "Mac" Forbes. Admittedly, the addition of Forbes in 1923 was not a real problem because he had been among those specifically referenced as members of the club by Lovett in *Old Boston Boys*.[49] His absence on the ball in 1906 was later explained away by Scudder in the 1924 commemorative booklet because Forbes had been "loaned to them [the opposing English and Latin School team] to captain their side" against his Oneida friends thus not being one of the famous 1863 championship team members.[50] This reveals little historical clarity on the club's size, however. Only two Oneida matches appeared in the press in the 1860s, and on neither occasion was it clear that they played with fifteen players.[51] Yet again Scudder made a retroactive change and shrouded Forbes's absence on the ball. Maybe at the time of the 1923 commemoration, the son of a prominent investor and prosperous railroad developer of the same name could not be left out rather than because, according to Scudder, the fantastic Forbes's "reputation was international."[52]

The addition of Forbes and the swapped Davis and Tucker brothers were only the 1923 alterations. By 1926, the club's definitive fifty-two-man roster had been published, including and omitting a host of other individuals. Scudder's new list did not match completely with Lovett's narrative description from 1906, which weaved the Oneidas in and out of the wider school football scene never defining a fixed roster. Save for the specific account of the 1863 match, Lovett had never clearly distinguished between those who were Oneida Club members versus who played football on the Common with school teams or more informally. His goal in 1906, after all, was just to remember a bygone world of boyhood games, not elect a hall of fame. Concretely, this meant his account was not statistically bulletproof. Proofreading notwithstanding, Lovett's papers contain correspondence that points out errors even after the first edition.[53] Yet nothing suggests a correction around the additional thirty-six names added by Scudder in 1926. Lovett had given a list of boys who "congregated there [Boston Common] daily for football, hockey, or what not."[54] But Lovett is unclear if this included Oneida Club members or not. Among the twenty-one additional names he gave in his chapter on the club, just four were eventually added to Scudder's final list in 1926.[55] Most of the other names cited by Lovett simply disappeared, with dinner organizer Cabot and Ned Fenno perhaps the most glaring.[56] In their place, others like Forbes or the substituted Davis and Tucker brothers, all absent from the 1904 dinner, were given seats at the Oneida table.[57] Similarly, the choice to include Henry Cabot Lodge, James Arthur Beebe, Stephen "Ren" Thayer, and Edward "Ned" Burgess in the 1926 list was never explained, and all were posthumous and, it must be said, illustrious additions. Lodge's memoirs mentioned football twice but never as part of the club.[58] None of their obituaries so carefully pasted during the following decades into Lovett's copy of *Old Boston Boys* ever mentioned them as Oneidas. But by 1926 these men—and most of the Oneidas—were long dead and would not be able to argue the matter even if they had wished to.

The dubbing of those Oneidas not mentioned by Lovett is equally perplexing. Whether it was John Henry Brooks—the brother alive in 1906—or the miraculous inclusion of Bishop William Lawrence, omission in Lovett's account in 1906 or during the 1923 commemorations did not preclude one from making Scudder's final cut in 1926. Like Alanson Tucker, despite not even subscribing to the first edition, the younger Brooks (John Henry) somehow appeared posthumously.[59] The bishop, who had been the club's champion in 1923, had had multiple opportunities to be presented as a club member. The press at the Miller plaque ceremony interviewed Lawrence, who even confessed to be "not enough of an athlete . . . to belong to the champion Oneida team."[60] But the banker bishop, who had presided over the aforementioned three Boston funerals (Parkman, Lodge, and Haughton), appeared somehow on Scudder's extended list only after his name-dropped reputation had been useful to champion the club *again*, this time for the final monument pigskin carving. Ten others with obvious social prominence were still alive when the monument was unveiled—curiously conspicuous by their absence in the press, however—and none had featured before Scudder's list.[61] The final addition was in 1927 with the last Oneida document, Lovett's poem, which listed brunch host Billy Fields as an honorary club member, salvaging his memory among the forgotten of 1906.

While it is not for any outsider to judge who was worthy of Oneida membership, it does reveal the unfixed nature of the club's roster. In effect, it was not really until 1926 that the surviving monument men sat down and tried to define who was a club member and who was not. Even at the key anniversary moment for which a stone tablet had been commissioned and an event planned, the club was still in some sense a fluid group, and an exclusive and final list was not established until the monument project had been completed. This lack of clarity created all sorts of problems for the media, who played their own role in shaping the narrative of the club. If the book reviews for *Old Boston Boys* at the start of the century had never actually referred to the club or its membership, the 1920s papers were only interested in the most recognizable and had a hard time keeping the Oneidas' names straight.[62] Even if the Oneidas could not be responsible for reporting mistakes, the inability to define a coherent and full list of club members until *after* erecting a monument does not resonate well with being an *organized* football club.

As a process, commemoration is riddled with problems in identifying who counts, when, and where. Decades after the Oneidas, the national Vietnam War Memorial was unveiled, and the addition of names—effectively altering the date of American involvement—illustrates how a monument "challenges memory as a knowable object."[63] When Scudder's imagination lit in 1923 with an idea to memorialize the Oneidas and captain Miller in a didactic exercise for Nobles schoolboys, the editor thought he knew his teammates from memory, the same geriatric reminiscence captured by Lovett almost two decades earlier. But the roster hid a nascent problem that featured in writing on the ball. As a result, by the end of their commemoration project Scudder had retroactively changed who was welcome in the Oneida clubhouse.

If there were questions regarding some of the names, number, and identities of club members, a further historical problem was the club's foundation date—also changed between 1922 and 1923—as it became associated with the claim to being first. In 1906 Lovett had pinned the start: "In 1863 the Oneida Football Club was organized and composed. . . ."[64] However, from the 1923 school tablet to Scudder's 1924 *An Appreciation* booklet for Miller, his later *An Historical Sketch*, the press, and all the historiography after 1925, the club's foundation date was communicated everywhere as 1862.[65] So theoretically the earliest and most complete account of the Oneidas claimed its foundation in 1863. The club name had never appeared in connection to the earlier school team matches, whether reported by the press or corroborated by fellow student Francis Lincoln's eyewitness diary.[66] Fascinatingly, despite pages of correspondence in Lovett's papers around the writing and publication of *Old Boston Boys*—which include all sorts of praise, comments, and corrections from dozens of friends—there is not a single mention of Lovett having incorrectly identified the foundation date, nor was it corrected in the book's two later reprintings. Not even Means Lawrence, who later was one of the monument men, saw fit to mention the date or their famous club in his letter of congratulations.[67] Similarly silent are the 1922 donation documents at Historic New England. Not a single piece of evidence refers to the change or discusses Lovett's previous 1863 claim as erroneous.[68] Yet when Scudder's memorialization projects took off in early 1923, the date subsequently given was always 1862, and the club was always affirmed as first.

Dates are not arbitrary. 1862 was not a haphazard choice. If the Oneidas were not responsible when the newspapers incorrectly related the date on multiple occasions—most often as either 1873 or 1852—they were responsible for choosing what they *engraved* on memorials and *wrote* in documents designed to affirm their story.[69] Prince's 1923 Harvard history had ingeniously placed the Boston tradition parallel to a "revival" of football in England, which "organized the Football Association in 1863, but the followers of the Rugby rules did not get together until 1871 when the Rugby Football Union was formed."[70] From 1923 onward the new 1862 foundation became central to the Oneida story, thereby quipping the English—despite the absence of any conclusive evidence—of the potential title of earliest *organizers* of the game.[71] Since the archive before 1923 does not testify to the 1862 founding date, all we have is the Oneidas' word. Yet even they could not be patent in their own mathematical calculations. Whether it was the start date or the actual duration of the club's existence, Scudder seems to have been loose with his numbers and the first news story (about the 1922 donation) had even claimed that the 1863 championship match was "the last game of the famous Oneida team."[72] But when commemorating firsts, the end is less important than the beginning.

The most peculiar, and possibly surreptitious, nebulosity in the Oneida narrative is also perhaps the most obvious. One of the principal arguments made by the monument architect Jones in the pigskin saga was that he claimed the initial designs called for a round ball. This was why he warned the city's art commission when the Oneidas were trying to insist on having the oval pigskin carved. The architect had insisted that "what they [the Oneidas] propose is entirely out of scale with the monument and is the wrong shape and completely changes its character" because, in his words, "the photographs of the model submitted in the fall [of 1925] had an old fashioned round ball roughly indicated, but this was not studied carefully at the time and was not satisfactory to me."[73] Who submitted the initial plans, and why would Jones disapprove of the old-fashioned *round* ball if he had produced the design? Was Jones reacting to "rough" designs created by the Oneidas? Is it possible that the Oneidas submitted first designs in September of 1925 with a round ball—recalling their old painted one on public display at Otis House—but subsequently revised the plans insisting on a "football of appropriate proportions with the lacing showing"?[74] It is obvious that a monument to the founders of *American* football would bewilder if it had a *round* ball instead of an *oval* one. Few contemporary passersby in 1925 would know, or remember, that the oval shape of 1920s football had not been the standard a half century earlier.[75] Such inconsistencies between round artifacts and oval monument carvings were precisely what had led to the problematic interpretations and refurbishments during the 1996 soccer grab. Unfortunately, none of the original plans have survived, so we are left with Jones's word against the Oneidas. But the Oneidas clearly desired the oval shape, however anachronistic, for the ball on their monument.

In all these ambiguities, one ought to assume good faith on the part of the Oneidas. When they began commemoration, there was no intention to memorialize a specific roster of players. Scudder spoke only of the championship team because the purpose was to provide a role model to Noble and Greenough schoolboys in the way Webb Ellis was mythically championed to Rugby students.[76] Even as far back as 1906, the ball had never been intended to be the definitive list of club members nor displayed in a museum but just a fond souvenir for friends. But when those same preciously kept private mementos became *public* artifacts gifted to the SPNEA, libraries, and historical societies, the stakes changed. With the 1925 monument on Boston Common, the Oneida story became part of the wider public Brahmin preservation movement shaping the future writing of history. With it came questions of historicity, authenticity, and coherence. The ambiguity began to reveal cracks in the story: the "reproduced" ball, substituted players, an undefined roster, the club's foundation date, and the shape of their graven ball.

If most of these ambiguities were invisible to the public, any errors or inconsistencies could just be considered memory problems with legitimate senescent justification. The 1920s correspondence from Scudder, a man who visibly spent hours working on the commemoration, does leave the reader with a sense of grandfatherly forgetfulness—in apologizing for neglecting to give Miller's tactical drawing to the Massachusetts Historical Society (MHS). But the archive also reveals a determined lucidity of purpose. Scudder's attention to detail—how and where to paste news clippings into the donated typescript—was almost obsessive as he thanked the MHS secretary for "the interest you have taken in this not important paper."[77] But Scudder and his friends knew exactly what they were doing with their supposedly "unimportant" matter. As they had done for other commemorative projects, they were engaging simultaneously in heritage preservation and scripting their place in sports history and wider Bostonian and American narratives. As with the Brahmin generation around them, the Oneidas knew the relevance of monuments, origin stories and myths as well as their dangers.[78] But Miller of all people should have been warned about the perils of tampering with truths. For it was his son who had disproved the evolutionary findings of the Piltdown man discovery a decade earlier, unveiling one of the greatest scientific hoaxes of all time.[79]

The Oneidas were both conscious of the societal importance of memorials and myths in shaping history and aware of their potential manipulation. But in this case, were they honest about themselves and their own achievements? They appear to have ruled out deliberate fabrication and seem to profess sincere virtue. When Lovett was preparing *Old Boston Boys*, his nephew, artist Dana Gibson, agreed to collaborate on the visuals while excluding the possibility of any manipulation: "The [manuscript] is delightful. I am already seeing what I can do. It's too good in itself—too true a story of those time [*sic*] to allow any fake pictures to set it and throw you out of step. So I shan't touch any part that is found to be authentic."[80] The letter is undated, and it is impossible to know if Gibson was involved in Sam Cabot's "reproduction" of the Oneida ball, but it underscores an awareness of what was authentic and what was not. Even if eulogies tend to extol the deceased, Lovett's tribute had called Cabot "such a pure, white-souled man" who had a "wonderful power of radiating, as it were, sincerity, honesty of purpose, truthfulness."[81] So it seems that, provided there was a modicum of honesty, the fine line of authenticity could be navigated with a clean Brahmin conscience.

But ambiguities abound, and their many artifacts, documents, and claims remained open to interpretation—Hancock's sign of a persistent hoax. As we know, the Oneidas were engaging in heritage preservation, which is not the same as history. As the artifact problems illustrate, writing truthful history is an unforgiving task, an "art of making an argument about the past by telling a story accountable to evidence."[82] And the evidence to which that Oneida story is accountable is precisely all those many artifacts and documents that they themselves had created, preserved, and deposited. In 1926, Scudder may have thought he was writing the definitive history of the Oneidas, but in fact he was just preserving more heritage and creating usable primary sources. An author, however, has no say on what Daniel Boorstin has called the "afterlife" of a document, that adventurous time after its author's death that is "vagrant, unpredictable, and often astonishing."[83] Scudder's document, and its narrative, then influenced the nearly decisive choice for an American football hall of fame in 1949, and later was reimagined as the origin point for soccer in America—a usable sporting past if ever there was one. Sometimes, however, documents and their public narrative can also reveal historical mysteries that were destined to remain secret, and instead their doubts are magnified in the light of private revelation.

Following their successful commemoration, the seven survivors shared, in the intimacy of the Oneidas' inner circle, a moment central to their story, one that unveiled a tactic hitherto hidden. The last known Oneida artifact was Lovett's poem, which he read to his friends at a luncheon in May of 1927. Entitled *A Pilgrimage*, Lovett wrote it for a meeting of six of the seven Oneidas at the home of William De Yongh Field. The poem, as far as we know, exists in one copy, preciously kept in off-site storage at Harvard's Widener

Library. No other copies were deposited in the other so many institutions where the Oneidas had donated their ball, handkerchief, multiple booklets, articles, and sketches. The Harvard copy is the only publicly available one.

The 1927 poem is wonderfully crafted verse with Lovett speaking to their old 1863 ball. Toward the end, Lovett explains that a monument had been erected but includes a fascinating admission:

> Then—"A Football Monument," I
>   said, "has lately been erected
> To the old Oneida Team." At this
>   he was visibly affected.
>
> Then I told of the graven Football
>   and the phrase, as on a scroll,
> That no opponent, anywhere, "Had
>   ever crossed our goal."
> He caught at "Graven Football"
>   and asked, naively, if I knew
> If *his* likeness was intended. "Sure,"
>   I said, "a good likeness too."
> Yes, I know, just shameless lying but
>   there's this upon my side:—
> If it made the Football happy, was I
>   not justified?
>
> Then all at once, he brightened up,
>   "Why!" excitedly, said he:—
> "Ef thet's the aim, then I kin the claim
>   this Moniment's for ME!"
> "My dear old sport," I answered,
>   "your reasoning's quite correct,
> Present your claim" (I lied again)
>   "twill be given due respect
> And *YOUR* Monument will long
>   endure, singing its Football Song
> When the remaining few of our dear
>   old Crew,
> Shall have silently passed along."

. . .
> The aged Football stretched himself
> and drew a long, deep breath.
> "Well, bless me!" he murmured,
> softly, "ef I ain't tickled 'most to
> death.
> To think an old, worn out Football,
> not wuth a single cent,
> Should be honored, on Bos'n Com'n,
> With a Marble Moniment!"[84]

As if one "shameless" lie was not enough, Lovett confessed to a second. What was the double lie about the ball's *true* likeness and the claim it presented? Was this an admission that the "graven ball" actually *should* have been round? Was it an acknowledgment that their game, the Boston Oneida game, was not what the monument actually portrayed? Did they finally privately admit to themselves that this escapade in establishing their sporting heritage had gotten out of control and that their old Boston Game was so different from the American football phenomenon dominating college campuses? They had always seemed to have understood the difference. In 1906, Scudder had endorsed *Old Boston Boys* and qualified their football—with a phrase singularly applied to that sport—"as it was played then."[85] Later, Robert Apthorp Boit's memoirs in 1915 noted, "Of course football then was a different game from that played today. We played with a round inflated rubber ball. But we had our rules, and good ones."[86] Such a different game, indeed, that Lawrence was described at the 1923 tablet unveiling as a "great dribbler of the ball in the days when it could not be carried."[87] And if their artifacts were so true, then why had Miller expressed some doubt in his June 1905 corrections to Lovett's manuscript. Why had he not simply cited the list of names painted on the ball in his possession so as to give Lovett the definitive championship roster—just three weeks before sending that ball to Cabot for a photograph?[88]

There is a certain irony in the Oneidas' private confession, bordering on what John Darlington has noted when "the thread of history is broken and the lessons it can teach us become meaningless, or worse, twisted to tell a different story—a lie."[89] Maybe this examination of conscience was a sort of collective mea culpa—admittedly an odd notion for Boston Brahmin Protestants.[90] Was it important to clear their conscience before their final hours and admit some twisted truth that their game was not really the college one that had been embossed in painted letters, preserved in archives, and immortalized in stone as such? To an extent, they had been complicit in media hyperbole beginning with the 1922 ball donation. The earliest newspaper article specifically about the Oneidas had trumpeted the 1863 date and the club as the first and "only team playing football . . . according to those who have delved into American football lore"—an audacious claim given that no publication to date affirmed this and Scudder had not written to Camp or Davis until a year later.[91] Perhaps the poem was Lovett's artful attempt to weave privy guilt into verse expressing the mischief that had ever so animated their memorial adventure. Lovett was among friends after all, and his poem was just the final verse in an Oneida prosody party. At Billy Field's house in May 1927, they gathered for a gammoned brunch to fete what Scudder had already encouraged them to celebrate after their monument had been erected. In the spring of 1926, the retired editor had reminded his four monument friends that November 7, 1862, was their "athletic birthday."[92] Not 1863, but 1862. Forget that the legendary match had taken place on November 7, 1863. Forget that they had apparently lied (twice) to their old ball. Forget what shape it was, its mysterious painted letters, or how its graven form became oblong. It was no matter, and Lovett's poetry breathed an air of levity into their final stanzas together. Besides, Scudder's letter about their "athletic birthday" had been penned on April 1st, and if the Oneidas were not hoaxers, they were anything but April fools.

11
CONCLUSION

Boys Will Be Boys

> We must not take this occasion too seriously. This is not a war memorial or the record of any great achievement in the history of Boston. It simply commemorates the primitive play of some Boston boys. This parade-ground was their playground, and in their sport they conceived the plan for organized football, which has now become accepted by thousands of eager contestants and watched by millions of shouting enthusiasts.
>
> —Peabody, 1925

Not "too seriously" had said Oneida member Frank Peabody at the 1925 unveiling. How ironic a statement for a public monument, and one whose legacy subsequently underwent multiple refurbishments over the next century. Why then did the Harvard professor insist so intently and publicly that their memorial was not "the record of any great achievement"?[1] Had not Peabody made, but a few moments earlier in his speech, the unmistakable parallel of the Oneidas to Revolutionary War rebels? Admittedly, a number of the Old Boston Boys could trace their lineage back to independence or before, and such a pedigree was more than enough to justify donations to the SPNEA or memorials in schools and parks. But the Oneidas' memorializing journey went beyond commemorating ancestry and became a retroactive self-fulfilling prophecy. Unveiling memorials, placing artifacts in museums, and depositing written material in libraries and archives was not simply preserving proof of a forgotten history. It *became* the truth that the Oneidas were the first organized football club in the United States *because* a stone monument was erected where they had played, an old rubber ball sat in a museum, and documentation—held by such august institutions as the SPNEA, the Bostonian Society, and the Massachusetts Historical Society—said so. Once Walter Camp and Parke Davis retrospectively proclaimed their primacy, the case was closed, even if it flew in the face of a culture bathed in Darwinian evolutionary ideas that eroded belief in all forms of creation myths.

The authors of a history of hoaxes underline the "universal penchant for believing what one wants to hear . . . [which] opens the door for the unscrupulous to exploit their less cynical peers."[2] In the enthusiastic context of preserving old New England's material culture, added to the impeccable credentials and social standing of the Oneidas, why would anyone question the legitimacy of their story? Faced with seven elderly men who claimed to have been at the heart of the American sporting revolution alongside the Bigelow, Lawrence, Lodge, and Wolcott names, among others, it is impossible to see the custodians of Boston's museums, libraries, and archives as anything but credulous. When the Oneidas presented a story of invention, a foundation myth for American sport with a list of fifty-two famous, wealthy, and upstanding citizens, Boston's Brahmin population were being told exactly the kind of nativist story of achievement and innovation that they wanted to hear in a disorienting world that seemed to dispense with their glorious past.

On the surface, the Oneidas do not appear to have done anything exceptional. They simply surfed the waves of commemoration common to their time following the lead of the SPNEA, the Pilgrim tercentenary, and all the memorials felicitating fellow Brahmin. Art historian Kirk Savage reminds us, however, that monuments "do not arise as if by natural law to celebrate the deserving, they are built by people with sufficient power to marshal (or impose) public consent for their erection."[3] If the Oneida tablet expresses some humility in not being sculpted in the club members' likenesses—only their names are listed, and on the *back* of the monument no less—the Boston Common commemorative escapade was different from other memorials on this salient public space. Of all the pre-1925 memorials honoring Brahmins—Sumner (1877), Quincy (1878), Garrison (1886), Ellery Channing (1902), Wolcott (1906), Hale (1912), and Wendell Phillips (1914–15) among others—none were commissioned during their lifetimes.[4] They were all, without exception, *post*mortem endeavors of a living community wishing to recognize the deceased. Admittedly, the Oneidas were discrete enough to avoid pasting their faces onto their monument, and its unveiling focused on remembering Wolcott's ultimate Civil War sacrifice to preserve the Union. Yet the surviving footballers were there, front and center,

Conclusion

in the most important park in Boston giving speeches about themselves and their deceased friends. They stood, photographed for posterity, by the only city memorial commissioned and unveiled by the *living* being honored.

As a result of their commemorative enterprise, the slippery idea called tradition now holds that all football in the United States—oval or round—began with the Oneidas in Boston. The club is not entirely factitious in the vein of Hobsbawm's "invented traditions," but they were hardly alone playing midcentury football.[5] Despite Lovett's view in 1906 that "when, where, and by whom [ball games were] first played is beyond our ken," over time the Oneidas had become convinced they were the origin.[6] By the 1920s, modern football was said to owe a debt to the hallowed fields of Rugby School and its legendary rebel, William Webb Ellis. As descendants of other (Revolutionary) rebels, the Oneida monument men saw themselves embodying that same tradition made famous by *Tom Brown's Schooldays*. After all, the 1923 Miller tablet "was suggested by the one at Rugby."[7] So just as one young English boy invented rugby, another Bostonian one begot football as "organized" and, in inventing the Boston Game, had created the American one. The Oneidas' private correspondence shows how in celebrating their honored captain they held Miller up as a reflection of Ellis in archetypal fashion: "Fortunately, his appreciation, Nov. 7 [the 1923 tablet at Nobles], and crowning, Nov. 21 [the 1925 monument unveiling], were not delayed 100 years, as in the case of his English prototype."[8] Despite disavowing a public crowning, they did privately admit to one. Their story then became another of the "re-imagined narratives and creation stories" written and rewritten on the palimpsest of history with partisans of both codes—soccer and gridiron football—carving and recarving the monumental and exclusive claim to an Oneida ancestry.[9]

Yet we are told that their indomitable persistence in commemorating themselves so publicly should be taken frivolously. Why "not too seriously"? And why do it all to begin with? In the crime novel, it is the final chapter that reveals what drives the narrative: motive. The mystery moves along, piece by piece exposing the means and the opportunity, but the motive remains fugitive until the end with the proverbial "why" known only in the imagination of the author. Like in fiction, narrative is inseparable from history—notwithstanding the frontiers between the two—and so there is a temptation in the historiographical enterprise to identify those elusive reasons behind all human endeavor.[10] Yet the academy has long been cautious of feeding the enemy of true history: judgment.[11] Perhaps this is why Barbara Tuchman counseled not to write to give lessons and leave the "why" of history alone until it emerges of itself to "suddenly appear and tap one on the shoulder."[12] Even if the Oneidas could never have predicted the surprise future legacies, why did they erect a monument only to dedicate it so facetiously and hide in beguiled poesy? What motives might lie—in all senses of the word—behind Lovett's verse?

Several possibilities suggest why seven old men planted a monument on the most important public space in downtown Boston sixty years after some boyhood games claiming to be the founders of "foot ball" (soccer and gridiron) in America. Yes, they rode a wave of nativist preservation, were inspired by Rugby School commemoration, and fought for city pride in rivalry with Yale's Walter Camp memorial efforts. But that was the context, means, and opportunity, not the true motive. While the monument men did bask in the reflected glory of Brahmin society, the seven survivors were not all as grand as the Wolcotts (deceased soldier and erstwhile governor), Senator Lodge, or Bishop Lawrence. Before the commemoration started in 1923, only Professor Peabody had a reputation that could rival the greatest Oneida names. Scudder, Means Lawrence, and Bowditch were Harvard men, but neither Arnold, Lovett, nor Miller had the illustrious degree or were listed as graduates of any university (until Miller's honorary one in 1924). While Peabody, as a schoolboy, was clearly the brightest, academic success was no guarantee for remembrance, as shown by the fate of one of Lovett's other schoolmates—Helen Magill White—the first girl to study at the Latin School and later first woman PhD in America.[13] The trio of pioneering baseballers had similarly faded out of living memory: Arnold into complete anonymity, even if Lovett's polished writing was appreciated and printed in occasional columns, and the wealthy but small-town upstate Miller had made a significant impact in dairy farming. But neither Arnold, Lovett, nor Miller appeared as elite Boston socialites, and until commemoration began, none of their talents had garnered great publicity. Even afterward, Scudder felt obliged to share with Lovett that he encountered a fellow Union Club member asking for one of his friend's poems, reassuring its author, "You see, old fellow, you are not so much of a back number as you think, but are still a going concern. Long may you wave!"[14]

Among the monument men, there was one thing that five of them—incidentally, the group of friends that comes out most strongly in the archive—shared: a missing crimson "H." Although some were degree holders, Arnold, Lovett, Means Lawrence, Miller, and Scudder never obtained the coveted

Conclusion

Harvard athletics letter and went unrecognized in the six-hundred-page school history printed just months before any mention of Oneida commemoration. The remaining two, Bowditch and Peabody, were both recognized Harvard sportsmen, Ned with a letter in rowing and Frank having played in the first-ever baseball game versus Yale.[15] Many deceased Oneidas and Old Boys were also "H" men, but *not* these five monument instigators. Degreeless Arnold and Lovett could only claim having played *against* Harvard, even if Lovett's amateur gentleman reputation had been enough for selection as the only noncollegian alongside forty baseball alumni from Harvard, Yale, and Dartmouth for an Old-Timers game against former Boston professionals in 1897.[16] This context explains Scudder's letter to his "lifelong and always most faithful friends" in which he urges the commemoration dates of November 7 (1923) and 21 (1925) be "celebrated by us as our red letter days."[17] The same missive that had "crowned" Miller as an American Webb Ellis reveals that in commemorating their sporting heritage, the Oneidas sought to fill a significant gap in their athletic pedigrees. Without erecting a stone tablet on Boston Common, six of the seven monument men (aside from Professor Peabody) would likely have disappeared into the book of hidden history where most of humanity wanders forgotten.

So in an act of conspicuous nosism, the Oneidas expressed an excess of collective hubris and planted a monument on the most important public space sixty years later—the entire escapade causing them to be viewed in retrospect as the founders of "foot ball" (soccer and gridiron) in the United States. Had they only celebrated their boyhood games at a dinner among friends and in a privately printed book, or even just the school plaque at Noble and Greenough, we could simply look back and smile at an exaggerated sense of collective significance. After all, until 1925 they had, in their gentlemanly modesty, consistently exercised self-effacement, always honoring someone else or at least he who was absent. Privately, the Oneidas knew they had become mischievous, but the seven self-memorializing oldsters convinced themselves and cozened everyone around them that they were the missing link in the evolutionary chain of football history and, therefore, worthy of remembrance. Was this group of teenage schoolboys really the first to organize football, a sport that later evolved into the oval collegiate phenomenon or the rounder "beautiful game"? Was their heritage preservation—so deliberately donated and duplicated across institutions—just a process resulting in the a posteriori invention of the "Boston Game"? Or does the ambiguity and manipulation of artifacts rather reveal that they pulled off the great football hoax? Belief begins at the fringes of history.

If the archive expresses one leitmotif in their story, however, it is friendship. Above all, the Oneida story speaks to their brotherly amity and that, particularly in those autumn years, this is where they found meaning in their lives. Their correspondence reveals the sharing of life's joys and hardships across time, from cribbage games to family sickness.[18] In the words of Means Lawrence, "As the shades of night are falling, it is good for us to gather closer together and tighten the bonds of affection and friendship."[19] They stood firm together, particularly the closest five, honoring one another whether it was captain Miller or their otherwise anonymous teammate Arnold.[20] Materially speaking, degreeless Lovett and Arnold were hardly in the 1 percent later in life as revealed by their degrading financial situations and continued employment into their seventies, with both renting rather than owning homes in the upscale Back Bay. In contrast to Scudder, who seemed to live a more than comfortable retired life, twice-widowed Lovett lodged with his unmarried daughter in a "little apartment" in Cambridge.[21] Such was Lovett's situation that by the 1930s, Miller was sending him checks, fresh fruit and vegetable baskets, quilts, and slippers and even paid for Lovett family members' medical treatment.[22] The motive of friendship was expressed in acts of true solidarity and verse like "Old Friends" (see image 12).

The Oneida story sparkles with complexities, alternate narratives, and the contested nature of history and memory, making its legacy more complicated than the seven men could ever have imagined. The idea that six decades after their deaths the custodians of American soccer would believe to possess the Oneida inheritance would have doubtless bewildered them. That a lone campaigner, Tom McGrath, would leap to their defense until the pigskin was restored on the monument may have seemed even more bizarre. That their monument was subject to such drama is curious given how plain and underwhelming (more akin to a graveyard headstone) it is, specifically in comparison to the grander Boston Common memorials to wars, politicians, artistic figures, and moments of social change. Perhaps more telling and informative of the true meaning of their self-memorialization is the context in which the Oneidas played their ball game, the years of the Civil War and Reconstruction, and their collective journey into a Gilded Age adulthood through a period so transformational for their Brahmin world. They were also the first generation liberated from a self-conscious cultural inferiority

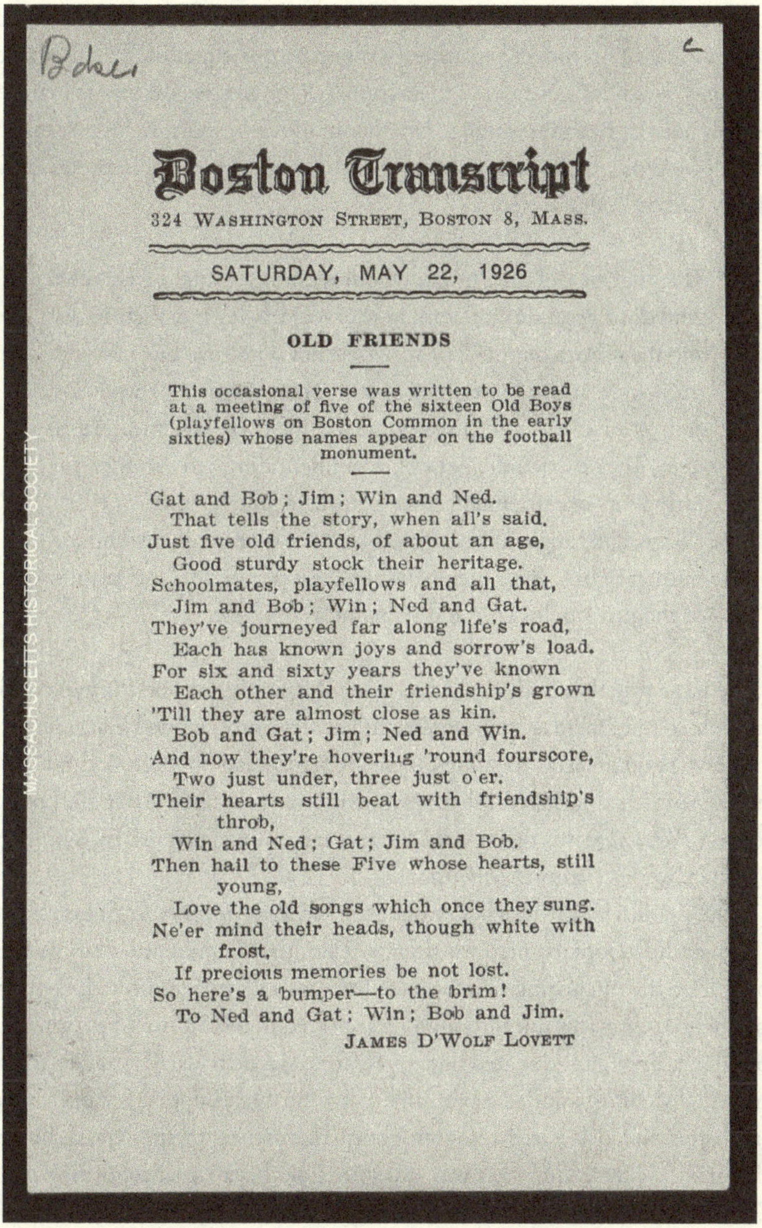

Boston Transcript

324 Washington Street, Boston 8, Mass.

SATURDAY, MAY 22, 1926

OLD FRIENDS

This occasional verse was written to be read at a meeting of five of the sixteen Old Boys (playfellows on Boston Common in the early sixties) whose names appear on the football monument.

Gat and Bob; Jim; Win and Ned.
   That tells the story, when all's said.
Just five old friends, of about an age,
   Good sturdy stock their heritage.
Schoolmates, playfellows and all that,
   Jim and Bob; Win; Ned and Gat.
They've journeyed far along life's road,
   Each has known joys and sorrow's load.
For six and sixty years they've known
   Each other and their friendship's grown
'Till they are almost close as kin.
   Bob and Gat; Jim; Ned and Win.
And now they're hovering 'round fourscore,
   Two just under, three just o'er.
Their hearts still beat with friendship's throb,
   Win and Ned; Gat; Jim and Bob.
Then hail to these Five whose hearts, still young,
   Love the old songs which once they sung.
Ne'er mind their heads, though white with frost,
   If precious memories be not lost.
So here's a bumper—to the brim!
   To Ned and Gat; Win; Bob and Jim.

               JAMES D'WOLF LOVETT

IMAGE 12. On May 22, 1926, the *Boston Transcript* published a poem penned by James D'Wolf Lovett that honored the close, lifelong ties that existed between the monument men. Courtesy of the Massachusetts Historical Society.

complex well-described by Sam Haynes; the Oneidas only knew an American Republic that "no longer regard[ed] Britain as our superior."[23] This shaped how they, as adults, considered their country's progressive destiny as manifest in their nativist Brahmin origins, whether in life or in sport. In an 1888 speech to the New England Society, the then member of the House of Representatives Henry Cabot Lodge stated,

> The Pilgrim and the Puritan whom we honor tonight were men who did a great deal of work in the world. They had their faults and their shortcomings, but they were not slothful in business and they were most fervent in spirit. They formed prosperous commonwealths and built on government by law and not of men. They carried the light of learning undimmed through the early years of settlement. They planted a school-house in every village, and fought always a good fight for ordered liberty and for human rights. Their memories shall not perish, for "the actions of the just smell sweet and blossom in the dust."[24]

In the same way that Lodge called to mind Pilgrim values and Puritan contributions, so the Oneidas' memorialization analogously claimed that no matter their own faults and shortcomings, these seven men had not been slothful. Their fervent spirit had fathered the game of American football. After all, Lovett's poem *A Pilgrimage* was their sacred sermon as sporting puritans. In Winthrop's city, they were a "shining *club* upon a hill."

There could hardly be a better case study in *lieux de mémoire*. It began with a dinner and a book printed for friends. Then they commemorated the club, institutionally anchoring it in a place (the school) with a direct link to the founder of rugby (mythical though he appeared in deed if not in person), followed by a booklet—donated but largely for didactic ends. Most audaciously, they finally commissioned a monument on the most important public space in Boston and deposited a sketch about themselves in the Massachusetts Historical Society. Yes, this was only possible because of who they were. Countless other groups of friends who gathered to play similar games never had the time, resources, or social standing to commemorate it and might be jealous. But if hyperbole has no place in the telling of history, it is not unwelcome in commemoration among friends. Moreover, memorials often meld forgetting with remembering in a healing process, and they have, to quote

Conclusion

Jay Winter, their own "life history," which sheds meanings and takes on "new significance in subsequent years."[25] So we pass no judgment on the Oneidas and leave envy to the covetous, particularly as those most entitled to it—like the omnipresent yet never crowned teammate Ned Fenno—showed none.[26] Besides, measuring historic greatness is a complex exercise, and in the words of distinguished psychologist Dean Simonton, "significant events and people are those that later generations think worthy of entering the permanent record of human acts."[27] For the Oneidas, only time will tell if they truly duped Clio.

The Oneida tale forces the historian to ask a question different from that which feeds the ongoing football history "origins debate."[28] Instead, we have wondered how and why a handful of men sought such a sacrosanct place in sport history. In an exercise of what William McNeill coined "mythistory," we have decrypted the origin story, separated its legends from its facts, seeking to understand what the Oneidas themselves, knew, believed, and commemorated.[29] Escalating into a most fascinating case of memorialization, sporting or otherwise, the Oneida saga sits on history's fertile verge and borders on what historian Daniel Boorstin has aptly named pseudoevents: those man-made events intended, at least on some level, to deceive. Rather than spontaneous historical happenings, such events are planted with the express purpose of being reported by an avid press and introduce sufficient ambiguity, which often results in self-fulfilling prophecy.[30] Historian William Baker described how the Webb Ellis myth arose from "innocent curiosity" when various actors "transformed hearsay into fact, trivia into significance" despite the fact that "an evolutionary explanation of the myth of the species would have been more plausible."[31] But a plaque or a monument rarely allows sufficient space for nuance and contextualization.

It is the historian's role then, in the words of Jed Smith (curator at the Museum of Rugby, Twickenham), to "show where the myth is at variance with the evidence but also to explain why a myth persists, despite the finest disregard for the rules of evidence."[32] In the case of the Oneida story, it was born of the same "innocent curiosity" as the Ellis legend but with a legitimate basis in fact that was recorded contemporaneously and then commemorated. It is in the course of commemoration that the Oneida "truth" was stretched, gulling everyone along the way. That complex construction of an unintended heritage started from personal motivations to honor faithful friends—more than fictive kin—under the specter of the sinking sands of time. The desire to memorialize was fueled by the unconscious irrepressible forces of collegiate rivalry, and the result was undoubtedly distorted by the hyperbolizing power of the media. Eminent biologist Stephen Jay Gould, whose discussion of evolutionary hoaxes and baseball history reminds us how origin myths offer humanity the "heroes and sacred places" we deeply desire, once cited P. T. Barnum: "No humbug is great without truth at the bottom."[33] In the spirit of Gould's clemency toward baseball's Doubleday story, we too are content to treat the Oneida tale gently. Hoaxes may, after all, be malicious *or* humorous. Lest we forget, at their 1922 ball donation reunion dinner, "talk waxed warmer . . . and the laughter of unrestrained youth filled the room."[34] In playfully crafting a national sporting origin story into what might be a most mischievous hoax, the Oneidas were old friends, just boys being boys, reminding us not to take it "too seriously."

So while historians continue to decrypt origin myths and endeavor to write an always more transcending history, perhaps we should now leave the Old Boston Boys to *requiescat in pace* with their parochial memories and their adopted sporting progeny, however much the association and American football siblings each act as if an only child. Voltaire once said that "history is, after all, nothing but a pack of tricks which we play upon the dead."[35] In writing their own history while still living, the Oneidas may have tricked the round rubber ball into an oval stone one. But over time and distance, the ball always runs faster than the man, and in death even the Oneidas themselves were outplayed. Unscored upon in life, their goal line was finally crossed *post mortem*.

EPILOGUE

In honor of the club's bard, James D'Wolf Lovett, the gentleman once called the "Shakespeare of baseball," we hope these few stanzas of our own New England–inspired verse might be received as a tribute to the Oneidas' *Pilgrimage*, just as jovial and warmly Frosty in style . . .

The Code Not Taken

Two codes diverged in a yellow wood,
And sorry he could not claim them both,
Being one ball, oblong it stood
And looked down Bos'n Com'n as far as he could
Where hid a sphere in the undergrowth.

Graven stone pigskin, as just as fair,
And having perhaps the better claim,
Because for gridiron the '20s did care;
With '94 the passing there
Had worn the tablet to soccer fame.

Five old friends in Camp's shadow yet lay,
On Brahm'n mem'ry had trodden black.
Oneida, yet first for another day!
As Beacon Hill breeds to the Back Bay,
I doubted if round should ever come back.

I shall be telling this with a smile
Somewhere pages and pages hence:
Two games devised in a yellow wood, and I—
I spied the club's poetic guile,
'A Lunch'n roast made all the difference.

NOTES

INTRODUCTION

1 Peter Hancock, *Hoax Springs Eternal: The Psychology of Cognitive Deception* (Cambridge: Cambridge University Press, 2015), 18.
2 Any references to the weather in this book come directly from historical newspapers and Raymond S. Bradley et al., *The Climate of Amherst Massachusetts 1836–1985* (Amherst: University of Massachusetts, Dept. of Geology and Geography, 1987).
3 Field entered the Boston Public Latin School in 1858 with Lovett. School records list him as a merchant but without any university degree. Field appears in multiple US Census records. From 1880 to 1930, the de Yongh Field farm in Weston was listed with two servants and a farm laborer as well as a country house in Mattapoisett staffed by a cook, a chambermaid, a housekeeper, and three laborers. By 1920, the house in Weston only had one servant left, and in 1930, the couple lived alone, with the house valued at $25,000. Henry F. Jenks, *Catalogue of the Boston Public Latin School. Established in 1635. With an Historical Sketch* (Boston: Boston Public Latin Association, 1886), 213.
4 Unfortunately, the archive does not reveal which of the seven attended the lunch. Beyond geographic conjecture, the "closeness" of the friendship circle suggests that Bowditch was the missing teammate. At some point in 1927, Bowditch and his wife moved to Murray Bay in Canada, where he died in 1929. "Edw. Bowditch Dies in Canada," *Times-Union, Albany NY*, July 21, 1929, 10-A.
5 In comparison with Miller, who lived on a grand country estate and whose fortune was estimated in the "millions," Arnold lived in a rental as an adult in what the censuses reveal to be mostly immigrant neighborhoods.
6 On the longevity of Peabody's theological work, see Grace Cumming Long, "The Ethics of Francis Greenwood Peabody: A Century of Christian Social Ethics," *Journal of Religious Ethics* 18, no. 1 (1990): 55–73.
7 All the biographical details have come, unless otherwise noted, from the various Harvard Class Secretary's Reports, obituaries, or the sources used

in the appendix available on the Digital Humanities Platform. The "partial list" appears in Winthrop Saltonstall Scudder, *An Historical Sketch of the Oneida Football Club of Boston 1862–1865* (deposited October 18, 1926), Massachusetts Historical Society.
8. Van Wyck Brooks, "On Creating a Usable Past," *Dial*, April 18, 1918, 337–41.
9. *Boys' Life*, October 1926, 19.
10. James D'Wolf Lovett, *A Pilgrimage—Read at a Meeting of the Oneidas, Saturday, May 28, 1927* (Boston: n.p., 1927). Kept in off-site storage, the booklet is available for consultation in the Phillips Reading Room, Widener Library, Harvard University. On the page opposite the first page of the poem is a stamp reading "Harvard College Library, 23 July 1927."
11. See multiple dates and publications, but for example, "Comics Supplement," *Sunday Star Ledger*, February 8, 1976, 1.
12. Sam W. Haynes, *Unfinished Revolution—the Early American Republic in a British World* (Charlottesville: University of Virginia Press, 2010), 43.
13. James M. Lindgren, "'A Constant Incentive to Patriotic Citizenship': Historic Preservation in Progressive-Era Massachusetts," *New England Quarterly* 64, no. 4 (December 1991): 602.
14. Erika Doss, *Memorial Mania: Public Feeling in America* (Chicago: University of Chicago Press, 2010), 27.
15. For America as a "city upon a hill," see Daniel T. Rodgers, *As a City on a Hill: The Story of America's Most Famous Lay Sermon* (Princeton, NJ: Princeton University Press, 2018); and Abram C. Van Engen, *A City upon a Hill* (New Haven, CT: Yale University Press, 2020). On exceptionalism, see Charles W. Dunn, ed., *American Exceptionalism: The Origins, History, and Future of the Nation's Greatest Strength* (Lanham, MD: Rowman and Littlefield, 2013); and Ian Tyrrell, *American Exceptionalism: A New History of an Old Idea* (Chicago: University of Chicago Press, 2021).
16. Seth C. Bruggeman, ed., *Born in the USA: Birth, Commemoration and the American Public Memory* (Amherst: University of Massachusetts Press, 2012), 5.
17. Quote translated from the French. Maurice Halbwachs, *Les cadres sociaux de la mémoire* (Paris: Félix Alcan, 1925), 206.
18. Jay Winter, *Remembering War: The Great War between Memory and History in the Twentieth Century* (New Haven, CT: Yale University Press, 2006), 136.

CHAPTER 1

1. For the establishment and objectives of what is now Historic New England, see James M. Lindgren, *Preserving Historic New England: Preservation,*

Progressivism and the Remaking of Memory (New York: Oxford University Press, 1995).

2 The gift was recorded as being from "Mr. Edward L. Arnold and others, Boston. Rubber football of the Oneida Football Club of Boston, a trophy won in 1863." *Old-Time New England* 14, no. 1 (July 1923): 35.

3 John R. Betts, "The Technological Revolution and the Rise of Sport, 1850–1900," *Mississippi Valley Historical Review* 40, no. 2 (1953): 244.

4 Hayes, C. The original rubber store, under Goodyear's patent. Established C. Hayes, 26 School St., Boston, 1861. See "The Original Rubber Store," Library of Congress, accessed April 29, 2024, https://www.loc.gov/item/rbpe.06802500/.

5 See, for example, "The Oldest Football," Soccer Ball World, accessed November 9, 2021, https://soccerballworld.com/oldest-football-charles-goodyears-soccer-ball/.

6 The US Patent Office records hold patents awarded to a C. Goodyear going back to 1835 and multiple awards in 1844, 1845, 1851, and 1852. Charles Goodyear, Improvement in making hollow articles of India rubber, US Patent 5,536, filed November 11, 1847, and issued April 25, 1848.

7 Charles Goodyear, *The Applications and Uses of Vulcanized Gum Elastic* (New Haven, CT: Goodyear, 1853), 199.

8 See Goodyear's own advertising, Goodyear Tyres Barbados, "Did you know? The first modern football was designed and built in 1855 by Charles Goodyear! The football was made of vulcanized rubber panels, glued at the seams, very similarly shaped to today's basketball. Prior to this, balls were dependent on the size and shape of a pig's bladder," Facebook, accessed April 24, 2024, https://www.facebook.com/GoodYearBarbados/photos/a.134370246749947/909457612574536/.

9 Clarence Deming, "Three Ages of Football," *Outing* 41 (October 1902): 57.

10 On the importance of ball technology as a causative factor in the development of football codes, see Gavin Kitching, "'Old' Football and the 'New' Codes: Some Thoughts on the 'Origins of Football' Debate and Suggestions for Further Research," *International Journal of the History of Sport* 28, no. 13 (2011): 1733–49.

11 "Foot Ball," *Boston Herald*, November 10, 1863, 4; "Foot Ball," *Boston Daily Advertiser*, November 9, 1863, 1.

12 "A Match Game," *Boston Evening Transcript*, November 9, 1863, 3.

13 James D'Wolf Lovett, *Old Boston Boys and the Games They Played* (Boston: Riverside Press, 1906).

14 Lovett, *Old Boston Boys*, 92–100.

15 Winthrop Saltonstall Scudder, *An Historical Sketch of the Oneida Football Club of Boston 1862–1865* (deposited October 18, 1926), Massachusetts Historical Society.

16 Lovett, *Old Boston Boys*, 84–85.

17 "Foot Ball," *Boston Herald*, October 13, 1860. William W. Newell from Cambridge entered Dixwell's at age fifteen but, in 1860, appears to have been in his first year at Harvard Divinity School. *A Catalog of the Officers and Students of Harvard University for the Academical Year 1860–61* (Cambridge, MA: Sever and Francis, 1860), 52.

18 Winthrop Saltonstall Scudder, ed., *Gerrit Smith Miller—an Appreciation—Supplement to the Nobleman* (Dedham, MA: Noble and Greenough School, 1924), 24.

19 Roger Tamte details the history of rules changes whereby touchdowns became more important than kicked goals from the field. Roger Tamte, *Walter Camp and the Creation of American Football* (Urbana: University of Illinois Press, 2018), 311–16.

20 Lovett, *Old Boston Boys*, 97.

21 Lovett, *Old Boston Boys*, 97–99.

22 Lovett, *Old Boston Boys*, 95–98. For more on Farragut's famous words "Damn the torpedoes, full speed ahead," see Robert M. Browning Jr., "'Damn the Torpedoes': What Did Farragut Really Say at Mobile Bay?," *Naval History Magazine* 28, no. 4 (July 2014), https://www.usni.org/magazines/naval-history-magazine/2014/july/damn-torpedoes.

23 Lovett mentions several Old Boys who died in the war: Mason, Huntington Wolcott, Will Freeman, and Cabot Russell. Lovett, *Old Boston Boys*, 75, 105, 121.

24 Lovett, *Old Boston Boys*, 123–24.

25 Lovett, *Old Boston Boys*, 24.

26 "Memorial Service for Roger Wolcott," *Boston Daily Globe*, April 19, 1901, 6.

27 Matthew R. Sagan, *The Boston Book of Sports: From Puritans to Professionals* (Milton Keynes: Xlibris, 2009), 22; Stephen Hardy, *How Boston Played: Sport, Recreation, and Community, 1865–1915* (Knoxville: University of Tennessee Press, 2003), 112; David M. Nelson, *The Anatomy of a Game: Football, the Rules, and the Men Who Made the Game* (Newark: University of Delaware Press, 1994), 25, 179.

28 For a critically important overview of the spread of the various football codes, see Tony Collins, *How Football Began: A Global History of How the World's Football Codes Were Born* (London: Routledge, 2018).

29 Mike Cronin, *Sport and Nationalism in Ireland: Gaelic Games, Soccer and Irish Identity since 1884* (Dublin: Four Courts Press, 1999); Mike Cronin, Mark Duncan, and Paul Rouse, *The GAA: A People's History* (Cork: Collins Press, 2009).

30 Tony Collins, *Rugby's Great Split: Class, Culture and the Origins of Rugby League* (London: Routledge, 1998).

31 On early football history, see Adrian Harvey, *Football: The First 100 Years; The Untold Story* (Abingdon, UK: Routledge, 2005); Gary James, *The Emergence*

of Footballing Cultures: Manchester 1840–1919 (Manchester, UK: Manchester University Press, 2019); and Gavin Kitching, "The Origins of Football: History, Ideology and the Making of 'The People's Game,'" *History Workshop Journal* 79, no. 1 (Spring 2015): 127–53.

32 For essentially an exact reprint of the 1871 English Rugby Union rules, see the 1876 typescript: *The Foot Ball Association of Canada—Organized 1873. Rules. Rugby Union* (Montreal: Gazette Printing House, 1876).

33 "Foot Ball," *Harvard Advocate* 14, no. 5 (December 6, 1872): 68.

34 See chapter 5 "The End of the Universal Game," in Collins, *How Football Began*, 31–37.

35 Lovett, *Old Boston Boys*, 86.

36 Lovett, *Old Boston Boys*, 87.

37 Lovett, *Old Boston Boys*, 17.

38 See, for example, Julie Des Jardins, *Walter Camp: Football and the Modern Man* (New York: Oxford University Press, 2015); and Tamte, *Walter Camp*.

CHAPTER 2

1 Both Daniel Rodgers and Abram Van Engen agree that the sermon was foremost a warning against failure, particularly morally and spiritually, before becoming an aspiration to future political greatness as a new nation-state. See Daniel T. Rodgers, *As a City on a Hill: The Story of America's Most Famous Lay Sermon* (Princeton, NJ: Princeton University Press, 2018), 39–41; and Abram C. Van Engen, *A City upon a Hill* (New Haven, CT: Yale University Press, 2020), 46–48.

2 Mark Peterson, *The City State of Boston: The Rise and Fall of an Atlantic Power, 1630–1865* (Princeton, NJ: Princeton University Press, 2019), 23.

3 On the growth and development of Boston, see Lawrence W. Kennedy, *Planning the City upon a Hill* (Amherst: University of Massachusetts Press, 1992).

4 On the first two centuries of Boston Latin, see Phillips Brooks, *The Oldest School in America—an Oration* (Boston: Houghton Mifflin, 1885); and Henry F. Jenks, *The Boston Public Latin School 1635–1881* (Cambridge, MA: Moses King, 1881).

5 For an early History of Harvard, see Benjamin Pierce, *A History of Harvard University: From Its Foundation Year of 1636 to the Period of the American Revolution* (Cambridge, MA: Brown, Shattuck, 1833).

6 On the growth and development of Beacon Hill as a socially elite enclave already somewhat partitioned between a poorer north slope and the more genteel southern slope, see Jeffrey Klee, "Civic Order on Beacon Hill,"

Buildings and Landscapes: Journal of the Vernacular Architecture Forum 15 (2008): 43–57.

7 Recording the foundation, Dixwell used just four words: "Began my private school." See entry for September 29, 1851, Epes Sargent Dixwell diaries, box 17, folder Diary Extracts, 1833–1884, Wigglesworth Family papers, Massachusetts Historical Society. Dixwell was a direct descendant of John Dixwell (1607–88), the regicide who approved the execution of Charles I. After the Restoration, Dixwell fled England and settled in New Haven, where he lived under an assumed name until his death.

8 In his autobiography, Dixwell states that the specific reason he left Boston Latin was due to a law passed by Boston City Council requiring all who received city salaries to reside within the city limits. Dixwell lived in Cambridge and was unwilling to move into Boston and quit his post as a result. Mary C. D. Wigglesworth, *An Autobiographical Sketch by Epes Sargent Dixwell*, 45, box-L 1907, Wigglesworth Family papers, Massachusetts Historical Society.

9 Beginning in 1851, the full register of students lists 295 enrolled boys. In his unfinished autobiography Dixwell included a nonexhaustive list of boys who, under his tutelage, had graduated from the Private Latin School (138) or his private school (102) and then Harvard. See Wigglesworth, *Autobiographical Sketch*, 61–66; and *Register of Pupils at the Private Latin School*, Epes Sargent Dixwell volumes, 1851–1881, box 24, folder E. S. Dixwell Register of Pupils, 1851–1871 [catalog record mislabeled as 1881], Wigglesworth Family papers, Massachusetts Historical Society.

10 Wigglesworth, *Autobiographical Sketch*, 50.

11 Extracts of the Latin curriculum are available in Henry F. Jenks, *Catalogue of the Boston Public Latin School. Established in 1635. With an Historical Sketch* (Boston: Boston Public Latin Association, 1886), 41, 65–69, 77–80.

12 John E. Rexine, "The Boston Latin School Curriculum in the Seventeenth and Eighteenth Centuries: A Bicentennial Review," *Classical Journal* 72, no. 3 (February–March 1977): 266.

13 See curriculum note "Private Latin School" for 1861–62, *Francis H. Lincoln's School Records, 1861–63*, Solomon and Francis H. Lincoln papers, Hingham Historical Society.

14 William Lawrence, *Fifty Years*, 2nd ed. (Boston: Houghton Mifflin, 1923), 12.

15 Karl Schriftgiesser, *The Gentleman from Massachusetts: Henry Cabot Lodge* (Boston: Little, Brown, 1944), 21. In his first two years, Lodge's study marks ranked him third and sixteenth overall, though his conduct placed him near the bottom of the fifty some students. See ranking lists, *Francis H. Lincoln's School Records, 1861–63*, Solomon and Francis H. Lincoln papers, Hingham Historical Society.

16 Henry Cabot Lodge, *Early Memories* (New York: Charles Scribner's Sons, 1913), 81–82.

17 Dixwell's own contemporary diary entries in the 1850s and '60s note multiple successful students but not one failure. His autobiography includes a partial list of the boys he taught who graduated from Harvard between 1856–75. See Wigglesworth, *Autobiographical Sketch*, 44, 64–66.
18 Wigglesworth, *Autobiographical Sketch*, 7; Mary Thacher Higginson, *Thomas Wentworth Higginson: The Story of His Life* (Boston: Houghton Mifflin, 1914), 22.
19 Robert Apthorp Boit, *Chronicles of the Boit Family and Their Descendants and of Other Allied Families* (Boston: S. J. Parkhill, privately printed, 1915), 159.
20 Richard Farnum, "The American Upper Class and Higher Education, 1880–1970," in *Social Class and Democratic Leadership*, ed. Harold J. Baltzell (Philadelphia: University of Pennsylvania Press, 1989), 73.
21 Ronald Story, "Harvard Students, the Boston Elite, and the New England Preparatory System, 1800–1876," *History of Education Quarterly* 15, no. 3 (Autumn 1975): 285.
22 Story, "Harvard Students," 286.
23 John S. Lawrence, *Amory Appleton Lawrence* (Boston: privately printed, 1914), 13.
24 Story, "Harvard Students," 290.
25 William Lawrence, *Memories of a Happy Life* (Boston: Houghton Mifflin and Riverside Press, 1913), 3.
26 "Good Old Days of Sport in Boston Knew No Football, Boxing, or Golf," *Boston Globe*, October 6, 1929, A45.
27 Frederick A. Bushee, "The Growth of Population in Boston," *Publications of the American Statistical Association* 6, no. 46 (June 1899): 240.
28 On the reinvention of Boston in the nineteenth century, see Edward L. Glaeser, "Reinventing Boston: 1630–2003," *Journal of Economic Geography* 5, no. 2 (2005): 119–53.
29 Thomas O'Connor, *Civil War Boston: Home Front and Battlefield* (Boston: Northeastern University Press, 1997), 6.
30 On the growth of Boston before and after the Civil War, see Stephen Puleo, *A City So Grand: The Rise of an American Metropolis, Boston 1850–1900* (Boston: Beacon Press, 2010).
31 For the inception of the idea see chapter 3 in William A. Newman and Wilfred E. Holton, *Boston's Back Bay: The Story of America's Greatest Nineteenth Century Landfill Project* (Boston: Northeastern University Press, 2006), 51–78.
32 James D'Wolf Lovett, unnamed memoirs typescript, November 1933, folders 19, 20, 21, 22 (writings 1–4), James D'Wolf Lovett papers, 1896–1935, Massachusetts Historical Society, 23.
33 Nancy S. Seasholes, *Gaining Ground: A History of Landmaking in Boston* (Cambridge, MA: MIT Press, 2003).

34. An architectural analysis of the houses built in the Back Bay can be found in Bainbridge Bunting, *Houses of Boston's Back Bay* (Cambridge, MA: Belknap Press, 1967), and online there is a wealth of material on https://backbayhouses.org/ (accessed May 5, 2021).
35. Newman and Holton, *Boston's Back Bay*. On the cultural institutions, see Paul Dimaggio, "Cultural Entrepreneurship in Nineteenth-Century Boston: The Creation of an Organisational Base for High Culture in America," *Media, Culture and Society* 4 (1982): 33–50; and chapter 8 in Ted Clarke, *Beacon Hill, Back Bay and the Building of Boston's Golden Age* (Charleston, SC: History Press, 2010).
36. See chapter 2 in Betty Farrell, *Elite Families: Class and Power in Nineteenth Century Boston* (Albany: State University of New York Press, 1993).
37. For an early history of the Common and a discussion of its gentrification, see Nehemiah Adams, *Boston Common* (Boston: Ticknor and Williams, 1842).
38. Peterson, *City State of Boston*, 605.
39. Lodge, *Early Memories*, 19.
40. Margaret Bendroth, "Rum, Romanism and Evangelism: Protestants and Catholics in Late-Nineteenth Century Boston," *Church History* 68, no. 3 (1999): 631.
41. For an assessment of violence in Boston prior to the war, see Patrick T. J. Browne, "The Most Atrocious Crusade against Personal Freedom. Anti-Abolitionist Violence in Boston on the Eve of War," *New England Quarterly* 94, no. 1 (2021): 47–81.
42. *Boston Post*, December 3, 1859.
43. Higginson's wife, Mary Channing, was William Ellery Channing Eustis's first cousin once removed, and Samuel Gridley Howe (husband to the *Battle Hymn of the Republic*'s composer, Julia Ward Howe) later became father-in-law to Henry Richards.
44. Miller to Lovett, January 14, 1932, box 1, folder 7, Gerrit Smith Miller papers, #3700, Division of Rare and Manuscript Collections, Cornell University Library. For grandfather Gerrit Smith's role in the Brown raid, see Edward J. Renehan Jr., *The Secret Six: The True Tale of the Men Who Conspired with John Brown* (Columbia: University of South Carolina Press, 1997).
45. See entries for November 6 and December 20, 1860, in Epes Sargent Dixwell diaries.
46. On Irish attitudes to the Civil War, see Daniel Downer, "Fighting for Lincoln? Irish Attitudes towards Slavery during the American Civil War," *History Ireland* 21, no. 3 (2013): 26–29.
47. See entry for April 15, 1861, in Epes Sargent Dixwell diaries.
48. Richard F. Miller, "Brahmin Janissaries: John A. Andrew Mobilizes Massachusetts' Upper Class for the Civil War," *New England Quarterly* 75, no. 2 (June 2002): 207.

Notes to Pages 33–36

49 Miller, "Brahmin Janissaries," 228.
50 A total of 12,976 Massachusetts men died in the Civil War including 246 Harvard alumni. Mostly part of the Twentieth Volunteer Regiment (known as "the Bloody 20th"), the university sent 1,662 men to battle on both sides (death rate of nearly 15 percent), while the state saw a total of 159,165 men serve overall (8 percent death rate). Corydon Ireland, "Blue, Gray, and Crimson," *Harvard Gazette*, March 21, 2012, https://news.harvard.edu/gazette/story/2012/03/blue-gray-and-crimson/.
51 Miller, "Brahmin Janissaries," 230.
52 Schriftgiesser, *Gentleman from Massachusetts*, 23.
53 Nathaniel Bowditch was Assistant Adjunct General and member of the First Massachusetts Cavalry Brigade, was wounded during a charge at Kelly's Ford on March 17, 1863, and died a day later. The death of his son profoundly affected Henry Bowditch. See Frances M. Clarke, *War Stories: Suffering and Sacrifice in the Civil War North* (Chicago: University of Chicago Press, 2011), 28–50.
54 Lawrence, *Memories of a Happy Life*, 9.
55 William Lawrence, *Roger Wolcott* (Boston: Houghton Mifflin, 1902), 21.
56 See entry for October 24, 1862, in Epes Sargent Dixwell diaries.
57 Lodge, *Early Memories*, 112.
58 See entries for July 13–18, 1863, in Epes Sargent Dixwell diaries.
59 On the riot, see Ian J. Jesse, "In Search of Excitement: Understanding Boston's Civil War 'Draft Riot,'" *Revere House Gazette* 124 (2016): 1–4; Michael S. Hindus, "A City of Mobocrats and Tyrants: Mob Violence in Boston, 1747–1863," *Issues in Criminology* 6, no. 2 (1971): 55–83; and William F. Hanna, "The Boston Draft Riot," *Civil War History* 36, no. 3 (September 1990): 262–73. For Cabot, see L. Vernon Briggs, *History and Genealogy of the Cabot Family: 1475–1927* (Boston: Charles E. Goodspeed, 1927), 2:698. See also John A. Blanchard, *The H Book of Harvard Athletics 1852–1922* (Cambridge, MA: Harvard Varsity Club, 1923), 443.
60 H. H. Lloyd, *Battle History of the Great Rebellion* (New York: H. H. Lloyd, 1866), 325.
61 On page 3 of the *Evening Transcript*, the Oneida match was recounted just a few lines down from the Rappahannock story. See "Foot Ball," *Boston Daily Advertiser* and *Boston Evening Transcript*, November 9, 1863.
62 See entries for December 6–7, 1863, and March 29, 1864, in Epes Sargent Dixwell diaries; Mary Caroline Crawford, *Famous Families of Massachusetts* (Boston: Little, Brown, 1930), 2:330–31.
63 See David M. Rosen, *Armies of the Young: Child Soldiers in War and Terrorism* (New Brunswick, NJ: Rutgers University Press, 2005), 5. For differing accounts on conscription in the North, see Peter Levine, "Draft Evasion in the North During the Civil War, 1863–1865," *Journal of American History* 67 (March 1981): 816–34; and James W. Geary, "Civil War Conscription in

the North: A Historiographical Review," *Civil War History* 32 (September 1986): 208–28.
64 Lodge, *Early Memories*, 125.
65 See entry for February 8, 1865, in Epes Sargent Dixwell diaries.
66 Lodge, *Early Memories*, 129.
67 Lawrence, *Memories of a Happy Life*, 12.
68 Lodge, *Early Memories*, 125. See the Dixwell seating plan, *Francis H. Lincoln's School Records, 1861–63*, Solomon and Francis H. Lincoln papers, Hingham Historical Society.
69 O'Connor, *Civil War Boston*, 250.
70 Drew Gilpin Faust, "Memory's Past and Future: Harvard's Memorial Hall," in *Civil War Places: Seeing Conflict through the Eyes of Its Leading Historians*, ed. Gary W. Gallagher and J. Matthew Gallman (Chapel Hill: University of North Carolina Press, 2019), 107–14.
71 O'Connor, *Civil War Boston*, 250.

CHAPTER 3

1 Mona Domosh, *Invented Cities: The Creation of Landscape in Nineteenth Century New York and Boston* (New Haven, CT: Yale University Press, 1998), 129.
2 Michael Rawson, *Eden on the Charles: The Making of Boston* (Cambridge, MA: Harvard University Press, 2010), 72.
3 On visual and cultural representations of the Common and the question of social order, see chapter 2 in Justin T. Clark, *City of Second Sight: Nineteenth Century Boston and the Making of American Visual Culture* (Chapel Hill: University of North Carolina Press, 2018).
4 "City of Boston," *Boston Daily Advertiser*, January 22, 1862.
5 Stephen Pendery, "Probing the Boston Common," *Archaeology* 43, no. 2 (March/April 1990): 47.
6 Permit dated May 26, 1866, in James D'Wolf Lovett Sports Scrapbook, 1861–1945, Revolutionary Spaces (formerly the Bostonian Society; hereafter cited as Revolutionary Spaces).
7 Robert Carver, *Book of Sports* (Boston: Lilly, Colman, and Holden, 1834).
8 The use of the Common for sport was contested and became, at times, highly politicized. See Stephen Hardy, *How Boston Played: Sport, Recreation, and Community, 1865–1915* (Knoxville: University of Tennessee Press, 2003), chap. 5.
9 Peter Morris, *But Didn't We Have Fun? An Informal History of Baseball's Pioneer Era, 1843–70* (Chicago: Ivan R. Dee, 2008), 46–47.

Notes to Pages 41–43

10. For an account of early baseball in Boston, see "The National Game," *Boston Journal*, February 20, 1905. The article was signed Tri-Mountain, but baseball historian John Thorn suggests it was Lovett.
11. David Q. Voigt, "The Boston Red Stockings: The Birth of Major League Baseball," *New England Quarterly* 43, no. 4 (1970): 531–49; "Brief Locals," *Bunker Hill Times*, January 10, 1874, 3; see also Harold Kaese, *The Boston Braves, 1871–1953* (Boston: Northeastern University Press, 2004), 3–16.
12. Melvin I. Smith, *Evolvements of Early American Foot Ball: Through the 1890/91 Season* (Bloomington, IN: AuthorHouse, 2008).
13. See chapters 2 and 3 in Brian Bunk, *From Football to Soccer: The Early History of the Beautiful Game in the United States* (Urbana: University of Illinois, 2021), 31–74.
14. Smith, *Evolvements*, 30.
15. Smith, *Evolvements*, 32.
16. *The Old Schoolboys of Boston* (Boston: privately printed, 1903), 76–77. Formed in 1880, the Old Schoolboys of Boston was open to any gentleman having been a student of a Boston public high school at any period fifty years prior to his one-time one-dollar membership application. This deliberately restricted the group by age but not by education, class, or pedigree. Evidence of the strong educational impetus of Boston society, this appears to be a remarkably democratic institution in its social reach including the Adams, Appleton, Hale, and other old family names. It predated the private schools' era of the 1850s and '60s, which later became finishing schools for Harvard.
17. Smith, *Evolvements*, 45.
18. "Editor's Table," *Harvard Magazine* 6, no. 50 (December 1859): 128.
19. "'College Record-Statistics of the Class of 1860," *Harvard Magazine* 7, no. 57 (September 1860): 19.
20. See Section 10 of the "City of Boston. An Ordinance in Relation to the Common, Public Garden and Common Lands," *Boston Daily Evening Transcript*, January 11, 1862, 3.
21. "Foot Ball," *Boston Herald*, October 13, 1860.
22. Many histories of football in the US do not even attempt to understand what went before. See, for example, Timothy P. Brown, *How Football Became Football: 150 Years of the Game's Evolution* (West Bloomfield, MI: Brown House, 2020) begins with the 1869 Princeton versus Rutgers game as if no form of the game preexisted that moment.
23. Kathleen Bachynski, *No Game for Boys to Play: The History of Youth Football and the Origins of Public Health Crisis* (Chapel Hill: University of North Carolina Press, 2019), 11.
24. Robert Pruter, *The Rise of American High School Sports and the Search for Control, 1880–1930* (Syracuse: Syracuse University Press, 2013), 5.

25 One of the counterhistorical approaches taken against the public school role in the development of codified football and the search for a definitive point of origin can be seen in the work of Adrian Harvey, *Football: The First 100 Years; The Untold Story* (Abingdon, UK: Routledge, 2005); and Peter Swain and Adrian Harvey, "On Bosworth Field or the Playing Fields of Eton and Rugby? Who Really Invented Modern Football?," *International Journal of the History of Sport* 29, no. 10 (2012): 1425–45.

26 Fabrice Neddam, "Constructing Masculinities under Thomas Arnold of Rugby (1828–1842): Gender, Educational Policy and School Life in an Early-Victorian Public School," *Gender and Education* 16, no. 3 (2004): 303–26.

27 Clifford Putney, *Muscular Christianity: Manhood and Sports in Protestant America, 1880–1920* (Cambridge, MA: Harvard University Press, 2001), 1.

28 For the later development of American boarding schools, see Axel Bundgaard, *Muscle and Manliness: The Rise of Sport in American Boarding Schools* (Syracuse: Syracuse University Press, 2005).

29 Of the 295 boys listed on the register, only four were from beyond greater Boston: one from South Carolina, one from Virginia, one from Ohio, and Miller. See *Register of Pupils at the Private Latin School*, Epes Sargent Dixwell volumes, 1851–1881, box 24, folder E. S. Dixwell Register of Pupils, 1851–1871 [catalog record mislabeled as 1881], Wigglesworth Family papers, Massachusetts Historical Society.

30 What is notable is how comparatively late, with respect to Britain, the US developed boarding schools that featured a games curriculum. See Christopher F. Armstrong, "The Lessons of Sports: Class Socialization in British and American Boarding Schools," *Sociology of Sport Journal* 1, no. 4 (1984): 314–31.

31 The development of sport, particularly of baseball, is noted during the Civil War but usually in the context of the army. See Lawrence W. Fielding, "War and Trifles: Sport in the Shadows of Civil War Army Life," *Journal of Sport History* 4, no. 2 (1977): 151–68.

32 For an account of the development and importance of Boston's associational life, see Frederic Cople Jaher, *The Urban Establishment: Upper Strata in Boston, New York, Charleston, Chicago and Los Angeles* (Urbana: University of Illinois Press, 1982).

33 Samuel Williams, *The Boy's Treasury of Sports, Pastimes and Recreations* (Boston: J. P. Hill, 1848) 28.

34 J. G. Woods, *Every Boy's Book: A Complete Encyclopedia of Sports and Amusements* (New York: G. Routledge, 1855), 35.

35 For a retrospective account, see Georg Henry Tripp, *Student Life at Harvard* (Boston: Lockwood, Brooks, 1876), 51–65.

36 "Foot Ball," *Boston Herald*, October 13, 1860.

37 John Allen Krout, *Annals of American Sport* (New Haven, CT: Yale University Press, 1929), 236.

38 George White, Henry Walker Herrick, Harrison Wier, and George Harvey, *The American Boy's Book of Sports and Games* (New York: Dick and Fitzgerald, 1864), 101–3.

39 J. G. Woods, *Every Boy's Book* (New York: Routledge, 1868), 224–26.

40 For more about the book's reach and impact globally, see Tony Collins, "Tom Brown's Schooldays by Thomas Hughes (1857)," in *A History of Sport in Europe in 100 Objects*, ed. Daphné Bolz and Michael Krüger (Hildesheim, Germany: Arete Verlag, 2023), 28–31.

41 Ticknor and Fields announced a sixth edition in print by 1858. See *Boston Post*, December 29, 1858, 3.

42 Henry Cabot Lodge, *Early Memories* (New York: Charles Scribner's Sons, 1913), 69.

43 "English School Life," *Harvard Magazine* 3, no. 7 (September 1857): 297–302. See "New Publications," *Boston Evening Transcript*, March 22, 1864, 3. The magazine was available on Newspaper Row from A. Williams and Co. at 100 Washington Street.

44 See A. T. Michell, *Rugby School Register, Volume II. From August, 1842, to January, 1874* (Rugby: A. J. Lawrence, 1902), 142, 156. See 1850 US Census for family records. George Henry stayed in the UK for university (Cambridge), finishing his MA in 1862 before returning to Harvard law school and graduating in 1865. President of the Cambridge boat club, he continued in the sport and was part of Oneida Ned Burgess's winning 1885 America's Cup crew. John Tudor returned to the US and served as a general in the army.

45 W. B. Morewood to father, October 25, [no year], box AM-275, Morewood family papers, 1827–1976, Berkshire County Historical Society. After several years of tutoring and preparation in Rugby, Morewood entered the "Big School" in 1863. Morewood was not a Brahmin but did marry Herman Melville's niece Maria Gansevoort. See Mitchell, *Rugby School Register*, 232.

46 Hardy, *How Boston Played*, 111.

47 See entry for Saturday October 18, 1862, Francis H. Lincoln's Diary, 1862, Solomon and Francis H. Lincoln papers, Hingham Historical Society.

48 Mary C. D. Wigglesworth, *An Autobiographical Sketch by Epes Sargent Dixwell*, 43, box-L 1907, Wigglesworth Family papers, Massachusetts Historical Society.

49 Smith, *Evolvements*, 192–96.

50 *Boston Morning Journal*, June 7, 1862, 4. The game was also reported in the *Boston Post*, June 7, 1862, 4.

51 In contrast to his student Lincoln, Headmaster Dixwell did not see the match as important enough to record in his diary; the only entry for that day discussed war notes and the purchase of a new piano. See diary entries for Thursday, June 5, and Saturday, October 18, 1862, in Francis H. Lincoln's Diary, 1862; see entry for June 6, 1862, Epes Sargent Dixwell diaries, box 17,

folder Diary Extracts, 1833–1884, Wigglesworth Family papers, Massachusetts Historical Society.
52 "Foot Ball," *Boston Daily Advertiser*, November 9, 1863, 1.
53 Smith, *Evolvements*, 49. No contemporary source records Wolcott as captain, even though Boit noted the attribution of the title to Wolcott in his memoirs, though it appears it was in relation to military drill. See Robert Apthorp Boit, *Chronicles of the Boit Family and Their Descendants and of Other Allied Families* (Boston: S. J. Parkhill, privately printed, 1915), 144.
54 Smith, *Evolvements*, 49–50.
55 Pruter, *Rise of American High School Sports*, 16.
56 Occasionally, other school games are similarly labeled in ambiguous terms, even qualified by a "maybe" or simply "no data available." Despite a mammoth list of sources, none of the individual matches are specifically referenced. Smith, *Evolvements*, 50–54, 198–200.
57 Bunk, *From Football to Soccer*, 74.
58 For a discussion of another rare club mention predating the Oneidas (the St. George's Club) which may, or may not, have played regularly throughout the mid-1840s and '50s, see David Kilpatrick, "New York Soccer Pioneers," in *Soccer Frontiers: The Global Game in the United States, 1863–1913*, ed. Chris Bolsmann and George Kioussis (Knoxville: University of Tennessee Press, 2021), 65–89. See also Ed Farnsworth's five-part series "The Origins of Soccer in Philadelphia," Society for American Soccer History, February 19, March 3, March 12, April 10, and April 16, 2020, https://www.ussoccerhistory.org.
59 An extensive search of the papers for the 1862–65 period reveals a number of school matches, including some referred to by Smith, but only two ever mentioning the Oneidas by name. See "Football," *Boston Evening Transcript*, October 31, 1864, 3. A repeat of the article appeared the following day on page 4.
60 Smith, *Evolvements*, 52.
61 See December 1862 in Epes Sargent Dixwell diaries.
62 There is an intriguing question about weather during the 1865–72 period when looking at the study of Amherst, Massachusetts, in which there was nearly a two-degree drop in average autumn temperatures. The months of October in 1870 and '71 saw around a six-degree rise compared to the same months in 1865, 1868, or 1869. Temperatures warmed in 1870 and 1871 and up to 1875, the period during which Harvard revived football games. Raymond S. Bradley et al., *The Climate of Amherst Massachusetts 1836–1985* (Amherst: University of Massachusetts, Dept. of Geology and Geography, 1987), 51, 55, 103.
63 Morton Henry Prince, "History of Football at Harvard, 1800–75," in *The H Book of Harvard Athletics 1852–1922*, ed. John A. Blanchard (Cambridge, MA: Harvard Varsity Club, 1923), 344.

64 Tony Collins, "The Invention of Sporting Tradition: National Myths, Imperial Pasts and the Origins of Australian Rules Football," in *Myths and Milestones in the History of Sport* Stephen Wagg, 15 (London: Palgrave Macmillan, 2011). For the near failure of the FA, see Tony Collins, *How Football Began: A Global History of How the World's Football Codes Were Born* (London: Routledge, 2018), 4–9.

65 Kilpatrick notes the first printing of a version of rules similar to the FA's by the *New York Clipper* in October of 1864. See Kilpatrick, "New York Soccer Pioneers," 72; and *Beadle's Dime Book of Cricket and Football*, 1881 reprint (1866; repr. New York: Beadle, 1881). See also Northern Illinois University Library's excellent digital Beadle collection: https://ulib.niu.edu/badndp/bibindex.html.

66 The winter was frigid, with another snowstorm impeding Dixwell from even walking home a few weeks earlier. See entries for January 17 and February 19 along with multiple entries in March and April 1867, Epes Sargent Dixwell diaries.

67 Overall enrollment dropped from fifty-eight in 1867–68 to thirty-two in 1868–69 and again to twenty-nine the year after. From Scudder's list of club members (1926), Dixwell's pupil register shows, among others, Bigelow, Burgess, Dwight, Eustis, Gray, the Lawrence brothers, Lodge, Mills, Minot, and Rotch. See E. S. Dixwell, *Tuition Book of the Private Latin School, 1851–1872*, box 24, Wigglesworth Family papers, Massachusetts Historical Society.

68 Former Dixwell classmates Bowditch, Peabody, Thies, and Watson all entered Harvard in 1865, while Forbes enrolled at MIT. The new Harvard freshmen were reunited with Brooks and Boit, both one class ahead. As for those who never attended college, Arnold and Lovett may have begun working. Davis and Hall's paths remain to be fully uncovered.

69 The clippings in Lovett's scrapbook record that Miller had pitched for the Lowells (playing alongside Lovett) as late as September 25 but did not appear again in regular baseball games in Boston. See entry for December 1, 1865, Epes Sargent Dixwell diaries.

CHAPTER 4

1 Winthrop Saltonstall Scudder, *An Historical Sketch of the Oneida Football Club of Boston 1862–1865* (deposited October 18, 1926), Massachusetts Historical Society, 6.

2 Ronald Story, "Harvard Students, the Boston Elite, and the New England Preparatory System, 1800–1876," *History of Education Quarterly* 15, no. 3 (Autumn 1975): 281.

3. Theodore Roosevelt, *The Works of Theodore Roosevelt* (New York, Charles Scribner's Sons, 1926), 13:559–70.
4. Joan D. Hedrick, "Harvard Indifference," *New England Quarterly* 49, no. 3 (1976): 362.
5. Karl Schriftgiesser, *The Gentleman from Massachusetts: Henry Cabot Lodge* (Boston: Little, Brown, 1944), 25.
6. See *A Catalog of the Officers and Students of Harvard University for the Academical Year 1866–67* (Cambridge, MA: Sever and Francis, 1866), 24, 38; and Ronald Story, *The Forging of an Aristocracy: Harvard and the Boston Upper Class, 1800–1870* (Middletown: Wesleyan University Press, 1980), 101.
7. Henry Cabot Lodge, *Early Memories* (New York: Charles Scribner's Sons, 1913), 180.
8. For an overview of the end of the Bloody Monday game and football's later revival, see Ronald A. Smith, *Sports and Freedom: The Rise of Big Time College Athletics* (New York: Oxford University Press, 1988), 67–99.
9. On a specific variant of such games at Dartmouth, see Scott Meacham, "Old Division Football, the Indigenous Mob Soccer of Dartmouth College," *Dartmo* (2006), https://www.dartmo.com/football/Football_Meacham.pdf.
10. This did include rule "3d. There shall be no carrying of the ball." See "The Game of Foot-Ball," *Hartford Courant*, November 6, 1858, 2. See also Melvin I. Smith, "1858: A Pivotal Year in Early American 'Foot-Ball,'" *College Football Historical Society (CFHS) Journal* 23, no. 2 (February 2010): 15–16.
11. *Orders and Regulations of the Faculty of Harvard College* (Cambridge, MA: Harvard College, 1852), 8.
12. "The Football Game Is Over—*Gaudeamus igitur!*," *Harvard Magazine*, 7, no. 57 (September 1860): 36.
13. Between 1855 and 1860, the *Harvard Magazine* included a number of back-and-forth editorials extolling football's virtues but also pleading to rid the college of it. See particularly the "The Football Game" in June 1858, the July 1858 reply "Sixty-One Up!" and a final plea in the "Senior's Corner" to keep the game in September of 1859 or the three page amalgam of Latin and English in March 1860, "An Epic for Harvard."
14. "The Football Game," *Harvard Magazine* 4, no. 5 (June 1858): 182.
15. "The Harvard Foot-Ball Match," *Boston Daily Advertiser*, September 18, 1858, 1.
16. Steven Apostolov, "Native Americans, Puritans and Brahmins: Genesis, Practice and Evolution of Archaic and Pre-Modern Football in Massachusetts," *Sport in Society* 20, no. 9 (2017): 1268.
17. For a biography of Ropes, see John Codman Ropes and Florian Dexheimer, eds., *The Civil War Letters of Lieutenant Henry Ropes, 20th Massachusetts Volunteer Infantry* (Scotts Valley: Create Space, 2018), 386–91.

18 "The Harvard Foot-Ball Match," *Boston Daily Advertiser*, September 18, 1858, 1.
19 "Atoms," *Harvard Advocate* 1, no. 2 (May 25, 1866): 28; "Out-Door Sports," *Harvard Advocate* 4, no. 2 (October 22, 1867): 28–29.
20 James W. Reed, "Morton Henry Prince," *American National Biography* (New York: Oxford University Press, 1999), https://doi.org/10.1093/anb/9780198606697.article.1200744, accessed November 10, 2021.
21 Morton Henry Prince, "History of Football at Harvard, 1800–75," in *The H Book of Harvard Athletics 1852–1922*, ed. John A. Blanchard (Cambridge, MA: Harvard Varsity Club, 1923), 346–48.
22 Prince, "History of Football at Harvard," 349.
23 Prince, "History of Football at Harvard," 342.
24 "Death of George Wigglesworth," *Daily Boston Globe*, November 28, 1930, 15.
25 James Dwight, Robert Means Lawrence, and Frederick Shattuck were at the medical school until 1874, 1873, and 1872, respectively, while Alanson Tucker and the younger Walter Burgess and Arthur Mills only graduated in 1872.
26 "College Library," *College Courant*, January 15, 1870, 29. See also Robert Pruter, *The Rise of American High School Sports and the Search for Control, 1880–1930* (Syracuse, NY: Syracuse University Press, 2013), 5. Pruter also cites the influence of Thomas Wentworth Higginson's *Atlantic Monthly* article "Saints and Their Bodies" from March 1855 in spreading a games ethic.
27 "Personal," *Cornell Era*, October 21, 1870, 45; "Exchanges," *Harvard Advocate* 10, no. 3 (November 11, 1870): 44.
28 *Cornell Era* 3, no. 30 (May 26, 1871): 236.
29 Thomas Hughes, "Recollections of American Universities," *Every Saturday*, March 25, 1871, 286. For the British printing, see *The Dark Blue* (London: Sampson Low, Son and Marston, March 1871), 59–67, Harvard University Archives.
30 Mark Bernstein, *Football: The Ivy League Origins of an American Obsession* (Philadelphia: University of Pennsylvania Press, 2001), 6.
31 The cup donation was reported in the *Yale Record* 1, no. 16 (January 8, 1873): 144. See "University Items," *Cornell Era* 3, no. 9 (November 11, 1870): 69; and "Exchanges," *Harvard Advocate* 10, no. 5 (December 9, 1870): 75.
32 Emphasis in original. Henry Van Dyke to Perry Walton, November 19, 1929, Mss. L667.49, Boston Athenaeum.
33 See Christian K. Anderson, "Myths and Stories from College Football's First One Hundred Years," in *The History of American College Football: Institutional Policy, Culture and Reform*, ed. Christian K. Anderson and Amber C. Fallucca (New York: Routledge, 2021), 1–15.
34 *Yale Literary Magazine*, no. 314 (November 1870): 97–98. For the match report versus Columbia, see *Yale Record* 1, no. 8 (October 30, 1872): 73; Bernstein, *Football*, 8.

35 On the issue of rules in these early games, see David M. Nelson, *The Anatomy of a Game: Football, the Rules, and the Men Who Made the Game* (Newark: University of Delaware Press, 1994), 26–32; and Smith, *Sports and Freedom*, 67–83.

36 "Foot-Ball," *Harvard Advocate* 14, no. 5 (December 6, 1872): 68–69.

37 Nelson, *Anatomy of a Game*, 30–32.

38 Prince, "History of Football at Harvard," 357–58.

39 Henry R. Grant to the Secretary of the Yale football association, October 11, 1873, Harvard University Archives in Bernstein, *Football*, 9. See *Yale Record* 2, no. 8 (October 29, 1873): 96.

40 See "Foot-Ball," *Harvard Advocate* 15, no. 3 (April 1, 1873): 40–41; "Foot-Ball," *Harvard Advocate* 16, no. 4 (October 31, 1873): 52–53; and "Exchanges," *Harvard Advocate* 15, no. 8 (May 23, 1873): 123.

41 In some Yale records, Morse was incorrectly identified as William Morse. Also in the Harvard boat were Arthur L. Devens, who entered Dixwell in 1865, and Daniel C. Bacon, who played in the inaugural football clash with Yale in 1876. On the Yale side, Willis F. McCook rowed in the 1873 race and had played football at least in 1872, while William C. Hall had both rowed and played football in 1874.

42 James Wellman and Walter Peet, *The Story of the Harvard-Yale Boat Race 1852–1912* (New York: Harper Brothers, 1912), 6–9.

43 *Yale Record* 2, no. 14 (December 10, 1873): 167–69.

44 Burns has argued that this match is critical in the importation of rugby-style handling in the evolution of American football. In a largely unknown but useful source, Spirn contended that the choice to renege on kicking and opt for McGill's rugby had more to do with affection for Englishness and science. Spirn is on to something as the *Magenta* dedicated more than a page to the fox hunt and social parts of the McGill trip and subsequently announced that the Harvard club was about to "send to London for jerseys and stockings . . . black and gold striped." See "The Foot-Ball Match," *Magenta*, May 22, 1874, 93–94; "Fox-Hunt," *Magenta*, November 6, 1874, 38–39; Adam Burns, "From the Playing Fields of Rugby and Eton: The Transnational Origins of American Rugby and the Making of American Football," *Sport History Review* 52, no. 2 (2021): 315–31; and Samuel Spirn, "'A Scientific Fit for Gentlemen'—Why Rugby Supplanted Soccer in the Early History of American Football, 1860–77" (honors thesis, Harvard University, 2003), 45–62.

45 See "Brevities," *Harvard Magenta*, October 23, 1874, 36; and "Foot-Ball," *Harvard Advocate* 18, no. 3 (October 30, 1874): 35–36.

46 As part of the trajectory of the game's development, see Ronald A. Smith, "American Football Becomes the Dominant Intercollegiate National Pastime," *International Journal of the History of Sport* 31, nos. 1–2 (2014): 109–19.

47 The growth of college football and its popularity saw infrastructure sprout around the fields to facilitate paid entry and allow for bigger crowds; see Patrick Tutka and Chad Siefried, "The Early Synedochical Anchors of College Football: Fields and Facilities, 1869–1903," *Sport History Review* 52, no. 2 (2021): 189–216. On the Harvard versus Yale rivalry, see Bernard M. Corbett and Paul Simpson, *The Harvard Yale Rivalry: The Only Game That Matters* (New York: Three Rivers Press, 2005).
48 For a discussion of this move in the context of the transnational development of football, see Tony Collins, "Unexceptional Exceptionalism: The Origins of American Football in a Transnational Context," *Journal of Global History* 8, no. 2 (2013): 209–30.
49 Nelson, *Anatomy of a Game*, 33–51.
50 Wellman and Peet, *Story of the Harvard-Yale*, 6–9.
51 Prince, "History of Football at Harvard," 359–63.
52 *Yale Record*, 4, no. 10 (1875), 114.

CHAPTER 5

1 William Lawrence, *Roger Wolcott* (Boston: Houghton Mifflin, 1902), 19, 25.
2 Lawrence, *Roger Wolcott*, 30.
3 Ronald Story, "Harvard Students, the Boston Elite, and the New England Preparatory System, 1800–1876," *History of Education Quarterly* 15, no. 3 (Autumn 1975): 291.
4 For the financial wealth and business interests of Harvard students in the context of sport, see Allen L. Sack, "The Commercialisation and Rationalisation of Intercollegiate Football: A Comparative Analysis of the Development of Football at Yale and Harvard in the Later Nineteenth Century" (PhD diss., Pennsylvania State University, 1974).
5 See Noam Maggor, *Brahmin Capitalism: Frontiers of Wealth and Populism in America's First Gilded Age* (Cambridge, MA: Harvard University Press, 2017).
6 Robert J. Allinson, "Introduction: Boston in the Late 1800s/Early 1900s," in *The Atlas of Boston History*, ed. Nancy S. Seasholes (Chicago: University of Chicago Press, 2019), 91.
7 On philanthropy and culture, see Frederic Cople Jaher, *The Urban Establishment: Upper Strata in Boston, New York, Charleston, Chicago and Los Angeles* (Urbana: University of Illinois Press, 1982), 107–17.
8 Robert Holmes, "Remembering the first high school football games," *Boston Globe*, November 21, 2012.
9 See Paul Goodman, "Ethics and Enterprise: The Values of a Boston Elite, 1800–60," *American Quarterly* 18, no. 3 (1966): 437–51.

10 Stephan Thernstrom, *The Other Bostonians: Poverty and Progress in the American Metropolis, 1880–1970* (Cambridge, MA: Harvard University Press, 1973), 104.
11 John S. Lawrence, *Amory Appleton Lawrence* (Boston: privately printed, 1914), 15.
12 Olivier Zunz, *Philanthropy in America: A History* (Princeton, NJ: Princeton University Press, 2014), 8.
13 Hugh Davids Scott Greenway, quoted in Samuel Hornblower, "Fifteen Minutes: The Old Boys' Clubs," *Harvard Crimson*, April 27, 2000, https://www.thecrimson.com/article/2000/4/27/fifteen-minutes-the-old-boys-clubs/, accessed June 13, 2020.
14 For an overview of how the elite Bostonians acquired wealth, see David Grayson Allen, *Investment Management in Boston: A History* (Amherst: University of Massachusetts Press, 2015), 29–57.
15 Zunz, *Philanthropy in America*, 8.
16 Hornblower, "Fifteen Minutes."
17 On Eliot and his legacy, see Jennings L. Wagoner, "Charles W. Eliot, Immigrants and the Decline of American Idealism," *Biography* 8, no. 1 (1985): 25–36.
18 Alexander W. Williams, *A Social History of the Greater Boston Clubs* (Barre, MA: Barre Publishers, 1970), 143.
19 Neil Harris, "The Gilded Age Revisited: Boston and the Museum Movement," *American Quarterly* 14, no. 4 (1962): 549.
20 The Tavern Club, *The Rules of the Tavern Club of Boston with a List of the Officers and Members* (Cambridge, MA: Riverside Press, 1891).
21 Oneida members were Beebe, J. S. and W. S. Bigelow, Iasigi, A. A. Lawrence, R. M. Lawrence, Minot, Rotch, Sparks, Tucker, Wharton, and R. Wolcott. See *A Brief History of the Somerset Club of Boston, with a List of Past and Present Members, 1852–1913* (Boston: Somerset Club, 1914).
22 Members included Beebe, Bigelow, Brooks, Duff, Eustis, Forbes, Jackson, Jones, A. A. Lawrence, R. M. Lawrence, W. Lawrence, Lodge, Minot, Parkman, Peabody, Scudder, Watson, and Roger Wolcott.
23 Apthorp, W. Bigelow, Boit, Dixwell, Eustis, A. A. Lawrence, W. Lawrence, Lovett, Parkman, Shattuck, and Roger Wolcott.
24 Doris A. Birmingham, "The St Botolph Club: Home of the Impressionists," *Archives of American Art Journal* 31, no. 3 (1991): 26.
25 Jennifer C. Lena, *Entitled: Discriminating Tastes and the Expansion of the Arts* (Princeton, NJ: Princeton University Press, 2019), 1.
26 This was part of a wider embrace that had begun with the previous generations of the arts, as representative of cultural standing; see Justin T. Clark, *City of Second Sight: Nineteenth Century Boston and the Making of American Visual Culture* (Chapel Hill: University of North Carolina Press, 2018), 82–113.
27 Harris, "Gilded Age Revisited," 549.

28 The Bigelow collection is a centerpiece of the Museum of Fine Arts and has even returned to tour Japan, such is the depth of the collection. "MFA Exhibit Tours Japan, Will Not Be Seen in Boston," *Boston Globe*, March 24, 2013.
29 Paul Dimaggio, "Cultural entrepreneurship in nineteenth century Boston: the creation of an organizational base for high culture in America," *Media, Culture and Society* 4 (1988): 38.
30 Palmer E. Presbey to Lovett, March 23, 1896, folder 1 (1896–1905), James D'Wolf Lovett papers, 1896–1935, Massachusetts Historical Society.
31 Charles Peverelley, *The Book of American Pastimes, Containing a History of the Principal Base-Ball, Cricket, Rowing, and Yachting Clubs*, 2nd ed. (New York: American News Company, 1868), 465.
32 Lovett's scrapbook contains dozens of 1860s news clippings in which these Oneidas played against one another in baseball.
33 See, for example, Lovett to Miller, April 23, 1934, box 1, folder 26, Gerrit Smith Miller papers, #3700, Division of Rare and Manuscript Collections, Cornell University Library.
34 See James O'Connell, *The Hub's Metropolis: Greater Boston's Development from Railroad Suburbs to Smart Growth* (Boston: MIT Press, 2013), chap. 3.
35 Anthony Mitchell Sammarco, *Milton* (Charleston, SC: Arcadia, 2004).
36 See Ned Bowditch to Miller, November 29, 1887, box 11; Ned Bowditch to Miller, September 13, 1887, box 11; Lovett to Miller, January 16, 1896, box 12; and Lovett to Miller, July 30, 1896, box 12, Gerrit Smith Miller papers, Special Collections Research Center, Syracuse University Libraries.
37 Dixwell's son recalled (Roger) Wolcott, Forbes, Miller, Watson, and Means Lawrence and his bishop cousin William in attendance. See John Dixwell to Lovett, January 3, 1915, folder 8 (1911–16), James D'Wolf Lovett papers.

CHAPTER 6

1 Cabot, although not on the Oneida memorial or extended list, had himself been listed in 1858 as one of the boys "who played on the Common," so he was clearly familiar with, if not a participant in, the football of the period. See Samuel Barber, *Boston Common: A Diary of Notable Events, Incidents and Neighbouring Occurrences* (Boston: Christopher Publishing House, 1914), 192.
2 For Lovett's anonymous two-column piece, see "The Listener," *Boston Evening Transcript*, February 24, 1904, 31.
3 James D'Wolf Lovett, *Old Boston Boys and the Games They Played* (Boston: Riverside Press, 1906), iii–iv.

4 Lovett, *Old Boston Boys*, 81–100.
5 Dana Gibson to Uncle Jim Lovett, n.d., folder 14, n.d. (2), James D'Wolf Lovett papers, 1896–1935, Massachusetts Historical Society.
6 Baseball historian John Thorn has suggested that Lovett may have authored a brief early history of baseball, serialized for the *Boston Journal* beginning February 20, 1905, the issues of which incidentally are all carefully preserved in Lovett's scrapbook. John Thorn, "Early Baseball in Boston," *Our Game*, July 6, 2012, https://ourgame.mlblogs.com/early-baseball-in-boston-d86107fb8560, accessed December 16, 2017.
7 Gat Miller to Sam Cabot, July 2, 1905, folder 5 (1905–1906), James D'Wolf Lovett papers.
8 Lovett, *Old Boston Boys*, image plate between pp. 92–93.
9 See leaflet "Opinions from a Few of the Old Boys" reprinted in the back of the 1906 edition of Lovett, *Old Boston Boys*. James D'Wolf Lovett papers, folder 23 (Misc. Printed). For a background on the press, which by 1910 was printing ten to fifteen thousand books per day and published the *Atlantic Monthly*, see *The Riverside Press: Cambridge, Massachusetts* (Cambridge, MA: Riverside Press, 1911).
10 Win Scudder to Jim Lovett, June 7, 1906, folder 3 (1906), James D'Wolf Lovett papers.
11 See *List of Subscribers for the Deluxe Edition of Old Boston Boys 250 Copies*, dated 1906, inside the Massachusetts Historical Society copy of James D'Wolf Lovett, *Old Boston Boys and the Games They Played* (Boston: Riverside Press, 1906).
12 The stamp on the inside cover of the Library of Congress copy notes "Two copies received May 28, 1906" with the copyright entry date listed as April 28, 1906. Sue Miller, Gat's wife, wrote to Lovett on June 16 thanking Lovett for the book. See Sue Miller to Jim Lovett, June 16, 1906, folder 13, n.d. (1), James D'Wolf Lovett papers.
13 It has been claimed that the letter was by Roosevelt's hand. This is incorrect; it was written by his secretary, William J. Loeb Jr. See William Loeb to James Lovett, June 4, 1906, folder 3 (June 1–11), James D'Wolf Lovett papers. See folder 4 for other congratulatory letters; *List of Subscribers for the Deluxe Edition*.
14 See Josephine Gibson to "Uncle Jim" Lovett, n.d., folder 17, n.d. (3), James D'Wolf Lovett papers; and Sue Miller to Jim Lovett, June 16, 1906, folder 13, n.d. (1), James D'Wolf Lovett papers.
15 Mary Eliot to Lovett, June 17, 1906, folder 17, n.d. (3), James D'Wolf Lovett papers. Eliot was married to Amory Eliot, Harvard president Charles W. Eliot's nephew. See Walter Eliot, *A Sketch of the Eliot Family* (New York: Press of Livingston Middleditch, 1897), 95.
16 James D'Wolf Lovett to Mary Clark Eliot, June 20, 1906, letters, 1906–1934, to Mary Eliot, Boston Athenaeum. Emphasis in original.

17 "The Old Boys of Boston. And the Fun They Used to Have on the Common and the Charles," *Sunday Herald*, June 24, 1906, James D'Wolf Lovett Sports Scrapbook, 1861–1945, Revolutionary Spaces.
18 "Old Boston Boys—the Games They Played in Days Gone By," *Boston Evening Transcript*, June 28, 1906, 13, James D'Wolf Lovett Sports Scrapbook.
19 "New Literature," *Boston Daily Globe*, August 22, 1906, 7.
20 Lovett, *Old Boston Boys*, 211–19.
21 See entry for June 10, 1906, volume 12, Robert Apthorp Boit diaries, 1876–1918, Massachusetts Historical Society.
22 See Edwin Howland Blashfield to James Lovett, folder 5 (1905–1906), James D'Wolf Lovett papers; Henry Cabot Lodge to Samuel Cabot, April 10, 1906, folder 2 (1906-Jan–May), James D'Wolf Lovett papers; and F. H. Viaux to Samuel Cabot, February 4, 1906, folder 7 (1906-Oct–Dec), James D'Wolf Lovett papers.
23 Henry Chadwick to Jim Lovett, October 25, 1906, James D'Wolf Lovett papers, 1896–1935, folder 6 (1907–10), Ms. N-1599, Massachusetts Historical Society.
24 A. G. Spalding to James Lovett, April 23, 1909, folder 2 (1906-Jan–May), James D'Wolf Lovett papers.
25 Lovett kept a news clipping referring to the box score: his amateur side lost 41–10 with Lovett pitching for a "Select Nine' against 'Boston baseball stars," which included both Wright brothers, Cal McVey, and pitcher A. G. Spalding. "Bostons Go South This Week," undated news clipping (probably 1896), James D'Wolf Lovett Sports Scrapbook.
26 Phil Bergen, "Early Base Ball in Boston—Lovett of the Lowells," *National Pastime* 16 (1996): 62–68.
27 See Charles Norman Fay to James Lovett, May 3, 1911, and James Lovett to Charles Norman Fay, May 9, 1911, folder 8 (1911–16), James D'Wolf Lovett papers.
28 George Wright to Alice Lovett, January 3, 1936, James D'Wolf Lovett Sports Scrapbook.
29 Edmund H. Sears, *James D'Wolf Lovett. A Tribute by Edmund H. Sears* (privately printed, n.d.), 5, James D'Wolf Lovett Sports Scrapbook. The five-page booklet is one of the last pieces in Lovett's scrapbook.
30 Lovett to Mary Clark Eliot, June 20, 1906, letters, 1906–1934, to Mary Eliot, Boston Athenaeum.
31 See Albert W. Dennis, *Who's Who along the North Shore of Massachusetts Bay* (Salem, MA: Salem Press, 1908) and *Men of Boston and New England* (Boston: Boston American Publishers, 1913).
32 The new legislation required immigrants to speak English before obtaining citizenship and moved the authority on naturalization from the state level to the Federal government under a new Federal Bureau of Immigration and

Naturalization. "New Naturalization Law—Important Measure Passed by Congress," *Boston Evening Transcript*, June 28, 1906, 11.

33 Henry James, *The American Scene* (London: Chapman and Hall, 1907), 87. For the chapter specific to Boston, see 226–55.

34 James M. Lindgren, "'A Spirit That Fires the Imagination': Historic Preservation and Cultural Regeneration in Virginia and New England, 1850–1950," in *Giving Preservation a History—Histories of Historic Preservation in the United States*, 2nd ed., ed. Randall Mason and Max Page (New York: Routledge, 2019), 49–57. The project was led by Boston Brahmin William Sumner Appleton Jr., whose father had been one of Dixwell's first students. See William T. R. Marvin, *William Sumner Appleton* (New England Genealogical Register, 1874; repr., Boston: Press of David Clapp and Son, 1904), 4.

35 Montague Shearman and James Vincent, *Foot-Ball—Its History for Five Centuries* (London: Leadenhall Press, 1885), 2. See chapter 4 for the schools discussion, 47–66.

36 Shearman and Vincent, *Foot-Ball*, 64.

37 Shearman and Vincent, *Foot-Ball*, 11–13, 48 and 64.

38 Old Rugbeian Society, *The Origin of Rugby Football. Report (with Appendices) of the Sub-Committee of the Appointed in July, 1895* (Rugby: A. J. Lawrence, 1897), 3.

39 Old Rugbeian Society, *Origin of Rugby Football*, 22.

40 The Ellis myth has been discussed widely by William J. Baker, Tony Collins, Lincoln Allison, Rusty MacLean, and Dai Richards.

41 "The Origin of the Rugby Game," *Birmingham Daily Post*, January 20, 1900, 9.

42 L. E. S., *Some Notes on the History and Development of the Old Rugbeian Society. Especially in Its Early Years*, Rugby School Archives (no printing information, typescript dated October 1935), 62. The school's records have no documentation (yet found) about the Ellis tablet and its unveiling. Aside from the school newspaper, *The Meteor*, which did include passing mention of the plaque in the annual report of the Old Rugbeian Society for November 1900, the only other records postdate the plaque by thirty some years.

43 Jenifer Macrory, *Running with the Ball—the Birth of Rugby Football* (Collins Winslow, 1991), 34–35.

44 Digital searches for British papers from 1900 do not reveal immediate news beyond the Midlands. See "Old Rugbeian Society—Annual Report of the Committee," *Meteor*, no. 407 (November 15, 1900): 135–36.

45 See "The Football Field," *Manchester Guardian*, December 10, 1900, 3.

46 Searching newspaper databases through the *Boston Globe*, *Herald*, and *Post* reveals nothing about the tablet in Rugby during 1900–1901. While the *Boston Evening Transcript* is silent in early January (no editions available on January 5, 7, or 14 on Google), city papers did report on a statue to the former

governor Roger Wolcott as well as the death of former Rugby headmaster Thomas Arnold's wife. See *Boston Evening Transcript*, January 2, 1901; and *Boston Daily Advertiser*, March 3, 1901.

47 Soccer was not entirely absent from the moment the first printed FA rules appeared in the United States (1866) and the time of the Oneida dinner in 1904. See Chris Bolsmann and George Kioussis, eds., *Soccer Frontiers: The Global Game in the United States, 1863–1913* (Knoxville: University of Tennessee Press, 2021); Brian Bunk, *From Football to Soccer: The Early History of the Beautiful Game in the United States* (Urbana: University of Illinois, 2021); Tom McCabe, *The Dear Old Mug: A Quest to Find America's Oldest Soccer Trophy* (Kearny, NJ: Soccertown Media, 2024); and SASH (Society for American Soccer History), "American Soccer History Archives," accessed May 13, 2024, https://www.ussoccerhistory.org/ASHA/ASHA/.

48 Peverelley's 1868 *Book of American Pastimes* made no mention of football within its 593 pages. Despite not referring to them in their full-page ad in Peverelley's book, Peck and Snyder's 1868 catalog did list imported English footballs. See Charles Peverelley, *The Book of American Pastimes, Containing a History of the Principal Base-Ball, Cricket, Rowing, and Yachting Clubs*, 2nd ed. (New York: American News Company, 1868), appendix, 10.

49 Similar to his 1874 *Football Our Winter Game* (printed in London by Field Office), the US printing of Alcock's *The Book of Rules of the Game of Foot Ball* had only short mentions of football's background. See Charles W. Alcock, *The Book of Rules of the Game of Foot Ball, as Adopted and Played by the English Football Associations* (New York: Peck and Snyder, 1871).

50 Dixwell referred to Higginson's arrest following the 1854 trial of enslaved man Anthony Burns. See entry for June 9, 1854, Epes Sargent Dixwell diaries, box 17, folder Diary Extracts, 1833–1884, Wigglesworth Family papers, Massachusetts Historical Society. See David R. Maginnes, "The Case of the Court House Rioters in the Rendition of the Fugitive Slave Anthony Burns, 1854," *Journal of Negro History* 56, no. 1 (January 1971): 31–42.

51 Rowing and baseball comprise the lion's share. F. O. Vaille and H. A. Clark, eds., *The Harvard Book: A Series of Historical, Biographical, and Descriptive Sketches by Various Authors. Illustrated with Views and Portraits* (Cambridge, MA: Welch, Bigelow, 1875), 2:186–87, 191–267, 268–340.

52 *Princeton Book—a Series of Sketches Pertaining to the History, Organization and Present Condition of the College of New Jersey* (Boston: Houghton, Osgood; Cambridge, MA: Riverside Press, 1879), 396, 432–40.

53 Henry Chadwick, *The Sports and Pastimes of American Boys—a Guide and Text-Book of Games of the Playground, the Parlour, and the Field Especially Adapted for American Youth* (New York: George Routledge and Sons, 1884), 97, 107.

54 The 1888 edition was revised in 1892. Richard M. Hurd, *A History of Yale Athletics 1840–1888* (New Haven, CT: Yale University, 1888; repr. with appendix 1892), 5, 53–59.

55 Early Yale publications built a myth around Schaff as "formerly of Rugby." Born in Pennsylvania, he was schooled near Stuttgart in his father's native Germany but never appears in the Rugby School registers. Schaff explained that an old schoolmate living in England sent him a rugby ball in 1871 to use at Yale. From there the myth was born. Not even the publication of his class's 1901 yearbook, which gave a complete picture of Schaff's role, could alter the legend that appeared in Camp's later books. Frederick J. Shepard, ed., *The History of the Yale Class of 1873* (Buffalo, NY: n.p., July 1901), 278–83.

56 Roger Tamte, *Walter Camp and the Creation of American Football* (Urbana: University of Illinois Press, 2018), xiii.

57 Michael Oriard, *Reading Football: How the Popular Press Created an American Spectacle* (Chapel Hill: University of North Carolina Press, 1993), 35.

58 Walter Camp, *Walter Camp's Book of College Sports*, 3rd ed. (New York: Century Company and De Vinne Press, 1893), 88.

59 Camp begins by linking American football to the 1871 Rugby Union rules before following immediately, "Of the Association game one can say but little as regards its American following. It is quite extensively played in this country, but more by those who have themselves played it in Great Britain than by native-born Americans. Its popularity is extending, and at some day it will very likely become as well understood in this country as the derived Rugby is to-day. Its essential characteristic is, that it is played with the feet, in distinction from the Rugby, in which the ball may be carried in the hands." Walter Camp, *American Football* (New York: Harper and Brothers, 1891), 3–4, 8.

60 See John Henry Bartlett and John Pearl Gifford, eds., *Dartmouth Athletics: A Complete History of All Kinds of Sports and the College* (Concord, NH: Republican Press Association, 1893); Amos Alonzo Stagg and Henry L. Williams, *A Scientific and Practical Treatise on American Football for Schools and Colleges* (Hartford, CN: Press of Case, Lockwood, and Brainard Company, 1893); James Church, ed., *University Foot-Ball—the Play of Each Position Treated by a College Expert* (New York: Scriber's Sons, 1893); and Henry Chadwick, *The Reliable Book of Outdoor Games Containing Official Rules for Playing Base Ball, Foot Ball, Cricket, Lacrosse, Tennis, Croquet, etc.* (New York: F. M. Lupton, 1893).

61 Chadwick referred to the American college game having the "worst features of the Rugby game and the least attractive methods of the Association game" and actually advocated most in favor of Gaelic rules, popular in the New York immigrant clubs. Camp's book, based on the one thousand questionnaires he received, sought to establish an empirical basis to defend football in the face of claims of excessive violence. Walter Camp, *Football Facts and Figures—a Symposium of Expert Opinion on the Game's Place in American Universities* (New York: Harper and Brothers, 1894).

62 Walter Camp and Lorin Deland, *Football* (Cambridge, MA: Riverside Press, 1896), 3.
63 Though no references are given, the account is not dissimilar to the 3rd edition of Shearman and Montague's 1887 history. See Camp and Deland, *Football*, 17.
64 See George W. Orton, *A History of Athletics at Pennsylvania, 1873–1896* (Philadelphia: Avil Printing Company, Athletic Association of the University of Pennsylvania, n.d. [presumed 1897 from handwritten note]); Lewis Sheldon Welch and Walter Camp, *Yale: Her Campus, Class-Rooms, and Athletics* (Boston: L. C. Page, 1899); and Frank Presbey and James Hugh Moffatt, eds., *Athletics at Princeton: A History* (New York: Frank Presbey Company, 1901).
65 Walter Camp, *Sports and Games* (New York: P. F. Collier and Son, 1903), 213.
66 Thomas Zeiler, "A Night at Delmonico's: The Spalding Baseball Tour and the Imagination of Empire," *International Journal of the History of Sport* 23, no. 1 (February 2006): 28–45.
67 See the Baseball Hall of Fame website: https://baseballhall.org/discover-more/stories/short-stops/spalding-road-trip, accessed March 28, 2021.
68 Harold Seymour, *Baseball: The Early Years* (New York: Oxford University Press, 1989), 8–12.
69 Lovett, *Old Boston Boys*, 128.
70 "Old Boston Boys—the Games They Played in Days Gone By," *Sunday Herald*, June 24, 1906, 13, James D'Wolf Lovett Sports Scrapbook.
71 On the baseball myth, see Peter Levine, *A. G. Spalding and the Rise of Baseball: The Promise of American Sport* (New York: Oxford University Press, 1986); and Brian Martin, *Baseball's Creation Myth: Adam Ford, Abner Graves and the Cooperstown Story* (Jefferson, NC: McFarland, 2013).
72 Sam W. Haynes, *Unfinished Revolution—the Early American Republic in a British World* (Charlottesville: University of Virginia Press, 2010), 28.
73 See chapters 4–7 in John Watterson, *College Football: History, Spectacle, Controversy* (Baltimore: Johns Hopkins University Press, 2000); John H. Moore, "Football's Ugly Decades, 1893–1913," *Smithsonian Journal of History* 2 (Fall 1967): 49–68; Ronald A. Smith, "Harvard and Columbia and a Reconsideration of the 1905–06 Football Crisis," *Journal of Sport History* 8, no. 3 (Winter 1981): 5–19; Roberta J. Park, "From Football to Rugby—and Back, 1906–1919: The University of California-Stanford University Response to the 'Football Crisis of 1905,'" *Journal of Sport History* 11, no. 3 (Winter 1984): 5–40; and John J. Miller, *The Big Scrum: How Teddy Roosevelt Saved Football* (New York: Harper Collins, 2011).
74 See entry for November 30, 1905, vol. 11, Robert Apthorp Boit diaries, 1876–1918.

75 Brian Ingrassia, *The Rise of Gridiron University: Higher Education's Uneasy Alliance with Big-Time Football* (Lawrence: University of Kansas Press, 2015), 40.
76 J. Mott Hollowell, "For a more open game," *Boston Evening Transcript*, November 29, 1904, 5.
77 Dana Gibson to Uncle Jim Lovett, n.d., folder 14, n.d. (2), James D'Wolf Lovett papers.
78 The copy in the Library of Congress still includes news clippings from unnamed newspapers glued onto the first inside cover pages. See "Boston Gossip of Latest Books," *New York Times*, July 18, 1908.
79 A. G. Spalding to James Lovett, November 11, 1911, folder 8 (1911–16), James D'Wolf Lovett papers.
80 Cabot's certificate was signed by another Oneida, F. C. Shattuck. See also Commonwealth of Massachusetts, *Return of a Death—1906 (Samuel Cabot) 26 November*, in Massachusetts Deaths, 1841–1915, 1921–1924—FamilySearch.org, number 10257, 183. The other Oneidas who passed away during these years were Arthur Mills (1907), Alanson Tucker (1909), Amory Appleton Lawrence (1912), William Foster Apthorp, John Henry Brooks (both 1913), James Arthur Beebe (1914), John Power/Paouaa Hall (1916), James Dwight (1917), Robert Apthorp Boit, Frederick Russell Sturgis, William Fisher Wharton (all 1919), and Frank Jackson (1921).
81 This was the first American-printed football book to address the game's history before the English period working through *pheninda* in classical Athens, imperial Rome's *harpastum*, and carnivalesque Florentine *calcio*. In ingenious writing, Camp recognizes Webb Ellis but also handily situates his originality in a broader narrative of games through Western civilization. Walter Camp, *The Book of Foot-Ball* (New York: Century, 1910), 11–14. See also Tamte, *Walter Camp*, 112–13.
82 Incidentally, while the cover illustration shows an early helmet-covered player with a ball under the arm being tackled by an opponent, the inside cover still shows a player kicking the ball. Camp, *The Book of Foot-Ball*, 62–65.
83 Parke H. Davis, *Football, the American Intercollegiate Game* (New York: Charles Scribner's Sons, 1911), 3.
84 Davis, *Football*, 40–42, 45–51, 64.
85 It is worth noting that Deland, a Bostonian, never attended Harvard nor played football. He had become famous for inventing the flying wedge during his brief tenure as Harvard coach.
86 Davis, *Football*, 41, 66.
87 C. M. Van Stockum's extensive bibliography published in 1914 listed no less than 170 books written on football (all forms of it) in English, German, French, and Dutch. See C. M. Van Stockum, *Sport. Attempt at a Bibliography of Books and Periodicals Published during 1890–1912 in Great-Britain, the*

United States of America, France, Germany, Austria, Holland, Belgium and Switzerland (New York: Dodd and Livingston, 1914), 34–37.
88 Charles Gondouin and Jordan, *Le Football: Rugby—Américain—Association* (Paris: Pierre Lafitte, 1910), 245–48.
89 William Edwards's *Football Days*, prefaced by Walter Camp and published in 1916, appears to be the first memoir to meaningfully include school football (Phillips Exeter and St. Paul's in New Hampshire, Phillips Andover in Massachusetts, or Lawrenceville in New Jersey). While none of Edwards's testimonies harken back prior to the 1870s, Phillips Andover's school history published in 1917 mentioned intramural school matches popular long before the Civil War. Student Thomas White Nickerson is said to have learned of rugby in Boston schools before bringing the game to Andover in 1874. Graduating from Harvard (1880), there is no record of him in the Latin or Dixwell registers up to 1871. Even Henry Sheldon's extensive treatise on the life of students at schools and universities, which gives much space to football, makes virtually no mention of the mid-nineteenth century. See William H. Edwards, *Football Days—Memories of the Game and the Men behind the Ball* (New York: Moffat, Yard, 1916); Claude M. Fuess, *An Old New England School—a History of Phillips Academy Andover* (Boston: Houghton Mifflin, 1917), 469–74; and Henry D. Sheldon, *Student Life and Customs* (New York: D. Appleton and Company, 1901).
90 Henry F. Jenks, *Catalogue of the Boston Public Latin School. Established in 1635. With an Historical Sketch* (Boston: Boston Public Latin Association, 1886), 93.
91 *The Hawes School Memorial, Containing an Account of Five Re-Unions of the Old Hawes School Girls' Association, and a Series of Biographical Sketches of the Old Masters* (Boston: David Clapp and Son, 1889), 35.
92 *The Old Schoolboys of Boston* (Boston: privately printed, 1903), 76–77, 154–57.
93 Of all the book reviews about the 1908 edition, only one mentions the Oneida Club specifically (but even cricket was the subject of more lines in the article than football). See "Sporty Boys, Those of Boston in 1858—in the Stories James Lovett Tells of Them," *Boston Advertiser*, n.d. [probably 1908], 8, folder 15 (1906–35), James D'Wolf Lovett papers.
94 "The Listener," *Boston Evening Transcript*, February 24, 1904, 31.
95 See folders 6 (1907–10), 8 (1911–16), 9 (1917–21), James D'Wolf Lovett papers.

CHAPTER 7

1. William Sumner Appleton Jr. to Francis G. Peabody, November 18, 1922, Accession File 1922.768, "The Rubber Football," Historic New England.
2. *Six of the Seven Survivors of the Oneida Football Game of November 7, 1863*, November 15, 1922, photograph, gifted by W. S. Scudder, November 24, 1922, Accession File 1922.768, "The Rubber Football."
3. Lovett, Bowditch, Scudder, Means Lawrence, Peabody, and Arnold to Gat Miller, November 18, 1922, Accession File 1922.768, "The Rubber Football."
4. *Bulletin of the Society for the Preservation of New England Antiquities* 1, no. 1 (May 1910): 8. Cited hereafter as *Bulletin of the SPNEA*.
5. *Bulletin of the SPNEA* 4, no. 1 (Serial no. 9, August 1913): 18.
6. See *Bulletin of the SPNEA* 7, no. 1 (Serial no. 14, May 1916): 32; *Bulletin of the SPNEA* 7, no. 2 (Serial no. 15, December 1916): 32; and *Bulletin of the SPNEA* 8, no. 1 (Serial no. 16, March 1917): 7–16.
7. Life members from 1910 included Russell Gray and Oscar Iasigi's wife, while others took occasional yearly memberships or support pledges: Francis G. Peabody, William Sturgis Bigelow, Russell Gray, Henry Cabot Lodge, Fred C. Shattuck, and other non-Oneidas like Horatio Curtis, James Barr Ames, and Robert F. Clark.
8. See *Bulletin of the SPNEA* 10, no. 1 (Serial no. 20, October 1919): 36; and *Old-Time New England* 12, no. 1 (Serial no. 20, July 1921): 40.
9. *Old-Time New England* 11, no. 1 (Serial no. 21, July 1920): iii.
10. *Bulletin of the SPNEA* 3, no. 1 (Serial no. 6, March 1912): 12.
11. James M. Lindgren, *Preserving Historic New England: Preservation, Progressivism and the Remaking of Memory* (New York: Oxford University Press, 1995), 10. On the foundation of historical societies, see Alea Henle, "Preserving the Past, Making History: Historical Societies in the Early United States" (PhD diss., University of Connecticut, 2012).
12. Van Engen argues that three distinct views arose between 1870–1930: that the Pilgrims and Puritans had initiated civil and religious liberty, the more antagonistic view that liberty had been achieved only by escaping strict Puritan culture, and that American wealth was the result of the industrious and enterprising Puritans. See chapter 13 in Abram C. Van Engen, *A City upon a Hill* (New Haven, CT: Yale University Press, 2020).
13. *Report of the Pilgrim Tercentenary Commission* (Boston: Wright and Potter, 1917), 9.
14. From Virginia, Astor married into the Shaw family—of Robert Gould Shaw fame—before later moving abroad. Her sister Irene married James D'Wolf Lovett's nephew Charles Dana Gibson, becoming one of the inspirations for his famous Gibson Girls. *Pilgrim Tercentenary: Observances at Plymouth,*

December 21, 1920, and the Summer of 1921 (Plymouth, MA: Plymouth Cordage Co., 1921), 2.

15 Van Engen explains this brilliantly staged event but for some reason states that the Coolidge, Massachusetts, governor and soon to be vice president read the poem. The 1923 report notes that it was Lodge, visibly in on the stunt, who read aloud Daniel Webster's famous 1820 Plymouth bicentenary oration. Van Engen, *A City upon a Hill*, 202–6; and original source in Frederick William Bittinger, *The Story of the Pilgrim Tercentenary Celebration at Plymouth in the Year 1921* (Plymouth, MA: Memorial Press, 1923), 15–23.

16 Sam W. Haynes, *Unfinished Revolution—the Early American Republic in a British World* (Charlottesville: University of Virginia Press, 2010), 14.

17 It is worth noting that, while the focus was on Plymouth, in the same breath Lodge mentioned the Jamestown colony along with the Pilgrims as joint "cornerstones" of America, something neither Daniel Rodgers nor Abram Van Engen recognize. For analysis of Lodge's views on immigration, see John A. Garraty, *Henry Cabot Lodge: A Biography* (New York: Knopf, 1953), 140–45; Brian Gratton, "Race or Politics? Henry Cabot Lodge and the Origins of the Immigration Restriction Movement in the United States," *Journal of Political History* 30, no. 1 (2018): 128–57; and Rachel Leah Hershfield, "The Immigration Restriction League: A Study of the League's Impact on American Immigration Policy, 1894–1924" (master's thesis, University of Calgary, 1993).

18 "University Asked to Join in Pageant at Princeton," *Harvard Crimson*, October 29, 1919.

19 See "1919 Marks 50th Anniversary of Intercollegiate Football," *Harvard Crimson*, November 22, 1919; and *The Nassau Literary Magazine* 75, no. 3 (December 1919): 131–34.

20 Save for a handful of syndicated articles, searches in *Chronicling America* reveal no mention of the 1839 origin point. In 1916, the *Newark Evening Star* (NJ) and the *Bridgeport Evening Farmer* (CT) ran similar articles on the twenty-third anniversary since Doubleday's death; only the former called for a great celebration around his birthday "centenary three years hence." Two years on, the *El Paso Herald* (TX) and the *Montgomery Advertiser* (AL) printed shorter pieces on the now twenty-fifth anniversary but made no mention of the upcoming centenary for the game's founding. A rare lengthy piece in 1919 ignored the anniversaries entirely. Even Harold Seymour is silent. See "Little New York Village Is Birthplace of Baseball," *Newark Evening Star*, January 24, 1916, 13; "New York Village Is Birthplace of Baseball," *Bridgeport Evening Farmer*, January 24, 1916, 10; "New York Village Is Birthplace of Baseball," *Montgomery Advertiser*, January 24, 1918, 9; "New York Village Is Birthplace of Baseball," *El Paso Herald*, January 24, 1918, 10; and F. K., "History of Baseball—a Retrospective Analysis of the National Game from

Its Inception to the Present Date," *Mirror* (Stillwater, MN), April 3, 1919, 1, 3.

21. James Wellman and Walter Peet, *The Story of the Harvard-Yale Boat Race 1852–1912* (New York: Harper and Brothers, 1912).
22. Books like Daly's and Haughton's, if they included any background at all, mentioned concisely how American collegiate football was an offshoot of early Rugby Union. See Charles Daly, *American Football—with Many Diagrams by the Author and Portraits of Prominent Players and Coaches* (New York: Harper and Brothers, 1921); and Percy D. Haughton, *Football and How to Watch It* (Boston: Marshall Jones, 1922).
23. "'The H Book' Will Be Ready for Distribution within Three Weeks," *Harvard Crimson*, January 20, 1923.
24. Morton Henry Prince, "History of Football at Harvard, 1800–75," in *The H Book of Harvard Athletics 1852–1922*, ed. John A. Blanchard (Cambridge, MA: Harvard Varsity Club, 1923), 344.
25. Prince, "History of Football at Harvard," 344–46.
26. Coinciding with the second of Morton's father's terms as mayor of Boston, the 1880 Census listed the Prince family at number 311 Beacon Street, while recent widower Lovett resided two doors down in his sister Anna's home (number 317 Beacon Street). Widow Anna Gibbs lived there from 1879 to 1884, while the Prince family lived at 311 Beacon from 1872 to 1899. See Tom High, "315–17 Beacon Street," Back Bay Houses, accessed April 29, 2024, https://backbayhouses.org/315-317-beacon/.
27. Davis wrote two pieces that appeared only in the Harvard magazine, the second a few months later on the 1874 Harvard-McGill match. Davis had clearly mined the Harvard student newspapers and other sources, though he provided few references. Interestingly, Davis drew a direct distinction between the hazing "football fightum" of Harvard and the situation at Yale and Princeton where "the game flourished remarkably, but it was a game that was an orderly football contest, adapted from the 'association' code of football play." Davis also drew a link between Boston, "its British foundation," and how a "highly ingenious style of football play had arisen in Boston, known as 'Old Boston.' During the decade of the '60s, when the country was at war, the boys of the Boston Latin School, Dixwell's School, and at Andover and Exeter, played this game, and boy-like, at each institution made changes in the 'Old Boston' game suitable for their grounds and exigencies of play." Parke H. Davis, "The Beginnings of Football at Harvard," *Harvard Alumni Bulletin* 18, no. 12 (December 15, 1915): 213–19. See also "The Harvard-McGill Football Game of 1874," *Harvard Alumni Bulletin*, 18, no. 24 (March 15, 1916): 450–55.
28. Prince, "History of Football at Harvard," 371.
29. In 1926, Scudder credited the late Volkmann for calling to his attention Bussy's article. Winthrop Saltonstall Scudder, *An Historical Sketch of the*

Oneida Football Club of Boston 1862–1865 (deposited October 18, 1926), Massachusetts Historical Society, 1.
30 *Boston Evening Transcript*, March 3, 1923, 1.
31 J. P. Collins and Philip Bussy, "Rugby's Birth, Its Yesterdays and Its Today," *Boston Evening Transcript*, March 3, 1923, 4.
32 The first reports regarding a centenary celebration appear to be in February. "Rugby Football Centenary," *Advertiser* (UK), February 3, 1922, 6.
33 Around the 1922 annual Rugby Football Union meeting in London that summer, leading French paper *L'Auto* made many calls for an international match and France's participation, even soliciting French readers for suggestions until January 1923. "L'Assemblée générale de la Rugby Union," *L'Auto* (France), June 22, 1922, 3; "Rugby Union Meeting," *Advertiser* (UK), June 23, 1922, 6; see *L'Auto* in January 1923 for at least ten articles.
34 See "For 'Footballers,'" *Boston Herald*, September 9, 1922, 15.
35 Parke H. Davis, *Football, the American Intercollegiate Game* (New York: Charles Scribner's Sons, 1911), 27. Davis's account was more detailed than Camp's and was reproduced in the Boston papers featuring large photos of Rugby School and the plaque. "By Parke H. Davis of the Intercollegiate Rules Committee," *Boston Sunday Post*, November 27, 1910, 18.
36 "A Football Centenary," *Boston Herald*, January 23, 1923, 16.
37 Collins and Bussy, "Rugby's Birth, Its Yesterdays," 4.
38 Among the Oneidas were Edward Bowditch, William Ellery Channing Eustis, Arthur Hunnewell, John Wayland McBurney, Francis Greenwood Peabody, and Robert Clifford Watson. The wider group in Lovett's *Old Boston Boys* included James Barr Ames, George Bass, Arthur Burnham, Arthur T. Cabor, Joseph S. Fay, Edward "Ned" Fenno, Alden P. Loring, Francis Ogden Lyman, Francis Rawle, and Robert Gould Shaw.
39 Tony Collins, *A Social History of English Rugby Union* (Abingdon, UK: Routledge, 2009), 65–71.
40 While Scudder simply states that the merger was "on account of his failing health," the circumstances of Volkmann's retirement were more sinister. Despite his excellent reputation, he was falsely suspected during the first World War of being a German spy due to his accent. In 1918, his school was destroyed by an unexplained fire. See Winthrop Saltonstall Scudder, ed., *Gerrit Smith Miller—an Appreciation—Supplement to the Nobleman* (Dedham, MA: Noble and Greenough School, 1924), 7; *Cornell University Class of 1877 Report* (Ithaca, NY: Cornell University, 1923), 72; Melissa D. Burrage, *The Karl Muck Scandal: Classical Music and Xenophobia in World War I America* (Rochester: University of Rochester Press, 2019), 111–14.
41 Report from Richard Saltonstall to Board of Trustees, October 1, 1914, box 18, folder 10, papers of Abbott Lawrence Lowell, Harvard University Archives. See also Richard T. Flood, *The Story of Noble and Greenough School 1866–1966* (Dedham, MA: Noble and Greenough School, 1966), 56–81.

42 James D'Wolf Lovett, *Old Boston Boys and the Games They Played* (Boston: Riverside Press, 1906), 81–82, 93.
43 "Miller, Gerrit Smith," *The National Enyclopaedia of American Biography* (New York: James T. White, 1958) 42:100; and "Obituaries," *New York History*, 20, no. 1 (January 1939): 63–64.
44 W. Freeman Galpin, "Gerrit Smith Miller, a Pioneer in the Dairy and Cattle Industry," *Agricultural History* 5, no. 1 (January 1931): 1–6.
45 "Miller, Gerrit Smith," *National Enyclopaedia*.
46 Steven B. Levine, "The Rise of American Boarding Schools and the Development of a National Upper Class," *Social Problems* 28, no. 1 (October 1980): 63–94.
47 "Deaths—A. L. K. Volkmann," *Boston Herald*, August 22, 1923, 11.
48 See letterhead from *Memorandum*, December 7, 1923, Noble and Greenough School archives; *The Constitution, By-Laws and House Rules of the Union Club of Boston Incorporated, with a List of Officers and Members, October 1, 1921* (Boston: Union Club, privately printed, 1921), 59, 61, 67, 71, 79; and "Theodore T. Scudder," *Boston Globe*, January 14, 1953, 3.
49 Camp's letter is dated September 22 and refers to Scudder's sent three days prior. There is no copy of Davis's reply in 1923, only a later letter referring back to it. See Scudder, *Historical Sketch*, 2–3.
50 Lovett, *Old Boston Boys*, 91–93.
51 In all the Boston papers reviewed, the earliest mention of the Oneidas is from the November 1863 match. City papers did include mention of a seventeen-a-side Dixwell–Latin School game on June 6, 1862. "Football Match," *Boston Herald*, June 7, 1862, 4.
52 None of the clippings in Lovett's richly annotated copy of *Old Boston Boys* mention an 1862 foundation date. His scrapbook contains one undated clipping (from an unnamed source) noting that "in 1862 or '63, he was also a leading member of the Oneida Foot-Ball Club." Pasted in between baseball game clippings dated to the summer of 1868, there is no indication, however, as to when Lovett obtained it or when he created the scrapbook, which was not donated until after his death in 1935.
53 "The Rugby Centenary," *Times* (UK), October 23, 1923.
54 "Rugby Football—Centenary Match at Rugby," *Times* (UK), April 6, 1923, 5; "The Rugby Centenary—a Historic Match," *Times* (UK), October 23, 1923, 7; "Schoolboy Who Revolutionised the Game," *Observer* (UK), October 28, 1923, 14; "Rule-Breaking and Game Making," *Manchester Guardian*, October 30, 1923, 8.
55 *Supplement to the Rugby Advertiser*, November 2, 1923, Rugby School Archives.
56 Phil Dine, *French Rugby Football: A Cultural History* (Oxford: Berg, 2001), 27.
57 *The Centenary of Rugby Football—1823–1923—Menu & Toasts*, November 1, 1923. Rugby School Archives.

Notes to Pages 123–126

58 "To honor the founder of organized football," *Boston Globe*, November 7, 1923.
59 Scudder, *Gerrit Smith Miller*, 12, 26–30.
60 *Memorandum regarding Miller, Dixwell, Lovett, Watson and Volkmann Medals and Funds, to Be Submitted to the Board of Trustees of Noble and Greenough School*, December 7, 1923, 1–2, Noble and Greenough School archives.
61 "Unveil Tablet in Honor of Founder of Football in the United States," *Boston Globe*, November 8, 1923, 23; "To Honor Star of Other Days," *Boston Herald*, November 7, 1923, 10.
62 "Tablet Honors Football Founder," *New York Times*, November 8, 1923.
63 "To Honor the Founder of Organized Football," *Boston Globe*, November 7, 1923.
64 "Dedicate Tablet to 'Gat' Miller, Football's Founder," *Boston Herald*, November 8, 1923, 10.
65 "Unveil Tablet in Honor of Founder of Football in the United States," *Boston Globe*, November 8, 1923, 23.
66 "Sixty Years of Football," *Boston Transcript*, November 7, 1923, James D'Wolf Lovett Sports Scrapbook, 1861–1945, Revolutionary Spaces.
67 "Founder of Football Living in Peterboro and Raising Holsteins," December 1, 1923, unnamed newspaper, folder 2-2, Smith-Miller Family Collection, 1879–1961, Madison County Historical Society, Oneida, NY.
68 The *Omaha Morning Bee* mistakenly noted the club as founded fifty-two years earlier (1871), November 14, 1923, 8.
69 "To Honor the Founder of Organized Football," *Boston Globe*, November 7, 1923.
70 The inside cover of the Bostonian Society's copy records that the booklet was gifted on March 13, 1924. See Scudder, *Gerrit Smith Miller*, inside cover, Revolutionary Spaces.
71 Copy 1 in the Library of Congress has a handwritten note on the inside cover: "Gift Editor March 6, 1924." See Scudder, *Gerrit Smith Miller*, Library of Congress.
72 "Unveil tablet in honor of founder of football in the United States," *Boston Globe*, November 8, 1923, 23.
73 Scudder, *Gerrit Smith Miller*, 17, 25. The booklet lauds the Peterboro man (who entered Harvard in 1865) for not wanting to play against his old Lowell team for that season's championship match. Miller, who had beaten Harvard with Lowell the year before, was by all accounts an accomplished pitcher and first-baseman. See *Harvard College Class of 1869 Secretary's Report No. 1* (Boston: n.p., 1869), 21; Blanchard, *H Book*, 251; and *Harvard College Class of 1866 Secretary's Report No. 1* (Boston: n.p., 1866), 15–16.
74 Scudder, *Gerrit Smith Miller*, 29.
75 Scudder, *Gerrit Smith Miller*, 30.

76 "Unveil Tablet in Honor of Founder of Football in the United States," *Boston Globe*, November 8, 1923, 23.
77 "President Eliot on Football," *School Journal*, February 18, 1905.
78 John Miller states that Eliot had "little to say about the game" after retiring in 1909. See Charles W. Eliot, *Harvard Memories* (Cambridge, MA: Harvard University Press, 1923); and John J. Miller, *The Big Scrum: How Teddy Roosevelt Saved Football* (New York: Harper Perennial, 2011), 220–21.
79 "Unveil Tablet in Honor of Founder of Football in the United States," *Boston Globe*, November 8, 1923, 23.
80 "Football as an Organized Game Is Honored by Having Gerrit Smith Miller as Its Founder—1862," signed print, November 7, 1923, James D'Wolf Lovett Sports Scrapbook.
81 Michael Oriard, *Reading Football: How the Popular Press Created an American Spectacle* (Chapel Hill: University of North Carolina Press, 1993), 57–89.
82 For his honorary degree, master of arts, the text referred to *Gulliver's Travels*: "Swift reckoned a benefactor to mankind the man who made two blades of grass to grow in place of one, and we honor him who has made our cattle yield two quarts of milk for every one they gave before." See *Harvard Graduates Magazine* 33, no. 129 (September 1924): 109–10.
83 "Dedicate Tablet to 'Gat' Miller, Football's Founder," *Boston Herald*, November 8, 1923, 10.
84 "The First Organized Football Club in the United States," *Old-Time New England* 15, no. 1 (July 1924): 8–13; "Reviews—Gerrit Smith Miller: An Appreciation by Winthrop S. Scudder; Kriemhild Herd, a Chapter in Holstein History by Frank Norton Decker," *Quarterly Journal of the New York State Historical Association* 7, no. 3 (July 1926): 233–34.
85 Daniel Boorstin, *Hidden History* (New York: Vintage Books, 1989), 259–62, 284–96.
86 "Original Football Team," clipping from *John Hancock Field*, November 1923, James D'Wolf Lovett Sports Scrapbook.
87 See folder 10 (1922–24), James D'Wolf Lovett papers, 1896–1935, Massachusetts Historical Society.
88 Appleton to J. Lovett, September 10, 1924, folder 10 (1922–24), James D'Wolf Lovett papers.
89 This repeated much of another long essay—silent on the Oneidas and Boston schoolboys—by Allanson Shaw a month earlier. See the "Rugby Football Centenary," *New York Times Magazine*, October 12, 1924, 4, 15.
90 "Who Started All This Football, Anyway?," *Literary Digest*, November 22, 1924, 50, 52.

CHAPTER 8

1. James D'Wolf Lovett, *A Pilgrimage—Read at a Meeting of the Oneidas, Saturday, May 28, 1927* (Boston: n.p., 1927). 7.
2. See David J. Lunt, "The Heroic Athlete in Ancient Greece," *Journal of Sport History* 36, no. 3 (2009): 375–92; Christopher Stride and Ffion Thomas, "Tension in the Union of Art and Sport: Competition for Ownership of the Baseball Statuary and Its Influence upon Design," *NINE: A Journal of Baseball History and Culture* 24, nos. 1–2 (2015–16): 1–28; and Chris Stride, John P. Wilson, and Ffion Thomas, "Honouring Heroes by Branding in Bronze: Theorizing the UK's Football Statuary," *Sport in Society* 16, no. 6 (2013): 749–71.
3. Both Ed Mahan (1892–1975) and Ed Casey (1894–1966) were Harvard alumni and from assimilated Irish families (Casey attended Phillips Exeter). In 1924, Ted Coy (1888–1935, son of first Hotchkiss headmaster) was a well-known figure and Bill Mallory (1901–1945, from Memphis) had just graduated following an undefeated final season at Yale.
4. See Pierre Nora, "Between Memory and History: Les Lieux de Mémoire," *Representations*, no. 26, Special Issue: Memory and Counter-Memory (Spring 1989): 7, 12. For the original, see Pierre Nora, *Les Lieux de mémoire*, 3 tomes: t. 1, *La République* (1 vol., 1984); t. 2, *La Nation* (3 vols., 1986); and t. 3, *Les France* (3 vols., 1992) (Paris: Gallimard, Bibliothèque illustrée des histoires).
5. Haughton had been a Harvard player himself at the turn of the century and then coached Cornell but earned his fame leading his alma mater. See "Percy D. Haughton Dies Suddenly—Famous Coach, Taken Ill on Football Field, Was a Victim of Angina Pectoris," *Boston Evening Globe*, October 28, 1924, 1A; "Last Tribute Paid to Percy Haughton," *Boston Globe*, October 31, 1924, 13A; and "News from the Classes—1899," *Harvard Graduates Magazine* 33, no. 130 (December 1924): 336–37.
6. See HM 137 microfilm reel 48, folder 55, "Scrapbook: Newspaper Clippings on Camp's Death, 1925," box 70, Walter Chauncey Camp papers (MS 125), Manuscripts and Archives, Yale University Library.
7. See "Recalls Death of Percy Haughton," *Boston Globe*, March 14, 1925; and "Camp Was Known as the 'Father of Football,'" *Boston Globe*, March 14, 1925, HM 137 microfilm reel 48, folder 55, "Scrapbook: Newspaper Clippings on Camp's Death, 1925," Walter Chauncey Camp papers.
8. For example, see "Camp Was Known as the 'Father of Football,'" *Boston Globe*, March 14, 1925, 4; "Walter Camp Is Taken by Death—End Comes as He Sleeps in Hotel in New York—'Father of Football' Active in Many Lines of Endeavor," *Boston Sunday Globe*, March 15, 1925, 1; "Football Has Lost Its Father Declares Yost," *Boston Sunday Globe*, March 15, 1925, 2; "Walter Camp Is Found Dead in Room at New York Hotel—'Father of

Football' Victim of Angina Pectoris Attack While Asleep," *Boston Herald* March 15, 1925; and "The Caesar of Football," *Boston Globe*, March 16, 1925.

9   Parkman, Lodge, and Lawrence were childhood friends. For Haughton, the bishop led the prayers for mercy. "Funeral in Trinity of Henry Parkman—Throng Present—Bishop Lawrence Celebrated," *Boston Daily Globe*, June 26, 1924, A8; "Senator Lodge Buried Simply; Crowds Mourn—Friend of Boyhood Leads Services," *Chicago Daily Tribune*, November 13, 1924, 10; "Last Tribute Paid to Percy Haughton," *Boston Daily Globe*, October 31, 1924, 13A.

10 Egg Rock's Wildlife Sanctuary still carries the senator's name. See photo with caption "Only Bust for Which Senator Lodge Posed," *Chicago Daily Tribune*, November 13, 1924; "Bird Sanctuary Proposed on Egg Rock near Nahunt," *Christian Science Monitor*, February 19, 1925, 3; and "'Henry Cabot Lodge Bird Sanctuary' on Egg Rock," *Boston Daily Globe*, February 26, 1925, 9. See "Henry Cabot Lodge," *Proceedings of the Massachusetts Historical Society*, 3rd ser., 58 (October 1924–June 1925): 97–110.

11 "Henry Cabot Lodge," *Harvard Graduates Magazine* 33, no. 131 (March 1925): 439–55; "Percy Duncan Haughton," *Harvard Graduates Magazine* 33, no. 131 (March 1925): 464–76; "Necrology," *Harvard Graduates Magazine* 33, no. 129 (September 1924): 198.

12 "Harvard to Honor Haughton Memory; Classmates and Former Pupils on Football Squads Plan to Erect Memorial," *New York Times*, November 21, 1924, 24.

13 "All New Haven Mourns—Memorial to Athletic Leader Will Probably Be Erected," *New York Times*, March 15, 1925, 22.

14 "Columbia Seeks Funds for Haughton Memorial," *Boston Daily Globe*, April 28, 1925, 24; Daniel French to Charles H. Walker, November 5, 1925, Walker, Charles Howard, 1857–1936, letters received, 1925–1927, Boston Athenaeum.

15 Clarence W. Mendell to Mrs. Walter Camp, April 28, 1925, HM 137 microfilm reel 48, folder 9, "Mrs. Walter Camp Correspondence 1921–1934," box 66, Walter Chauncey Camp papers. Folder 9 begins at microfilm slide 0183.

16 Walter Powell to Mr. Walter Camp Jr., May 21, 1925, HM 137 microfilm reel 48, folder 9, "Mrs. Walter Camp Correspondence 1921–1934," box 66, Walter Chauncey Camp papers. Folder 9 begins at microfilm slide 0183.

17 The Camp papers are full of letters about the memorial. See booklet, *A National Memorial to Walter Camp*, 67, HM 137 microfilm reel 48, folder 21, "Yale Memorial Gateway," Walter Chauncey Camp papers. Folder 21 begins at microfilm slide 0721.

18 See chapter 6 in Brian Ingrassia, *The Rise of Gridiron University: Higher Education's Uneasy Alliance with Big-Time Football* (Lawrence: University of Kansas Press, 2015).
19 Scudder to Parker, June 28, 1926, Clubs—Oneida Football Club, Boston, vertical file, Revolutionary Spaces. Hereafter cited as Oneida vertical file, Revolutionary Spaces.
20 "The First Organized Football Club in the United States," *Old-Time New England* 15, no. 1 (July 1924): 8–13.
21 Miller, Lawrence, Lovett, and Scudder to Bigelow, September 8, 1926, Oneida Monument file, Boston Art Commission archives, Boston city hall.
22 Reported in Boston, Yale's plans were presented but action delayed, which contrasts the speed of the Oneida project, completed in just two months. See "Discuss Walter Camp Memorial," *Boston Sunday Globe*, September 13, 1925; "Football Coaches Plan Camp Memorial," *New York Times*, September 13, 1925; and Parker to Robert D. Andrews, October 5, 1925, Boston Art Commission archives.
23 "Monument to Oneida Football Team to Be Placed on the Common," *Boston Globe*, October 30, 1925, 23.
24 Miller, Lawrence, Lovett, and Scudder to Andrews, Jones, Biscoe, and Whitmore, November 13, 1925, Boston Art Commission archives.
25 "Monument to Oneida Football Team to Be Placed on the Common," *Boston Globe*, October 30, 1925, 23.
26 "Monument Honoring Nation's First Football Team Unveiled as Crowd of 54,000 Flocks to Stadium," *Boston Traveler*, November 21, 1925, James D'Wolf Lovett Sports Scrapbook, 1861–1945, Revolutionary Spaces.
27 "Dedicate Monument on Boston Common Where First Football Team Played," *Boston Globe*, November 21, 1925, 5.
28 "Monument Honoring Nation's First Football Team Unveiled as Crowd of 54,000 Flocks to Stadium," *Boston Traveler*, November 21, 1925, James D'Wolf Lovett Sports Scrapbook.
29 "Dedicate Stone in Memory of First Football in U.S.," *Boston Sunday Globe*, November 22, 1925, 15.
30 See "Monument to First Football Team Dedicated on Common," *Boston Herald*, November 22, 1925, 10; "Dedicate Stone in Memory of First Football in U.S.," *Boston Sunday Globe*, November 22, 1925, 15; and "Shaft Unveiled to Oneida Club—Memorial to First Football Team in United States on Common," *Christian Science Monitor*, November 21, 1925.
31 See "Monument Honoring Nation's First Football Team Unveiled as Crowd of 54,000 Flocks to Stadium," *Boston Traveler*, November 21, 1925; and "Dedicate Stone in Memory of First Football in U.S.," *Boston Sunday Globe*, November 22, 1925, 15.
32 *New York Times*, November 22, 1925, 6, Sports section.

33　H. F. Mahoney, "Boston A. A. Games Feb. 6—Football Monument Unveiled at Boston—Other Notes," *New York Sun*, December 12, 1925.

34　Ramon Coffman penned a regular column in the 1920s *Wisconsin State Journal*, syndicated across the country and covering many topics. He wrote nearly eight hundred articles for the *Washington Post*, some under the pen name Uncle Ray.

35　"Uncle Ray's Corner—a Little Saturday Talk—Early Football in America," *Washington Post*, November 21, 1925, 10. Coffman's piece also appeared that day in the *Wisconsin State Journal*, 8.

36　"Uncle Ray's Corner—a Little Saturday Talk—the Rugby Football Rules," *Washington Post*, November 14, 1925, 10.

37　See "Monument to First Football Team Dedicated on Common," *Boston Herald*, November 22, 1925, 10; and "Football Came Down to Us from Romans," *Boston Herald*, November 22, 1925, section C, 5.

38　"Dedicate Monument on Boston Common Where First Football Team Played," *Boston Globe*, November 21, 1925, 15.

39　"To Erect Monument on Common to First Organized Football Club," *Boston Herald*, October 30, 1925, 26.

40　Jones to Parker, May 18, 1926, Boston Art Commission archives.

41　Miller, Means Lawrence, Lovett, and Scudder to Boston Art Commission, June 28, 1926, Boston Art Commission archives.

42　Parker to Scudder, August 12, 1926, Boston Art Commission archives.

43　Jones to Parker, August 23, 1926, Boston Art Commission archives.

44　Scudder to Parker, August 18, 1926, Boston Art Commission archives; Scudder to Parker, August 19, 1926, Boston Art Commission archives.

45　See Scudder to Parker, August 24, 1926, Boston Art Commission archives; and Scudder to Jones, September 9, 1926, Boston Art Commission archives.

46　Boston Art Commission secretary Henry Forbes Bigelow was a member of the Union Club from at least 1907 until 1915, like the Noble and Greenough Trustees Board members and so many others in the Brahmin world and Oneidas James Arthur Beebe, brothers Amory Appleton and William Lawrence, their cousin Robert Means Lawrence, William Ellery Channing Eustis, and John Duff. Others were admitted later: Walter Denison Brooks (1918), Francis G. Peabody (1916), and Scudder (1918). Moreover, it was Scudder's Riverside Press that published the Union Club's biannual rules. See reports between 1875–1921, Union Club of Boston, *The Constitution, By-Laws and House Rules of the Union Club of Boston Incorporated, with a List of Officers and Members*.

47　Jones to Parker, September 3, 1926, Boston Art Commission archives.

48　See "Walter Camp's Memory to Be Honored on Many Gridirons Today," *Boston Globe*, October 16, 1926, 8. See First National Bank of Boston check no. 5838 from J. D'Wolf Lovett to Andrews, Jones, Biscoe and Whitmore, and First National Bank of Boston check no. 5839 from J. D'Wolf Lovett to J. Coletti, folder 11 (1925–27), James D'Wolf Lovett papers, 1896–1935, Massachusetts Historical Society.

49. While no evidence points to Jones being Irish, the red-haired man could only have referred to Jones. Scudder to Parker, October 18, 1926, Boston Art Commission archives.
50. Winthrop Saltonstall Scudder, *An Historical Sketch of the Oneida Football Club of Boston 1862–1865* (deposited October 18, 1926), Massachusetts Historical Society, 10.
51. Both memorials were unveiled in November of 1927. See "Memorial to Camp Dedicated at Yale," *New York Times*, November 4, 1927, 165; and "Memorial to Percy D. Haughton Unveiled at Soldiers Field," *Boston Sunday Globe*, November 20, 1927, 31.
52. Scudder to Parker, January 29, 1927, Boston Art Commission archives.
53. Scudder to Parker, February 19, 1927, Boston Art Commission archives.
54. Jim Lovett to Gat Miller, December 9, 1927, box 1, folder 2, Gerrit Smith Miller papers, #3700, Division of Rare and Manuscript Collections, Cornell University Library. Emphasis in original.
55. Lovett explained that "before commencing the afternoon's games, it was the custom to place our coats, vests, etc., in a pile upon one side of the ground." James D'Wolf Lovett, *Old Boston Boys and the Games They Played* (Boston: Riverside Press, 1906), 95, 98.
56. The story can be traced back to a contemporary account about Boston Latin's schoolboys, subsequently argued as apocryphal. Artist Henry Bacon painted the famous scene entitled "Boston Boys and General Gage" in 1875, on display at the 1878 Centennial International Exhibition in Philadelphia. See Henry F. Jenks, *Catalogue of the Boston Public Latin School. Established in 1635. With an Historical Sketch* (Boston: Boston Public Latin Association, 1886), 40, 88; and H. Barbara Weinberg, "Cosmopolitan and Candid Stories, 1877–1915," in *American Stories: Paintings of Everyday Life, 1765–1915*, ed. H. Barbara Weinberg and Carrie Rebora Barratt (New Haven, CT: Yale University Press, 2009), 179.
57. "Monument Honoring Nation's First Football Team Unveiled as Crowd of 54,000 Flocks to Stadium," *Boston Traveler*, November 21, 1925, James D'Wolf Lovett Sports Scrapbook.
58. J. P. Collins and Philip Bussy, "Rugby's Birth, Its Yesterdays and Its Today," *Boston Evening Transcript*, March 3, 1923, 4.
59. Scudder to Jim and Alice Lovett, October 18, 1926, Oneida vertical file, Revolutionary Spaces.
60. Miller, Arnold, Lovett, and Means Lawrence to Scudder, March 29, 1926, Oneida vertical file, Revolutionary Spaces. The file only holds the first page of the letter, the second of which can be found in Lovett's papers at the Massachusetts Historical Society.

61 See handwritten note, page 2. Miller, Arnold, Lovett, Means Lawrence to Scudder, March 29, 1926, folder 11 (1925–27), James D'Wolf Lovett papers.

62 See Miller, Arnold, Lovett, and Means Lawrence to Scudder, March 29, 1926, folder 11 (1925–27), James D'Wolf Lovett papers.

63 See A. M. Weyand, *American Football—Its History and Development* (New York: D. Appleton, 1926), xv, 2; and Harford Powel Jr., *Walter Camp—the Father of American Football* (Boston: Little, Brown, 1926).

64 See "In Memory of the Nestor of American Football," *New York Herald Tribune*, October 17, 1926; and list of "Walter Camp Day Games," HM 137 microfilm reel 48, folder 21, "Yale Memorial Gateway 1925–1929, undated," box 67, Walter Chauncey Camp papers. Folder 21 begins at microfilm slide 0721.

65 Citing Scudder's *An Historical Sketch*, held in the Massachusetts Historical Society, the article recalled the Noble and Greenough tablet, the monument, and named several illustrious members including Bishop Lawrence, the deceased Lodge and Parkman, as well as Roger Wolcott. "The Famous Oneidas," *New York Times*, December 12, 1926, 10.

66 Stagg's four-page account of the Oneidas discussed the monument, the men still living, and, strangely, underlined that the ball could *not* be carried during play. Manchester's is one of the rare sporting texts of this early historiography to list (an impressive list of) sources, but not Lovett's *Old Boston Boys* or Scudder's *An Historical Sketch*, which may explain why he never discussed the Oneidas. Da Grosa repeats the same narrative about a Rugby School student (presumably David Schaff) who brought the game with him to Yale. See W. W. Stout and A. A. Stagg, *Touchdown—as Told by Amos Alonzo Stagg to Wesley Winans Stout* (New York: Longmans, Green, 1927), 24–27; Herbert Manchester, *Four Centuries of Sport in America 1490–1890* (New York: Derrydale, 1931), 128–29, 149–51; and John Da Grosa, "The Progress of American Football," *Spalding's Official Intercollegiate Foot Ball Guide, 1935*.

67 "Work Begins at Yale on the Memorial to Walter Camp," *Yale University News Statement*, June 8, 1927, HM 137 microfilm reel 48, folder 21, "Yale Memorial Gateway 1925–1929, undated," box 67, Walter Chauncey Camp papers. Folder 21 begins at microfilm slide 0721.

68 One rare publication where Camp's ownership of the game was less definitive was the 1929 Carnegie Report. Camp was mentioned without the usual "father" qualification and alongside a succinct Oneida account. Howard J. Savage, *American College Athletics* (New York: Carnegie Foundation for the Advancement of Teaching, 1929), 19.

69 "Winthrop Scudder Dies in New York—Art Editor Played on America's First Football Team," *Boston Herald*, August 15, 1929, 15; "Winthrop Scudder, Art Editor, Dies Here—Former Cambridge Resident Played Football Ten Years before Yale-Harvard Games," *New York Times*, 15 August 15, 1929, 18; "Winthrop S. Scudder, 82, Dies Here of Pneumonia—Former Boston Art

Notes to Pages 147–148

Editor Was Pioneer Football Star," *New York Herald Tribune*, August 15, 1929, 19; "Old Football Star Dies in New York; Played Years Ago," *Elmira Star-Gazette* (NY), August 15, 1929, 24.

70 See "Yachts and Yachtsmen—More Than 60 Years in the Sport—Walter Burgess Began Racing Career at Beverly in 1869," *Daily Boston Globe*, December 6, 1931, B58; and "William E. C. Eustis," *Daily Boston Globe*, October 30, 1932, A10.

71 Jim Lovett to Gat Miller, November 16, 1931, box 1, folder 7, Gerrit Smith Miller papers, #3700.

72 Jim Lovett to Gat Miller, November 21, 1931, box 1, folder 7, Gerrit Smith Miller papers, #3700.

73 Lovett thanked Eliot for the "royal feast on lobster salad and thought of your great kindness in remembering us." See Lovett to Mary Clark Eliot, September 18, 1934, letters, 1906–1934, to Mary Eliot, Boston Athenaeum.

74 Emphasis in original. See Jim Lovett to Gat Miller, December 1, 1931, box 1, folder 7, Gerrit Smith Miller papers, #3700. See also Jim Lovett to Gat Miller, January 20, 1933, box 1, folder 11, Gerrit Smith Miller papers, #3700.

75 James D'Wolf Lovett, unnamed memoirs typescript, November 1933, folders 19, 20, 21, 22 (writings 1–4), James D'Wolf Lovett papers, foreword.

76 George C. Carens, "The Pulse: Looking Back at 90 Years; Lovett Is a Nonagenarian; Glorious Days on Common," *Boston Evening Transcript*, May 31, 1934, James D'Wolf Lovett Sports Scrapbook.

77 The claim of club founder bothered Lovett enough for him to write Miller about it two weeks later: "I was <u>much</u> disappointed that your name did not appear in Caren's article, as the first organizer of football and captain of the Oneida club and also the captain who pitched the Lowells to the championship of New England. But I did not see the proof of the article as it <u>would</u> have been." Emphasis in original. See Jim Lovett to Gat Miller, June 15, 1935, box 1, folder 22, Gerrit Smith Miller papers, #3700.

78 Emphasis in original. Jim Lovett to Gat Miller, March 7, 1935, box 2, folder 2, Gerrit Smith Miller papers, #3700.

79 Jim Lovett to Gat Miller, n.d., box 2, folder 2, Gerrit Smith Miller papers, #3700.

80 "Dr. Lawrence Is Dead at 87—Aged Boston Physician Was Pioneer Football Player with Oneidas," *Boston Herald*, March 8, 1935, 31.

81 Jim Lovett to Gat Miller, August 5, 1935, box 2, folder 6, Gerrit Smith Miller papers, #3700.

82 Jim Lovett to Gat Miller, September 7, 1935, box 2, folder 6, Gerrit Smith Miller papers, #3700.

83 Lovett's funeral was reported on the front page of the *Globe*, but just as one line in the summary of "Today's Globe Contents." See *Boston Daily Globe*, October 3, 1935, 1.

84 "Early Football Star Dies at 91—James D'Wolf Lovett Was in First Recorded Game in America," *Boston Herald*, October 1, 1935, 13; "Funeral Tomorrow for J. D'W. Lovett," *Boston Globe*, October 1, 1935, 19.

85 Lovett even referred to the hope that "Frank P." would elucidate some unnamed mystery. See Jim Lovett to Gat Miller, March 13, 1934, box 1, folder 22, Gerrit Smith Miller papers, #3700.

86 "Prof. F. G. Peabody Dead in Cambridge," *Boston Globe*, December 29, 1936, 17; "Peabody Funeral to Be Held Today," *Boston Herald*, December 30, 1936, 13; "Harvard's Peabody," *Boston Herald*, December 30, 1936, 12; "Prof. Peabody's Rites Thronged," *Boston Herald*, December 31, 1936, 11.

87 "A Cambridge Clergyman," *New York Times*, December 31, 1936, 16.

88 "Obituaries," *New York History* 20, no. 1 (January 1939): 63–64.

89 The First National Bank of Boston regularly produced ink blotter calendars with historic images of Boston and New England; the calendars are regularly auctioned off on eBay today. The first ad to show the Oneidas appears to have been in the *Boston Transcript* of November 21, 1935, of which a copy was preserved in Lovett's scrapbook. "'Their Goal Was Never Crossed': A Tribute to America's First Football Team," *Boston Evening Transcript*, November 21, 1935, 2. This bank was different from the Old Boston Bank of which Oneida Robert Apthorp Boit was a director.

90 Francis Peabody Magoun Jr., *History of Football—from the Beginnings to 1871* (Bochum, Germany: Verlag Heinrich Pöppinghaus O. H. G., 1938), 86.

91 Magoun completed his bachelors (1916) and PhD (1923) at Harvard before serving there as an instructor, assistant professor, associate professor, and tutor. He had taken interest in football origins history, researching and publishing two scholarly pieces in 1929 and 1931. See his piece on literary references from the twelfth to the sixteenth century in "Football in Medieval England and in Middle-English Literature," *American Historical Review* 35, no. 1 (October 1929): 33–45; on the origins of football in Scotland, see "Scottish Popular Football, 1424–1815," *American Historical Review* 37, no. 1 (October 1931): 1–13. For Magoun's Harvard career, see *Historical Record of Harvard University 1636–1936* (Cambridge, MA: Harvard University Press, 1937), 316.

92 Selim Hobart Peabody and Charles Henry Pope, *Peabody (Paybody, Pabody, Pabodie) Genealogy* (Boston: Charles H. Pope, 1909).

93 Rhea's work impresses not only by its four-hundred-plus pages but in its bibliography and notes. Foster Dulles Rhea, *America Learns to Play; a History of Popular Recreation, 1607–1940* (1940; repr. Gloucester, MA: Peter Smith, 1959), 197.

94 While apparently privately published, the New York based Hill had his book advertised—on the eve of the attack on Pearl Harbor—in the Boy Scouts monthly and endorsed by Grantland Rice. See *Boys' Life*, December 1941, 48.

95 Dean Hill, *Football thru the Years* (New York: Gridiron Publishing, 1940).
96 Hill, *Football thru the Years*, 11.
97 "Bishop Lawrence Dead at 91," *Boston Daily Globe*, November 7, 1941, 1, 18; "Bishop Lawrence Funeral Today at St. Paul's," *Boston Daily Globe*, November 8, 1941, 1, 4; "Massachusetts Bishop Dies in 92d Year," *Atlanta Constitution*, November 7, 1941, 29.
98 "Dr. Lawrence Dies; Bishop Emeritus," *New York Times*, November 7, 1941, 23.
99 "Leaders of Church, State Pay Bishop Lawrence Last Tribute," *Boston Herald*, November 9, 1941, 1, 8.
100 "Henry E. Richards," *Daily Boston Globe*, January 27, 1949, 25; "H. Richards Dies; Retired Architect," *New York Times*, January 27, 1949, 23.
101 Richards's older brothers were not the first Bostonians or Americans to attend Rugby, nor the last. See 1867, 1870, and 1874 Registers of Students at Rugby School.
102 The 1906 rules segmented the game into individual plays and, by the 1920s, the control of time was complete down to the one-minute intermissions between quarters. For the 1906 rules, see Walter Camp, ed., *Spalding's Official Foot Ball Guide 1906* (New York: American Sports Publishing, 1906), 114–15. See also John S. Watterson, *College Football: History, Spectacle, Controversy* (Baltimore: Johns Hopkins University Press, 2000), especially chapters 5, 6, and 7; and Roger Tamte, *Walter Camp and the Creation of American Football* (Urbana: University of Illinois Press, 2018), 311–16.
103 See chapter 7 in Ludovic Ténèze, "Histoire du football: Le Board et l'analyse des transformations des lois du jeu" (PhD diss., Université de Paris Descartes, 2011).

CHAPTER 9

1 Bill Cunningham, "How Sports Began Here Century Ago," *Boston Sunday Herald*, June 13, 1948, 1, 3.
2 The Oneidas were also briefly cited in Bill Graham's inaugural *North American Soccer Guide*, albeit without any explicit soccer link. Milt Miller, "Soccer Shots," *Long Island Star Journal*, December 15, 1948, 17; Bill Graham, *North American Soccer Guide—1948–49* (New York: William Graham, 1948), 72.
3 Morris Allison Bealle, *The History of Football at Harvard, 1874–1948* (Washington DC: Columbia, 1948).
4 Victor J. Danilov, *Hall of Fame Museums: A Reference Guide* (Westport, CT: Greenwood Press, 1997), 114. For more on the Baseball Hall of Fame, see Bill James, *Whatever Happened to the Hall of Fame? Baseball, Cooperstown, and the Politics of Glory*, 1st Fireside ed. (New York: Simon and Schuster,

1995), 148, 294–99; and Tom Stanton, *The Road to Cooperstown: A Father, Two Sons, and the Journey of a Lifetime* (New York: Thomas Dunne Books / St. Martin's Griffin, 2003), 226.
5 "Pick Site for Hall of Fame—Rutgers Will House Football Shrine," *Chicago Daily Tribune*, September 13, 1949, 1 of Sports section; "Rutgers Is Selected for Home of Football's Hall of Fame," *Washington Evening Star*, September 12, 1949, A14.
6 Ed Farnsworth, "The Origin of the National Soccer Hall of Fame," *Society for American Soccer History*, May 6, 2021, https://www.ussoccerhistory.org/the-origin-of-the-national-soccer-hall-of-fame, accessed August 25, 2021. The Pennsylvania Historical Society holds some documents related to the Old Timers' Association and celebratory dinners but with no record of the 1950 event. See list for table 12, "Old Timers' Testimonial Dinner—Guests," box 142, folder 4, the Lighthouse Records 1893–2000, the Historical Society of Pennsylvania.
7 The governing body found "the venture was an excellent one and should be encouraged" but stopped short of endorsing it. Minutes of the United States Soccer Football Association of the National Commission, January 15, 1950, USSFA annual report 1950, 6.
8 Report of the Chairman of the international players selection committee, USSFA annual report 1950, 19.
9 Report of the Executive Secretary, USSFA annual report 1951, 5.
10 "Noble & Greenough Gives 26 Diplomas," *Boston Globe*, June 7, 1951, 13. See Richard T. Flood, *The Story of Noble and Greenough School 1866–1966* (Dedham: Noble and Greenough, 1966), 13.
11 Arthur J. O'Keefe to John Bellows, July 31, 1951, Oneida Monument file, Boston Art Commission archives, Boston city hall.
12 A service order was issued by the City of Boston on August 28, signed by Bellows. City of Boston—County of Suffolk Service Order for the Art Department, Faneuil Hall, Oneida Monument file, Boston Art Commission archives.
13 "Crimson Pranksters Daub Paint on Camp Memorial," unnamed and undated newspaper clipping, HM 137 microfilm reel 48, folder 21, "Yale Memorial Gateway 1925–1929, undated," box 67, Walter Chauncey Camp papers (MS 125), Manuscripts and Archives, Yale University Library. Folder 21 begins at microfilm slide 0721.
14 "Culprits Daub Eli Gate with Crimson Hues," *Crimson*, November 27, 1951.
15 Several invoices appear in the archive from 1951 and 1952. See City of Boston—County of Suffolk Standard Invoice Voucher number 89549, Purchase order S5, Vendor's Invoice No. 11634, Boston Art Commission archives.
16 Report of the National Commission meeting, February 13, 1954, USSFA annual report 1954, 2.

17 See Bill Graham, "15 Soccer Aces Named to Hall of Fame Shrine," *Brooklyn Eagle*, February 1, 1950, 20; and Harry Saunders, "Introducing the Father of Organized Soccer in This Country," *Soccer News*, February 1951, 7. For discussion of another man honored simultaneously with the fatherly title, Tom Cahill, see chapter 15 in Tom McCabe, *The Dear Old Mug: A Quest to Find America's Oldest Soccer Trophy* (Kearny, NJ: Soccertown Media, 2024).
18 Minutes of the 1963 United States Soccer Football Association Annual General Meeting, USSFA annual report 1963, 23–24.
19 Boston Redevelopment Authority, *Commemorative Plaques in Boston* (City of Boston, 1961), 14.
20 Bill Graham, ed., *1962–1963 Official United States Soccer Football Association Annual Guide—with Complete 1961–62 Records* (New York: United States Soccer Football Association, 1962), 22.
21 USSFA, *Soccer Football Rules Season 1960–61* (New York: United States Soccer Football Association, 1960), 16.
22 Robert Charles Baptista, "A History of Intercollegiate Soccer in the United States of America" (PhD diss., Indiana University, 1962), 51–53.
23 Baptista, "History of Intercollegiate Soccer," 61.
24 Allison Danzig, *The History of American Football: Its Great Teams, Players, and Coaches* (Englewood Cliffs, NJ: Prentice-Hall, 1956), see especially 4–9.
25 Denise DeHass, *NCAA—1981–82-2006–07: Sports Sponsorship and Participation Rates Report* (Indianapolis: National Collegiate Athletic Association, 2008), 87, 201.
26 Chris Bolsmann has uncovered a number of unpublished dissertations that were often focused on coaching but never printed widely. Chris Bolsmann, introduction to *Soccer Frontiers: The Global Game in the United States, 1863–1913*, ed. Chris Bolsmann and George Kioussis (Knoxville: University of Tennessee Press, 2021), 3, 13.
27 James Francis Robinson, "The History of Soccer in the City of Saint Louis" (PhD diss., Saint Louis University, 1966), 11–14.
28 John Allen, *Soccer for Americans* (New York: Grosset and Dunlap, 1967), 17; Julie Menendez and Matt Boxer, *Soccer* (New York: Ronald Press, 1968), 3.
29 This is particularly telling as both authors were immigrants themselves. Menendez and Boxer, *Soccer*, v.
30 Tim Cohane, "New England Fountainhead of Football—Harvard and Yale Share Most of Game's Early Milestones," and "Boston Schoolboys Paved Football Road," *Boston Globe*, September 21, 1969, 73; Francis Rosa, "Oneida Rallied on Common . . . and Football Was Born," *Boston Sunday Globe*, August 30, 1970, 88–89.
31 Forrest C. Tyson, "A Study of the Factors Affecting the Growth of Youth Soccer in Selected Cities in the United States" (PhD diss., Ohio State University, 1976), 16.

32. Alan Peterson, *A Guide to Soccer in the State of Massachusetts* (Danvers, MA: Massachusetts Soccer Association, 1973), 13.
33. For recent histories that have shed light on this period, see Roger Allaway, *Rangers, Rovers and Spindles: Soccer, Immigration, and Textiles in New England and New Jersey* (Haworth, NJ: St. Johann Press, 2005); David Wangerin, *Distant Corners American Soccer's History of Missed Opportunities and Lost Causes* (Philadelphia: Temple University Press, 2011); and McCabe, *Dear Old Mug*.
34. John Allen, *Soccer for Americans*, 28; Menendez and Boxer, *Soccer*, v.
35. "Can Soccer Score in America?," *Boys' Life*, October 1967, 32–34, 36–37. See also "Russian Youth," *Boys' Life*, March 1963, 14. Soccer appeared only a handful of times between 1911 and the 1960s in contrast to the regularly visible American football.
36. Kevin Tallec Marston, "An International Comparative History of Youth Football in France and the United States (C.1920–C.2000): The Age Paradigm and the Demarcation of the Youth Game as a Separate Sector of the Sport" (PhD diss., De Montfort University, 2012), 175–223.
37. Kevin Tallec Marston, "Rethinking 'Ethnic' Soccer: The National Junior Challenge Cup and the Transformation of American Soccer's Identity (1935–1976)," *Soccer & Society* 18, nos. 2–3 (2017): 330–47.
38. Sam Foulds and Paul Harris, *America's Soccer Heritage* (Manhattan Beach, CA: Soccer for Americans, 1979), iii.
39. Chuck Cascio, *Soccer U.S.A.* (Washington, DC: Robert B. Luce, 1975), 47–51.
40. Foulds and Harris, *America's Soccer Heritage*, 19.
41. The Boston chapter is preceded by general origins and two pages on early New England Pasuckquakkohowog as played by the Native Americans. Foulds and Harris noted that the Oneidas' "rules were very similar to the code adopted by the Football Association of England in 1863" but failed to mention that the boys did on occasion run with the ball. Foulds and Harris, *America's Soccer Heritage*, 19–20.
42. The USSFA dropped "football" from its name in 1975. Mark Simonson, *Soccer in Oneonta* (Charlestown, SC: Arcadia Publishing, 2004), 7, 75–116.
43. Neil Morris, "Two Halls of Fame 15 Miles Apart. . . . One Thrived, One Failed," Southern Soccer Scene, September 23, 2013, https://www.southernsoccerscene.com/2013/09/23/two-halls-of-fame-15-miles-apart-one-thrived-one-failed/, accessed August 6, 2021.
44. Zander Hollander, *The American Encyclopedia of Soccer* (New York: Everest House, 1980), 21.
45. Sam Foulds, "Manning: America's Grand Old Man of Soccer," *Soccer America*, July 9, 1981.
46. Wayne Rasmussen, "Historical Analysis of Four Attempts to Establish Professional Soccer in the United States 1894 and 1994" (PhD diss., Temple University, 1995).

47 Franklin Foer, *How Soccer Explains the World* (New York: Harper Collins, 2005), 241.
48 Ciccarelli explored the historical and sociological reasons behind multiple professional league failures. Daniel Ciccarelli, "A Review of the Historical and Sociological Perspectives Involved in the Acceptance of Soccer as a Professional Sport in the United States" (PhD diss., Temple University, 1983).
49 Len Oliver, "Cultural Implications of the Soccer Phenomenon in America," in *Cultural Dimensions of Play, Games and Sport*, ed. Bernard Mergen (Champaign, IL: Human Kinetics, 1986), 192–93.
50 Len Oliver, "American Soccer Didn't Start with Pelé: Philadelphia Soccer in the 1940s and 50s," *Journal of Ethno-Development* 1, no. 3 (1992): 72–81.
51 See chapter 13, "Creating a Usable Past," in Abram C. Van Engen, *A City upon a Hill* (New Haven, CT: Yale University Press, 2020).
52 The September–October issue included a two-page article by Raymond Ernenwein on the Oneidas but never mentioned the word soccer. See *National Soccer Hall of Fame Newsletter* 4, no. 3 (May–June 1984): 1, folder 2-3, in 2001.A032, Smith-Miller Family Collection, 1879–1961, Madison County Historical Society, Oneida, NY.
53 David Wangerin, *Soccer in a Football World: The Story of America's Forgotten Game* (Philadelphia: Temple University Press, 2006).
54 For the 1986 bid, see George Kioussis, "A Bid Denied: The U.S. Application to Host the 1986 World Cup," *Soccer & Society* 21, no. 8 (2020): 946–59.
55 Will Lunn to Joseph Blatter, March 17, 1992, USA Miscellaneous box, folder—History of USSF, FIFA Archives.
56 Sam T. N. Foulds, "Editorial Comment," *Historical Quarterly*, 1st issue for the Society for American Soccer History (Winter 1993–94).
57 Sophye Zoukee, *Adopt a Statue Casebook* (Boston: City of Boston, Boston Foundation, and Friends of the Public Garden and Common, n.d.), 31. The cover letter inside includes a stamp dated January 23, 1990.
58 The official monthly newsletter, *Soccer Watch '94*, proclaimed Boston as the nation's oldest soccer hub. The Port Authority of New York and New Jersey produced a special World Cup issue proudly placing the 1862 Oneidas as precursors to the English FA. See *Soccer Watch '94*, June 1994, 8; *Omnibus*, June/July 1994, 19, 38.
59 Albert Colone to Thomas Menino, March 21, 1995, Boston Art Commission archives.
60 Albert Colone to Mildred Farrell, November 17, 1995, Boston Art Commission archives.
61 Albert Colone to Mildred Farrell, November 17, 1995; Mildred Farrell to Albert Colone, November 27, 1995, Boston Art Commission archives.
62 "Calichman's Appeal Is Denied, So He'll Miss Title Match," *Boston Globe*, October 17, 1996, C5.

63 "America's First Soccer Team," undated news clipping, National Soccer Hall of Fame archives—Sam Foulds Collection—EO199—box 272.

64 "Membership Notes," *SASH Historical Quarterly* 14 (Spring [incorrectly labeled Fall] 1997): 3.

65 In his article, Gardner was actually critical of using the Oneidas in this way, saying it gave off "a whiff of another fairy-tale world, that of marketing." Paul Gardner, "Don Garber's Making Sense," *Soccer America*, December 20, 1999, 7.

66 Interview with Tom McGrath, April 15, 2021.

67 Interview with Tom McGrath, April 15, 2021.

68 Tom McGrath to Sarah Hutt, email "Oneida," July 16, 2003, Boston Art Commission archives.

69 See "Memo to File," July 18, 2003, from Adrienne Sage, Assistant Registrar SPNEA, Accession File 1922.768, "The Rubber Football," Historic New England.

70 Tom McGrath to Adrienne Sage, July 10, 2003, Accession File 1922.768, "The Rubber Football."

71 Connelly's thirty-four-page document appraised the ball at a market value of $96,000. See Robert J. Connelly, *Appraisal for Jack Huckel—Early Soccer Ball (Football)*, January 30, 2004, Accession File 1922.768, "The Rubber Football." See also Adrienne Sage to Jack Huckel, July 18, 2003, Accession File 1922.768, "The Rubber Football."

72 Adrienne Sage to Jack Huckel, November 5, 2004, Accession File 1922.768, "The Rubber Football."

73 Interview with Tom McGrath, April 15, 2021; Sarah Hutt to Tom McGrath, email "RE: Oneida," July 16, 2003, Boston Art Commission archives.

74 Mildred Farrell to Albert Colone, October 28, 1997, Accession File 1922.768, "The Rubber Football."

75 "An Editorial: The Hall of Fame," *SASH Historical Quarterly* 15 (Summer 1997): 1.

76 Albert Colone to Mildred Farrell, November 17, 1995, Boston Art Commission archives.

77 The archives reveal a shift in the SPNEA's views on the ball and the Oneidas, initially supportive of the soccer link in the 1990s until it became Historic New England in the early 2000s. Quote refers to an internal email regarding the NCAA centenary project: Adrienne Sage to Sally Hinkle, email "Fwd: Re: Ball," November 4, 2005, Accession File 1922.768, "The Rubber Football." On the SPNEA and its name change, see Gretchen Buggeln, "*Cherished Possessions: A New England Legacy*: An Exhibition Review," *Winterthur Portfolio* 40, no. 2/3 (Summer/Autumn 2005): 153.

78 Jessica Zdeb, "The 'Boston Game' and Modern American Football," *Historic New England* (Fall 2005): 1, Accession File 1922.768, "The Rubber Football."

79 Joseph N. Crowley, *In the Arena—the NCAA's First Century* (Indianapolis: NCAA, 2006), 2.
80 1994 NSHOF Membership brochure, 2, Boston Art Commission archives.
81 Tom McGrath to Sarah Hutt, email "Oneida," July 16, 2003, Boston Art Commission archives.
82 Memo, Tom McGrath to Sarah Hutt, undated but with the 2004 email correspondence, Boston Art Commission archives.
83 Memo to file, Adrienne Sage, July 18, 2003, Accession File 1922.768, "The Rubber Football."
84 Tom McGrath to Sarah Hutt, August 27, 2004, Boston Art Commission archives.
85 Tom McGrath to Sarah Hutt, July 10, 2003, Boston Art Commission archives.
86 Henry Lee to Sarah Hutt, March 21, 2007, Boston Art Commission archives.
87 See Ivan Myjer to Sarah Hutt, email "Oneida football," May 22, 2007, Boston Art Commission archives; Proposal—Project: Oneida Football Monument, Boston Common, submitted by Ivan Myjer, May 22, 2007, Boston Art Commission archives; and Henry Lee to Sarah Hutt, May 25, 2007, email "Re: Oneida Football," Boston Art Commission archives.
88 Mildred Farrell to Albert Colone, January 22, 1996, Boston Art Commission archives.
89 Robert Holmes, "Remembering the first high school football games," *Boston Globe*, November 21, 2012.
90 US Soccer Federation, *100 Years of Soccer in America* (New York: Universe Publishing, 2013).
91 See Application by the Friends of the Public Garden, "Oneida Football Monument" addressed to the Landmarks Commission, file dated December 18, 2013, attached to undated email from Sarah Hutt to Karin Goodfellow, forwarded by Karin Goodfellow to Christian Guerra, email, "Re: Oneida Football Monument," January 15, 2014, Boston Art Commission archives.
92 Elizabeth Vizza to Karin Goodfellow, March 25, 2014, Boston Art Commission archives.
93 Karin Goodfellow, Lynne Kortenhaus, and Ekua Holmes to Sarah Hutt, April 8, 2014, Boston Art Commission archives.
94 Interview with Tom McGrath, April 15, 2021. See Invoice C-0511-1 for Project: Oneida Football Monument, dated September 30, 2014, Boston Art Commission archives.
95 Christopher Stride and Ffion Thomas, "Tension in the Union of Art and Sport: Competition for Ownership of the Baseball Statuary and Its Influence upon Design," *NINE: A Journal of Baseball History and Culture* 24, nos. 1/2 (2015–16): 1–28.

CHAPTER 10

1. "L'idole des origines," Marc Bloch, *Apologie pour l'Histoire ou Métier d'Historien*, 2nd ed. (Paris: Cahier des Annales, 3, Librairie Armand Colin, 1952), 19–23.
2. Scudder was actually quoting from British writer Phillip Bussy, who had written the "history of football" for the 1924 Miller tablet pamphlet. *Old-Time New England* 15, no. 1 (July 1924): 7.
3. Winthrop Saltonstall Scudder, *An Historical Sketch of the Oneida Football Club of Boston 1862–1865* (deposited October 18, 1926), Massachusetts Historical Society, 5.
4. Richard Holt, "Afterword: History and Heritage in Sport," in *Sport, History, and Heritage: Studies in Public Representation*, ed. Jeffrey Hill, Kevin Moore, and Jason Wood (Woodbridge, UK: Boydell, 2012), 263.
5. Pierre Nora, "Between Memory and History: Les Lieux de Mémoire," *Representations*, no. 26 (1989): 7–24.
6. Tony Collins, *How Football Began: A Global History of How the World's Football Codes Were Born* (Abingdon, UK: Routledge, 2019), 2.
7. Gavin Kitching, "The Origins of Football: History, Ideology and the Making of 'The People's Game,'" *History Workshop Journal* 79, no. 1 (Spring 2015): 127.
8. Nearly eighty years before Ruiz, Frederick Lorz pranked the International Olympic Committee at the 1904 St. Louis marathon, before legitimately winning the Boston marathon the following year. See David E. Martin and Roger W. H. Gynn, *The Olympic Marathon* (Champaign: Human Kinetics, 2000), 43–52; and Paul C. Clerici, *Boston Marathon: History by the Mile* (Charleston, SC: Arcadia Publishing, 2014). If Ruiz had obviously prepared to concoct that sporting untruth—by first defrauding the New York marathon organizers in 1979 in order to qualify—it is unclear whether she actually had planned to win in the Boston race. According to one of Ruiz's confidants, she entered the end of race too early, thereby miscalculating her plan, and finished first. Bryan Marquard, "As in Life, Apparent Death of Rosie Ruiz Shrouded in a Bit of Mystery," *Boston Globe*, August 7, 2019.
9. Peter Hancock, *Hoax Springs Eternal: The Psychology of Cognitive Deception* (Cambridge: Cambridge University Press, 2015), 180–83.
10. James M. Lindgren, *Preserving Historic New England: Preservation, Progressivism and the Remaking of Memory* (New York: Oxford University Press, 1995), 67.
11. In the half century before the Oneida monument, more than fifty plaques, statues, and memorials had been erected or placed across the city center including nine in the Public Garden and seven on the Common. Many honored Boston Brahmins with statues or monuments, beginning with Charles Sumner in 1877 and imitated by a host of others in the half century

that followed. On Beacon Hill, Boston Common, in the Public Garden, or around the heart of the city were memorialized Josiah Quincy (in 1878), William Lloyd Garrison (1886), William Ellery Channing (1902), Edward Everett Hale (1912), Wendell Phillips (1915), and Curtis Guild Jr. (1917). See Sophye Zoukee, *Adopt a Statue Casebook* (Boston: City of Boston, Boston Foundation, and Friends of the Public Garden and Common, n.d.). Charles Sumner's case is interesting. His statue was erected in 1878 (four years after his death), but he was remembered oddly by his family history. In Appleton's 1879 history, Sumner was described as having an "unfortunately irregular" relationship with his family. Though his father (Charles Pinckney, born Job) was prominent and well-respected, "few of [Pinckney's] kids lived up to promise" (from grandfather Job—unmarried). Sumner had become famous after his caning in the Brooks-Sumner affair and was close with Ellery Channing. William Sumner Appleton, Record of the descendants of William Sumner (Boston: David Clapp and Son, 1879), 176–77.

12 Erika Doss, *Memorial Mania: Public Feeling in America* (Chicago: University of Chicago Press, 2010), 20; James D'Wolf Lovett, *Old Boston Boys and the Games They Played* (Boston: Riverside Press, 1906), 94. See "Joint Memorial," *Boston Daily Globe*, December 30, 1906, 31; and "Memorial to Gov. Wolcott," *New York Times*, January 1, 1907, 3.

13 Among others, Boston erected statues and memorials to Thomas Cass, the Irish-born Civil War colonel of the "Irish Fighting Ninth"; Christopher Columbus; and Leif Erikson. See Helen Weston Henderson, *A Loiterer in New England* (New York: George H. Doran, 1919), 416–21; William Eleroy Curtis, *Christopher Columbus—His Portraits and His Monuments—Part II* (Chicago: W. H. Lowdermilk, 1893), 46; and Torgrim Sneve Guttormsen, "Valuing Immigrant Memories as Common Heritage: The Leif Erikson Monument in Boston," *History & Memory* 30, no. 2 (Fall/Winter 2018): 87.

14 Daniela G. Jäger, "The Worst 'White Lynching' in American History: Elites vs. Italians in New Orleans, 1891," *AAA: Arbeiten aus Anglistik und Amerikanistik* 27, no. 2 (2002): 161–79.

15 In Zoukee's list, there were a handful of occasions in which two memorials were dedicated the same year in the center of the city (1867, two on the Common; 1877, one on the Common, one in the Public Garden; 1912, two in Post Office Square). However, 1925 is the only year in which three memorials were unveiled in the same downtown space.

16 Statues were erected in Chicago, New York, and Washington, DC, between 1900 and 1920. They were not immune to vandalism, and a week after the unveiling in Yonkers, someone had stolen the large bronze sword off the statue. "Sword of Statue Gone—Mystery Surrounds Despoiling of Kosciuszko Schaft in Yonkers Convent Yard," *Evening Star* (Washington, DC), June 7, 1912, 11.

17 "Polish People Planning Kosciuszko Memorial," *Boston Globe*, January 31, 1925, 2.
18 Gat Miller to Sam Cabot, July 2, 1905, folder 5 (1905–06), James D'Wolf Lovett papers, 1896–1935, Massachusetts Historical Society.
19 Lovett, *Old Boston Boys*, 95.
20 Advertisement by Alfred Hale and Co. at 23 School Street, Boston for Rubber Foot Balls, *Boston Herald*, March 28, 1862, 37.
21 "Baseballs of the 60's," unnamed newspaper clipping, n.d. but probably 1910, James D'Wolf Lovett Sports Scrapbook, 1861–1945, Revolutionary Spaces.
22 Lovett refers to the *Boston Herald* and the *Boston Evening Transcript* in *Old Boston Boys* but regarding baseball, not the Oneidas.
23 Miller to Lovett, June 10, 1906, folder 3 (1906), James D'Wolf Lovett papers.
24 Lovett, *Old Boston Boys*, 93.
25 Both Brooks brothers actually overlapped at Dixwell's (1861–62), but the elder Walter had left by 1862–63, leaving only one boy on the tuition roll and questions as to the older brother's whereabouts in 1862 and '63 when the Oneida Club was formed. Unlike Walter, who had passed away almost thirty years earlier, John Henry remained in Boston and was still alive when Lovett wrote *Old Boston Boys*. It is unclear where Walter went between 1862 and 1864. He did enter Harvard's 1868 class in the fall of 1864 but then moved to Williams College, though he was listed among the twenty-six students who did not graduate. However, Teele's *History of Milton* lists him as a Williams alum (class of 1868) in the long list of the city's college graduates. See entries for 1861–62 and 1862–63, E. S. Dixwell, *Tuition Book of the Private Latin School, 1851–1872*, box 24, Wigglesworth Family papers, Massachusetts Historical Society; *A Catalog of the Officers and Students of Harvard University for the Academical Year 1864–65* (Cambridge, MA: Sever and Francis, 1864), 21; *General Catalog of the Officers, Trustees, Alumni, Honorary Graduates and of Students Not Graduated of Williams College 1885* (Williamstown: Williams College, 1885), 82; and A. K. Teele, *The History of Milton, Mass. 1640 to 1887* (n.p.,), 356.
26 "Walter D. Brooks," *Boston Globe*, April 7, 1877, 4.
27 Another Brooks (Arthur) was listed among those who played games. Lovett, *Old Boston Boys*, 93–96.
28 One paper referred to the club insignia being visible on the red handkerchiefs, though no other reference to this exists elsewhere. "Founder of Football Living in Peterboro and Raising Holsteins," December 1, 1923, unnamed newspaper, folder 2-2 in 2001.A032, Smith-Miller Family Collection, 1879–1961, Madison County Historical Society, Oneida, NY.
29 See articles by John Thorn, "Early Baseball in Boston," *Our Game*, July 6, 2012, https://ourgame.mlblogs.com/early-baseball-in-boston, accessed December 16, 2017; and Janey Murray, "Gerrit Smith Miller: A Pioneer in

Baseball, Football and Farming," National Baseball Hall of Fame, accessed March 28, 2021, https://baseballhall.org/discover/baseball-history/gerrit-smith-miller-a-pioneer-in-baseball-football-and-farming.

30 See Chris Bolsmann and Dilwyn Porter, *English Gentlemen and World Soccer—Corinthians, Amateurism and the Global Game* (Abingdon, UK: Routledge, 2018), 101–16.

31 "To Honor Founder of Organized Football," *Boston Globe*, November 7, 1923, 15; "Dedicate Tablet to 'Gat' Miller, Football's Founder," *Boston Herald*, November 8, 1923, 10. Thanks to regional syndication across New England, a handful of newspaper articles recount that the team's "only uniform was a red silk handkerchief." See "To Honor Star of Other Days," *Boston Herald*, November 7, 1923, 10; "Football Founder to Have Memorial," *New Britain Herald* (CT), November 7, 1923, 2; "Pay Tribute to Founder of Organized Football," *Berkshire Evening Eagle* (MA), November 8, 1923, 12; and "Founder of Organized Football," *Biddeford Daily Journal* (ME), November 10, 1923, 6. For one article that appears singularly informed by more local sources, see "Founder of Football Living in Peterboro and Raising Holsteins," December 1, 1923, unnamed newspaper, folder 2-2, Smith-Miller Family Collection, 1879–1961, Madison County Historical Society, Oneida, NY.

32 It was credited to Ned Arnold. See list of "Gifts and Loans to the Museum, March 1, 1922, to February 28, 1923," *Old-Time New England* 14, no. 1 (July 1923): 35.

33 The *Boston Herald* ran an article in September 1922 discussing footballers' fashion in England with players wearing "gally colored handkerchiefs for which high prices are sometimes paid." See "For 'Footballers,'" *Boston Herald*, September 9, 1922, 15.

34 Winthrop Saltonstall Scudder, ed., *Gerrit Smith Miller—an Appreciation—Supplement to the Nobleman* (Dedham, MA: Noble and Greenough School, 1924), 24.

35 Racing in that shell had been Jonathan Dwight, first cousin of Oneida James Dwight, and Charles Jackson Paine, a third cousin of dinner organizer Sam Cabot who later designed America's Cup yachts alongside Oneida Ned Burgess. "The Boating Reputation of Harvard," *Harvard Magazine* 4, no. 5 (June 1858): 195. See also "College Record: A College Regatta," *Harvard Magazine* 4, no. 5 (June 1858): 215; and "Notes on Our Naval History," *Harvard Magazine* 4, no. 6 (July 1858): 247–59.

36 "College Record: Statistics of the Class of 1861," *Harvard Magazine* 7, no. 10 (July 1861): 362; "College Union Regatta," *Harvard Magazine* 5, nos. 6–7 (July and September 1859): 280; *A History of American College Regattas* (Boston: Wilson, 1875), 7–9, 22–24.

37 John A. Blanchard, ed., *The H Book of Harvard Athletics 1852–1922* (Cambridge, MA: Harvard Varsity Club, 1923), 3–5, 8.

38 Close friends Ned Fenno and Robert Swain Peabody both rowed to victory in 1866. The latter had attended the 1904 dinner but died in 1917, while Fenno lived until 1931 and remained close with Lovett and Miller. Rowing alongside Cliff Watson (d. 1902) in the victorious 1868 race was fellow Oneida J. W. McBurney (d. 1885). Championship teammate Watson was remembered as the dear friend of Miller's whose heart would have been warmed by the sight of the "reproduced" ball.

39 *National Soccer Hall of Fame Newsletter* 4, no. 3 (May–June 1984): 1.

40 Donations to the society were extensive every year, and the official bulletin of the society, *Old-Time New England*, included the annual inventory of gifts, which totaled several thousand items in 1922–23. See *Old-Time New England* 14, no. 1 (July 1923): 35–47.

41 Tessa Morris-Suzuki, *The Past within Us: Media, Memory, History* (London: Verso, 2005), 119. For a discussion of images in sport history and the manipulation of photographs, see Murray G. Phillips, Mark E. O'Neill and Gary Osmond, "Broadening Horizons in Sport History: Films, Photographs, and Monuments," *Journal of Sport History* 34, no. 2 (Summer 2007): 271–93.

42 Gary Osmond, "Photographs, Materiality and Sport History: Peter Norman and the 1968 Mexico City Black Power Salute," *Journal of Sport History* 37, no. 1 (Spring 2010): 121.

43 The *Boston Traveler* and *Boston Globe* have slightly different photographs, taken probably a few seconds apart, but they are generally the same pose. "Monument Honoring Nation's First Football Team Unveiled as Crowd of 54,000 Flocks to Stadium," *Boston Traveler*, November 21, 1925, James D'Wolf Lovett Sports Scrapbook; "Dedicate Monument on Boston Common Where First Football Team Played," *Boston Globe*, November 21, 1925, 15, James D'Wolf Lovett Sports Scrapbook.

44 *The Six Survivors*, November 21, 1925, photograph, James D'Wolf Lovett Sports Scrapbook.

45 Scudder, *Historical Sketch*, 7.

46 Listed were Edward L. Arnold, Robert A. Boit, Edward Bowditch, Walter Brooks, Frank Davis, John P. Hall, Robert M. Lawrence, James D'W. Lovett, Gerrit S. Miller (Capt.), Francis G. Peabody, Winthrop S. Scudder, Louis Thies, Lawrence Tucker, R. Clifford Watson, and Huntington F. Wolcott. "This Rubber Football Was Won on Boston Common by the Oneida Football Club of Boston, 7 November 1863," November 15, 1922, Accession File 1922.768, "The Rubber Football," Historic New England. All three editions of *Old Boston Boys* have the same list of fifteen names. See Lovett, *Old Boston Boys*, 92–93.

47 See Lovett, *Old Boston Boys*, 82, 92–95.

48 When triangulating census data, Dixwell's school registers and tuition book, Dixwell's autobiography and student lists, *Old Boston Boys*, and the subscription list, it is two sets of brothers who appear to be the best fit.

The Tucker brothers overlapped at Dixwell's (1860–61), but by 1862 William W. Tucker was paying tuition for only one boy, almost certainly Alanson, since he appears second in the school register. The Tucker family appears in the 1850 Massachusetts and 1865 US census with merchant William W. Tucker and his two boys (listed as students in 1865) in a household with five servants. In 1865, the family appears just opposite the entry for Henry P. Sturgis, father of Oneida Frederick Russell Sturgis. Both Tucker brothers died before the monument (Alanson in 1909, Lawrence in 1912). Similarly, census listings included a Davis family living in Milton with merchant William H. Davis, who had three sons who attended Dixwell's and appeared on the school registers; the oldest was William P. followed by Frank W. and George K. There is another possibility with a Frank Dupont Davis (Harvard class of 1870)—son of Rear Admiral Charles Davis—born in Cambridge and whose sister Anna Mills Davis married Henry Cabot Lodge. Frank does not appear on the Dixwell or Public Latin School registers of the period; neither does any other George Davis—the only George being the brother of Frank W. and son of William H. from Milton.

49 Lovett, *Old Boston Boys*, 91.
50 Scudder wrote, "In this match, the Oneidas allowed their opponents sixteen men, they, themselves, playing their usual fifteen. Mac Forbes, the extra man, one of the best players in the Oneidas, was loaned to them to captain their side but, in spite of this handicap in the number of men, the Allies were beaten in three straight games." See Lovett, *Old Boston Boys*, 91; and Scudder, *Gerrit Smith Miller*, 23.
51 The retrospective accounts by Lovett forty years on noted that the club had played with fifteen players, at least on that championship occasion. But even for that match, the newspaper reports from 1863 reported games played sixteen-a-side. The only other Oneida reference in the press was from 1864 stating that time the teams were twelve boys to a side. For the school games reported in the Boston papers between 1862 and 1868—including the two reported Oneida matches—the numbers of players varied from ten to twelve, sixteen, and even seventeen a side. *Boston Daily Advertiser*, November 9, 1863, 1. The two sentences in the *Boston Evening Transcript* did not mention the number of players. *Boston Evening Transcript*, October 31, 1864, 3.
52 Scudder, *Historical Sketch*, 4.
53 For example, Stratton wrote about some errors in the Harvard class years of three baseball players. Charles E. Stratton to Jim Lovett, June 5, 1906, folder 3 (1906), James D'Wolf Lovett papers.
54 Lovett, *Old Boston Boys*, 95–96.
55 According to Lovett, the boys who gathered to play were "William Walley, Sam Cabot, Arthur Brooks, George Lyman, Charlie and Rollins Morse, George Mifflin, Cabot Russell, Sam and Gus Bradstreet, Henry and

Joe Fay, Billy Field, Lem Stanwood, Malcolm Greenough, Frank Manning, Frank Nicholson, Tom Motley, and a host of others." Lovett, *Old Boston Boys*, 96.

56 Among those left out were the Blaikie and Frothingham brothers, Tom Nelson, Jack Oviatt, Ned Fenno, Sam Cabot, and James Barr Ames. The omission of Sam Cabot is rather surprising. Even if he was five years younger than the core Oneidas and thus not a contemporary player with the older boys, he had been the one to organize the original 1904 dinner. Lovett had even described him as "a tough customer to run foul of, and whoever he tackled might as well give it up first," and even wrote a newspaper tribute after his death. Harvard professor James Barr Ames was another name mentioned in passing by Lovett in the football section but left out of the 1926 list—despite the fact that he had ordered copy number two of *Old Boston Boys*. In Lovett's chronicling of legendary games, he described a number of reunion dinners hosted by Cliff Watson at the Union Club where sporting memories were shared. One specific match had been recounted by Watson for "four of us veterans, Gat Miller, Jim Ames, John Hall and myself [Lovett]." Four of the five were Oneidas—and whose names were on the ball—but James Barr Ames was only remembered in baseball. Ames even read drafts of the book before its publication and praised them highly without corrections or criticism. See Lovett, *Old Boston Boys*, 85; and *List of Subscribers for the Deluxe Edition of Old Boston Boys 250 Copies*, dated 1906, inside the Massachusetts Historical Society copy of James D'Wolf Lovett, *Old Boston Boys and the Games They Played* (Boston: Riverside Press, 1906). See James Barr Ames to Jim Lovett, June 5, 1905, folder 1 (1896–1905), James D'Wolf Lovett papers; and "Samuel Cabot," *Boston Evening Transcript*, November 28, 1906, news clipping in Lovett's donated copy of *Old Boston Boys*, James D'Wolf Lovett papers, 99.

57 George died by suicide in 1893. Both Tuckers had died after *Old Boston Boys* had been published but well before the 1923 events and were buried in Mount Auburn Cemetery, Alanson in 1909 and Lawrence in 1912. See death certificate for Alanson, "Massachusetts Deaths, 1841–1915, 1921–1924," database with images, FamilySearch (https://familysearch.org/ark:/61903/1:1:N4CP-VJ6: April 6, 2020), Alanson Tucker, May 1, 1909; citing Boston, Massachusetts, 433, State Archives, Boston; FHL microfilm 2,257,896. For Lawrence, see "Massachusetts Deaths, 1841–1915, 1921–1924," database with images, FamilySearch (https://familysearch.org/ark:/61903/1:1:N4QC-VX3: April 6, 2020), Susan E. Lawrence in entry for Lawrence Tucker, May 16, 1912; citing Boston, Massachusetts, 491, State Archives, Boston; FHL microfilm 2,396,420.

58 Henry Cabot Lodge, *Early Memories* (New York: Charles Scribner's Sons, 1913), 19, 86.

59 "John H. Brooks Dead," *Boston Globe*, July 22, 1913, 8.

Notes to Pages 197–198

60 "Dedicate Tablet to 'Gat' Miller, Football's Founder," *Boston Herald*, November 8, 1923, 10, and reprinted in other papers.
61 Scudder states that it is only "a partial list." The other Oneidas alive in 1925, beyond the seven monument men, were J. Bigelow (died 1930), W. Bigelow (1926), Brown (1929), W. Burgess (1931), Dixwell (1931), Gray (1929), Hardy (1930), W. Lawrence (1941), Revere (1932), Richards (1949), and Shattuck (1929).
62 None gave a definitive number in 1923, saying that the club had been composed of either fifteen or sixteen boys. The *Transcript* gave no names at all aside from Miller's, and while the *Globe* and the *Herald* did print fifteen names, they both missed one each, swapping Boit for Forbes. The big loser in the papers was Ned Arnold, omitted in almost every article. Both papers listed eight deceased members; the *Globe* listed Forbes but left out Boit, while the *Herald* included Boit but omitted Forbes. Finally, with the 1925 monument, the papers seemed to print a consistent story of sixteen club members notwithstanding slighting the most *un*well-known Arnold.
63 Kim Servart Theriault, "Re-membering Vietnam: War, Trauma, and 'Scarring Over' after 'the Wall,'" *Journal of American Culture* 26, no. 4 (December 2003): 429. See also Doss, *Memorial Mania*, 150–52.
64 Lovett, *Old Boston Boys*, 91.
65 The one exception was Laura Wiggins's article about the plaque's unveiling printed at the end of Scudder's booklet. Wiggins referred to the memento round robin signed for Miller, but she stated 1863 instead of 1862. See Scudder, *Gerrit Smith Miller*, 30.
66 The schools listed were Boston Public Latin, Dixwell's, Boston English, and Chauncy Hall. See "Foot Ball," *Boston Herald*, October 13, 1860; "Football Match," *Boston Herald*, June 7, 1862, 4; "Foot-Ball," *Boston Daily Advertiser*, November 21, 1864, 1; "Local Varieties," *Boston Herald*, October 8, 1865, 4; and "Football," *Boston Herald*, October 14, 1865, 2.
67 Means Lawrence to Lovett, June 5, 1906, folder 3 (1906), James D'Wolf Lovett papers.
68 The only vague mention comes from one undated and passing reference to Lovett as a member of the Oneidas in "1862 or '63" but without any foundation date. "James D'W Lovett," undated and unnamed clipping, James D'Wolf Lovett Sports Scrapbook.
69 Reporting on the school plaque in 1923, two papers—*Boston Traveler, Boston Herald*—reported the date correctly as well as the *Boston Globe* (though it misprinted the dates about Miller's school attendance from the plaque printed as 1860–63). Testament to their status as newspapers of record, the 1862 date was printed in the paragraph in the *New York Times* as well as farther south in the Washington, DC–based *Evening Star*—papers that gave no date for the club's foundation. Errors were printed in the *Biddeford Journal, New Britain Herald, Berkshire Evening News* (all stating 1873), or

the *Omaha Bee* (1871). If in 1925, the local papers were correct regarding the 1862 date (*Boston Traveler, Boston Herald, Boston Globe*), the situation was worse elsewhere. Some printed no foundation date at all (*Berkshire Evening News*) or embarrassingly wrote that the club was founded in 1852, found in the *New York Times* as well as the *Evening Star*.

70 Morton Henry Prince, "History of Football at Harvard, 1800–75," in *The H Book of Harvard Athletics 1852–1922*, ed. John A. Blanchard (Cambridge, MA: Harvard Varsity Club, 1923), 313.

71 The date was on everyone's minds. Both Camp and Davis had underlined the importance of 1863 as a starting date for organized football beyond intramural school contests. In his commemorative 1924 booklet, Scudder included Bussy's article on the history of football, which gave the founding of the English FA as an important date in the efforts to unify the various rules across schools. The Boston media had also hinted as much when the *Globe* noted how the Oneidas predated the earliest collegiate game in 1869 and were the "first exponent of which there is any record of organized football in this country" and slipped in that "England followed suit in 1863." See Walter Camp and Lorin Deland, *Football* (Cambridge, MA: Riverside Press, 1896), 3–4; and Parke H. Davis, *Football, the American Intercollegiate Game* (New York: Charles Scribner's Sons, 1911), 30–31.

72 Scudder's edited 1923 booklet only describes matches from "the two seasons of 1862 and 1863" (despite no newspaper evidence for 1862) and discussed an 1864 offer extended to Harvard that went "a long time" without reply. Scudder concludes that "this was the last of the four years of the Oneida Football Club's existence." How he managed to count four years in between 1862 and 1864 (1865 if we count the "long time" they waited for a match with Harvard) is a mystery. Scudder, *Gerrit Smith Miller*, 23–25; "Gerrit S. Miller, Peterboro, Captained First Football Team in United States," November 25, 1922, unnamed newspaper, folder 2-2 in 2001.A032, Smith-Miller Family Collection, 1879–1961, Madison County Historical Society, Oneida, NY.

73 Jones to Parker, May 18, 1926, Oneida Monument file, Boston Art Commission archives, Boston city hall.

74 Miller, Lawrence, Lovett, and Scudder to Andrews, Jones, Biscoe, and Whitmore, November 13, 1925, Oneida vertical file, Revolutionary Spaces.

75 Ball shape was not regulated until the 1890s, and even Walter Camp's biography by Harford Powel never mentions the oval shape and recalls the normalcy of a round ball in the 1870s such that chapter 1 is entitled "The Round Black Rubber Football." The rules of the American Intercollegiate Association, as printed in *Spalding's Official Foot Ball Guides*, did not include a specific regulation on ball shape until the 1890s. The *Guides* included advertisements for many types of ball shapes and sizes until the 1898 rules stipulated that the ball "should have the shape of a prolate spheroid." See

Walter Camp, ed., *Spalding's Official Foot Ball Guide* (New York: American Sports Publishing, 1899), 173–74.

76 Scudder even contradicted himself. He wrote about "twelve Dixwell boys" but then immediately listed thirteen names before adding the non-Dixwell boys (for a total of sixteen names) and still mentioning that the club played with its "usual fifteen." It does not seem to be a simple typo. The errors were repeated in the reedited version of the SPNEA *Old-Time New England* bulletin in July 1924. It is odd that no one caught the simple calculation error. Even Lovett, it seems, could not get the numbers straight either. In a clipping from the John Hancock insurance company internal newsletter, pasted into his scrapbook, the short piece noted fifteen players, referred to the old ball, and stated that "four of the seven surviving Oneidas were at the dedication." This is interesting since someone, presumably Lovett, corrected the second erroneous fact with a note in the margin but left the overall incorrect team number (fifteen rather than sixteen) untouched. The note in the article has the word four crossed out with five handwritten in the left margin. See Scudder, *Gerrit Smith Miller*, 23; *Old-Time New England* 15, no. 1 (July 1924): 11; and "Original Football Team," *John Hancock Field*, November 1923, James D'Wolf Lovett Sports Scrapbook.

77 Scudder to Tuttle, November 12, 1926, and December 14, 1926, in "An Historical Sketch of the Oneida Football Club of Boston 1862–65," folder of Mixed Material, Ms. S-686b, Massachusetts Historical Society.

78 Four years before *An Historical Sketch*, Scudder published a commemorative booklet detailing the memorial erected in honor of the Cambridge poet Longfellow (whose son Ernest was a classmate to many Oneidas). So deserving of a monument, an association was created, funds raised, and a bust sculpted and then dedicated in 1914 by Charles W. Eliot. Means Lawrence wrote a book about the origins and history of customs, superstitions, and beliefs that included numerous references to memorials, monuments, and myths and even referenced another work with examples of athletes and statues. Later, in 1916, Means Lawrence also published a history of local St. Paul's Cathedral, the bibliography of which revealed his knowledge of Boston and New England history, landmarks and memorials. Winthrop S. Scudder, *The Longfellow Memorial Association 1882–1922: An Historical Sketch* (Cambridge, MA: privately printed by the association, 1922); Robert Means Lawrence, *The Magic of the Horse-Shoe: With Other Folk-Lore Notes* (London: Gay and Bird, 1898).

79 Miller Jr. published his "The Jaw of the Piltdown Man" in the Smithsonian collections on November 24, 1915. After a riposte in 1917 to Miller Jr.'s first paper in 1915, the Oneida captain's son produced two more papers in 1918 and 1920 culminating in different schools of interpretation. See William L. Straus, "The Great Piltdown Hoax," *Science* 119, no. 3087 (February 26, 1954): 265–69.

80 Gibson to Lovett, n.d., folder 14 (n.d.), James D'Wolf Lovett papers.
81 Lovett, *Old Boston Boys*, 99; "Samuel Cabot," *Boston Evening Transcript*, November 28, 1906, news clipping in Lovett's donated copy of *Old Boston Boys*, Massachusetts Historical Society, 99.
82 Jill Lepore, *The Story of America: Essays on Origins* (Princeton, NJ: Princeton University Press, 2012), 15.
83 Daniel J. Boorstin, ed., *An American Primer* (Chicago: University of Chicago Press, 1966), xvii.
84 James D'Wolf Lovett, *A Pilgrimage—Read at a Meeting of the Oneidas, Saturday, May 28, 1927* (Boston: n.p., 1927). Italics and capitals as in original.
85 The endorsements only appear in the back of the 1906 edition, presumably for the promotion of the book. None of the currently digitally available copies of *Old Boston Boys* include them. The full quote is as follows: "Your vivid and humorous descriptions of swimming, boating, skating, coasting, baseball, and football—as it was played then—have recalled much that I had almost forgotten of my happy boyhood days in Boston and Brookline." See Lovett's donated copy of *Old Boston Boys*, Massachusetts Historical Society.
86 Robert Apthorp Boit, *Chronicles of the Boit Family and Their Descendants and of Other Allied Families* (Boston: S. J. Parkhill, privately printed, 1915), 143–44.
87 "Unveil Tablet in Honor of Founder of Football in the United States," *Boston Globe*, November 8, 1923, 23.
88 Miller wrote, "In your MSS on page 88 you mention 'Bob' Peabody and Roger Wolcott as members of the Oneida foot ball team. Frank Peabody and 'Hunty' Wolcott were on that team. Roger was a member of the club and may have played on the team in some of the other matches. Bob Peabody was in college when the O.F.B. Club was formed and was not a member." Gat Miller to Jim Lovett, June 11, 1905, folder 1 (1895–1906), James D'Wolf Lovett papers.
89 John Darlington, *Fake Heritage. Why We Rebuild Monuments* (New Haven, CT: Yale University Press, 2020), 11.
90 Miller and Peabody were listed as Unitarian, while Lawrence, Lovett, and Scudder all had Episcopalian funeral services. Nothing is known for Arnold.
91 "Gerrit S. Miller, Peterboro, Captained First Football Team in United States," November 25, 1922, unnamed newspaper, folder 2-2 in 2001.A032, Smith-Miller Family Collection, 1879–1961, Madison County Historical Society, Oneida, NY.
92 Win Scudder to Miller, Lovett, Means Lawrence, Arnold, April 1, 1926, folder 11 (1925–27), James D'Wolf Lovett papers.

CHAPTER 11

1 "Monument Honoring Nation's First Football Team Unveiled as Crowd of 54,000 Flocks to Stadium," *Boston Traveler*, November 21, 1925, James D'Wolf Lovett Sports Scrapbook, 1861–1945, Revolutionary Spaces.
2 Ian Tattersall and Peter Nevraumont, *Hoax: A History of Deception; 5000 Years of Fakes Forgeries and Fallacies* (New York: Black Dog, 2018), 9.
3 Kirk Savage, "The Politics of Memory: Black Emancipation and the Civil War Monument," in *Commemorations: The Politics of National Identity*, ed. John R. Gills (Princeton, NJ: Princeton University Press, 1994), 135.
4 Erected in 1877, the Soldiers and Sailors Monument on Flagstaff Hill is the largest of the memorials on the Common and includes scenes with recognizable individuals, including the face of the great poet Henry Wordsworth Longfellow living at the time, though he is not the focus of the memorial. According to biographer Christoph Irmscher, Longfellow was a "deeply private man" and declined public invitations. See Christoph Irmscher, *Longfellow Redux* (Urbana: University of Illinois Press, 2006), 8.
5 Eric Hobsbawm, "Introduction: Inventing Traditions," in *The Invention of Tradition*, ed. Eric Hobsbawm and Terence Ranger (Cambridge: Cambridge University Press, 2000), 2. Melvin Smith's extensive research records a plethora of pre-Oneida sporting contests before the American Civil War.
6 James D'Wolf Lovett, *Old Boston Boys and the Games They Played* (Boston: Riverside Press, 1906), 126.
7 Winthrop Saltonstall Scudder, ed., *Gerrit Smith Miller—an Appreciation—Supplement to the Nobleman* (Dedham, MA: Noble and Greenough School, 1924), 12.
8 Win Scudder to Miller, Lovett, Means Lawrence, Arnold, April 1, 1926, folder 11 (1925–27), James D'Wolf Lovett papers, 1896–1935, Massachusetts Historical Society.
9 Tony Collins, "The Invention of Sporting Tradition: National Myths, Imperial Pasts and the Origins of Australian Rules Football," in *Myths and Milestones in the History of Sport*, ed. Stephen Wagg (London: Palgrave Macmillan, 2011), 8.
10 For a discussion of the differences between history and the novel, see Pierre Nora, "Histoire et roman: Où passent les frontières?," *Le Débat* 3, no. 165 (2011): 6–12.
11 See Marc Bloch, *Apologie pour l'Histoire ou Métier d'Historien*, 2nd ed. (Paris: Cahier des Annales, 3, Librairie Armand Colin, 1952), 21, 80–83.
12 Barbara Tuchman, "In Search of History," *Radcliffe Quarterly* (May 1963): 43.
13 Between 1861 and 1863, academic rank for the fifty-some pupils at Dixwell's was balanced alongside conduct (misdemeanors). Peabody was number

one (or two) academically. Arnold was in the top twenty scholastically but near bottom in conduct (before leaving in 1862). Means Lawrence's bottom half rank did not impede him from later entering Harvard, while Miller's mediocre academics contrasted with top conduct. Helen Magill White became the first girl to study at the Public Latin School in the same years as Lovett. The daughter of Edward and Sarah Magill, Quakers and firm believers in education, Helen's father taught at the Latin School and had the precocious and gifted girl enrolled. Neither Magill nor Lovett were ever listed on any of the school's later historical registers. Only Pauline Holmes (a relation of Justice Oliver Wendell Holmes) revived her memory in 1935 in a footnote though missing Helen's pioneering doctoral achievement. See ranking lists, *Francis H. Lincoln's School Records, 1861–63*, Solomon and Francis H. Lincoln papers, Hingham Historical Society; and Pauline Holmes, *A Tercentenary History of the Boston Public Latin School, 1635–1935* (Cambridge, MA: Harvard University Press, 1935), 494.

14 Scudder to Lovett, October 18, 1926, Oneida vertical file, Revolutionary Spaces.

15 Lovett gets one passing mention, credited for helping design the first baseball diamond on Boston Common and pitching against Harvard in their second and third recognized games. John A. Blanchard, *The H Book of Harvard Athletics 1852–1922* (Cambridge, MA: Harvard Varsity Club, 1923), 150, 251, 596, 604.

16 "Old-Timers Prepare for 1879 Ball Game," unnamed newspaper clipping, James D'Wolf Lovett Sports Scrapbook. Title error in original.

17 Win Scudder to Miller, Lovett, Means Lawrence, and Arnold, April 1, 1926, folder 11 (1925–27), James D'Wolf Lovett papers.

18 The Miller-Lovett correspondence from the 1880s and 90s held at Syracuse ranges from regular discussion of health challenges faced by family members, Miller's son Garry's scientific advances and a love of cribbage games—the latter continuing as a theme of their time spent together and recounted in later correspondence held by the Massachusetts Historical Society and at Cornell.

19 Lawrence to Scudder, March 29, 1926, Oneida vertical file, Revolutionary Spaces.

20 Ned Arnold was generally omitted by the press. Practically invisible in the 1923 coverage, he fared marginally better in 1925 and was a peripheral figure at best making the official picture and caption. See *Boston Globe*, November 21, 1925. Even the Getty image archive contains a 1925, nearly identical to those used by the papers but featuring only the five other teammates.

21 FamilySearch.org holds tax records for both Arnold and Lovett showing their trust funds of the 1870s and 1880s much diminished by the turn of the century. Neither owned fancy Back Bay homes, living as boarders

or in rentals. Both worked late in life in insurance. See Jim Lovett to Gat Miller, August 21, 1933, box 1, folder 16, Gerrit Smith Miller papers, #3700, Division of Rare and Manuscript Collections, Cornell University Library.
22. Lovett wrote, "What a <u>wonderful</u> comfort and the help, the $100 you gave us in the fall, has been to us this winter in taking care of doctor's bills for treatments we both had to have. <u>You will never know what it meant to us!</u>" (emphasis in original). See Jim Lovett to Gat Miller, May 1, 1933, box 1, folder 11, Gerrit Smith Miller papers.
23. Sam W. Haynes, *Unfinished Revolution—the Early American Republic in a British World* (Charlottesville: University of Virginia Press, 2010), 279.
24. "Address of the Hon. Henry Cabot Lodge," in *The New England Society in the City of Brooklyn—Ninth Annual Report* (Brooklyn: n.p., 1889), 23.
25. See Jay Winter, *Sites of Memory, Sites of Mourning: The Great War in European Cultural History* (Cambridge: Cambridge University Press, 1995), 79, 115.
26. Fenno, who missed the 1904 dinner due to illness, featured all throughout the football section of *Old Boston Boys* but was never named subsequently to the Oneida roster. Fenno, who had ordered two copies of Lovett's book in 1906, left correspondence testifying to his participation in the games of the era and never sought to correct the manuscript. But rather than emit jealousy or argue for club recognition, the Harvard letterman (rowing) only expressed gratefulness and continued admiration for the "hero . . . of the football matches on the Common . . . [who] carried us to victory." Ned Fenno to Lovett, September 20, 1930, folder 12 (1930–35), James D'Wolf Lovett papers.
27. Dean Keith Simonton, *Greatness: Who Makes History and Why* (New York: Guildford Press, 1994), 6.
28. The "Origins of Football Debate" involves scholarly work about early codification of football in the nineteenth century. This debate has run for nearly twenty years essentially on the pages of the *International Journal of the History of Sport* and *Sport in Society*. It has been principally argued by Graham Curry, Eric Dunning, and Adrian Harvey and includes contributions from Peter Swain, Gary James, and others.
29. William H. McNeill, "Mythistory, or Truth, Myth, History, and Historians," *American Historical Review* 91, no. 1 (1986): 1–10.
30. Daniel Boorstin, *The Image: A Guide to Pseudo-Events in America*, 25th anniversary ed. (New York: Vintage Books, 1992), 11–12.
31. William J. Baker, "William Webb Ellis and the Origins of Rugby Football: The Life and Death of a Victorian Myth," *Albion* 13, no. 2 (1981): 119, 125.
32. Jed Smith, "Discredited Class-War Fable or Priceless Promotional Asset? The Duality of Rugby Union's William Webb Ellis Foundation Myth," in *Sport, History, and Heritage: Studies in Public Representation*, ed. Jeff Hill, Kevin Moore, Jason Wood (Woodbridge, UK: Boydell Press, 2012), 31.

33 Stephen Jay Gould, "The Creation Myths of Cooperstown," *Natural History* (November 1989).
34 "Gerrit S. Miller, Peterboro, Captained First Football Team in United States," November 25, 1922, unnamed newspaper, folder 2-2 in 2001.A032, Smith-Miller Family Collection, 1879–1961, Madison County Historical Society, Oneida, NY.
35 This quote is itself an exercise in "mythistory." Anderson explains that this quotation comes from Durant's *Story of Philosophy*, which references British statesman John Morley's monograph on Voltaire. If Morley did cite Voltaire's *Œuvres* directly, he took liberties in his translation. The original text is in a letter from Voltaire to l'abbé Morellet (not Mme du Chatelet as per Anderson) discussing texts considered as heretical: "Il eft bien trifte que l'on impute quelquefois à des vivans, et même à de bons vivans, les ouvrages des morts." Charles Anderson, "The Exchange," *RQ* 26, no. 2 (Winter 1986): 149.

INDEX

Page numbers in *italics* refer to figures.

abolition, 31–32
affluence and wealth, 74–80, 82, 86, 87, 210, 217n5, 248n26, 280–81nn21–22
age, 25–26, 143–44; Oneida Football Club later in life, 1–3, 5, 86, 126–27, 133, 147
amateurism vs. professionalism, 95–96, 98, 105, 117
ambiguity, history and, 179, 181, 184, 189, 193, 200, 209, 213
American Encyclopedia of Soccer (Hollander), 168–69
American Intercollegiate Association, 276n72
American Youth Soccer Organization (AYSO), 167
Ames, James Barr, 274n56
Andrew, John Albion, 32–33, 73
anniversaries, 113–15, 119, 247n20; Rugby School centenary match, 117–19, 123, 137, 183
antiquarian movements, 113–31, 133, 170. *See also* artifacts; preservation, historical
Appleton, William Sumner, Jr., 111
Appreciation, An (Scudder). See *Gerrit Smith Miller—an Appreciation*
Apthorp, William Foster, 77, 79, 82, 236n23, 244n80
Arbella sermon, 23, 221n1
archives, 137, 151–52, 163–65, 174–75, 186, 194, 198–200

Aristonico Caristo, 131
Arnold, Edward "Ned" Lincoln, 16, 84–85, *112*, 129, 208–9, 210, 280n20; modest means of, 87, 217n5, 280–81n21
art, 83–84
art commission. See Boston Art Commission
artifacts, 111–14, 159, 161, 170, 183–84, 188
association football. See soccer
Athenaeum, Boston, 82–83
Australia, 18
AYSO. See American Youth Soccer Organization

Back Bay, Boston, 27, 29–30, 40, 85
ball, Oneida championship, 184–89, 204; as artifact, 159, 161, 170, 184; loan to NSHOF, 170, *171*, *172*, 174–76; Miller and, 93, 183, 185, 186; painted names on, 184–87, 189, 194–95, *195*, 199, 203–4; photographs of, *10*, 93, 111, *112*, 184, *195*; SPNEA and, 9–12, *10*, 111–13, 145, 183, 184–88
balls (sporting goods), 11–12, 46, 60–61, 70, 108, *162*, 276n75; as artifacts, 159, 161, 170, 184
bans, football, 40, 42, 47, 51, 57, 58, 60, 70, 99, 102, 108, 163. *See also* Bloody Monday
Baptista, Robert Charles, 161–65

baseball, 40–42, 52, 85, 115, 208, 237n32, 247n20; Lovett and, 41, 95–96, 148, 238n6; The Lowells (baseball team), 41, 84, 87, 251n73, 259n77; Miller and, 87, 251n73; origins, 104, 163
Beacon Hill, Boston, 30, 39
Beebe, James Arthur, 16, 78, 79, 85, 86, 196, 236nn21–22, 244n80, 256n46
Bigelow, Henry Forbes, 256n46
Bigelow, Joseph Smith, 77, 78, 79, 86, 236n21, 275n61
Bigelow, William Sturgis, 75, 77, 79, 80, 146, 236n21, 236n23, 246n7, 275n61
birthday, athletic, 204
Black people, 17
Bloch, Marc, 179
Bloody Monday (hazing), 42, 47, 57, 63, 70–71, 232n8
boarding schools, 44–45, 122, 228n29
Board of Overseers, Harvard, 80–81
Boit, Robert Apthorp, 26, 60, 79, 95, 105, 203, 230n53, 231n68, 236n23, 272n46
Book of Foot-Ball, The (Camp), 107, 242n61, 244nn81–82
Book of Sports (Carver), 40–41
books, sporting, 46–48, 151–52, 165, 176, 241n48, 244n81, 244–45n87, 245n89, 248n22; college, 101–7, 242n61. *See also* historiography; *individual titles*
Boston, 5, 23–38, 40, 76, 85, 97. *See also* Brahmin elite
Boston Art Commission, 137, 141–42, 173–74, 176–77, 256n46
Boston Athletic Association, 181, 185
Boston Boys. *See* high schools; Oneida Football Club; *individual schools*
Boston Common, 14, 30, 39–41, 50, *150*, 226n8, 257n55; Friends of the Boston Public Garden and Common, 174, 176–77; memorials in, *x*, 210, 268–69n11, 269n15; as playground, 42–46, 48–54, 143–44, 205
Boston English High School, 50, 123
Boston Evening Transcript, 13, 117–19, *150*, 186, *211*

Boston Game, the, 13–16, 41–54, 59, 61, 64, 203–4, 248n27, 264n41; Harvard and, 61–62, 68–72, 116; as missing link, 163–66, 209; origins and foundation myths and, 2–5, 50–53, 119, 122, 143, 207, 213–14. *See also* Oneida Football Club
Boston Grammar School (England), 24
Boston Public Garden. *See* Public Garden, Boston
Boston Public Latin School, 15–16, 50, 116, 121, 208, 217n3, 279–80n13
Boston Red Stockings, 41, 96
Bowditch, Edward "Ned," 1, 24, 87, *112*, 208–9
Bowditch, Henry Pickering, 36, 225n50
Bowditch, Mary Ingersoll, 24
Bowditch, Nathaniel, 33, 225n50
Bowdoin Square Club, 41
Boys' Life magazine, 2, 166
Brahmin elite, 2, 3, 24, 30, 39–40, 73–87, 206, 208, 212–13; Harvard and, 55–57, 74, 227n16; heritage, as "old stock," 27–28, 97, 120–22, 181–82; war and, 32–33, 34, 37–38; worldview of, 75–77, 210–12
Brazil, 159
Britain, 18, 19; high schools in, 44, 57, 98–100, 107, 117, 228n25; high schools in, vs. US, 44–45, 48, 52, 67–68, 108, 119, 122, 228n29
Brooks, John Henry, 85, 187, 194, 196–97, 270n25
Brooks, Walter Denison, 85, 187, 194, 270n25, 272n46
Brown, John, 31–32, 36
Brown, Joseph Taylor, 275n61
Brown, Tom (fictional character), 48, 62, 117
Burgess, Edward, 77, 79, 196, 229n44, 271n35
Burgess, Walter, 77, 84, 147, 233n25, 275n61
Bushee, Frederick A., 27
businesses, family, 77–79
Bussy, G. F. Philip, 117–19, 144, 268n2

Index

Cabot, Samuel, 16, 91–93, 196, 201, 237n1, 271n35, 274n56
Cabot, Stephen, 34–35
Cambridge, MA, 85, 222n8
Camp, Walter, 20–21, 67, 71, 102–3, 122, 135, 242n59, 258n68; memorial to, 136–37, 146, 152, 160, 255n22
Canada, 18, 66, 69, 234n44
carrying. *See* handling code, vs. kicking
Carver, Robert, 40–41
Catholicism, 27, 28
Cazenovia, NY, 158, 163, 187
cemeteries, Mount Auburn, 75
centenary match, Rugby School, 117–19, 123, 137, 183
Chadwick, Henry, 102, 242n61
champions and heroes, 4, 37, 100, 126, 129–31, 181, 183–84, 197, 200, 214
championship match of 1863 (Oneida Football Club), 13, 20, 35–36, 93, 123, 185–86, 193–95, 199–200, 203, 273nn50–51. *See also* rosters, Oneida Football Club
character, 123–24, 126–27, 140–41
Charleston, SC, 36
city upon a hill, 5, 23, 212, 221n1, 265n51
Civil War, 13, 16–17, 31–38, 51–52, 144, 225n50; Brahmin elite and, 32–33, 34, 37–38; effect on sports of, 45, 59–60, 108–9; immigration and, 31, 34; Oneida Football Club and, 33–37, 38
class, social, 18, 29, 34, 39, 40, 46, 79, 166, 167, 169. *See also* Brahmin elite
clubs, 80–87. *See also individual clubs*
codification. *See* rules and regulations
Coffman, Ramon, 140, 256n34
Coletti, Joseph, 142, 143
colleges, 25–26, 67–68. *See also individual institutions*
college sports, 18–21, 57–72, 100–107, 119–20, 125, 161–65, 235n47, 242n61; first intercollegiate football match, 63–65, 107–8, 152; rowing, 65–66, 67, 74, 115, 188–89, 229n44, 271n35, 272n38
Collins, Tony, 19, 180

Colone, Albert, 172, 174–75
Columbia University, 64, 136
commemoration. *See* memorialization
Common. *See* Boston Common
Confederacy, 30–38
Cosmos (soccer team), 167
cultural inferiority, American, 4, 210–12
Cunningham, Bill, 157–58

Danzig, Allison, 163–64
Davis, Frank, 193–94, 196, 272n46
Davis, George Kuhn, 193–93, 196
Davis, Parke H., 107–8, 116, 122, 161, 248n27, 249n35
Deland, Lorin, 103, 108, 244n85
Deming, Clarence, 12
de Yongh Field, William, 1, 201, 217n3
dissertations, 162–66, 263n26
Dixwell, Epes Sargent, 24–25, 32, 49, 50, 53, 82, 222nn7–9, 223n17, 229n51
Dixwell, John, 222n7, 236n22, 275n61
Dixwell Latin School, 15–16, 24–26, 34, 42, 49–51, 53, 222n7, 231nn67–68, 272–73n48, 279–80n13. *See also* Oneida Football Club
Doss, Erika, 4, 182
Doubleday, Abner, 105, 115, 214, 247n20
draft, 33, 34, 36
Duff, John Robertson, 236n22, 256n46
Dwight, James, 77, 85, 86, 231n67, 233n25, 244n80, 271n35
Dyke, Henry Van, 63, 101–2

education, 24, 118–19, 227n16. *See also* colleges; high schools; *individual schools and institutions*
Eliot, Charles William, 56, 77, 81, 126–27, 142, 183
Eliot, Mary Clark, 94
elite, Boston. *See* Brahmin elite
Ellis, William Webb, 99–101, 117, 118, 183, 207, 240n42, 240–41n46, 244n81; memorial to, 99, 117, 118, 183, 240n42, 240–41n46
emblems and insignia, 187–88, 270n28
end of game, 14, 15

endzones, 14
England. *See* Britain
English Football Association (FA), 19, 52, 101, 172, 231n64
English High School, Boston, 50, 123
Eustis, William Ellery Channing, 78, 85, 86, 147, 224n43, 231n67, 236nn22–23, 249n38, 256n46
exceptionalism, American, 4–5, 217n15,

FA. *See* English Football Association
Farrell, Mildred, 173
"fathers" of football: gridiron, 20, 67, 71, 102, 105, 117, 130–31, 135, 146, 149, 151, 152, 212, 258n68; soccer, 160, 169
Fédération Internationale de Football Association (FIFA), 170
Fenno, Ned, 196, 272n38, 281n26
Field, Billy, 197, 204, 217n3
FIFA. *See* Fédération Internationale de Football Association
First National Bank of Boston, 149, *150*, 189, 260n89
firsts, 98, 104, 115, 119, 122, 143. *See also* origins and foundation myths
football, association. *See* soccer
football, gridiron, 14–15, 19, 127, 153; Gaelic, 18, 180, 242n61; "mob" version, 99, 108, 163, 164; rugby roots, 100, 102–3; violence in, 47, 58–59, 70–71, 105
Football Days (Edwards), 245n89
Foot-Ball—Its History for Five Centuries (Shearman and Vincent), 98
footballs (sporting goods). *See* ball, Oneida championship; balls; Oneida Football Monument: ball on
Forbes, John Malcolm "Mac," 189, 195–96, 236n22, 273n50, 275n62
Forbes, William Hathaway, 189
forward pass, 14, 19
Foulds, Sam, 160–61, 164, 167–70, 172, 173, 264n41
foundations. *See* Oneida Football Club: foundation date; Oneida Football Club: founder of; origins and foundation myths

France, 117, 123, 249n33
French Rugby Federation, 123
friendship, 2, 146, 210, *211*, 213–14, 217n4
Friends of the Boston Public Garden and Common, 174, 176–77
Frontier Thesis, 4, 17
full backs, 14, 15
funerals, 33, 37, 58, 87, 135, 153, 197

Gaelic football, 18, 180, 242n61
Gage, Thomas, 144
Gansevoort, Maria, 229n45
Georgia Institute of Technology, 152
Gerrit Smith Miller—an Appreciation (Scudder), 125–27, 129–30, 133, 145, 188, 193, 195–96, 198, 251n73, 276n72
Gettysburg, 34, 35, 59
Gibson, Dana, 92, 200–201
Gilded Age, 3, 81, 86, 87, 93, 97, 181–82, 210
Gilman, Arthur, 29
goalposts, 14
goals, 14, 15–16, 57, 60, 67, 70, 220n19
goods, sporting, 11, 101. *See also* balls
Goodyear, Charles, 11–12, 219n6
Gray, Russell, 82, 85, 112, 231n67, 246n7, 275n61
Great Britain. *See* Britain
Greece, 107, 131, 134, 244n81
gridiron, 14, 19. *See also* Boston Game, the; football, gridiron; Harvard game, the
Guild, Curtis, 42, 109
Gulliver's Travels (Swift), 252n82

Hall, John Paouaa, 14, 272n46, 274n56
halls of fame, 158–60, 168–76, 201. *See also* National Soccer Hall of Fame
Hancock, Peter, 181, 184, 189, 201
handkerchiefs, 183, 188, 202, 270n28, 271n31, 271n33
handling code, vs. kicking, 16, 42, 45, 47–78, 99–100, 102–4, 160–64, 234n44, 244n82
Hardy, Arthur Sherburne, 275n61
Harris, Paul, 167–68, 264n41

Index

Harvard College/University, 24, 26, 55–72, 114–15, 126–27, 225n50; *Advocate*, 18, 60, 62, 65; bans, football, 42, 47, 51, 58, 60; books and histories and, 57–72, 101–3, 115–17, 119, 189; Boston Game and, 61–62, 68–72, 116; Brahmin elite and, 55–57, 74, 227n16; football clubs, 60, 62, 176; high schools and, 25–26, 227n16, 231n68; *Magazine*, 58, 232n13; McGill, match vs., 66, 69–70, 234n44, 248n27; Oneida Football Club and, 53–55, 74, 80–81, 126–27, 129, 208–9, 231n68, 233n25; Yale and, 19, 65–67, 71–72, 115, 139–40, 141, 160, 188–89. *See also* bans, football; Bloody Monday; Boston Game, the; college sports; Harvard game, the; origins and foundation myths; rules and regulations

Harvard game, the (rule set), 59–61, 64, 69, 70–71, 101, 164

Haughton, Percy D., 134–35, 136, 143

Haynes, Sam, 4, 105, 212

hazing, 42, 47, 248n27

H Book of Harvard Athletics (Prince), 115–17, 119–20, 189

heritage: Brahmin elite as "old stock," 27–28, 97, 120–22, 181–82; history and, 4, 5, 170–81, 201, 205–6; preservation of, 4, 111–14, 119, 170–81, 200, 201, 205–6, 209

heroes. *See* champions and heroes

Higginson, Thomas Wentworth, 25, 31, 45, 101, 233n26, 241n50

high schools, 26, 42–45, 50–53, 74, 92, 275n66; boarding schools, 44–45, 122, 228n29; British, 44, 57, 98–100, 107, 117, 228n25; British vs. US, 44–45, 48, 52, 67–68, 108, 119, 122, 228n29; Harvard and, 25–26, 227n16, 231n68; interclass matches, 50–53, 64; interscholastic matches, 50, 230n56, 230n59, 245n89, 276n71. *See also* championship match of 1863

Hill, Dean, 152, 260n94

Historical Sketch, An (Scudder), 143, 146, 183, 190–93, 198, 201

Historic New England Library and Archives. *See under* Society for the Preservation of New England Antiquities

historiography, 41, 100, 107, 118, 151–53, 163, 169, 183, 258n66; dissertations, 162–66, 263n26; local vs. national, 123–25, 139–40, 145–46; universities and, 101–7, 109, 115–16, 158. *See also* books, sporting; *individual titles*

history, 203, 207–8, 210, 212–13, 214, 268n2; heritage and, 4, 5, 170–81, 201, 205–6; vs. memory and memorialization, 2–5, 15, 20, 152, 212–13; mythistory, 213–14, 282n35; of New England, 111–14, 206

History of American Football, The (Danzig), 163–64

History of Football—from the Beginnings to 1871 (Magoun), 151

hoaxes, 5, 174, 181, 184, 200, 201, 204, 206, 210, 214

Holmes, Robert, 177

Hughes, Thomas, 62–63, 229n40

Hutt, Sarah, 174, 176, 177

Iasigi, Oscar, 66, 77, 85, 236n21, 246n7

identity, 30–31, 49, 114, 181–82. *See also* heritage

idols of origins, 126, 179–80. *See also* champions and heroes

IFAB. *See* International Football Association Board

immigrants and immigration, 23–24, 29–31, 97, 114, 121, 181–82, 239–40n32, 242n61; Irish, 27–28, 31, 34, 253n3

India rubber balls, 11–12, 46

industrialization, 27, 98, 109, 113

inheritances, 79, 82, 85

injury, 19, 71, 105

Intercollegiate Football Association, 67, 102

intercollegiate sports. *See* college sports; *individual sports and institutions*

International Football Association Board (IFAB), 18, 154

interscholastic matches. *See* championship match of 1863; high schools: interscholastic matches
Ireland, 18, 27
Irish immigrants, 27–28, 253n3; Civil War and, 31, 34
Ivy League, 57, 101. *See also individual institutions*

Jackson, Frank, 85, 236n22, 244n80
Jackson, Pat, 16
John Evans and Co., 160
Jones, I. Howland, 138, 141–43, 199
Jones, Robert Gould, 85, 236n22

kicking, 12, 15–16; code, vs. handling, 16, 42, 45, 47–78, 99–100, 102–4, 160–64, 234n44, 244n82
Knickerbocker Base Ball Club, 41
Kościuszko, Tadeusz, 182

Latin School, Boston Public, 15–16, 24, 50, 116, 208, 217n3, 279–80n13
Latin School, Dixwell, 15–16, 24–26, 42, 49–51, 53, 222n7, 231nn67–68, 272–73n48, 279–80n13
Lawrence, Amory Appleton, 25, 26, 77, 236nn21–23
Lawrence, William, 25–26, 34, 37, 73, 80, 126, 135, 140–41, 152–53, 197, 203, 208, 236nn22–23, 275n61
Lee, Henry, 176
Lee, Robert E., 35
leisure time, 43–46, 51–52, 54
lieux de mémoire, 180, 212. See also *milieux de mémoire*
Lincoln, Abraham, 37
linebackers, 14
line of scrimmage, 14
lists of Oneida club members. *See* rosters, Oneida Football Club
Lodge, Henry Cabot, 25, 30, 34, 37, 48, 55–56, 196, 208, 212, 236n22; death of, 134, 135; Plymouth bicentenary oration, 114, 247n15; as student, 74, 222n15

Longfellow, Henry Wadsworth, 277n78, 279n4
Lovett, Alice, 139, 145, 157, 191
Lovett, James "Jim" D'Wolf, 1, 29, *112*, 129, 139, 208–9, *211*; baseball and, 41, 95–96, 148, 238n6; death of, 148, 149; Miller and, 87, 121, 251n73, 276n72, 280n18; modest means of, 210, 248n26, 280–81nn21–22; writing of, 86, 147–48, 197, 208, 215. *See also* rosters, Oneida Football Club; scrapbook, Lovett's; *individual titles by*
Lowell, Abbot Lawrence, 81
Lowell, John A., 41, 85
Lowells, The (baseball team), 41, 84, 87, 251n73, 259n77
lurking/offside, 13, 16, 49

Magoun, Francis Peabody, 151, 260n91
Major League Soccer (MLS), 172
Manning, Gus Randolph, 160, 169
marathons, 181, 268n8
marriages, 77
Massachusetts, 113, 225n50
Massachusetts Association of Baseball Players, 41
Massachusetts Historical Society, 55, 143
Massachusetts Soccer Association, 166
matches. *See* centenary match, Rugby School; championship match of 1863; college sports: first intercollegiate football match; high schools: interclass matches; high schools: interscholastic matches; McGill University, match vs. Harvard
McBurney, John Wayland, 249n38, 272n38
McGill University, match vs. Harvard, 66, 69–70, 234n44, 248n27
McGrath, Tom, 173–78, 210
Means Lawrence, Robert "Bob," 1, 74, 87, *112*, 138, 148, 208, 236nn21–22, 272n46
medals, scholarship, 124, 159
memoirs, 92, 95, 96, 98, 109, 147, 153. *See also individual titles*
memorialization, 120, 134, 213–14; history and, 2–5, 15, 20, 152, 212–13; local vs.

Index

national, 123–25, 146, 149–53; motivation and, 5, 207–8, 209–10, 213–14; posthumous, 151–53, 181; private, 92, 98, 100, 106, 109–10, 125, 127–30; public, 133–34, 200, 201–4, 209–10; self-, 1–5, 86–87

memorials, 5, 134, 177–78, 189, 197, 210, 269n16, 277n78, 279n4; in Boston, x, 182–83, 210, 268–69n11, 269n15; to Camp, 136–37, 146, 152, 160, 255n22; to Ellis, 99, 117, 118, 183, 240n42, 240–41n46; to Haughton, 136, 143; to Miller, 122–30, 133, 145, 158, 183, 193–95, 197, 203, 207, 268n2; repair and restoration of, 143–44, 159–60, 174, 176–78; statue mania and, 4, 182, 206, 268–69n11. *See also* Oneida Football Monument

memory, 20, 152, 197–98; collective, 4, 92, 95, 115, 129, 134; history and, 2–5, 15, 20; *lieux de mémoire*, 134, 180, 212

Messrs. Lawrence and Co., 77

milieux de mémoire, 134. See also *lieux de mémoire*

Miller, Gerrit "Gat" Smith, 14, 31–32, 87, 148–49, 170, 200, 207–8, 217n5; baseball and, 87, 251n73; as founder of Oneidas/football, 2, 121, 123–24, 127–29, 259n77; Harvard and, 126–27, 129; Lovett and, 87, 121, 280n18; memorial to, 122–30, 133, 145, 158, 183, 193–95, 197, 207, 268n2. *See also Gerrit Smith Miller—an Appreciation*

Miller, Milt, 158

Miller, Perry, 23

Miller, Sue, 94

Mills, A. G., 104

Mills, Arthur, 231n67, 233n25, 244n80

Mills Commission, 105

Milton, MA, 85–86

Minot, George Richards, 62, 78, 85, 231n67, 236nn21–22

MLS. *See* Major League Soccer

modernization, 59, 69, 71, 76, 113, 153. *See also* rules and regulations: codification of

montages, 190–92

monuments. *See* memorials; Oneida Football Monument

morality, 44–45, 127, 140–41

Morewood, William Barlow, 48, 229n45

Morse, Henry L., 66, 234n41

motivations for memorialization, 5, 207–8, 209–10, 213–14

Mount Auburn Cemetery, 75

Muscular Christianity, 44–45, 125–26, 140–41

mythistory, 213–14, 282n35. *See also* origins and foundation myths

NASL. *See* North American Soccer League

National Collegiate Athletic Association (NCAA), 125, 164, 176

National Football League (NFL), 125

National Football Shrine and Hall of Fame, 158

National Soccer Hall of Fame (NSHOF), 168–76, *171*

Native Americans, 264n41

nativism, 106, 206, 208, 212. *See also* heritage

Naturalization Act, 97, 239–40n32

NCAA. *See* National Collegiate Athletic Association

Nelson, Tom, 16

Newell, William, 15–16, 220n17

New England, 2, 85, 111–14, 174–75, 206. *See also* Society for the Preservation of New England Antiquities

newspapers, 33, 50–52, 94–95, 140, 247n20; championship match of 1863, 51, 186, 273n51; local vs. national, 148–49, 151–53, 158–59; memorials and, 124, 126, 128–30, 139–41, 240–41n46. *See also individual papers*

New York, 65–66, 139–40, 167

NFL. *See* National Football League

Noble and Greenough School, 119, 120, 122–24, 159, 183. *See also* memorials: to Miller

North American Soccer League (NASL), 167, 169

North End, Boston, 30, 34–35, 97, 139

NSHOF. *See* National Soccer Hall of Fame

offside/lurking, 13, 16, 49
O'Keefe, Arthur J., 159
Old Boston Boys and the Games They Played
 (Lovett), 104–10, 115, 122, 183–88,
 194–97, 198, 249n38; descriptions of the
 Boston Game, 13–17, 46; as personal
 memoir, 19–20, 91–98; publication of,
 200–201, 238n12, 278n85
"Old Friends" (Lovett), 210, *211*
Old Rugbeian Society, 99–100, 123,
 240n42
Old Schoolboys club, 42, 227n16
Old Timers' Association, 262n6
Oliver, Len, 169
Olympic Games, 268n8
Oneida Football Club, 10–11, 43–54, 77,
 119, 143–44, *190*, *191*, *211*, 214; 1904
 dinner, 91, 109, 184–86, 196, 272n38,
 274n56, 281n26; 1927 luncheon, 1–3, 5,
 134, 197, 201–2, 217n4; aging, 1–3, 5, 86,
 126–27, 133, 147; championship match
 of 1863, 13, 20, 35–36, 93, 123, 185–86,
 193–95, 199–200, 203, 273nn50–51;
 Civil War and, 33–37, 38; deaths of, 37,
 134–35, 146–49, 151–53, 181, 244n80,
 274n57; depictions of, *150*, *162*, 189,
 260n89; Dixwell Latin School and, 49,
 50–51, 53, 231n67; as first club, 120–21,
 163–64; foundation date, 198–99, 204,
 250n52, 275n65, 275–76nn68–69,
 276nn71–72; founder of, 2, 121, 123–24,
 127–29, 259n77; Harvard and, 53–55,
 74, 80–81, 126–27, 129, 208–9, 231n68,
 233n25; as missing link, 163–66, 209;
 soccer and, 5, 157–78, *162*, *171*, 201, 210,
 265n48. *See also* ball, Oneida championship; Boston Game, the; memorialization; rosters, Oneida Football Club;
 individual members
Oneida Football Monument, *x*, 4, 86–87,
 144, 180, 193, 205–13; ball on, 138,
 141–43, 165, 172–78, 197, 199, 202–4;
 ceremonies and speeches for, 138–39,
 144, 173, 205, 207; creation of, 137–43,
 209; importance/unimportance of,
 138, 144–46, 205, 207; payment and
 funds for, 138, 142–43, 174–75, 177;
 photographs of, 190–93, *190*, *191*, *192*;
 repair and restoration of, 143–44,
 159–60, 174, 176–78; wreath proposed
 for, 138, 142
Oneonta, NY, 168–74
origins and foundation myths, 43, 98–100,
 115, 163, 179–80, 200, 206, 212–13;
 baseball, 104, 163; football, 5, 98–109,
 153, 163; football, Boston roots of, 2–5,
 50–53, 119, 122, 143, 207, 213–14; football, rugby roots of, 100, 102–3; idols of,
 126, 179–80; mythistory, 213–14, 282n35.
 See also firsts
Otis House, 111, 161, 167, 175, 176
ownership, 98, 106, 177–78, 258n68

Page, Walter Gilman, 113
painted balls, 184–87, 189, 194–95, *195*, 199,
 203–4
Parkman, Henry, 134, 135, 236nn22–23
Pasuckquakkohowog, 264n41
patriotism, 32, 37, 73, 104, 120, 138
Peabody, Francis "Frank" Greenwood, 1,
 87, *112*, 148–49, 205, 208–9, 236n22;
 speech for Oneida Football Monument,
 138, 144, 205, 207
Peabody, Robert Swain, 272n38
Pelé, 4, 167
Peterboro, NY, 31, 93, 121, 145, 147, 185, 186
Peterson, Alan, 166
Peterson, Mark, 23, 30
pheninda, 131
Philadelphia Old Timers, 159, 160
philanthropy, 79–80, 83
photographs, 93, 183, 188, 189–92, 272n43;
 of Oneida ball, *10*, 93, 111, *112*, 184, *195*
pig-bladder balls, 11, 12
Pilgrimage, A (Lovett), 2–3, 133, 134, 187,
 201–3, 212, 215, 218n10
Pilgrims, 113, 114, 115, 212, 246n12, 247n17
Piltdown man, 200
plaques. *See* memorials
Plymouth Rock, 113, 247n17
poetry, 143, 204, 208, *211*, 247n15, 277n78,
 279n4; "Old Friends" (Lovett), 210, *211*;

Index

A Pilgrimage (Lovett), 2–3, 133, 134, 187, 201–3, 212, 215, 218n10
politics, 5, 28, 30, 45, 76, 83, 84, 97
Powell, Walter, 136
preservation, historical, 113–31, 133; heritage and, 4, 111–14, 119, 170–81, 200, 201, 205–6, 209. *See also* Society for the Preservation of New England Antiquities
press. *See* newspapers
Prince, Morton Henry, 60, 65, 116–17, 119–20, 248n26
Princeton University, 63–64, 101–2, 114–15, 152, 248n27
private schools. *See* high schools; *individual schools and institutions*
professionalism vs. amateurism, 95–96, 98, 105, 117
Protestantism, 27, 30, 203
pseudoevents, 213
Public Garden, Boston, 26, 39, 40, 42, 182, 268–69n11, 269n15; Friends of the Boston Public Garden and Common, 174, 176–77
Public Latin School, Boston, 15–16, 50, 116, 121, 208, 217n3, 279–80n13
public schools. *See* high schools; *individual schools and institutions*
Puritanism, 23–24, 114, 212, 246n12

quarterbacks, 14

Rappahannock River, 35
Reconstruction era, 3, 17, 37, 51, 57, 60, 63, 210
Red Sox, Boston. *See* Boston Red Stockings
Reed-Johnson Immigration Act of 1924, 121
referees, 154
regattas, 65–66, 67
Republican Party, 83
Revere, Joseph Warren, 275n61
"revolutionary spirit," 118, 144–45, 205
Revolutionary War, 144, 182, 205, 207
Rhea, Foster Dulles, 151–52, 260n93

Richards, Henry, 48, 152, 153, 224n43, 275n61
riots, 36
Riverside Press, 93, 103, 256n46
Rome, 107, 244n81
Roosevelt, Theodore, 55, 93, 238n13
Ropes, Henry, 59
rosters, Oneida Football Club, 193, 237n1, 272n46, 273–74nn55–56, 278n88; Lovett's, 194–97, 203, 273n51, 277n76, 281n26; Scudder's, 55, 193–97, 199–200, 231n67, 273n50, 275nn61–62, 277n76
Rotch, Arthur, 82, 83, 85, 231n67, 236n21
Round Robin, 127, *128*
rowing, 65–66, 67, 74, 115, 188–89, 229n44, 271n35, 272n38
rubber, 11–12, 61
rugby, 12, 14, 98–105, 107, 242n59; divergence from soccer and football, 17–19, 43, 45, 68–72, 180, 242n61. *See also* Rugby School
Rugby Football Union, 19, 52, 198, 249n33
Rugby School, 44, 48, 98–100, 117–19, 127, 207, 229n45; centenary match, 117–19, 123, 137, 183; Old Rugbeian Society, 99–100, 123, 240n42. *See also* memorials: to Ellis
Ruiz, Rosie, 181, 268n8
rules and regulations, 40, 46–47; of the Boston Game, 13–16, 47–48, 49, 203–4, 264n41; Canadian, 66, 69–70, 234n44; codification of, 17–20, 41, 52, 59, 65–67, 153–54, 261n102, 281n28; college football and, 57, 63–72, 102, 248n27; divergence of, into soccer, football, and rugby, 17–19, 43, 45, 68–72, 180, 242n59; handling code, vs. kicking, 16, 42, 45, 47–78, 99–100, 102–4, 160–64, 234n44, 244n82; of the Harvard game, 59–61, 64, 69, 71–71, 101, 164; scoring, 14–16, 57, 60, 67, 70, 220n19
rush line, 14
Rutgers University, 63–64, 152
Ruth, Babe, 147

SASH. *See* Society for American Soccer History

Schaff, David, 102, 242n55
schoolboys. *See* high schools; Oneida Football Club; *individual schools*
Schooldays at Rugby. See *Tom Brown's Schooldays*
schools. *See* colleges; high schools; *individual schools and institutions*
scoring, 14, 15–16, 57, 60, 67, 70, 220n19
scrapbook, Lovett's, 51, 94, 106, 127, 137, 191, 231n69, 237n32, 250n52
Scudder, Winthrop "Win" Saltonstall, 87, 93, *112*, 118, 203, 208–9, 210, 236n22; luncheon and, 1, 3; memorialization effort and, 117, 119–20, 122, 142, 145, 146–47, 179, 200. *See also* rosters, Oneida Football Club; *individual titles by*
Second Battle of Rappahannock Station, 35
segregation, 29–31, 40
shape of ball. *See* ball, Oneida championship; balls; Oneida Football Monument: ball on
Shattuck, Frederick Cheever, 62, 74, 77, 81–82, 233n25, 236n23, 244n80, 246n7, 275n61
Shearman, Montague, 98
slavery, 17, 31
Smith, Melvin I., 41, 42, 51
soccer, 5, 17–19, 157–78, *162*, *171*, 201, 210, 265n48; divergence from rugby and football, 17–19, 43, 45, 68–72, 180, 242n61; as foreign, 165, 166, 167, 169–70
Soccer U.S.A. (Cascio), 167
socialism, 4, 166, 169
social networks, 29, 74–87, 93, 142
Society for American Soccer History (SASH), 170
Society for the Preservation of New England Antiquities (SPNEA), 10, 97, 111–13, 145, 161, 174, 183–88, 246n7; bulletins, 113, 129, 137, 179, 183, 188, 272n40, 277n76; as Historic New England Library and Archives, 9, 10, 11, 175–76, 184, 188, 198
Sombart, Werner, 4
Somerset Club, 82
South, the (US), 28, 30–38

Soviets, 166
Spalding, A. G., 104
Sparks, William Eliot, 236n21
SPNEA. *See* Society for the Preservation of New England Antiquities
sports and games, 40, 46, 228n29, 268n8; character and, 123–24, 126–27, 140–41; Civil War's effect on, 45, 59–60, 108–9; "fathers" of, 105, 117, 130–31, 135, 146, 152, 160, 169, 258n68; goods, sporting, 11, 101; time in, 15, 66, 153–54, 261n102; violence in, 47, 58–59, 70–71, 99, 105. *See also* balls (sporting goods); books, sporting; college sports; *individual sports*
statue mania, 4, 182, 206, 268–69n11. *See also* memorials
St. Botolph Club, 82–83
Sturgis, Frederic Russell, 77, 79, 244n80
Sumner, Charles, 268–69n11

tablets. *See* memorials
tackling, 13, 16, 61, 66, 99, 244n82, 274n56
Tavern Club, 82
Thayer, Stephen Van Rensselaer, 78, 85, 86, 112, 196, 236n21
Thies, Louis, 16, 231n68, 272n46
time, in sports, 15, 66, 153–54, 261n102
Tom Brown's Schooldays (Hughes), 48, 62, 101, 107, 207
touchdowns, 14, 70, 220n19
transitional eras, 17–20, 26–28, 76, 96–97, 210
Trinity College, 57
Tucker, Alanson, 193–94, 196, 236n21, 272–73n48
Tucker, Lawrence, 193–94, 196, 272–73n48
Tudor, John, 229n44
Turner, Frederick Jackson, 4, 17
Tyson, Forrest, 165

Union Army, 32–38
Union Club, 82, 256n46
United States, 4–5, 107–9, 207, 210–12. *See also* heritage; patriotism
United States Soccer Football Association / United States Soccer Federation

Index

(USSFA/USSF), 159, 160–61, 168, 262n7, 264n42
usable past, 2, 5, 86, 119, 158, 201, 265n51; artifacts and, 170, 183; soccer and, 161, 165, 201
USSFA/USSF. *See* United States Soccer Football Association / United States Soccer Federation

Victorians, 44–45
Vincent, James, 98
violence, 28, 30, 35; in sports, 47, 58–59, 70–71, 99, 105
Volkmann, Arthur L. K., 117, 119, 249n40
Voltaire, 214, 282n35

"wall game," 44
war, 16–17, 197, 249n40. *See also* Civil War; Revolutionary War
Watson, Robert Clifford, 14, 186, 236n22, 272n46
wealth and affluence, 74–80, 82, 86, 87, 210, 217n5, 248n26, 280–81nn21–22
weather, 52, 230n62, 231n66

Wharton, William Fisher, 74, 83, 85, 236n21, 244n80
White, Helen Magill, 208, 279–80n13
Wigglesworth, George, 61–62
Williams, Samuel, 46
Winthrop, John, 23
Winthrop, Robert C., 42
Wolcott, Huntington "Hunty" Frothingham, 17, 36, 37, 50, 73, 187, 208, 230n53
Wolcott, Roger, 17, 73, 80, 182, 187, 208, 236nn21–23
women and girls, 166–67, 170, *171*, 279–80n13
Woods, J. G., 46
World Cup, 159, 170, 172, 178
worldviews, 75–77, 210–12
wreaths, 138, 142
Wright, George, 139
Wright, Harry, 96

Yale University, 64, 102–3, 136–37, 234n41, 242n55, 248n27, 253n3; Harvard and, 65–67, 71–72, 115, 139–40, 141, 160, 188–89

MIKE CRONIN is the Academic Director of Boston College in Ireland and a Professor in Boston College's Irish Studies Program. He has published widely on Irish and sporting history and his publications include *Sport: A Very Short Introduction* (Oxford University Press, 2014) and, with Renée Fox and Brian Ó Conchubhair, *The Routledge International Handbook of Irish Studies* (Routledge, 2021).

KEVIN TALLEC MARSTON is Senior Research Fellow at CIES and long-time Visiting Lecturer at De Montfort University's International Centre for Sport History & Culture. He has published on sport history and governance, contributing chapters to edited collections as well as articles in *Contemporary European History* and the *International Sports Law Journal*. He is the author of two books on sport governance (CIES) and the Asian Football Confederation's commemorative history of women's football (2022).